Lecture Notes in Computer Science   8079

Commenced Publication in 1973
Founding and Former Series Editors:
Gerhard Goos, Juris Hartmanis, and Jan van Leeuwen

Juhani Karhumäki   Arto Lepistö
Luca Zamboni (Eds.)

Combinatorics on Words

9th International Conference, WORDS 2013
Turku, Finland, September 16-20, 2013
Proceedings

 Springer

Volume Editors

Juhani Karhumäki
Arto Lepistö
Luca Zamboni
University of Turku
Department of Mathematics and Statistics
Assistentinkatu 7
20014 Turku, Finland
E-mail:{karhumak, alepisto}@utu.fi; lupastis@gmail.com

ISSN 0302-9743   e-ISSN 1611-3349
ISBN 978-3-642-40578-5   e-ISBN 978-3-642-40579-2
DOI 10.1007/978-3-642-40579-2
Springer Heidelberg New York Dordrecht London

Library of Congress Control Number: 2013946036

CR Subject Classification (1998): F.1, F.2, D.2, E.1, F.3, F.4

LNCS Sublibrary: SL 1 – Theoretical Computer Science and General Issues

Typesetting: Camera-ready by author, data conversion by Scientific Publishing Services, Chennai, India

Printed on acid-free paper

Springer is part of Springer Science+Business Media (www.springer.com)

Preface

The 9th International Conference on WORDS was held at University of Turku during September 16–20, 2013.

WORDS is the main conference in the area of combinatorics on words. It was initiated in 1997 in Rouen. Since its inception, the conference has taken place every second year in the following locations: Rouen, Palermo, Turku, Montreal, Marseille, Salerno and Prague.

The scope of the conference is to cover diverse topics in the study of finite and infinite words. This includes combinatorial, algebraic, and algorithmic aspects of words, as well as applications in mathematics, theoretical computer science, and theoretical physics.

A unique feature of WORDS 2013 was to publish a refereed proceedings volume in Springer's *Lecture Notes in Computer Science* series. In addition, local proceedings containing presentations or abstracts of all accepted and invited papers are edited as a *TUCS report*. In accordance with the founding spirit of the conference, the local proceedings provide a forum for recent surveys and/or previously published contributions. Following the conference, a special issue of *Theoretical Computer Science* will be edited.

We received 43 submissions from 17 different countries. Of these, 34 papers were submitted to the refereed proceedings. Following a peer-review process, 20 submissions were selected for LNCS and 13 for the local proceedings. In addition to contributed presentations, the conference program included six invited talks given by J. Cassaigne (Marseille), M. Dekking (Delft), V. Halava (Turku), G. Levitt (Caen), N. Rampersad (Winnipeg), and M. Sciortino (Palermo).

We warmly thank all invited speakers and all authors of submitted papers for their contributions. We are also very grateful to all the PC members and the sub-referees for their hard work, as well as the Organizing Committee, in particular M. Bucci. Last but not least, we express our gratitude to the representatives of Springer, in particular A. Kramer and A. Hofmann, for their professional and smooth collaboration.

June 2013

J. Karhumäki
A. Lepistö
L. Zamboni

Organization

WORDS 2013 was hosted by the Department of Mathematcs of the University of Turku (Finland) under the auspices of the European Association for Theoretical Computer Science. It was organized by the FUNDIM Centre in connection with FiDiPro program of the Academy of Finland.

Program Committee

Francine Blancet-Sadri	University of North Carolina at Greensboro, USA
Arturo Carpi	University of Perugia, Italy
Maxime Crochemore	King's College, London, UK
James Currie	University of Winnipeg, Canada
Juhani Karhumäki	University of Turku, Finland - Co-chair
Dirk Nowotka	University of Kiel, Germany
Edita Pelantová	Czech Technical University in Prague, Czech Republic
Gwénaël Richomme	University of Montpellier 3, France
Michel Rigo	University of Liège, Belgium
Arseny Shur	Ural Federal University, Russia
Luca Zamboni	University of Turku, Finland - Co-chair

Steering Committee

Jean Néraud	Rouen, France
Dominique Perrin	Marne-la-Valle, France
Julien Cassaigne	Marseille, France
Maxime Crochemore	London, UK
Juhani Karhumäki	Turku, Finland - Chair
Jeffrey Shallit	Waterloo, Canada
Aldo de Luca	Naples, Italy
Antonio Restivo	Palermo, Italy
Michail Volkov	Ekaterinburg, Russia
Srecko Brlek	Montreal, Canada
Christophe Reutenauer	Montreal, Canada

Organizing Committee

Michelangelo Bucci   Juhani Karhumäki (Chair)
Svetlana Puzynina   Jetro Vesti
Mari Huova   Jarkko Peltomäki
Aleksi Saarela   Luca Zamboni

Additional Reviewers

M.-P. Béal   I. Gorbunova   B. Nagy
N. Bedaride   V. Halava   P. Ochem
G. Bell   Š. Holub   A. Parreau
M. Berlinkov   J. Honkala   R. Péchoux
J. Bernat   D. Jamet   E. Petrova
É. Charlier   T. Jolivet   A. Plyushchenko
M. Christodoulakis   T. Kamae   A. Saarela
F. D'Alessandro   J. Kari   C. Selmi
A. De Luca   K. Klouda   W. Steiner
F. Durand   J. Leroy   J.-Y. Thibon
S. Fazekas   F. Manea   J. Thuswaldner
F. Franek   Z. Masáková   O. Turek
A. Frid   R. Mercas   E. Vandomme
Y. Gamzova   T. Monteil   S. Widmer
A. Glen   M. Müller

Sponsoring Institutions

University of Turku Foundation
City of Turku
University of Turku
Finnish Academy of Sciences and Letters, Mathematics foundation
Turke Centre for Computer Science
European Association of Theoretical Computer Science

Table of Contents

Invited

Contributions

Which Arnoux-Rauzy Words Are 2-Balanced?

Julien Cassaigne

Institut de mathématiques de Luminy, case 907,
13288 Marseille Cedex 9, France
cassaigne@iml.univ-mrs.fr

Abstract. Arnoux-Rauzy words are one possible generalization of Sturmian words. They are infinite words with exactly one left special factor and one right special factor of each length, those special factors being extendable with any letter in the alphabet. Sturmian words are exactly binary Arnoux-Rauzy words.

We are interested here in the language of an Arnoux-Rauzy word, not in the word itself. Just as the language of a Sturmian word depends only on the associated slope, or equivalently on its continued fraction expansion, the language of an Arnoux-Rauzy word is defined by the associated directive sequence.

A classical property of Sturmian words is that they are 1-balanced: any two factors u and v of the same length of a given Sturmian word contain almost the same number of occurrences of any given letter, the difference being at most 1. Actually, this turns out to be a characterization of Sturmian words: an aperiodic infinite binary word is Sturmian if and only if it is balanced.

For Arnoux-Rauzy words, the situation is quite different. It was expected however that they would be C-balanced for some constant C (the maximum allowed difference in the number of occurrences), but we proved [1] that it is not the case, constructing an Arnoux-Rauzy word which is not C-balanced for any C. This was further improved in [2], where a large class of such words is given. On the other hand, it is easy to construct 2-balanced infinite words that are not Arnoux-Rauzy.

The question of characterizing Arnoux-Rauzy words with a given balance arises then naturally. We restrict here to 2-balance and a ternary alphabet, but even so it does not seem an easy problem. In [3] we obtained a sufficient condition, as well as a necessary condition, both of the type: the set of prefixes of the directive sequence is in a certain rational language.

We were able to obtain a characterization [4], at the expense of replacing C-balance with a stronger notion, strong C-balance. Also, we proved that the set of prefixes of directive sequences of 2-balanced ternary Arnoux-Rauzy words does not form a rational language. Therefore, a characterization of 2-balanced ternary Arnoux-Rauzy in terms of rational languages only is not possible.

References

1. Cassaigne, J., Ferenczi, S., Zamboni, L.Q.: Imbalances in Arnoux-Rauzy Sequences. Ann. Inst. Fourier (Grenoble) 50, 1265–1276 (2000)

J. Karhumäki, A. Lepistö, and L. Zamboni (Eds.): WORDS 2013, LNCS 8079, pp. 1–2, 2013.

2. Cassaigne, J., Ferenczi, S., Messaoudi, A.: Weak mixing of Arnoux-Rauzy Sequences. Ann. Inst. Fourier (Grenoble) 58, 1983–2005 (2008)
3. Berthé, V., Cassaigne, J., Steiner, W.: Balance properties of Arnoux-Rauzy words. Internat. J. Algebra Comput. 23, 689–703 (2013)
4. Cassaigne, J., Nardi, J.: Étude du 2-équilibre des mots d'Arnoux-Rauzy (in preparation)

Dynamical Equivalence of Morphisms

Michel Dekking

Department of Applied Mathematics
Delft University of Technology
The Netherlands
F.M.Dekking@tudelft.nl

Abstract. Infinite words can be fixed points of morphisms, and if the morphism is primitive, then such a word determines a unique dynamical system: the set of infinite words which have the property that each finite subword occurs in the fixed point word. The map on the dynamical system is the shift. Two dynamical systems are isomorphic if there exists a bi-continuous bijection between them which preserves the dynamics. We call two primitive morphisms dynamically equivalent if their dynamical systems are isomorphic. The task is to decide when two morphisms are dynamically equivalent. A morphism is called uniform if all the images of the letters have the same length. A first result is that the number of morphisms (of morphisms with the same length) dynamically equivalent to a given uniform morphism is finite, if the morphisms are one-to-one and if we ignore changes of alphabet. We will present the equivalence class of the Toeplitz morphism $0 \rightarrow 01$, $1 \rightarrow 00$. This is joint work with Ethan Coven and Mike Keane.

J. Karhumäki, A. Lepistö, and L. Zamboni (Eds.): WORDS 2013, LNCS 8079, p. 3, 2013.
© Springer-Verlag Berlin Heidelberg 2013

Deterministic Semi-Thue Systems and Variants of Post Correspondence Problem

Vesa Halava

Department of Mathematics and Statistics
University of Turku
FI-20014 Turku, Finland
vesa.halava@utu.fi

Abstract. We study recent undecidability result on deterministic semi-Thue systems, and it is applications in the variants of Post Correspondence Problem. Namely, we discuss the ideas of the new proofs for the circular PCP and the n-permutation PCP.

1 Introduction

This work is based on the recent articles written jointly with Tero Harju ([3], [4]) and Tero Harju and Mari Huova ([5]). We begin with the definitions and backround.

A *semi-Thue* system T is a pair (Σ, R) where $\Sigma = \{a_1, a_2, \ldots, a_n\}$ is a finite alphabet, the set of the elements of which are called *generators* of T, and $R \subseteq \Sigma^* \times \Sigma^*$ is a relation. The elements of R are called *rules* of T. We say that $T = (\Sigma, R)$ is a *Thue system*, if the relation R is symmetric, i.e., if $(x, y) \in R$, then also $(y, x) \in R$. Clearly, a Thue system corresponds to a semigroup with generators Σ and relations R.

We write $u \longrightarrow_T v$, if there exists a rule $(x, y) \in R$ such that $u = u_1 x u_2$ and $v = u_1 y u_2$ for some words u_1 and u_2. We denote by $\longrightarrow_T^*$ the reflexive and transitive closure of R, and by $\longrightarrow_T^+$ the transitive closure of R.

In the *word problem* for a semi-Thue system T we are given two words $u, v \in \Sigma^*$ and the task is to determine, whether or not there exists a *derivation in T* starting from u to v using the transformation rules in R, that is, whether or not $u \longrightarrow_T^* v$. The first proof for undecidability of the word problem were given independently by Post [18] and Markov [9].

The first concrete example of a finite Thue system with an undecidable word problem was given by Markov [9] in 1947. Markov's result and the proof of it were stated in the terminology of finitely presented semigroups. His example, which had 13 generators and 33 relations, was improved by Ceĭtin [1] (see also Scott [21]), who proved that there exists a Thue system T_7 over a 5-letter alphabet with seven relations that has an undecidable word problem. He applied undecidability result of the special Thue systems, with a reference to Novikov [15], were it was proved that the word problem is undecidable for finitely presented groups.

Makanin [8] made an improvement in 1966 to Ceĭtin's result. Namely, he used Ceĭtin's T_7 to prove that the word problem is undecidable for semigroups with 4 generators and 6 rules. There is a note at the end of Makanin's article that he has found

J. Karhumäki, A. Lepistö, and L. Zamboni (Eds.): WORDS 2013, LNCS 8079, pp. 4–13, 2013.

a 3–generator and 5–rule semigroup with an undecidable word problem. Makanin also notes that Matiyasevich had achieved a similar result in [10]. Finally, Matiyasevich [11] proved that there exists a three rule Thue-system T_3 with an undecidable word problem. From this Pansiot [16] noted that Thue system T_3 can be represented as a semi-Thue systems with only five rules over a 2-letter alphabet.

In 1996 Matiyasevich and Sénizergues proved that the word problem is undecidable for 3–rule semi-Thue systems using a similar approach as Matiyasevich had in T_3; see [12] and [13].

In this article we study the word problem in semi-Thue systems of a restricted type and its application in special variants of the *Post Correspondence Problem* (PCP). This work is based on recent results in [3], [4] and [5].

Here we shall use the following definition of the PCP: Let A and B be two alphabets, in the PCP we are given two morphisms $g, h: A^* \to B^*$, and the task is to determine whether or not there exist a nonempty word $w \in A^+$ such that

$$g(w) = h(w)?$$

Now, in [3] it was proved that the word problem is undecidable in the case of deterministic semi-Thue system. Indeed, the determinism appears there in a rather restricted form. We shall give here a bit more general definition of the determinism. Let $T = (\Sigma, R)$ be a semi-Thue system. Now T is called *(left) deterministic*, if, for all words $u \in \Sigma^*$, left derivation of u is unique in T. Note that a derivation is called *left derivation* if at each step of the derivation the rule of T is used on the leftmost possible position of the word. Moreover, it follows from the proofs and constructions in [3] that the word problem is undecidable for deterministic semi-Thue systems.

The semi-Thue systems constructed in [3] are *reversible*, since the derivation is also backwards deterministic. Using this reversibility, it was proved in [4] that it is undecidable for the deterministic semi-Thue systems whether or not there exist a nonempty derivation $u \to_T^+ u$, i.e., form u back to itself. Such a derivation is called *cyclic*. Moreover, this undecidability of the cyclic word problem was used in [4] to give a new proof for the *circular* Post Correspondence Problem. In the circular PCP we are given two morphism $g, h: A^* \to B^*$, but asked to determine whether or not there exist words $u, v \in A^*$ with $uv \neq \varepsilon$ such that

$$g(uv) = h(vu).$$

Here the words $w_1 = uv$ and $w_2 = vu$ are called *conjugates* of each other. Hence, the circular PCP could be stated by asking does the exist conjugate words w_1 and w_2 such that $g(w_1) = h(w_2)$? The phrase 'circular PCP' refers to the problem setting where the words are considered to be cyclic, i.e., the last letter is followed by the first letter.

The circular PCP was originally shown to be undecidable by Ruohonen in [19], where the proof employs an undecidable property of *linearly bounded automata*. The proof by Ruohonen is rather long and technical, and therefore, there was request for a simpler proof for this problem.

In [19] Ruohonen also proved that the *n-permutation* PCP, asking, for morphisms $g, h: A^* \to B^*$, whether or not there exists a word $w = w_1 w_2 \cdots w_n$ and permutation σ of the set $\{1, 2, \ldots, n\}$ such that

$$g(w_1 \cdots w_n) = h(w_{\sigma(1)} \cdots w_{\sigma(n)}),$$

is undecidable. A new proof for the *n*-permutation PCP was given in [5], using the undecidability of the cyclic word problem for deterministic semi-Thue systems proved in [4]. Note that the circular PCP is indeed the 2-permutation PCP and trivially 1-permutation PCP is the PCP.

Note that the technique for transforming semi-Thue systems to instances of the PCP was originally introduced by Claus [2]. The idea is to simulate a derivation of the semi-Thue system T on a word u with two morphisms g, h such that there exist a word w with $g(w) = h(w)$ if and only if there is a derivation in T starting from u and ending in the given word v. Here the word w corresponds to a required derivation according to T. Hence we may say that the morphisms g and h *simulate* derivations of T starting from a given word u.

Finally, note also that in some undecidability proofs, the existence of so called reversible Turing machine is required. These machines are very restricted in the sense that in each step of a computation the previous configuration of the computation can be uniquely determined. Reversible Turing machines are employed for example in the case of the injective PCP; see Lecerf [7] and Ruohonen [20]. Indeed, in the construction of the deterministic, or reversible, semi-Thue system the similar idea is used, and the reversibility is actually employed to achieve the cyclic computation back to the beginning. The idea of the reversible rewriting system was already used in [6] where Karhumäki and Saarela gave a new prove for the undecidability of the injective PCP and the deterministic and reversible semi-Thue systems were originally discovered from their construction.

2   Special Semi-Thue Systems

The special deterministic (and reversible) semi-Thue systems are constructed from the deterministic Turing machines in a following way. Let $\mathcal{M}$ be a Turing machine (TM) with a unique halting state, that is, $\mathcal{M}$ is a 7–tuple

$$\mathcal{M} = (Q, \Sigma, \Gamma, \delta, q_0, \star, H),$$

where Q is a finite set of states, q_0 is the initial state, $H \in Q$ is the halting state, Σ is the input alphabet, Γ is the tape alphabet with $\Sigma \subseteq \Gamma$, and $\delta: Q \times \Gamma \to Q \times \Gamma \times \{L, R\}$ is a partial function called the *transition function* where L and R are special direction symbols and $\star \in \Gamma$ is the blank symbol.

Note that the TM $\mathcal{M}$ is deterministic, but we allow δ to be a partial function, i.e., it may be undefined for some elements $(q, a) \in Q \times \Sigma$.

Each *transition* of $\mathcal{M}$ is of the form $\delta(p, a) = (q, b, D)$ that we shall also write more conveniently in the following form

$$(p, a) \longrightarrow (q, b, D) \quad \text{with } p, q \in Q, \ a, b \in \Gamma \text{ and } D \in \{L, R\}.$$

Here D refers to 'direction' and L and R refer to 'left move' and 'right move', respectively.

A configuration of a TM at some point in its computation is a word $u(q,a)v \in \Gamma^*(Q \times \Gamma)\Gamma^+$ where $u = \varepsilon$ or u begins with a nonblank letter, $v = \star$ or v ends with a nonblank letter. A configuration describes the global state of the Turing machine: uav is the shortest word from the tape containing all squares filled by nonblank symbols while the TM is currently in state q and reading the symbol a on its position.

A *step in a computation* or a *move* $\gamma \vdash \gamma'$ yielding from one configuration γ of $\mathcal{M}$ to the next one γ' is defined as follows. Let $\gamma = a_1 a_2 \cdots a_{i-1}(p, a_i)a_{i+1} \cdots a_n$.

(L) For a *left transition* $\delta(p, a_i) = (q, b, L)$, let

$$a_1 \cdots a_{i-1}(p, a_i)a_{i+1} \cdots a_n \vdash_{\mathcal{M}} \begin{cases} a_1 \cdots a_{i-2}(q, a_{i-1})ba_{i+1} \cdots a_n & \text{if } i > 1, \\ (q, \star)ba_{i+1} \cdots a_n & \text{if } i = 1. \end{cases}$$

(R) For a *right transition* $\delta(p, a_i) = (q, b, R)$, let

$$a_1 \cdots a_{i-1}(p, a_i)a_{i+1} \cdots a_n \vdash_{\mathcal{M}} \begin{cases} a_1 \cdots a_{i-1}b(q, a_{i+1}) \cdots a_n & \text{if } i < n, \\ a_1 \cdots a_{i-1}b(q, \star) & \text{if } i = n. \end{cases}$$

We notice that, since δ is a (partial) function, for each configuration $\gamma = u(q, a)v$, there exists at most one configuration γ' such that $\gamma \vdash_{\mathcal{M}} \gamma'$.

Let $\vdash_{\mathcal{M}}^*$ or $\vdash^*$ for simplicity, be the reflexive and transitive closure of the relation $\vdash_{\mathcal{M}}$. Also, $\gamma \vdash^* \gamma'$ is an *accepting* computation if the state in γ' is the halting state H.

We shall now start the construction of the semi-Thue system of the desired form for a given TM $\mathcal{M}$. The construction is from [3] where it is mentioned that it originates from an article by Karhumäki and Saarela [6] where the authors gave a new proof for the undecidability of the injective PCP.

Let $\mathcal{M} = (Q, \Sigma, \Gamma, \delta, q_0, \star, H)$ be a given Turing machine. We define three alphabets Δ, Θ and Λ. First let

$$\Delta = \Gamma \cup (Q \times \Gamma)$$

and

$$\Theta = \Delta \times (\{S\} \cup (Q \times \Gamma)),$$

where S is a new symbol. We write the second component from $\{S\} \cup (Q \times \Gamma)$ below the first component from Δ. For instance, if $q \in Q$ and $a \in \Gamma$, then

$$\underset{S}{(q, a)} \in \Theta \quad \text{and} \quad \underset{(q,a)}{a} \in \Theta.$$

Finally, let

$$\Lambda = \Delta \cup \Theta \cup \{\#, \$\}$$
$$= (\Gamma \cup (Q \times \Gamma)) \cup (\Delta \times (\{S\} \cup (Q \times \Gamma))) \cup \{\#, \$\},$$

where $\#$ and $\$$ are again new symbols.

We define the semi-Thue system $S_{\mathcal{M}}$ on Λ for a given TM $\mathcal{M}$ as

$$S_{\mathcal{M}} = (\Lambda, R_1),$$

where R_1 consists of the following rules for $a, b, c, b' \in \Gamma$ with $a, c, b' \neq \star$, and $q, q' \in Q$ and $y, z \in \Delta$.

$$\underset{S}{a z} \longrightarrow \underset{S}{a z}, \qquad\qquad z \neq (q_0, \star), \tag{1}$$

$$\underset{S}{a(q, b)} \longrightarrow \underset{(q,b)}{(q', a)b'}, \qquad\qquad \text{if } \delta(q, b) = (q', b', L), \tag{2}$$

$$\underset{S}{\#(q, b)} \longrightarrow \underset{(q,b)}{\#(q', \star)b'}, \qquad\qquad \text{if } \delta(q, b) = (q', b', L), \tag{3}$$

$$\underset{S}{(q, b)c} \longrightarrow \underset{(q,b)}{b'(q', c)}, \qquad\qquad \text{if } \delta(q, b) = (q', b', R), \tag{4}$$

$$\underset{S}{(q, b)\$} \longrightarrow \underset{(q,b)}{b'(q', \star)\$}, \qquad\qquad \text{if } \delta(q, b) = (q', b', R), \tag{5}$$

$$\underset{(q,b)}{a \ y} \longrightarrow \underset{(q,b)}{a \ y}, \tag{6}$$

$$\underset{(q,b)}{\# \ y} \longrightarrow \underset{S}{(q, b)\# y}. \tag{7}$$

The idea in the semi-Thue system $S_{\mathcal{M}}$ is the following. The special symbols # and \$ correspond to the endmarkers of the tape of $\mathcal{M}$. For the initial configuration $(q_0, \star)$ of $\mathcal{M}$ there corresponds the initial word $\#(q, \star)\$$. For a symbol (q, a), we simulate a move of the TM $\mathcal{M}$. First, by applying a rule from (2) - (5) we will have the symbol (q', x) in our word. Then the lower part (q, b) is shifted step by step to the left by the rules (6). On the marker # the pair (q, b), for which the transition of $\mathcal{M}$ was applied, is written to the left of # by the rule (7), and then we will be dealing with the symbol $\underset{S}{y}$. Finally, the underlying symbol S is shifted under the symbol (q', x) with the rule (1). Note also that the rules (3) and (5) work on the left and right boundary of the configuration by adding a symbol $\star$ by the boundary if the head of the Turing machine moves out of the old configuration.

It follows that the construction of the semi-Thue system $S_{\mathcal{M}}$ works in the following way, for details see [3]: Assume then that there is a halting computation for the initial configuration $(q_0, \star)$ of $\mathcal{M}$. This means that

$$(q_0, \star) \vdash^*_{\mathcal{M}} u(H, a)v$$

for some $u, v \in \Gamma^*$ and $a \in \Gamma$. Then in the semi-Thue system $S_{\mathcal{M}}$ the unique deduction stating from the initial word $\#(q_0, \star)\$$ is of the form

$$\underset{S}{\#(q_0, \star)\$} \longrightarrow^+_{S_{\mathcal{M}}} x_1 x_2 \cdots x_k \underset{S}{\#u(H, a)v\$},$$

where $x_i \in Q \times \Gamma$ for each i. Note that the word $x_1 x_2 \cdots x_k$ is indeed the the *history* of the derivation of $S_{\mathcal{M}}$. We shall define a modified semi-Thue system, using the history word $x_1 x_2 \cdots x_k$ to reverse the computation back to the initial configuration after meeting the unique halting state. The construction is as follows.

Define the alphabet

$$\overline{\Theta} = \left\{ \underset{y}{\overline{x}} \ \Big| \ \underset{y}{x} \neq \underset{S}{(H, a)}, \ a \in \Gamma \right\},$$

i.e., $\overline{\Theta}$ contains an overlined copy of the symbols in Θ that are not of the form $(H, a)_s$. Next define the new rules. Let

$$t = (z \underset{y}{x} w \longrightarrow z' \underset{y'}{x'} w') \in R_1$$

be a rule of $S_{\mathcal{M}}$, where z, z', w, w' may be empty. If $\underset{y'}{x'} \neq (H, a)_s$ for all $a \in \Gamma$, we define a new rule

$$\overline{t} = (z' \underset{y'}{\overline{x'}} w' \longrightarrow z \underset{y}{\overline{x}} w),$$

and if $\underset{y'}{x'} = (H, a)_s$ for some $a \in \Gamma$, then define

$$\overline{t} = (z' \underset{y'}{x'} w' \longrightarrow z \underset{y}{\overline{x}} w) = (z'(H, a)_s w' \longrightarrow z \underset{y}{\overline{x}} w). \qquad (8)$$

Therefore, in effect, the rule $\overline{t}$ does the reverse transition of the original rule t, but with a unique symbol from $\overline{\Theta}$ instead of Θ. The symbol $(H, a)_s$ is not overlined as seen in (8). Set

$$\overline{R_1} = \left\{ \overline{t} \mid t \in R_1 \right\}, \quad R = R_1 \cup \overline{R_1}, \quad \text{and} \quad \Xi = \Lambda \cup \overline{\Theta}. \qquad (9)$$

Let then

$$\overline{S}_{\mathcal{M}} = (\Xi, R).$$

Lemma 1. *The semi-Thue system $\overline{S}_{\mathcal{M}}$ is deterministic.*

Proof. The proof is omitted here, we only state the idea of the proof. The claim follows from the construction since in R each rule contains one letter from the set $\Theta \cup \overline{\Theta}$ and this symbol together with the surrounding symbols imply that there is a unique rule in R that can be used on the leftmost possible position of any word from Ξ^*.

For the proof of the following lemma, see [3].

Lemma 2. *Let $\mathcal{M}$ be a Turing machine and let $\overline{S}_{\mathcal{M}} = (\Xi, R)$ be defined as above for $\mathcal{M}$. Then there exists a halting computation for empty input in $\mathcal{M}$ if and only if*

$$\#(q_0, \star)_s \$ \underset{\overline{S}_{\mathcal{M}}}{\overset{*}{\longrightarrow}} \#\overline{(q_0, \star)}_s \$. \qquad (10)$$

Now using the undecidability of the *halting problem* of Turing machines on empty input (see, e.g., Manna [14]) Lemma 2 yields the following result.

Theorem 1. *The word problem is undecidable for deterministic semi-Thue systems.*

It is rather straightforward to modify the semi-Thue system $\overline{S}_{\mathcal{M}}$ to get the undecidability for cyclic derivation of the semi-Thue system. Indeed, it can be done by adding a single rule to it:

$$t_C = \#\overline{(q_0, \star)}_s \$ \longrightarrow \#(q_0, \star)_s \$. \qquad (11)$$

Denote this new semi-Thue system corresponding to the TM $\mathcal{M}$ by $C_{\mathcal{M}}$. Note that the rule t_C in (11) simply transforms the unique final configuration back to the initial configuration.

The next lemma is now obvious by the previous steps of the construction.

Lemma 3. *Let $\mathcal{M}$ be a Turing machine and $C_{\mathcal{M}}$ be the semi-Thue system as defined in the above. Then $\mathcal{M}$ halts on the empty input word if and only if there exists a cyclic derivation*

$$\#(q_0,\star)\$ \underset{S}{\to^*_{C_{\mathcal{M}}}} \#\overline{(q_0,\star)}\$ \underset{S}{\to_{C_{\mathcal{M}}}} \#(q_0,\star)\$ \tag{12}$$

according to C_M

3   Circular PCP

The standard reduction, as introduced by Claus [2], of a semi-Thue system to the PCP uses both initial and final words of the word problem. Here in the cyclic case these words will be equal. Therefore, we are able to construct a reduction where the PCP has a circular solution if and only if the derivation in $C_{\mathcal{M}}$ returns to the initial configuration $\#(q_0,\star)\$$.

Let d be a new symbol not in Ξ, defined in (9), and let ℓ_d and r_d be the *desynchronizing morphisms* defined by $\ell_d(x) = dx$ and $r_d(x) = xd$ for each letter $x \in \Delta_1$.

We define two morphisms, $g, h: (\Delta_1 \cup R \cup \{t_C\})^* \to (\Xi \cup \{d\})^*$ as follows. For any letter $a \in \Delta_1$, set

$$g(a) = \ell_d(a) = da \quad \text{and} \quad h(a) = r_d(a) = ad,$$

and for $t \notin \{t_I, t_C\}$, say $t = u_1\theta_1 v_1 \longrightarrow u_2\theta_2 v_2$, where $u_1, u_2, v_1, v_2 \in \Delta_1^*$ and $\theta_1, \theta_2 \in \Theta \cup \overline{\Theta}$, we set

$$g(t) = \ell_d(u_1\theta_1 v_1) \quad \text{and} \quad h(t) = r_d(u_2\theta_2 v_2).$$

For t_C, let

$$g(t_C) = \ell_d(\#\overline{(q_0,\star)}\$)d \quad \text{and} \quad h(t_C) = d\,r_d(\#(q_0,\star)\$).$$

We denote the first rule of the unique derivation in the semi-Thue system by t_I, i.e.,

$$t_I = \#(q_0,\star)\$ \underset{(q_0,\star)}{\longrightarrow} u_1(q',x)v_1, \tag{13}$$

for some $u_1, v_1 \in \Delta_1^*$, where $\Delta_1 = \Delta \cup \{\#, \$\} = \Lambda \setminus \Theta$. Now, for the letter t_I in (13), set

$$g(t_I) = \ell_d(\#(q_0,\star)\$) \quad \text{and} \quad h(t_I) = r_d(u_1(q',x)v_1).$$

The following theorem was proved in [4].

Theorem 2. *There exists a nonempty computation*

$$\#(q_0,\star)\$ \underset{S}{\longrightarrow^+} \#(q_0,\star)\$$$

in $C_{\mathcal{M}}$ if and only if there exists a non empty $w \in (\Delta_1 \cup R \cup \{t_C\})^*$ such that $w = uv$ and $g(uv) = h(vu)$ for some words u and v.

Proof. We only sketch the idea here. The idea is to use the fact that the right hand side of the rule t_C is equal to the left hand side of t_I together with the desynchronizing to force the symbol t_C to be the first symbol with respect to the morphism h in order to get equal images for h and g. Indeed, assume that there is the cyclic derivation in $C_{\mathcal{M}}$, say of the form

$$\#(q_0,\star)\$ \underset{S}{\longrightarrow} \beta_2 \longrightarrow \beta_3 \longrightarrow \cdots \longrightarrow \beta_k \longrightarrow \beta_{k+1} = \#(q_0,\star)\$, \tag{14}$$

and the rules used in the derivation are $t_I, t_2, \ldots, t_{k-1}, t_C$. Then clearly there exists words u_i, v_i for $i = 1, \ldots, k$, such that $g(u_i t_i v_i) = \ell_d(\beta_i)$ and $h(u_i t_i v_i) = r_d(\beta_{i+1})$, and $d\, r_d(\beta_k) = d\, h(u_{k-1} t_{k-1} v_{k-1}) = g(t_C) = \ell_d(\#(q_0,\star)\$)d$. Then, we have that for

$$w = t_I(u_2 t_2 v_2)(u_3 t_3 v_3)\cdots(u_{k-1} t_{k-1} v_{k-1})t_C = uv, \tag{15}$$

where $v = t_C$, and $g(w) = h(vu)$.

The proof for the other direction of the claim is omitted here, since the proof is quite long and technical.

For the complete proof of the following theorem, see [4].

Theorem 3. *The circular PCP is undecidable.*

4 n-Permutation PCP

For the n-permutation PCP, the idea of the construction is again rather straight-forward, but the proof becomes technical while showing that a solution for the n-permutation PCP implies a cyclic derivation in $C_{\mathcal{M}}$.

First, we take $n-1$ copies the semi-Thue system $C_{\mathcal{M}}$, meaning that we have $n-1$ copies of letters of the alphabet Ξ and rule symbols $R \cup \{t_C\}$. Denote by $\alpha^{(i)}$ the ith copy of $\alpha \in \Xi \cup R \cup \{t_C\}$ and for a word $w \in \Xi \cup \{d\}$, denote by $w^{(i)}$ the word where every letter of Ξ is replaced by the ith copy of it (note: there is only one copy of d). Now let τ be a permutation of the set $\{1, \ldots, n-1\}$ and set for all $\alpha \in \Delta_1 \cup R$

$$g(\alpha^{(i)}) = (g(\alpha))^i \quad \text{and} \quad h(\alpha^{(i)}) = (g(\alpha))^{(\tau(i))}$$

and for letters $t_C^{(i)}$ define

$$g(t_C^{(i)}) = (\ell_d(\#(q_0,\star)\$))^{(i)}_S \quad \text{and} \quad h(t_C) = (r_d(\#(q_0,\star)\$))^{(\tau(i)+1)}_S$$

for $i = 1, \ldots, n-2$, and for $i = n-1$, we define

$$g(t_C^{(n-1)}) = (\ell_d(\#\overline{(q_0,\star)}\$)d)^{(n-1)}_S \quad \text{and} \quad h(t_C) = (d\, r_d(\#(q_0,\star)\$))^{(1)}_S.$$

Assume that $C_{\mathcal{M}}$ has a cyclic computation of the form (14) and let w be as in (15). Now set $\omega = w^{(1)} w^{(2)} \cdots w^{(n-1)}$, then clearly

$$g(\omega) = (\ell_d(\#(q_0,\star)\$\beta_2 \cdots \beta_k))^{(1)}_S \cdots (\ell_d(\#(q_0,\star)\$\beta_2 \cdots \beta_k)d)^{(n-1)}_S$$

and

$$h(\omega) = (r_d(\beta_2 \cdots \beta_k))^{(\tau(1))} (r_d(\#(q_0, \star)\$))^{(\tau(1)+1)}_S$$

$$(r_d(\beta_2 \cdots \beta_k))^{\tau(2)} (r_d(\#(q_0, \star)\$))^{(\tau(2)+1)}_S \cdots$$

$$(r_d(\#(q_0, \star)\$))^{(\tau(n-2)+1)}_S (r_d(\beta_2 \cdots \beta_k))^{\tau(n-1)} (d\, r_d(\#(q_0, \star)\$))^{(1)}_S.$$

Define next the permutation σ by setting $\sigma(1) = n$ and $\sigma(i) = \tau^{(-1)}(i-1)$ for $i = 2, \ldots n$. Finally, set the words w_i' so that

$$\omega = w_1' t_C^{(1)} w_2' t_C^{(2)} \cdots w_{n-1}' t_C^{(n-1)},$$

and, further, set $w_i = w_i' t_C^{(i)}$ for $i = 1, \ldots, n-2$, $w_{n-1} = w_{n-1}'$ and $w_n = t_C^{(n-1)}$. It can be shown that,

$$g(w_1 \ldots w_n) = h(w_{\sigma(1)} w_{\sigma(2)} \cdots w_{\sigma(n)}).$$

As mentioned above, to prove that if there exists a solution for the instance (g, h) of n-permutation, then $C_{\mathcal{M}}$ has the cyclic derivation of the form (14), is rather long and technical. Therefore, we omit it the proof here, for the full proof of the following theorem, see [5].

Theorem 4. *The n-permutation PCP is undecidable.*

Note that actually the n-permutation PCP is undecidable for both existence of a solution for a fixed permutation and existence of solution for any n-permutation.

Acknowledgement. The author is grateful to Prof. Tero Harju for his valuable comments, especially for comments which were completely unrelated to this work or any other scientific work of the author.

References

1. Ceĭtin, G.C.: Associative calculus with an unsolvable equivalence problem. Tr. Mat. Inst. Akad. Nauk 52, 172–189 (1958) (Russian)
2. Claus, V.: Some remarks on PCP(k) and related problems. Bull. EATCS 12, 54–61 (1980)
3. Halava, V., Harju, T.: Word problem for deterministic and reversible semi-Thue systems, manuscript (submitted), TUCS Technical Report 1044, TUCS (2012)
4. Halava, V., Harju, T.: New Proof for the Undecidability of the Circular PCP (submitted) TUCS Technical Reports 1059, TUCS (2012)
5. Halava, V., Harju, T., Huova, M.: On n-permutation Post Correspondence Problem. (manuscript) to appear in TUCS Technical Reports series (2013)
6. Karhumäki, J., Saarela, A.: Noneffective Regularity of Equality Languages and Bounded Delay Morphisms. Discrete Mathematics & Theoretical Computer Science 12(4), 9–18 (2010)
7. Lecerf, M.Y.: Récursive insolubilité de l'équation générale de diagonalisation de deux monomorphismes de monoïdes libres $\varphi x = \psi x$. Comptes Rendus 257, 2940–2943 (1963)
8. Makanin, G.S.: The identity problem in finitely defined semigroups. Dokl. Akad. Nauk SSR 107(2), 285–287 (1966)

9. Markov, A.A.: On the impossibility of certain algorithms in the theory of associative systems. Dokl. Akad. Nauk 55, 587–590 (1947); 58, 353–356 (1947) (Russian)
10. Matiyasevich, Y.: Simple examples of unsolvable associative calculi. Trudy Mat. Inst. Steklov 93, 50–88 (1967) (Russian)
11. Matiyasevich, Y.: Simple examples of unsolvable associative calculi. Dokl. Akad. Nauk 173, 1264–1266 (1967) (Russian); Soviet Math. Docl. 8(2), 555–557 (1967) (English)
12. Matiyasevich, Y., Sénizergues, G.: Decision problems for semi-Thue systems with a few rules. In: Proceedings of the 11th IEEE Symposium on Logic in Computer Science, pp. 523–531 (1996)
13. Matiyasevich, Y., Sénizergues, G.: Decision problems for semi–Thue systems with a few rules. Theor. Comput. Sci. 330(1), 145–169 (2005)
14. Manna, Z.: Mathematical Theory of Computation. McGraw-Hill Computer Science Series. McGraw-Hill Book Co. (1974); Reprinted, Dover (2003)
15. Novikov, P.S.: On the algorithmic unsolvability of the problem of equality of words in group theory. Tr. Mat. Inst. Akad. Nauk 44, 1–144 (1955) (Russian)
16. Pansiot, J.J.: A note on Post's Correspondence Problem. Inform. Proc. Lett. 12, 233 (1981)
17. Post, E.: A variant of a recursively unsolvable problem. Bulletin of Amer. Math. Soc. 52, 264–268 (1946)
18. Post, E.: Recursive unsolvability of a problem of Thue. J. Symb. Logic 12, 1–11 (1947)
19. Ruohonen, K.: On some variants of Post's correspondence problem. Acta Informatica 19, 357–367 (1983)
20. Ruohonen, K.: Reversible machines and Post's correspondence problem for biprefix morphisms. J. Inform. Process. Cybernet. EIK 21, 579–595 (1985)
21. Scott, D.: A short recursively unsolvable problem. J. Symb. Logic 21, 111–112 (1956)

Subword Complexity in Free Groups

Gilbert Levitt

Laboratoire LMNO,
Université de Caen, F14032 Caen Cedex
France
levitt@math.unicaen.fr

Abstract. Subword complexity is a basic invariant for words on a finite alphabet. I will explain how one can define a complexity for points in the boundary of a finitely generated free group F or for a lamination on F. This complexity, or rather the way it grows, is invariant under automorphisms of F and may be interpreted geometrically. I will discuss a version of Pansiot's theorem about the complexity of fixed points of substitutions in the context of automorphisms of free groups. This is based on joint work with Arnaud Hilion.

J. Karhumäki, A. Lepistö, and L. Zamboni (Eds.): WORDS 2013, LNCS 8079, p. 14, 2013.
© Springer-Verlag Berlin Heidelberg 2013

Non-constructive Methods
for Avoiding Repetitions in Words

Narad Rampersad

Department of Mathematics and Statistics, University of Winnipeg
515 Portage Ave., Winnipeg MB, R3B 0M3, Canada
narad.rampersad@gmail.com

Abstract. We survey several different non-constructive methods for showing the avoidability of certain kinds of repetitions in words.

Many problems in combinatorics on words have the following form:

> Let S be a given set of words over an alphabet Σ. Does there exist an infinite word over the alphabet Σ that avoids S? That is, does there exist an infinite word $\mathbf{w}$ such that no factor of $\mathbf{w}$ is an element of S?

For example, one might take $S = \{xx : x \in \{0, 1, 2\}^*\}$; i.e., S is the set of *squares* over a 3-letter alphabet. In this case, the affirmative answer to the above question is a classical result of Thue [11].

Thue's demonstration of this result is constructive. He explicitly produces an infinite word with the desired property; this word is defined by iterating a *morphism*. The study of morphisms and *morphic words* is itself a very rich area, but this is by no means the only method for demonstrating avoidability in words. Here we focus on non-constructive methods, i.e., those based on some type of counting or probabilistic argument.

One of the earliest results on words to be proved using the probabilistic method is the following theorem due to Beck [1]:

Theorem 1. *For any real $\epsilon > 0$, there exist an integer N_ϵ and an infinite binary word $\mathbf{w}$ such that for every factor x of $\mathbf{w}$ of length $n > N_\epsilon$, all occurrences of x in $\mathbf{w}$ are separated by a distance at least $(2 - \epsilon)^n$.*

Beck's proof of this result is based on a lemma from probabilistic combinatorics known as the Lovász local lemma. In 2010, Moser and Tardos [7] gave an algorithmic version of the Lovász local lemma based on an argument known as *entropy compression*. Grytczuk, Kozik, and Micek [5] used this entropy compression method to prove the following theorem.

Theorem 2. *For every sequence $L_1, L_2, \ldots$ of 4-element sets, there exists a squarefree word $s_1 s_2 \cdots$ such that $s_i \in L_i$ for all $i \geq 1$.*

Bell and Goh [2] used another non-constructive method, based on generating functions, to prove some results concerning avoidability of patterns. Their approach was based on the following special case of a result of Golod (see Rowen [9, Lemma 6.2.7]):

J. Karhumäki, A. Lepistö, and L. Zamboni (Eds.): WORDS 2013, LNCS 8079, pp. 15–17, 2013.

Theorem 3. *Let S be a set of words over a k-letter alphabet, each word of length at least 2. Suppose that for each $i \geq 2$, the set S contains at most c_i words of length i. If the power series expansion of*

$$G(x) := \left(1 - kx + \sum_{i \geq 2} c_i x^i \right)^{-1}$$

has non-negative coefficients, then there are least $[x^n]G(x)$ words of length n over an k-letter alphabet that avoid S.

This next result, which confirmed a conjecture of Cassaigne [4], was proved in 2013 simultaneously and independently by Ochem and Pinlou [8] and by Blanchet-Sadri and Woodhouse [3].

Theorem 4. *Let p be a pattern with m distinct variables.*

1. *If $|p| \geq 3 \cdot 2^{m-1}$, then p is avoidable over a binary alphabet.*
2. *If $|p| \geq 2^m$, then p is avoidable over a ternary alphabet.*

Pinlou and Ochem obtained this result by applying the Moser–Tardos entropy compression method, and Blanchet-Sadri and Woodhouse proved the result by using the method of Theorem 3.

Another criterion for the avoidability of a set S over a k-letter alphabet, which is somewhat similar to that of Theorem 3, is the following, due to Miller [6].

Proposition 1. *Let S be a set of non-empty words over a k-letter alphabet Σ. If there exists $c \in (1/k, 1)$ such that*

$$\sum_{s \in S} c^{|s|} \leq kc - 1,$$

then there is an infinite word over Σ that avoids S.

From this one can derive the following result, which had previously been established by Rumyantsev and Ushakov [10] using an argument based on Kolmogorov complexity.

Corollary 1. *Let S be a set of non-empty words over a k-letter alphabet Σ and let $\alpha \in [0, 1)$. There is a positive integer d such that if S contains at most $k^{\alpha m}$ words of length m for each $m \geq d$, and none of length less than d, then there is an infinite word over Σ that avoids S.*

These are just some selected examples to illustrate applications of some of these non-constructive methods. There are, of course, many other results on words that have been shown using these types of techniques.

References

1. Beck, J.: An application of Lovász local lemma: there exists an infinite 01-sequence containing no near identical intervals. In: Hajnal, A., et al. (eds.) Infinite and Finite Sets. Colloq. Math. Soc. J. Bolyai, vol. 37, pp.103–107 (1981)
2. Bell, J., Goh, T.L.: Lower bounds for pattern avoidance. Inform. and Comput. 205, 1295–1306 (2007)
3. Blanchet-Sadri, F., Woodhouse, B.: Strict bounds for pattern avoidance (preprint)
4. Cassaigne, J.: Motifs évitables et régularités dans les mots. Thèse de doctorat, Université Paris 6, LITP research report TH 94-04
5. Grytczuk, J., Kozik, J., Micek, P.: New approach to nonrepetitive sequences. Random Structures Algorithms 42, 214–225 (2013)
6. Miller, J.: Two notes on subshifts. Proc. Amer. Math. Soc. 140, 1617–1622 (2012)
7. Moser, R.A., Tardos, G.: A constructive proof of the general Lovász local lemma. J. ACM 57, Art. 11 (2010)
8. Ochem, P., Pinlou, A.: Application of entropy compression in pattern avoidance. Preprint available at http://arxiv.org/abs/1301.1873
9. Rowen, L.: Ring Theory. Vol. II. Pure and Applied Mathematics, vol. 128. Academic Press, Boston (1988)
10. Rumyantsev, A.Y., Ushakov, M.A.: Forbidden substrings, Kolmogorov complexity and almost periodic sequences. In: Durand, B., Thomas, W. (eds.) STACS 2006. LNCS, vol. 3884, pp. 396–407. Springer, Heidelberg (2006)
11. Thue, A.: Über unendliche Zeichenreihen. Kra. Vidensk. Selsk. Skrifter. I. Mat. Nat. Kl. 7, 1–22 (1906)

Words, Trees and Automata Minimization

Giusi Castiglione and Marinella Sciortino

DMI, Università di Palermo, via Archirafi, 34 - 90123 Palermo, Italy
{giusi,mari}@math.unipa.it

Abstract. In this paper we explore some connections between some combinatorial properties of words and the study of extremal cases of the automata minimization process. An intermediate role is played by the notion od word trees for which some properties of words are generalized. In particular, we describe an infinite family of binary automata, called *word automata* and constructed by using standard sturmian words and more specifically Fibonacci words, that represent the extremal case of some well known automata minimization algorithms, such as Moore's and Hopcroft's methods. As well as giving an overview of the main results in this context, the main purpose of this paper is to prove that, even if a recently introduced polynomial variants of Brzozowski's algorithm is considered, such family of word automata represent the worst case for the number of steps and for its overall time complexity. This fact suggests that the standard sturmian words, and consequently the associated word automata, are able to capture some properties for which the minimization process becomes inherently more complex.

1 Introduction

In this paper we explore and describe some close connections between combinatorics on words and automata minimization algorithms. In particular, we are interested in some combinatorial properties of words that have been fundamental and useful to study extremal cases of important and well-known minimization algorithms, such as Hopcroft's algorithm and Brzozowski's algorithm.

More in detail, in [10,4] some combinatorial properties of standard sturmian words, circularly considered, have been related with the execution of Hopcroft's algorithm. It has been shown in [10,12] that a circular special factor of a word corresponds to a refining operation (called *split*) of the partition of the states of unary and binary automata constructed by using such a word. In the construction of these unary, and especially binary, automata the words are used to define the state's labels and the edge's labels. Such automata, also called *word automata* are in fact constructed from binary trees whose structures and labels are defined by the words. Such trees are called *word trees*.

It is well known (cf. [21]) that Hopcroft's algorithm is ambiguous and it can produce several and different executions on the same automaton having time complexity with different orders of magnitude. It has been proved in [13] that if the word automata are constructed by using word trees associated to standard sturmian words (also called *standard word trees*) all the executions have

J. Karhumäki, A. Lepistö, and L. Zamboni (Eds.): WORDS 2013, LNCS 8079, pp. 18–33, 2013.

running time with the same asymptotic growth rate. In particular, lower and upper bound for the running time of the algorithm can be expressed in terms of combinatorial properties of the trees and consequently of the standard sturmian words. Moreover, for certain subfamilies obtained from circular Fibonacci words, Hopcroft's algorithm is tight, i.e. all its executions have time complexity $\Theta(n \log n)$, where n is the number of states of the automaton.

Standard sturmian words have a crucial role in extremal cases of many algorithms in several context, such as data compression algorithms (cf. [27]), periodicity of words [16,15,17], pattern matching algorithm, suffix automata (cf. [22]). In this paper we show that the combinatorial properties of the standard sturmian words and the associated word trees, used for the construction of the word automata above mentioned, have a crucial role in the study of the extremal cases of the problem of minimizing finite state automata. In fact, it has been proved in [9] that such families of automata represent a challenge also for Brzozowski's minimization algorithm, in the sense that at least quadratic is the running time for the algorithm on these automata. However, Brzozowski's algorithm is exponential in the worst case because a determinization of a non-deterministic automaton is required, although in [3,28] it is experimentally verified that in practice Brzozowski's algorithm has a good performance and usually outperforms the other algorithms when applied on non-deterministic finite state automata. In this paper we prove that, even if new polynomial variants of Brzozowski's algorithm recently introduced in [19] are considered, the family of word automata associated to standard word trees and more specifically to word trees constructed from Fibonacci words represent the worst cases in the number of steps and in the overall time complexity, respectively. This fact suggests that the standard sturmian words, and consequently the associated word automata, are able to capture some properties for which the minimization process becomes inherently more complex.

2   Preliminaries

In this section we recall some basic definitions about words and automata that will be used in the paper.

Let Σ be a finite alphabet and v, u be two words in Σ^*. We say that v and u are *conjugate* if for some words $z, w \in \Sigma^*$ one has that $v = zw$ and $u = wz$. It is easy to see that conjugation is an equivalence relation. Note that many combinatorial properties of words in A^* can be thought as properties of the respective conjugacy classes.

We say that a word $v \in \Sigma^*$ is a *circular factor* of a word w if v is a factor of some conjugate of w. Equivalently, a circular factor of w is a factor of ww of length not greater than the length of w ($|w|$). Note that, while each factor of w is also a circular factor of w, there exist circular factors of a word w that are not factors of w. For instance, ca is a circular factor of abc without being factor of abc.

Moreover, a circular factor u of w is said to be *special* if both ua and ub are circular factors of w.

In this paper an important role is played by a well known family of words, the *standard sturmian words*. Let $d_1, d_2, \ldots, d_n, \ldots$ be a sequence of natural integers, with $d_1 \geq 0$ and $d_i > 0$, for $i = 2, \ldots, n, \ldots$. Consider the following sequence of words $\{s_n\}_{n \geq 0}$ over the alphabet $A = \{a, b\}$: $s_0 = b$, $s_1 = a$, $s_{n+1} = s_n^{d_n} s_{n-1}$ for $n \geq 1$. Each finite word s_n in the sequence is called *standard sturmian word*. It is uniquely determined by the (finite) directive sequence $(d_0, d_1, \ldots, d_{n-1})$. In the special case where the directive sequence is of the form $(1, 1, \ldots, 1, \ldots)$ we obtain the sequence of Fibonacci words. We denote by f_n the n-th finite Fibonacci word and $F_n = |f_n|$.

A finite state automaton is a 5-tuple $\mathcal{A} = (Q, \Sigma, \delta, I, F)$ where Q is a finite set of states, Σ is a finite alphabet, $I \subseteq Q$ is the set of initial states, $F \subseteq Q$ is the set of final states and δ is the transition function from $Q \times \Sigma$ to 2^Q.

The finite state automaton is *deterministic* iff it has a unique initial state and δ is a mapping from $Q \times \Sigma$ to Q.

Let $\mathcal{A} = (Q, \Sigma, \delta, q_0, F)$ be a *deterministic finite automaton (DFA)* over the finite alphabet Σ, where Q is a finite state set, δ is a *transition function* $Q \times \Sigma \to Q$, $q_0 \in Q$ is the *initial state* and $F \subseteq Q$ the set of *final states*. If C is a subset of Q and $a \in \Sigma$, with $\delta_a^{-1}(C)$ we denote the set $\{q \in Q | \delta(q, a) \in C\}$. $\mathcal{L}(\mathcal{A})$ denotes the language recognized by the automaton $\mathcal{A}$.

An automaton is *minimal* if it has the minimum number of states among all its equivalent deterministic finite state automata (i.e. recognizing the same language). For each regular language there exists a unique minimal DFA. It can be computed using the Nerode equivalence. Given a state $p \in Q$, we define the language

$$\mathcal{L}_p(\mathcal{A}) = \{v \in \Sigma^* \mid \delta(p, v) \in F\}.$$

The *Nerode equivalence* on Q, denoted by $\sim$, is defined as follows: for $p, q \in Q$, $p \sim q$ if $\mathcal{L}_p(\mathcal{A}) = \mathcal{L}_q(\mathcal{A})$. It is known that $\sim$ is a congruence of $\mathcal{A}$, i.e. for any $a \in \Sigma$, $p \sim q$ implies $\delta(p, a) \sim \delta(q, a)$, and it is the coarsest congruence of $\mathcal{A}$ that saturates F, i.e. such that F is a union of classes of the congruence. The Nerode equivalence can be computed by the Moore construction. For any integer $k \geq 0$, the Moore equivalence $\sim_k$ is defined the following way:

$$\mathcal{L}_p^k(\mathcal{A}) = \{v \in \mathcal{L}_p(\mathcal{A}) \mid |v| \leq k\}; \qquad p \sim_k q \Leftrightarrow \mathcal{L}_p^k(\mathcal{A}) = \mathcal{L}_q^k(\mathcal{A}), \; \forall p, q \in Q.$$

The *depth* of the finite automaton $\mathcal{A}$ is the smallest k such that the Moore equivalence $\sim_k$ equals the Nerode equivalence $\sim$. It is also the smallest k such that $\sim_k$ equals $\sim_{k+1}$.

Theorem 1 (Moore). *The depth of the deterministic finite state automaton* $\mathcal{A} = (Q, \Sigma, \delta, q_0, F)$ *is at most* $|Q| - 2$.

Let $\mathcal{P} = \{Q_1, Q_2, \ldots, Q_m\}$ be the partition corresponding to the Nerode equivalence. For $q \in Q_i$, the class Q_i is denoted by $[q]$. Then the minimal automaton that recognizes $\mathcal{L}(\mathcal{A})$ is $\mathcal{MA} = (Q_M, \Sigma, \delta_M, q_{0_M}, F_M)$, where: $Q_M = \{Q_1, Q_2, \ldots, Q_m\}$, $q_{0_M} = [q_0]$, $\delta_M([q], a) = [\delta(q, a)]$, $\forall q \in Q$, $\forall a \in \Sigma$ and $F_M = \{[q] \mid q \in F\}$.

3   From Words to Automata

This section is devoted to describe a family of automata constructed by using words. Such automata have turned interesting for the study of the minimization process, as it is also shown in this paper, because they have some features that make complex this process.

Standard sturmian words have been used to define families of unary automata representing the extremal case of Hopcroft's algorithm ([10,6]). Since the minimization of unary automata can be achieved in linear time (cf. [25]) but the solution does not seem to extend to larger alphabet, in this paper in order to study the key features that complicates the minimizazion process we are interested to a family of binary automata defined as follows.

Let $w = a_1 a_2 ... a_n$ be a word of length n over the binary alphabet $\Sigma = \{a, b\}$.

The *word automaton* associated to w, denoted by $\mathcal{A}_w$, is the DFA $(Q, \Sigma, \delta, 1, F)$ such that $Q = \{1, 2, \cdots, n\}$, $F = \{i \in Q \mid a_i = b\}$, and with, for every $i \in Q$ and every $x \in \Sigma$,

$$\delta(i, x) = \begin{cases} i + 1 & \text{if } i \neq n \text{ and } x = a_i \\ 1 & \text{otherwise} \end{cases}$$

In Fig. 1 a word automaton $\mathcal{A}_w$ with $w = \backslash f_5 = abaababa$ is depicted.

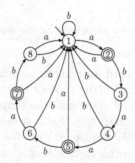

Fig. 1. The word automaton $\mathcal{A}_{f_5}$ associated to the word $f_5 = abaababa$

The minimization process of such automata can be studied by the combinatorial properties of particular trees, associated to words, that can be considered the skeleton of the word automata. Such tree, also called *word tree*, have been introduced in [12] and are defined below.

Let $\Sigma = \{a, b\}$ a binary alphabet. We use the notion of *binary labeled tree* over Σ defined as a map $\tau : \Sigma^* \to \Sigma$ whose domain $dom(\tau)$ is a prefix-closed subset of Σ^*. The elements of $dom(\tau)$ are called *nodes*. If $x, y \in dom(\tau)$ are nodes of τ such that $x = yi$ for some $i \in \Sigma$, we say that y is the *father* of x and in particular, if $i = a$ (resp. $i = b$) x is the *left son* (resp. *right son*) of y. A node without sons is called *leaf* and the node ϵ is called *the root* of the tree. Given a tree τ, the *outer frontier* of τ is the set $Fr(\tau) = \{xi \mid x \in dom(\tau), i \in \Sigma, xi \notin dom(\tau)\}$.

Let $w = w_1 w_2 ... w_n \in \Sigma^*$, by τ_w we denote the labelled tree that we call *word tree* such that $dom(\tau_w)$ is the set of prefixes of w and the map is defined as follows:

$$\begin{cases} \tau_w(\epsilon) = w_1 \\ \tau_w(w_1 w_2 ... w_i) = w_{i+1} \quad \forall 1 \le i \le n-1 \end{cases}$$

In Fig. 2 a word tree τ_w with $w = f_5 = abaababa$ is depicted.

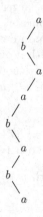

Fig. 2. The word tree τ_{f_5} associated to the word $f_5 = abaababa$

It is easy to note that the word automaton associated to w can be obtained from τ_w by adding a transition to the root of the tree for each missing edge. Moreover, the root is the initial state and the states corresponding to nodes labeled by a (resp. b) are non-final (resp. final) states.

Using the word tree is useful because, as described in the following sections, some refinements operations during the minimization algorithms applied on the word automata, can be connected to combinatorial properties of the *circular factors* of the word trees. In order to give such a definition we need to introduce the notion of *simultaneous concatenation* of labelled trees defined in [11]. The tree $\tau_1 \circ \tau_2$ is the *simultaneous concatenation* of τ_2 to all the nodes of $Fr(\tau_1)$, i.e. the root of τ_2 is attached to all the nodes of the outer frontier of τ_1.

Let τ be a tree, with τ^ω the infinite simultaneous concatenation $\tau \circ \tau \circ \tau \circ ...$ is denoted. Notice that, by infinitely applying the simultaneous concatenation, a complete infinite tree is obtained.

Let τ and τ' be two binary labeled trees. We have that τ is a *subtree* of τ' if there exist a node $v \in dom(\tau')$ such that:

i) $v \cdot dom(\tau) = \{vu | u \in dom(\tau)\} \subseteq dom(\tau')$
ii) $\tau(u) = \tau'(vu)$ for all $u \in dom(\tau)$.

In this case we say that τ is a subtree of τ' that *occurs* at node v.

In what follows we recall some notions and definitions about trees given in [12]. We define *factor* of a tree a finite complete subtree of the tree. The *height* of a finite tree τ, denoted by $h(\tau)$, is defined as $\max\{|u| + 1, u \in dom(\tau)\}$.

Let τ be a tree, σ and $\bar{\sigma}$ two factors of τ such that $\bar{\sigma}$ is the complete prefix of σ of height $h(\sigma) - 1$, then σ is called an *extension of* $\bar{\sigma}$ in τ. A factor σ of a tree τ is *extendable* in τ if there exists at least one extension of σ in τ.

A factor σ of τ is *2-special* if there exist exactly two different extensions of σ in τ.

We say that γ is a *circular factor* of τ if it is a factor of τ^{ω} with $h(\gamma) \leq h(\tau)$. A circular factor γ of τ is a *special circular factor* if there exist at least two different extensions of γ in τ^{ω} (that we can call *circular extensions* or simply extensions). A special factor is called *2-special circular factor* if it has exactly two different extensions.

Example 1. In Fig. 3(a) a tree τ and three of its circular factors are depicted. The single node labeled by b is a 2-special circular factor indeed it has two different extensions depicted in Fig. 3(b) and Fig. 3(c). The single node labeled by a has a unique extension depicted in Fig. 3(d).

The concept of circular factor can be easily understood by noting that in the case of unary tree it coincides with the notion of circular factor of a word.

We say that a finite tree τ is a *standard tree* if for each $0 \leq h \leq h(\tau) - 2$ it has only a 2-special circular factor of height h.

Remark 1. It has been proved in [12] that there exists a one-to-one correspondence between the set of circular factors of w and the set of circular factors of τ_w. Moreover, w is a standard sturmian word if and only if the word tree τ_w is a standard tree.

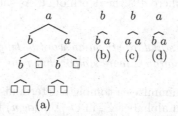

Fig. 3. A finite tree τ and its circular factors of height 2

As mentioned before, in the following sections a close connection between the sets of states of the word automaton and the circular factors of the associated word tree is used. For this purpose the following notation is fundamental. For any circular factor σ of τ_w, we define the subset Q_σ of states of $\mathcal{A}_w$ that are occurrences of σ in τ_w. Trivially, we have that $Q_\epsilon = Q$, $Q_b = F$ and $Q_a = Q \setminus F$.

4   A Worst Case of Minimization

The goal of this section is to show that the family of word automata constructing from standard sturmian words could represent a complex case for the minimization process regardless of the minimization algorithm is used. We will recall the results regarding the classical Moore's, Hopcroft's and Brzozowski's algorithm. Then we will give the main contribution that is to prove that, also for some polynomial variants of Brzozowski's algorithm, recently introduced in [19], the family of word automata associated to standard word trees and more specifically to word trees constructed from Fibonacci words represent the worst cases of the algorithm. Again we will use combinatorics on words to characterize the running time of the algorithm. This fact suggests that the standard sturmian words, and consequently the associated word automata, are able to capture some properties for which the minimization process becomes inherently more complex.

4.1   Minimization by Equivalence of States

A well known and important family of minimization algorithms work by operating a sequence of refinements of a partition of the set of states of the automaton. Moore's and Hopcroft's algorithms are two of the main minimization algorithms in this class. Although based on the same strategy, they are quite different in behavior and in complexity (cf. [21]).

Moore's algorithm (cf. [24]) starts from the partition $\Pi = \{F, Q \setminus F\}$ which corresponds to the equivalence $\sim_0$. The algorithm is iterative and, at each iteration, the partition corresponding to the equivalence $\sim_{i+1}$ is computed from the one corresponding to the equivalence $\sim_i$, using the fact that $p \sim_{k+1} q$ iff $p \sim_k q$ and for all $a \in \Sigma$, $\delta(p, a) \sim_k \delta(q, a)$. The algorithm halts when no new partition refinement is obtained, and the result is the Nerode equivalence. Each iteration is performed in time $\Theta(|Q|)$. The time complexity of Moore's algorithm applied to $\mathcal{A}$ is therefore $\Theta(d\,|Q|)$, where d is the depth of $\mathcal{A}$. As shown in [9] the following result can be proved.

Theorem 2. *Let w be a standard sturmian word of length n and let $\mathcal{A}_w$ be the correspondent word automaton. Moore's algorithm runs in $\Theta(n^2)$ on $\mathcal{A}_w$.*

Hopcroft's algorithm minimizes a complete deterministic finite state automaton with n states, over an alphabet Σ, in $O(|\Sigma|n \log n)$ time (cf. [20]). It is, up to now, the most efficient algorithm known in the general case.

In Figure 4 a brief description of the algorithm is given.

Given an automaton $\mathcal{A} = (Q, \Sigma, \delta, q_0, F)$, it computes the coarsest congruence that saturates F. The algorithm is based on the notion of split operation. More in detail, given a partition $\Pi = \{Q_1, Q_2, ..., Q_m\}$ of Q, we say that the pair (S, a), with $a \in \Sigma$, *splits* the class Q_j if $\delta_a^{-1}(S) \cap Q_j \neq \emptyset$ and $Q_j \not\subseteq \delta_a^{-1}(S)$. In this case, the class Q_j is split into $Q_j' = \delta_a^{-1}(S) \cap Q_j$ and $Q_j'' = Q_j \setminus \delta_a^{-1}(S)$. The partition Π is a congruence if and only if for any $1 \leq i, j \leq m$ and any $a \in \Sigma$, the pair (Q_i, a) does not splits Q_j.

HOPCROFT MINIMIZATION $(\mathcal{A} = (Q, \Sigma, \delta, q_0, F))$

1. $\Pi \leftarrow \{F, Q \setminus F\}$
2. **for all** $a \in \Sigma$ **do**
3. $\mathcal{W} \leftarrow \{(min(F, Q \setminus F), a)\}$
4. **while** $\mathcal{W} \neq \emptyset$ **do**
5.   *choose and delete any* (C, a) *from* $\mathcal{W}$
6.   **for all** $B \in \Pi$ **do**
7.   **if** B **is split from** (C, a) **then**
8. $B' \leftarrow \delta_a^{-1}(C) \cap B$
9. $B'' \leftarrow B \setminus \delta_a^{-1}(C)$
10. $\Pi \leftarrow \Pi \setminus \{B\} \cup \{B', B''\}$
11.   **for all** $b \in \Sigma$ **do**
12.   **if** $(B, b) \in \mathcal{W}$ **then**
13. $\mathcal{W} \leftarrow \mathcal{W} \setminus \{(B, b)\} \cup \{(B', b), (B'', b)\}$
14.   **else**
15. $\mathcal{W} \leftarrow \mathcal{W} \cup \{(min(B', B''), b)\}$

Fig. 4. Hopcroft's algorithm

Hopcroft's algorithm operates by a sequence $\Pi_1, \Pi_2, \ldots, \Pi_l$ of successive refinements of a partition of the states and it is based on the so-called "smaller half" strategy. Actually, it starts from the partition $\Pi_1 = \{F, Q \setminus F\}$ and refines it by means of splitting operations until it obtains a congruence, i.e. until no split is possible. To do that it maintains the current partition Π_i and a set $\mathcal{W} \subseteq \Pi_i \times \Sigma$, called *waiting set*, that contains the pairs for which it has to be checked whether some classes of the current partition are split. The main loop of the algorithm takes and deletes one pair (C, a) from $\mathcal{W}$ and, for each class B of Π_i, checks if it is split by (C, a). If it is the case, the class B in Π_i is replaced by the two sets B' and B'' obtained from the split. For each $b \in \Sigma$, if $(B, b) \in \mathcal{W}$, it is replaced by (B', b) and (B'', b), otherwise the pair $(min(B', B''), b)$ is added to $\mathcal{W}$ (where $min(B', B'')$ stands for the smaller of the two sets). Let us observe that a class is split by (B', b) if and only if it is split by (B'', b), hence, the pair $(min(B', B''), b)$ is chosen for convenience.

There can be several executions and several sequences of refinements that starting from the initial partition $\Pi_1 = \{F, Q \setminus F\}$ lead to the coarsest congruence of the input automaton $\mathcal{A}$. In fact, the algorithm has several degrees of freedom because, first of all, the pair (C, a) to be processed at each step is freely chosen. Another free choice intervenes when a set B is split into B' and B'' with the same size and it is not present in $\mathcal{W}$. In this case, the algorithm can, indifferently, add to $\mathcal{W}$ either B' or B''. Note that the time complexity of each execution is proportional to the sum of the cardinality of the elements of the waiting set.

Word automata represent an interesting case study for Hopcroft's algorithm from several points of view. The following theorem (cf. [12]) states that in case of standard word automata, the refinement process of Hopcroft's algorithm is unique whatever strategy is used for choosing and deleting any pair from the waiting set.

Theorem 3. *Let $\mathcal{A}_w$ be a standard word automaton. The refinement process $\Pi_1, \Pi_2, \ldots \Pi_m$ is uniquely determined. Furthermore, $m = h(\tau_w) - 1$ and for each $1 \leq k \leq h(\tau_m) - 1$,*

$$\Pi_k = \{Q_\sigma | \ \sigma \ \text{is a circular factor of } \tau_w \ \text{with } h(\sigma) = k\}$$

Note that the uniqueness of the refinement process does not necessarily implies the uniqueness of the execution. Let us denote by $C_H(n)$ the running time of the current execution of Hopcroft's algorithm to minimize $\mathcal{A}$ with n states. The following theorem proved in [13] expresses the running time of the best and the worst execution of Hopcroft's algorithm on a standard word automata in terms of the occurrences of 2-special circular factors of the standard word tree.

Theorem 4. *Let w be a standard word of length n and A_w the standard automaton associated to the standard tree τ_w. Each execution of Hopcroft's algorithm on this automaton has a running time satisfying the following inequalities:*

$$\sum_{\sigma \in sp(\tau_w)} \min(|Q_{\sigma'}|, |Q_{\sigma''}|) + n - 1 \leq C_H(n) \leq 2 \sum_{\sigma \in sp(\tau_w)} \min(|Q_{\sigma'}|, |Q_{\sigma''}|).$$

Previous theorem states that, when applied to word automata associated to standard sturmian words, all the executions of Hopcroft's algorithm have running time with the same asymptotic growth rate whatever strategy is used to implement the waiting set. The following theorem proved in [12] states that there exists an infinite family of standard word automata representing the worst case of the algorithm.

Theorem 5. *Let $\mathcal{A}_{f_n}$ be a standard automaton associated with the standard tree τ_{f_n}, where f_n is the Fibonacci word of order n. Each execution of Hopcroft's algorithm on this automaton has a running time that satisfies the following inequalities:*

$$\frac{K}{\phi} F_n \log F_n + F_n - 1 \leq C_H(F_n) \leq 2K F_n \log F_n,$$

where $K = \frac{3}{5 \log \phi}$.

The key element in the proof of the result is the fact that during the refinement process of Hopcroft's algorithm, each class of any partition has as cardinality a Fibonacci number and, recursively, when it is split, the cardinalities of the resulting classes are the two preceding Fibonacci numbers, respectively.

4.2   Brzozowski's Minimization Algorithm and Its Polynomial Variants

In this section we describe Brzozowski's algorithm introduced in [7] that is a method of automata minimization that takes as input a non deterministic finite state automaton. Its time complexity is exponential in the worst case (cf. [14]), but here we will consider also one of its variants that are recently introduced (cf. [19]) for deterministic automata and runs in polynomial time.

First, we give some preliminary definitions and notations.

Let $\mathcal{A} = (Q, \Sigma, \delta, I, F)$ be a finite state automaton. We say that a state of Q is *accessible* if it can be reached by sequence of transitions, that we call *path* starting from an initial state. By $d(\mathcal{A})$ we denote the deterministic finite state automaton equivalent to $\mathcal{A}$, $d(\mathcal{A}) = (Q_d, \Sigma, \delta_d, q_0, F_d)$, where:

- Q_d is the set of subsets p of Q
- $q_0 = I$
- $\delta_d(p, a) = \{\delta(p, a) \mid p \in p\}, \forall p \in Q_d, a \in \Sigma$
- $F_d = \{p \mid p \cap F \neq \emptyset\}$.

The mechanism of building $d(\mathcal{A})$ from $\mathcal{A}$ is called the *determinization*.

The *reverse* of the automaton $\mathcal{A} = (Q, \Sigma, \delta, I, F)$ is the automaton $r(\mathcal{A}) = (Q_r, \Sigma, \delta_r, I_r, F_r) = (Q, \Sigma, \delta_r, F, I)$, where for each $a \in \Sigma$ and $q \in Q_r$, $\delta_r(q, a) = \{p \in Q \mid q \in \delta(p, a)\}$.

Brzozowski's algorithm consists of computing twice a reversal operation followed by a determinization. More in detail, if $\mathcal{A}$ if the finite state automaton considered as input, $d(r(d(r(\mathcal{A}))))$ is its minimal equivalent automaton. Since the reverse operation can be also applied to non-deterministic finite state automata, this algorithm is able to minimize both deterministic and non-deterministic finite state automata. Obviously, the reverse of an automaton can easily be computed in linear time with respect to its size (number of states and transitions), the critical part of the algorithm is the determinization. Hence, the worst-case running time complexity of the algorithm is exponential because it depends on the number of states producing during the determinizations. However in [28,3] it is experimentally verified that in practice Brzozowski's algorithm has a good performance and usually outperforms the other algorithms when applied on non-deterministic finite state automata. In [9] the authors prove that for word automata associated to Fibonacci words such an operation has a quadratic lower bound. The result has been obtained by estimating the cardinality of "big" sets in the determinization and fundamental tools are the properties of Fibonacci words given in the following propositions.

Proposition 1. *Let f_n be the n-th Fibonacci word, with $n \geq 3$. If n is odd then the circular factor af_{n-1} has a unique occurrence in f_n at position F_n. If n is even then the circular factor af_{n-2} has a unique occurrence in in f_n at position F_{n-1}.*

Proposition 2. *Let f_n be the n-th Fibonacci word, with $n \geq 2$, and let u be a suffix of f_n that is also a prefix of f_n. Then u is equal to f_{n-2i}, for some $i > 0$.*

Note that, occurrences of circular factors in Fibonacci words are strictly connected to paths in the determinization of the reverse of $\mathcal{A}_{f_n}$ here denoted by $d(r(\mathcal{A}_{f_n}))$.

Remark 2. If $u = vx$, with $x \in \Sigma$, is a circular factor of the word f_n then there exists a path in $r(\mathcal{A}_{f_n})$ labeled by v^r. In particular, if $u = vb$ then there exists in $r(\mathcal{A}_{f_n})$ starting from an initial state and labeled with v^r.

One can find in $d(r(\mathcal{A}_{f_n}))$ some accessible states are closely related with the properties of the circular factors of f_n that label the relative paths, i.e. occurrences of some circular factors of f_n determine the cardinality of subsets reached by the corresponding paths.

Theorem 6. *Let $\mathcal{A}_{f_n}$ be the word automaton corresponding to the n-th Fibonacci word f_n. If n is odd, then in the automaton $d(r(\mathcal{A}_{f_n}))$ the state $\{F_n - 1\}^c$ is accessible by the path labelled by f_{n-1}. If n is even, then in the automaton $d(r(\mathcal{A}_{f_n}))$ the state $\{F_{n-1} - 1\}^c$ is accessible by the path labelled by f_{n-2}.*

One can deduce the following corollary that counts the number of sets in $d(r(\mathcal{A}_{f_n}))$ with cardinality $|Q| - 1$.

Corollary 1. *If n is odd then in the automaton $d(r(\mathcal{A}_{f_n}))$ the states $\{k\}^c$, with $1 \leq k \leq F_n - 1$, are accessible. If n is even then in the automaton $d(r(\mathcal{A}_{f_n}))$ the states $\{k\}^c$, with $1 \leq k \leq F_{n-1} - 1$, are accessible.*

Such results allow to provide a lower bound on the number of the sum of the cardinality of the states obtained after the first determinization. Consequently, this also represents a lower bound on the time complexity of Brzozowski's algorithm. Let us denote by $C_B(n)$ be the time complexity of Brzozowski's algorithm on an automaton having n states.

Theorem 7. *Let $\mathcal{A}_{f_n}$ be the word automaton corresponding to the n-th Fibonacci word f_n. Then*

$$c_B(F_n) = \Omega(F_n^2),$$

where $F_n = |f_n|$ is the number of states of $\mathcal{A}_{f_n}$.

Studies on generic and average complexities of Brzozowski's minimization algorithm have been proposed. Very recently, it has been proved in [26] that both these complexities are super-polynomial for the uniform distribution on deterministic automata.

However, a polynomial variant of the Brzozowski's algorithm has been recently introduced in [3] for deterministic finite state automata. The classical strategy proposed by Brzozowski is not based on refinement operations, but such variant shows Brozowski's method is not so far from Hopcroft's minimization algorithm. Connected results can be found in [1,2,23], where the theory of atomic NFA's is considered in order to obtain a more efficient minimization strategy.

MINIMIZATION BY PRD $(\mathcal{A} = (Q, \Sigma, \delta, q_0, F))$
1. $\Pi \leftarrow \{F, Q \setminus F\}$
2. $S = F$
3. $\mathcal{L} = \emptyset$
4. **for all** $a \in \Sigma$ **do**
5. $\mathcal{L} \leftarrow (S, a)$
6. **while** $\mathcal{L} \neq \emptyset$ **do**
7.   *choose and delete any* (S, a) *from* $\mathcal{L}$
8.   **for all** $B \in \Pi$ **do**
9.   **if** B **is split by** (S, a) **then**
10. $B' \leftarrow \delta_a^{-1}(S) \cap B$
11. $B'' \leftarrow B' \setminus \delta_a^{-1}(S)$
12. $\Pi \leftarrow \Pi \setminus \{B\} \cup \{B', B''\}$
13.   **for all** $b \in \Sigma$ **do**
14. $\mathcal{L} \leftarrow \mathcal{L} \cup \{(\delta_a^{-1}(S), b)\}$

Fig. 5. Minimization by Partial Reverse Determinization

Here we describe the minimization algorithm (see Fig. 5) for deterministic finite state automata given in [19], that is a variant of Brzozowski's algorithm but with time complexity bounded by $O(kn^2)$, where $k = |\Sigma|$ and $n = |Q|$. The minimization of a DFA is computed by a *partial determinization of the reverse* (PRD) and a contemporary refinement of the trivial partition in $\{F, Q \setminus F\}$ of Q till to obtain the Nerode equivalence. More precisely, it performs a determinization of the reverse of the automaton and uses the subsets to refine the partition. Such a determinization is partial since it takes into account only accessible sets of states of $d(r(\mathcal{A}))$ that are able to refine the current partition, i.e. that cause a split. The running time is computed by the sum of cardinalities of such sets because the subsets that do not cause a split are rejected. Note that such an algorithm uses instruments of Brzozowski's algorithm such as the determinization but also uses the split operation, like Hopcroft's algorithm. But in this case the sets used to splits are not the sets of the current partition but the sets obtained during the determinization.

Let $e \in \Sigma^*$ and let Q_e be the subset of Q such that $\delta_r(F, e) = Q_e$. In order to compute the running time of the algorithm we have to sum the cardinalities of sets that are in $\mathcal{L}$ during the process i.e. those sets Q_e, for some $e \in \Sigma^*$, that are stored in $\mathcal{L}$ during the process. We call *experiments* such words e such that Q_e causes a refinement. It is known that $\mathcal{L}$ contains at most $n-1$ elements, then the time complexity of the algorithm is $O(kn^2)$.

In this paper we consider the minimization by PRD algorithm of word automata. We prove that in order to minimize a standard word automaton, exactly $n-1$ elements in $\mathcal{L}$ are processed and that the time complexity is tight. The statement of the following theorem characterizes, analogously to Hopcroft's algorithm, the splits of sets and then the refinement process of the partitions on such automata. In particular, Theorem 8 relates the refinements produced during the PRD algorithm with the occurrences of 2-special factors of the standard word tree associated to the input automaton.

Theorem 8. *Let $\mathcal{A}_w$ be a word automaton, σ a circular factor of τ_w and $e \in \Sigma^*$, we have that (Q_e, a) split Q_σ for some $a \in \Sigma$ iff σ is a 2-special factor of τ_w.*

Moreover, one can prove that the refinement process is uniquely determined as a consequence of the fact that a standard word tree has a unique 2-special factor of each height.

In order to find the extremal case of PRD algorithm we give a characterization of the set of the experiments needed to minimize standard word automata.

Theorem 9. *Let $\mathcal{A}_w$ be the standard word automaton associated to a standard sturmian word of length n. Then, for each length $0 \leq l \leq n - 1$, there exists a unique experiment e of length l in the set of experiments that minimize $\mathcal{A}_w$ by PRD.*

The theorem is proved by using the following lemma that holds because a standard tree has not any 3-special factor (cf. Remark 1).

Lemma 1. *Let $\mathcal{A}_w$ be a standard word automaton and $e \in \Sigma^*$, if (Q_e, a) (resp. (Q_e, b)) refines Q_σ then (Q_e, b) (resp. (Q_e, a)) does not.*

Moreover, in case of standard word automaton we are able to exactly determine the experiments e that minimize the automaton.

Given a word $w \in \Sigma^*$, by $suf_l(w)$ we denote the set of suffixes u of w with $0 \leq |u| \leq l$. Then the following theorem holds.

Theorem 10. *Let $\mathcal{A}_w$ be a standard word automaton. The set of experiments that minimize $\mathcal{A}_w$ by PRD is $suf_{|w|-2}(w)$.*

In case of standard word automata associated to Fibonacci words, we are able to determine some crucial sets of states of the PRD that allow to give a quadratic bound of the running time. Hence we can conclude that to minimize word automata associated to Fibonacci words by PRD, $|Q| - 1$ experiments are needed. We use this fact in the sequel, together with the following proposition, in order to estimate the accessible part obtained by PRD algorithm applied on $\mathcal{A}_{f_n}$.

Proposition 3. *Let $\mathcal{A}_{f_n}$ be the word automaton associated to the n-th Fibonacci word f_n. If n is odd, then $Q_{f_{n-1}} = \{F_n - 1\}^c$. If n is even, then $Q_{f_{n-2}} = \{F_{n-1} - 1\}^c$.*

We can deduce the following corollary that allows us to determine what sets of cardinality $|Q| - 1$ are involved in the partial reverse determinization. Note that they are not all those with this cardinality that one can find in the reverse determinization and specified in the Corollary 1 but only those that contribute to the minimization.

Corollary 2. *If n is odd then the states $\{k\}^c$, with $F_{n-1} + 1 \leq k \leq F_n - 1$, are accessible in the PRD of $\mathcal{A}_{f_n}$. If n is even then the states $\{k\}^c$, with $F_{n-2} + 1 \leq k \leq F_n - 1$, are accessible in the PRD of $\mathcal{A}_{f_n}$.*

The following theorem establishes that word automata associated to Fibonacci words represent the extremal case of the polynomial variant of Brzozowski's algorithm introduced in [19]. It is a consequence of previous results and it is closely related to the combinatorial properties of standard sturmian words and its associated word trees. Let us denote by $C_{PRD}(n)$ the time complexity of minimization by PRD algorithm on an automaton of n states.

Theorem 11. *Let $\mathcal{A}_{f_n}$ be the word automaton associated to the n-th Fibonacci word f_n, with F_n states. Then*

$$C_{PRD}(F_n) = \Theta(F_n^2).$$

5   Conclusions and Further work

In recent years a bridge between combinatorics on words and the study of complexity of algorithms for the minimization of finite state automata has aroused great interest (cf. [6,5,12]. In particular, tools and notions from combinatorics on words have been fundamental to study the worst case of some minimization algorithms. In this paper we consider a family of binary automata constructed by using standard sturmian words that inherit combinatorial properties that plays an important role in the study of extremal cases of the process of minimization of an automaton. An intermediate role is played by the notion of word trees for which some properties of words are generalized. More in detail, we prove that a family of binary word automata, in which the states are final or not by following the letters of Fibonacci words, have combinatorial properties such that the minimization process of several algorithms become more complex. It would be interesting to give a characterization of the words for which such automata are always difficult to minimize. In this direction, results in [5] and the algorithms proposed in [2,23] could be considered. Finally, from the symmetric point of view, we highlight that the study of the executions of the minimization algorithms on word automata (and in particular Hopcroft's algorithm) has allowed to find new combinatorial properties of the circular sturmian words, by introducing the notion of reduction tree of a circular sturmian word that is a recursive tree that is intrinsically connected to the structure of words itself. It is possible to extend such a definition also to the case of words defined on alphabets with more than two letters (cf. [8]). This allows to define, on one hand, the notion of reduction tree of circular epichristoffel words (cf. [18]), on the other a variant of Hopcroft's algorithm for a more general class of fine state automata, the automata with output. These trees could provide new tools for investigate some still open issues related to epichristoffel words.

References

1. Brzozowski, J.A., Tamm, H.: Quotient complexities of atoms of regular languages. In: Yen, H.-C., Ibarra, O.H. (eds.) DLT 2012. LNCS, vol. 7410, pp. 50–61. Springer, Heidelberg (2012)
2. Brzozowski, J.A., Tamm, H.: Minimal nondeterministic finite automata and atoms of regular languages. CoRR, abs/1301.5585 (2013)
3. Almeida, M., Moreira, N., Reis, R.: On the performance of automata minimization algorithms. Technical Report DCC-2007-03, Universidade do Porto (2007)
4. Berstel, J., Boasson, L., Carton, O.: Continuant polynomials and worst-case behavior of Hopcroft's minimization algorithm. Theor. Comput. Sci. 410, 2811–2822 (2009)
5. Berstel, J., Boasson, L., Carton, O., Fagnot, I.: Sturmian trees. Theory of Computing Systems 46(3), 443–478 (2010)
6. Berstel, J., Carton, O.: On the complexity of Hopcroft's state minimization algorithm. In: Domaratzki, M., Okhotin, A., Salomaa, K., Yu, S. (eds.) CIAA 2004. LNCS, vol. 3317, pp. 35–44. Springer, Heidelberg (2005)
7. Brzozowski, J.A.: Canonical regular expressions and minimal state graphs for definite events. Mathematical Theory of Automata 12, 529–561 (1962)
8. Castiglione, C., Sciortino, M.: Moore automata and epichristoffel words. In: ICTCS 2012 - 13th Italian Conference on Theoretical Computer Science (2012)
9. Castiglione, G., Nicaud, C., Sciortino, M.: A challenging family of automata for classical minimization algorithms. In: Domaratzki, M., Salomaa, K. (eds.) CIAA 2010. LNCS, vol. 6482, pp. 251–260. Springer, Heidelberg (2011)
10. Castiglione, G., Restivo, A., Sciortino, M.: Hopcroft's algorithm and cyclic automata. In: Martín-Vide, C., Otto, F., Fernau, H. (eds.) LATA 2008. LNCS, vol. 5196, pp. 172–183. Springer, Heidelberg (2008)
11. Castiglione, G., Restivo, A., Sciortino, M.: Circular sturmian words and Hopcroft's algorithm. Theor. Comput. Sci. 410(43), 4372–4381 (2009)
12. Castiglione, G., Restivo, A., Sciortino, M.: On extremal cases of Hopcroft's algorithm. Theor. Comput. Sci. 411(38-39), 3414–3422 (2010)
13. Castiglione, G., Restivo, A., Sciortino, M.: Hopcroft's algorithm and tree-like automata. RAIRO - Theor. Inf. and Applic. 45(1), 59–75 (2011)
14. Champarnaud, J.-M., Khorsi, A., Paranthoën, T.: Split and join for minimizing: Brzozowski's algorithm. In: PSC 2002, pp. 96–104 (2002)
15. de Luca, A.: Combinatories of standard sturmian words. In: Mycielski, J., Rozenberg, G., Salomaa, A. (eds.) Structures in Logic and Computer Science. LNCS, vol. 1261, pp. 249–267. Springer, Heidelberg (1997)
16. de Luca, A., Mignosi, F.: Some combinatorial properties of sturmian words. Theor. Comput. Sci. 136(2), 361–385 (1994)
17. Mignosi, F., Restivo, A.: Characteristic sturmian words are extremal for the critical factorization theorem. Theor. Comput. Sci. 454, 199–205 (2012)
18. Paquin, G.: On a generalization of christoffel words: epichristoffel words. Theor. Comput. Sci. 410(38-40), 3782–3791 (2009)
19. García, P., López, D., Vázquez de Parga, M.: DFA minimization: from Brzozowski to Hopcroft. Technical report, Universidad Politécnica de Valencia. Informes técnicos de investigación DSIC-TLCC (2013), http://hdl.handle.net/10251/27623
20. Hopcroft, J.E.: An $n \log n$ algorithm for mimimizing the states in a finite automaton. In: Theory of Machines and Computations (Proc. Internat. Sympos. Technion, Haifa, 1971), pp. 189–196. Academic Press, New York (1971)

21. Berstel, J., Boasson, L., Carton, O., Fagnot, I.: Minimization of automata. CoRR, abs/1010.5318 (2010)
22. Sciortino, M., Zamboni, L.Q.: Suffix automata and standard sturmian words. In: Harju, T., Karhumäki, J., Lepistö, A. (eds.) DLT 2007. LNCS, vol. 4588, pp. 382–398. Springer, Heidelberg (2007)
23. Vazquez de Parga, M., Garcia, P., Lopez, D.: A polynomial double reversal minimization algorithm for deterministic finite automata. Theor. Comput. Sci. 487, 17–22 (2013)
24. Moore, E.F.: Gedaken experiments on sequential machines, pp. 129–153. Princeton University Press (1956)
25. Paige, R., Tarjan, R.E., Bonic, R.: A linear time solution to the single function coarsest partition problem. Theor. Comput. Sci. 40, 67–84 (1985)
26. De Felice, S., Nicaud, C.: Brzozowski algorithm is generically super-polynomial for deterministic automata. In: Béal, M.-P., Carton, O. (eds.) DLT 2013. LNCS, vol. 7907, pp. 179–190. Springer, Heidelberg (2013)
27. Mantaci, S., Restivo, A., Sciortino, M.: Burrows-Wheeler transform and sturmian words. Inf. Process. Lett. 86(5), 241–246 (2003)
28. Tabakov, D., Vardi, M.Y.: Experimental evaluation of classical automata constructions. In: Sutcliffe, G., Voronkov, A. (eds.) LPAR 2005. LNCS (LNAI), vol. 3835, pp. 396–411. Springer, Heidelberg (2005)

Auto-similarity
in Rational Base Number Systems

Shigeki Akiyama[1], Victor Marsault[2,*], and Jacques Sakarovitch[2]

[1] University of Tsukuba, 1-1-1 Tennodai, Tsukuba, Ibaraki, 350-8571 Japan
[2] Telecom-ParisTech and CNRS, 46 rue Barrault, 75013 Paris, France
victor.marsault@telecom-paristech.fr

Abstract. This work is a contribution to the study of set of the representations of integers in a rational base number system. This prefix-closed subset of the free monoid is naturally represented as a highly non regular tree whose nodes are the integers and whose subtrees are all distinct. With every node of that tree is then associated a minimal infinite word (and a maximal infinite word).

The main result is that a sequential transducer which computes for all n the minimal word associated with $n + 1$ from the one associated with n, has essentially the same underlying graph as the tree itself.

These infinite words are then interpreted as representations of real numbers; the difference between the numbers represented by the maximal and minimal word associated with n is called the span of n. The preceding construction allows to characterise the topological closure of the set of spans.

1 Introduction

The purpose of this work is a further exploration and a better understanding of the set of *words* that represent integers in a rational base number systems. These numeration systems have been introduced and studied in [1], leading to some progress in the results around the so-called Malher's problem (*cf.* [5]). We give below a precise definition of rational base number systems and of the representation of numbers in such a system. But one can hint at the results established in this paper by just looking at the figure showing the 'representation tree' of the integers – that is, the compact way of describing the words that represent the integers – in a rational base number system (Figure 1b for the base $\frac{3}{2}$) and by comparison with the representation tree (or trie) in an analogous integer base number system (Figure 1a for the base 3).

In the latter, all subtrees are the same and equal to the full ternary tree, whereas in the former, all subtrees are different. As a result, the language of the representations of the integers is not a regular language. It may even be shown that the language satisfies no iteration lemma of any kind ([6]). With the hope of finding some order or regularity within what seems to be closer to complete

---

* Corresponding author.

J. Karhumäki, A. Lepistö, and L. Zamboni (Eds.): WORDS 2013, LNCS 8079, pp. 34–45, 2013.
© Springer-Verlag Berlin Heidelberg 2013

randomness (which, on the other hand, is not established either) we consider the *minimal words* originating from every node of the tree.

In the case of an integer base, this is meaningless: all these minimal words are equal to 0^ω. In the case of a rational base these words are on the contrary all distinct and none are even ultimately periodic (as no ultimately periodic word can be found in this tree). In order to find some invariant of all these distinct words, or at least a relationship between them, we have studied the function that maps the minimal word w_n^- associated with n onto the one associated with $n+1$, and tried to describe this function by a (possibly infinite) transducer.

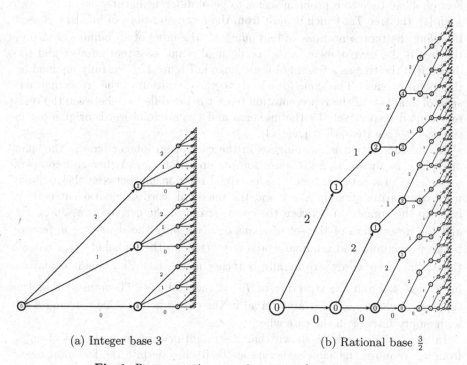

(a) Integer base 3   (b) Rational base $\frac{3}{2}$

Fig. 1. Representation trees in two number systems

The computation of such a transducer in the case of the base $\frac{3}{2}$, and more generally in the case of a base $\frac{p}{q}$ with $p = 2q - 1$, leads to a surprising and unexpected result. If $\mathcal{T}_{\frac{p}{q}}$ denotes the representation tree – viewed as an infinite automaton, – the transducer, denoted by $\mathcal{D}_{\frac{p}{q}}$, is obtained by replacing the label of every transition of $\mathcal{T}_{\frac{p}{q}}$ by a set of pairs of letters that depends upon this label only. In other words, the *underlying graphs* of $\mathcal{T}_{\frac{p}{q}}$ and $\mathcal{D}_{\frac{p}{q}}$ *coincide*, and $\mathcal{D}_{\frac{p}{q}}$ is obtained from $\mathcal{T}_{\frac{p}{q}}$ by a *substitution* from the alphabet of digits into the alphabet of pairs of digits, in this special and remarkable case.

The general case is hardly more difficult to describe, once it has been understood. Let $B_{p,q}$ be the digit alphabet with $2q - 1$ (consecutive) elementsand whose greatest element is $p - 1$. If $p > 2q - 1$, then $B_{p,q}$ is contained in A_p; it consists of A_p, enlarged with enough *negative* digits otherwise.

From $\mathcal{T}_{\frac{p}{q}}$ and with the digit alphabet $B_{p,q}$, we first define another 'automaton' denoted by $\widehat{\mathcal{T}_{\frac{p}{q}}}$: either by *deleting the transitions* of $\mathcal{T}_{\frac{p}{q}}$ whose labels do not belong to $B_{p,q}$ in the case where $p > 2q - 1$ or, in the case where $p < 2q - 1$ by *adding transitions* labelled with the new negative digits. Then, $\mathcal{D}_{\frac{p}{q}}$ is obtained from $\widehat{\mathcal{T}_{\frac{p}{q}}}$ exactly as above, by a *substitution* from the alphabet of digits into the alphabet of pairs of digits. This construction of $\mathcal{D}_{\frac{p}{q}}$, which we call the *derived transducer*, and the proof of its correctness are presented in Section 3. In the following Section 4, we turn to a problem seems to be of different nature.

In [1], the tree $\mathcal{T}_{\frac{p}{q}}$, which is built from the representations of integers, is used to *define* the representations of real numbers: the label of an infinite branch of the tree is the development 'after the decimal point' of a real number and the drawing of the tree as a fractal object — like in Figure 1b — is fully justified by this point of view. The same idea leads to the definition of the (renormalised) *span* of a node n of the representation tree: it is the difference between the reals represented respectively by the maximal and the minimal words originating in the node n (see Remark 1, page 44).

Again, this notion is meaningless in the case of an integer base p: the span of node n is always 1. And again, the notion is far more richer and complex in the case of a rational base $\frac{p}{q}$. The trivial relationship between the minimal word originating at node $n + 1$ and the maximal word originating at node n leads to the connexion between the construction of the derived transducer $\mathcal{D}_{\frac{p}{q}}$ and the description of the set of spans $\mathsf{S}_{\frac{p}{q}}$. Not only the *digit-wise difference* between maximal and minimal words is written on the alphabet $B_{p,q}$, but all these 'difference words' are infinite branches in the tree $\widehat{\mathcal{T}_{\frac{p}{q}}}$. This is explained in Section 4. From the structure of $\widehat{\mathcal{T}_{\frac{p}{q}}}$, it then follows (Theorem 3) that the topological closure of $\mathsf{S}_{\frac{p}{q}}$ is an interval in the case where $p \leqslant 2q - 1$, and a set with empty interior in the case where $p > 2q - 1$.

In conclusion, we have shown that a straightforward computation of w_{n+1}^- from w_n^- requires the same structure as $\mathcal{T}_{\frac{p}{q}}$ itself – despite the fact that every minimal word looks as complex as the whole tree – whether it be performed directly on the words, or indirectly via the span of the nodes. It is this phenomenon that we call *auto-similarity* of the structure $\mathcal{T}_{\frac{p}{q}}$. In this process, the number systems where $p = 2q - 1$ appear to mark the boundary between two different behaviours, in a more deeper way than that was described in the first study of rational base number systems [1].

This paper is meant to be self-contained and gives, in particular, all necessary definitions concerning rational base number systems. However, the reference [1] where these systems have been defined and the sets of representations first studied will probably be useful. In order to meet the space constraints, all proofs and even some figures have been removed. The reader may find them in a complete version downloadable from arXiv [2].

2   Preliminaries and Notations

2.1   Numbers and Words

Given two *real numbers* x and y, we denote by $\frac{x}{y}$ their division in $\mathbb{R}$ (even if x or y happens to be integers), by $[x, y]$ the corresponding interval of $\mathbb{R}$ and by $\lceil x \rceil$ the integer n such that $(n - 1) < x \leqslant n$. On the other hand, given two *positive integers* n and m, we denote by $n \div m$ and $n \% m$ respectively the quotient and the remainder of the Euclidean division of n by m, that is, $n = (n \div m) m + (n \% m)$ and $0 \leqslant (n \% m) < m$. Additionally, we denote by $[\![n, m]\!]$ the integer interval $\{n, (n + 1), \ldots, m\}$.

An *alphabet* is a finite set of symbols called *letters* or *digits* when they are integers. Given an alphabet A, we consider both the sets of *finite* and *infinite* words over A respectively denoted by A^* and A^ω and we denote the *empty word* by ε. For every positive integer p, we denote by A_p the canonical digit alphabet of the base p number system: $A_p = \{0, 1, \ldots, p - 1\}$. For clarity, we denote finite words by u, v and infinite words by w. The concatenation of two words u, v is either explicitly denoted by a low dot, as in $u.v$, or implicitly when there is no ambiguity, as in uv. A finite word u is said to be a prefix of a finite word v (resp. an infinite word w) if there exists a finite word v' (resp. an infinite word w') such that $v = uv'$ (resp. $w = uw'$). The set of subsets of an alphabet A is denoted by $\mathfrak{P}(A)$.

2.2   Automata and Transducers

We deal here with a very special class of automata and transducers only: they are infinite, their state set is $\mathbb{N}$, they are *deterministic* (or *letter-to-letter* and *sequential*), the initial state is 0, and all states are final.

As usual, an *automaton* $\mathcal{X}$ over A is denoted by a 5-tuple $\mathcal{X} = \langle \mathbb{N}, A, \delta, 0, \mathbb{N} \rangle$, where $\delta : \mathbb{N} \times A \to \mathbb{N}$ is the *transition function*. The partial function δ is extended to $\mathbb{N} \times A^*$, and $\delta(n, u) = m$ is also denoted by $n \cdot u = m$ or by $n \xrightarrow{u} m$. Given an integer n, every state $n \cdot a$ for some a in A is called a *successor* of n. A word u in A^* (resp. a word w in A^ω) is *accepted* by $\mathcal{X}$ if $0 \cdot u$ exists (resp. if $0 \cdot v$ exists for every finite prefix v of w). The *language* of *finite* words (resp. of *infinite* words) accepted by $\mathcal{X}$ is denoted by $L(\mathcal{X})$ (resp. by $\mathcal{L}(\mathcal{X})$).

For transducers, we essentially use the notation of [3], adapted for the infinite case. A *transducer* is an automaton whose transitions are labelled by (set of) pairs of letters. Formally, it is represented by a tuple $\mathcal{Y} = \langle \mathbb{N}, A \times B, \delta, \eta, 0, \mathbb{N} \rangle$ where $\langle \mathbb{N}, A, \delta, 0, \mathbb{N} \rangle$ is an automaton, called *the underlying input automaton* of $\mathcal{Y}$, A is called *the input alphabet*, B is the *output alphabet* and $\eta : \mathbb{N} \times A \to B$ is the *output function*. The transition function δ is extended as in automata, and η is extended to $\mathbb{N} \times A^* \to B^*$ by $\eta(n, \varepsilon) = \varepsilon$ and $\eta(n, ua) = \eta(n, u).\eta(n \cdot u, a)$, and $\eta(n, u)$ is also denoted by $n * u$ for short.

Moreover, given two finite words u and v, we denote by $n \xrightarrow{u|v} m$ the combination of $n \cdot u = m$ and $n * u = v$. We say that the *image* of a finite word u by $\mathcal{Y}$, denoted by $\mathcal{Y}(u)$, is the word v, if it exists, such that $0 \xrightarrow{u|v} k$

for some k. Similarly, the image of the infinite word w is w' if, for every finite prefix u of w, $\mathcal{Y}(u)$ is a prefix of w'.

2.3   Rational Base Number System

Let p and q be two co-prime integers such that $p > q > 1$. Given a positive ieger N, let us write $N_0 = N$ and define the sequence $(N_i)_{i \in \mathbb{N}}$ by all $i > 0$,

$$q N_i = p N_{(i+1)} + a_i \qquad \text{for all } i > 0 \ ,$$

where a_i is the remainder of the Euclidean division of $q \mathbb{N}_i$ by p, hence in the alphabet $A_p = [\![0, p-1]\!]$. Since $p > q$, the sequence $(N_i)_{i \in \mathbb{N}}$ is strictly decreasing and eventually stops at $N_{k+1} = 0$. Moreover, it holds that

$$N = \sum_{i=0}^{k} \frac{a_i}{q} \left(\frac{p}{q} \right)^i \ .$$

The *evaluation map* π is derived from this formula. Given a word $a_n a_{n-1} \cdots a_0$ over A_p, and indeed over any alphabet of digits, its *value* is defined by

$$\pi(a_n a_{n-1} \cdots a_0) = \sum_{i=0}^{n} \frac{a_i}{q} \left(\frac{p}{q} \right)^i \ . \tag{1}$$

Conversely, a word u in A_p^* is called a $\frac{p}{q}$-*representation* of an integer x if $\pi(u) = x$. Since the representation is unique up to leading 0's (see [1, Theorem 1]), u is denoted by $\langle x \rangle_{\frac{p}{q}}$ (or $\langle x \rangle$ for short) and can be computed with the modified Euclidean division algorithm above. By convention, the representation of 0 is the empty word ε. The set of all $\frac{p}{q}$-representations of integers is denoted by $L_{\frac{p}{q}}$:

$$L_{\frac{p}{q}} = \left\{ \langle n \rangle_{\frac{p}{q}} \,\middle|\, n \in \mathbb{N} \right\} \ .$$

It should be noted that a rational base number system is *not* a β-numeration — where the representation of a number is computed by the (greedy) Rényi algorithm (cf. [4, Chapter 7]) — in the special case where β is a rational number. In such a system, the digit set is $\{0, 1, \ldots, \lceil \frac{p}{q} \rceil\}$ and the weight of the i-th leftmost digit is $(\frac{p}{q})^i$; whereas the rational base number system, they are $\{0, 1 \ldots (p-1)\}$ and $\frac{1}{q}(\frac{p}{q})^i$ respectively.

It is immediate that $L_{\frac{p}{q}}$ is prefix-closed (since, in the modified Euclidean division algorithm $\langle N \rangle = \langle N_1 \rangle.a_0$) and right-extendable (for every representation $\langle n \rangle$, there exists (at least) an a in A_p such that q divides $(np + a)$ and then $\langle \frac{np+a}{q} \rangle = \langle n \rangle.a$). As a consequence, $L_{\frac{p}{q}}$ can be represented as an infinite tree, or 'trie' (cf. Figure 2).

It is known that $L_{\frac{p}{q}}$ is not rational (not even context-free), and the following automaton (accepting indeed the language $0^* L_{\frac{p}{q}}$) is infinite.

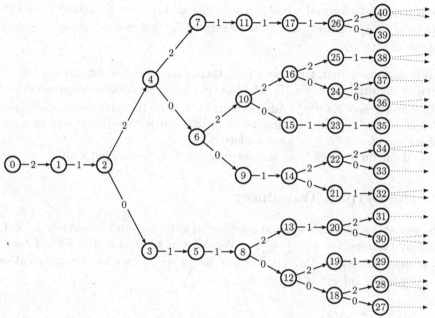

Fig. 2. The tree representation of the language $L_{\frac{3}{2}}$

Definition 1. *Let* $\tau_{\frac{p}{q}} : \mathbb{N} \times \mathbb{Z} \to \mathbb{N}$ *be the (partial) function defined[1] by:*

$$\forall n \in \mathbb{N}, \ \forall a \in \mathbb{Z} \qquad \tau_{\frac{p}{q}}(n, a) = \left(\frac{np + a}{q} \right) \qquad \text{if } (np + a) \text{ is divisible by } q. \qquad (2)$$

We denote[2] by $\mathcal{T}_{\frac{p}{q}}$ *the automaton* $\mathcal{T}_{\frac{p}{q}} = \left\langle \mathbb{N}, A_p, \tau_{\frac{p}{q}}, 0, \mathbb{N} \right\rangle$.

In $\mathcal{T}_{\frac{p}{q}}$, we then have the transitions $n \xrightarrow{a} \left(\frac{np+a}{q} \right)$ for every n in $\mathbb{N}$, and every a in A_p such that $(np + a)$ is divisible by q. The tree representation of $L_{\frac{p}{q}}$, as in Figure 2 augmented by an additional loop labelled by 0 on the state 0 becomes a representation of $\mathcal{T}_{\frac{3}{2}}$.

We call *minimal alphabet* the subalphabet $A_q = [\![0, q - 1]\!]$ of A_p and respectively *maximal alphabet* the subalphabet $[\![(p - q), (p - 1)]\!]$. Any letter of A_q is then called a *minimal letter*, *maximal letter* being defined analogously. The definition of $\tau_{\frac{p}{q}}$ implies that every state of $\mathcal{T}_{\frac{p}{q}}$ has a successor by a *unique* minimal (resp. maximal) letter.

---

[1] The function $\tau_{\frac{p}{q}}$ is defined on $\mathbb{N} \times \mathbb{Z}$ instead of $\mathbb{N} \times A_p$ in anticipation of future developments.

[2] In [1], $\mathcal{T}_{\frac{p}{q}}$ is denoted an infinite directed tree. The labels of the (finite) paths starting from the root precisely formed the language $0^* L_{\frac{p}{q}}$, as is $L\left(\mathcal{T}_{\frac{p}{q}}\right)$ in our case.

Definition 2 (minimal word). *A minimal word (in the $\frac{p}{q}$-system) is an infinite word in A_q^ω labelling an (infinite) path of $T_{\frac{p}{q}}$ (not necessarily starting from the initial state 0).*

It is immediate that, for every n in $\mathbb{N}$, there exists a unique infinite word in A_q^ω starting from the state n in $T_{\frac{p}{q}}$. We call this word *the* minimal word associated with n and denote it by w_n^-. Additionally, we will use the term *minimal outgoing label* of n, to designate the first letter of w_n^- and *minimal successor* of n the unique successor of n by a minimal letter.

We define in a similar way the *maximal word* w_n^+ associated with n.

3   The Derived Transducer

The goal of this section is to build a sequential letter-to-letter transducer $A_q \times A_q$ realising the function $w_n^- \mapsto w_{(n+1)}^-$. We call this transducer the *derived transducer* and denote it by $\mathcal{D}_{\frac{p}{q}}$. It will be obtained from $T_{\frac{p}{q}}$ by a local transformation and this is the subject of Section 3.1.

3.1   From $T_{\frac{p}{q}}$ to $\mathcal{D}_{\frac{p}{q}}$

The transformation of $T_{\frac{p}{q}}$ into $\mathcal{D}_{\frac{p}{q}}$ is a two-step process. First, the structure of $T_{\frac{p}{q}}$ is locally modified, by changing the alphabet, and a new automaton $\widehat{T_{\frac{p}{q}}}$ is obtained. The second step consists in replacing the labels in $\widehat{T_{\frac{p}{q}}}$ by a subset of $A_q \times A_q$ by means of a *substitution* (meaning that two transitions of $\widehat{T_{\frac{p}{q}}}$ labelled by the same letter will be replaced by the same set of pair of letters) and produces $\mathcal{D}_{\frac{p}{q}}$.

Changing the Alphabet. We write $B_{p,q} = [\![p - (2q-1), (p-1)]\!]$, that is $B_{p,q}$ is the alphabet whose maximal element is $p-1$ and containing $2q-1$ consecutive digits. In particular, if $p = (2q-1)$, $B_{p,q} = A_p$; if $p < (2q-1)$, $B_{p,q}$ contains negative digits; and if $p > (2q-1)$, $B_{p,q}$ is an uppermost subset of A_p. Note that $B_{p,q}$ is always of cardinal $(2q-1)$, an *odd number*, that the digit $(p-q)$ is then the *centre* of $B_{p,q}$ and that its maximal element $p-1$ coincides with the one of A_p.

The automaton $\widehat{T_{\frac{p}{q}}}$ is then defined by:

$$\widehat{T_{\frac{p}{q}}} = \left\langle \mathbb{N}, B_{p,q}, \tau_{\frac{p}{q}}, 0, \mathbb{N} \right\rangle \ .$$

This is possible, even if $B_{p,q}$ is larger than A_p because, in Equation 2, $\tau_{\frac{p}{q}}$ is defined on $\mathbb{N} \times \mathbb{Z}$, hence on $\mathbb{N} \times B_{p,q}$.

Figure 3 shows an example of the case when p is strictly smaller than $2q-1$, that is, transitions are added (thick arrows in the figure). The resulting automaton is a DAG (more complex than a tree with one loop).

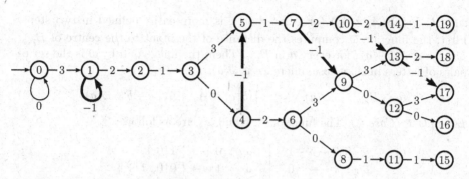

Fig. 3. Transforming $\mathcal{T}_{\frac{4}{3}}$ into $\widehat{\mathcal{T}_{\frac{4}{3}}}$

Figure 4a shows an example of the case when p is strictly greater than $2q-1$, that is, transitions are removed (dotted arrows in the figure). In this case, the resulting automaton is a forest (that is, an infinite union of trees). The accessible part is the tree rooted in 0. The other trees of the forest are not accessible; they are kept in $\widehat{\mathcal{T}_{\frac{p}{q}}}$, as they will come into play at Section 4. Furthermore, as already noted, if $p = (2q-1)$, $B_{p,q} = A_p$ and $\mathcal{T}_{\frac{p}{q}} = \widehat{\mathcal{T}_{\frac{p}{q}}}$.

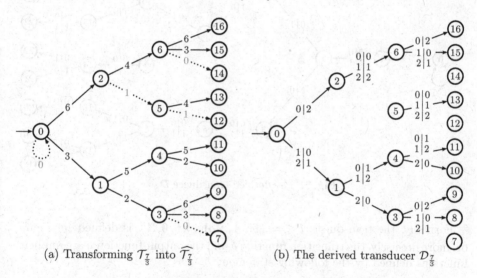

(a) Transforming $\mathcal{T}_{\frac{7}{3}}$ into $\widehat{\mathcal{T}_{\frac{7}{3}}}$ (b) The derived transducer $\mathcal{D}_{\frac{7}{3}}$

Fig. 4. From $\mathcal{T}_{\frac{7}{3}}$ to $\mathcal{D}_{\frac{7}{3}}$

This construction ensures that every state of $\widehat{\mathcal{T}_{\frac{p}{q}}}$ congruent to -1 modulo q has a unique successor and that every other state has exactly two successors.

Changing the Labels. Every label of $\widehat{\mathcal{T}_{\frac{p}{q}}}$ (which is a letter of $B_{p,q}$) is replaced by a *set* of pairs of digits in $A_q \times A_q$. The *label replacement function*

$\omega_{\frac{p}{q}} : B_{p,q} \to \mathfrak{P}(A_q \times A_q)$ (or ω for short), is more easily defined in two steps. First, the function $\overline{\omega}$ computes the distance of the input to the centre of $B_{p,q}$: $\overline{\omega}(a) = a - (p - q)$, for every a in $B_{p,q}$. Then, the image of a by ω is the set of pairs of letters in A_q whose difference is $\overline{\omega}(a)$:

$$\forall a \in B_{p,q} \quad \omega(a) \quad = \quad \{(b|c) \in A_q \times A_q \mid c - b = \overline{\omega}(a)\} . \tag{3}$$

Example 1 (Case $\frac{3}{2}$). The functions $\overline{\omega}_{\frac{3}{2}}$ and $\omega_{\frac{3}{2}}$ are as follows:

$$\overline{\omega}_{\frac{3}{2}} : 0 \longmapsto -1 \qquad \omega_{\frac{3}{2}} : 0 \longmapsto \{1|0\}$$
$$\overline{\omega}_{\frac{3}{2}} : 1 \longmapsto 0 \qquad \omega_{\frac{3}{2}} : 1 \longmapsto \{0|0, 1|1\}$$
$$\overline{\omega}_{\frac{3}{2}} : 2 \longmapsto 1 \qquad \omega_{\frac{3}{2}} : 2 \longmapsto \{0|1\}$$

and Fig. 5 shows $\mathcal{D}_{\frac{3}{2}}$ ($\mathcal{D}_{\frac{7}{3}}$ has been placed at Figure 4b in anticipation).

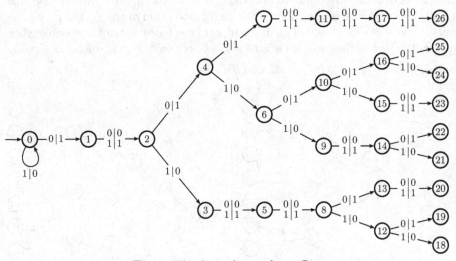

Fig. 5. The derived transducer $\mathcal{D}_{\frac{3}{2}}$

Formally, the transducer $\mathcal{D}_{\frac{p}{q}} = \langle \mathbb{N}, A_q \times A_q, \delta, \eta, 0, \mathbb{N} \rangle$ is defined *implicitly* or, more precisely, the transition function δ and the output function η are implicit functions defined by the following statement:

$$\forall n \in \mathbb{N}, \ \forall a \in B_{p,q}, \ \forall (b, c) \in \omega(a)$$
$$\tau_{\frac{p}{q}}(n, a) \text{ defined} \quad \Longrightarrow \quad n \xrightarrow{b|c} \tau_{\frac{p}{q}}(n, a) \quad \text{is a transition of } \mathcal{D}_{\frac{p}{q}},$$
$$\text{that is, } \delta(n, b) = \tau_{\frac{p}{q}}(n, a) \text{ and } \eta(n, b) = c. \tag{4}$$

In other words, the transitions of $\mathcal{D}_{\frac{p}{q}}$ are labelled as follows: if $n \equiv -1 \ [q]$, the state n has exactly one outgoing transition with labels $0|0, 1|1, \ldots, q-1|q-1$.

Otherwise, the state n has two outgoing transitions. If we write $k = a - (p - q)$ where a is the maximal outgoing label of n in $\mathcal{T}_{\frac{p}{q}}$: the label of the upper transition is $0|k, 1|k+1, \ldots, (q-1-k)|q-1$; while the label of the lower transition is $q-k|0, (q-k+1)|1, \ldots, q-1|k-1$.

The transducer constructed in this manner is sequential and input-complete, as stated by the following lemma.

Lemma 1. *For every state n of $\mathcal{D}_{\frac{p}{q}}$ and every letter b of A_q, there exists a unique state m and a unique letter c such that $n \xrightarrow{b|c} m$.*

Corollary 1. *For every infinite word w in A_q^{ω}, $\mathcal{D}_{\frac{p}{q}}(w)$ exists and is unique.*

3.2 Correctness of $\mathcal{D}_{\frac{p}{q}}$

It remains to establish that $\mathcal{D}_{\frac{p}{q}}$ has the expected behaviour, as stated below.

Theorem 1. *For every n in $\mathbb{N}$, $\mathcal{D}_{\frac{p}{q}}(w_n^-) = w_{(n+1)}^-$.*

The proof of Theorem 1 relies on the equivalent (and more explicit) definition of the transitions of $\mathcal{D}_{\frac{p}{q}}$, stated in the following proposition.

Proposition 1. *If $n \xrightarrow{b|c} m$ is a transition of $\mathcal{D}_{\frac{p}{q}}$, then*

$$c = (b - (n+1)p) \,\%\, q \qquad and \qquad m = \left\lceil \frac{(n+1)p - b}{q} - 1 \right\rceil .$$

In the case of finite words, a stronger version can be stated.

Theorem 2. *Given a base $\frac{p}{q}$ and two words u, v in A_q^*, the image of u by $\mathcal{D}_{\frac{p}{q}}$ is v if and only if there exists an integer n such that u is a prefix of w_n^- and v is a prefix of w_{n+1}^-.*

Theorem 2 is purposely stated on finite words and a similar statement for infinite words would be false: for every infinite word w of A_q^{ω}, $\mathcal{D}_{\frac{p}{q}}(w)$ exists, hence there are uncountably many pairs of infinite words $w \,|\, \mathcal{D}_{\frac{p}{q}}(w)$ accepted by $\mathcal{D}_{\frac{p}{q}}$ while there are only countably many pairs $w_n^- \,|\, w_{n+1}^-$.

4 Span of a Node

Lets us consider now the real value of infinite words. We denote by $\rho : A_p^{\omega} \to \mathbb{R}$, the *real evaluation function*, defined as follows:

$$\rho(a_1 a_2 \cdots a_n \cdots) \;=\; \sum_{i \geq 0} \frac{a_i}{q} \left(\frac{p}{q} \right)^{-i} . \tag{5}$$

We denote by $W_{\frac{p}{q}}$ the language of infinite words $\mathcal{L}(\mathcal{T}_{\frac{p}{q}})$. It is proven in [1, Theorem 2] that $\rho(W_{\frac{p}{q}})$ is the interval $[0, \rho(w_0^+)]$. By extension, we denote by $W_{\frac{p}{q},n}$ (or, for short, W_n) the language of infinite words $\langle n \rangle^{-1} W_{\frac{p}{q}}$. Intuitively, an infinite word w over A_p is in W_n if $n \cdot u$ exists in $T_{\frac{p}{q}}$ for every finite prefix u of w. Analogously to $W_{\frac{p}{q}}$, the following holds.

Lemma 2. *For every integer* n, $\rho(W_{\frac{p}{q},n})$ *is the interval* $[\rho(w_n^-), \ \rho(w_n^+)]$.

Definition 3. *For every integer* n, *the span of* n, *denoted by* $\mathtt{span}(n)$, *is the size of* $\rho(W_n)$: $\mathtt{span}(n) = (\rho(w_n^+) - \rho(w_n^-))$.

Remark 1. Let us stress that what we call the span of the node n is not, in the fractal drawing (Figure 1b), the width of the subtree rooted in n. This quantity is obviously decreasing exponentially with the depth of the node n and the set of these has 0 as unique accumulation point. What we call span is this quantity *renormalised* by multiplication by $(\frac{p}{q})^k$, where k is the depth of the node n.

Let a be a letter from the minimal alphabet $A_q = [\![0, (q-1)]\!]$ and b a letter from the maximal alphabet $[\![(p-q), (p-1)]\!]$. The integer $(b-a)$ is necessarily in $[\![p-(2q-1), p-1]\!] = B_{p,q}$. Hence, through this digit-wise subtraction, denoted by '$\ominus$', $(w_n^+ \ominus w_n^-)$ is a word over $B_{p,q}$, and is called *the span-word of* n. It is routine to check that the following statement is true.

Lemma 3. *For all integer* n, $\mathtt{span}(n) = \rho(w_n^+ \ominus w_n^-)$.

Let $\mathbf{S}_{\frac{p}{q}}$ be the set of real numbers $\mathbf{S}_{\frac{p}{q}} = \{\mathtt{span}(n) \mid n \in \mathbb{N}\}$; the following statement holds.

Theorem 3.

(i) *If* $p \leqslant 2q-1$, $\mathbf{S}_{\frac{p}{q}}$ *is dense in* $[0, \ \rho(w_0^+)]$.
(ii) *If* $p > 2q-1$, $\mathbf{S}_{\frac{p}{q}}$ *is nowhere dense.*

The key to Theorem 3 is the connexion between the span-words and $\widehat{T_{\frac{p}{q}}}$, achieved by Theorem 4 and Proposition 3.

Theorem 4. *All span-words are accepted by* $\widehat{T_{\frac{p}{q}}}$.

The proof of this theorem is a direct consequence of Proposition 2, below and requires more definitions. There exists a (trivial) map m from the minimal alphabet to the maximal alphabet, such that, for all integer n, $m(w_{n+1}^-) = w_n^+$.

$$
m : \quad A_q \quad \longrightarrow \quad [\![(p-q), (p-1)]\!]
$$
$$
a \quad \longmapsto \quad m(a) = \mathtt{maxLetter}(a+p)
$$

where $\mathtt{maxLetter}(x)$ is the greatest integer congruent to x modulo q and strictly smaller than p. By extending m to A_q^ω, Theorem 4 reduces to the statement that $\widehat{T_{\frac{p}{q}}}$ accepts $(m(w_{n+1}^-) \ominus w_n^-)$ for every n:

Proposition 2. *If* $w|w'$ *is a pair of infinite words accepted by* $\mathcal{D}_{\frac{p}{q}}$ *then* $\widehat{T_{\frac{p}{q}}}$ *accepts the word* $(m(w') \ominus w)$.

Analogously to the case of $\mathcal{D}_{\frac{p}{q}}$, $\widehat{\mathcal{T}_{\frac{p}{q}}}$ accepts uncountably many infinite words, therefore words that are not $(w_n^+ \ominus w_n^-)$ for any n. That being said, it seems to be the best result we can hope for, as the following two statements hold.

Proposition 3. *Every finite word accepted by $\widehat{\mathcal{T}_{\frac{p}{q}}}$ is the prefix of a span-word.*

Corollary 2. *The language of infinite words of $\widehat{\mathcal{T}_{\frac{p}{q}}}$ is the topological closure of the span-words.*

5 Conclusion

In the search of elucidating the structure of the set of representations of integers in a rational base number system, we have shown that the correspondence between two consecutive minimal words is achieved by a transducer that exhibits essentially the same structure as the one of the set of representations we started with. We have called this property an "*auto-similarity*" of the structure, as the structure is indeed not *self-similar*.

Let us note that the infinite transducer we have built realises the correspondence for *all minimal words*. It does not contradict the following conjecture that would express that each minimal word contains the complexity of the whole tree.

Conjecture 1. For every integer n, there exists a finite transducer that transforms w_n^- into w_{n+1}^-.

It is also remarkable that in this construction, the case $p = 2q - 1$ appears as the frontier between two completely different behaviours of the systems, in a much stronger way than it was described in our first work [1] on rational base number systems. It was hinted that there might be structural differences between two classes of rational base number systems. Indeed, those where $p \geqslant 2q - 1$ have an additional property, namely that, for every integer n, the span of n is never equal to 0. It was however never proved that this property was false when $p < 2q - 1$.

References

1. Akiyama, S., Frougny, C., Sakarovitch, J.: Powers of rationals modulo 1 and rational base number systems. Israel J. Math. 168, 53–91 (2008)
2. Akiyama, S., Marsault, V., Sakarovitch, J.: Auto-similarity in rational base number systems (full version), http://arxiv.org/abs/1305.6757
3. Berstel, J.: Transductions and Context-Free Languages. Teubner (1979)
4. Lothaire, M.: Algebraic Combinatorics on Words. Cambridge University Press (2002)
5. Mahler, K.: An unsolved problem on the powers of 3/2. J. Austral. Math. Soc. 8, 313–321 (1968)
6. Marsault, V., Sakarovitch, J.: On sets of numbers rationally represented in a rational base number system. In: Muntean, T., Poulakis, D., Rolland, R. (eds.) CAI 2013. LNCS, vol. 8080, pp. 89–100. Springer, Heidelberg (2013)

Infinite Words with Well Distributed Occurrences

Ľubomíra Balková[1], Michelangelo Bucci[2],
Alessandro De Luca[3], and Svetlana Puzynina[2,4]

[1] Department of Mathematics, FNSPE, Czech Technical University in Prague,
Trojanova 13, 120 00 Praha 2, Czech Republic
lubomira.balkova@gmail.com
[2] Department of Mathematics, University of Turku, FI-20014 Turku, Finland
{michelangelo.bucci,svepuz}@utu.fi
[3] DIETI, Università degli Studi di Napoli Federico II
via Claudio, 21, 80125 Napoli, Italy
alessandro.deluca@unina.it
[4] Sobolev Institute of Mathematics, Russia

Abstract. In this paper we introduce the *well distributed occurrences (WDO)* combinatorial property for infinite words, which guarantees good behavior (no lattice structure) in some related pseudorandom number generators. An infinite word u on a d-ary alphabet has the WDO property if, for each factor w of u, positive integer m, and vector $\mathbf{v} \in \mathbb{Z}_m^d$, there is an occurrence of w such that the Parikh vector of the prefix of u preceding such occurrence is congruent to $\mathbf{v}$ modulo m. We prove that Sturmian words, and more generally Arnoux-Rauzy words and some morphic images of them, have the WDO property.

Introduction

The combinatorial problem studied in this paper comes from random number generation. Pseudorandom number generators aim to produce random numbers using a deterministic process. No wonder they suffer from many defects. The most usual ones – linear congruential generators – are known to produce periodic sequences having a defect called lattice structure. Guimond et al. [2] proved that when two linear congruential generators are combined using infinite words coding certain classes of quasicrystals or, equivalently, of cut-and-project sets, the resulting sequence is aperiodic and has no lattice structure.

We have found a combinatorial condition – *well distributed occurrences*, or WDO for short – that guarantees absence of lattice structure if two arbitrary generators having the same output alphabet are combined using an infinite word having the WDO property. The WDO property for an infinite word u over an alphabet A means that for any integer m and any factor w of u, the set of Parikh vectors modulo m of prefixes of u preceeding the occurrences of w coincides with $\{0, 1, \ldots, m-1\}^{|A|}$ (see Definition 2.1). In other words, among Parikh vectors modulo m of such prefixes one has all possible vectors. Besides giving generators without lattice structure, the WDO property is an interesting combinatorial property of infinite words itself.

J. Karhumäki, A. Lepistö, and L. Zamboni (Eds.): WORDS 2013, LNCS 8079, pp. 46–57, 2013.
© Springer-Verlag Berlin Heidelberg 2013

We have proved first that Sturmian words have well distributed occurrences, and then we have shown this property for Arnoux-Rauzy words. The proof for Sturmian words is based on different ideas than the one for Arnoux-Rauzy words, therefore we will provide in the sequel both of them.

In the next section, we deal with pseudorandom number generation, thus establishing the motivation for our work. Next, in Section 2, we give the basic combinatorial definitions needed for our main results, including the WDO property. Finally, in the last two sections, we prove that the property holds for Sturmian and Arnoux-Rauzy words, respectively.

1 Motivation in Pseudorandom Number Generation

For the sake of our discussion, any infinite sequence of integers can be understood as a *pseudorandom number generator (PRNG)*; see also [2].

Let $X = (x_n)_{n\in\mathbb{N}}$ and $Y = (y_n)_{n\in\mathbb{N}}$ be two PRNGs with the same output $M \subset \mathbb{N}$ and the same period $m \in \mathbb{N}$, and let $u = u_0u_1u_2\ldots$ be a binary infinite word, i.e., an infinite sequence over $\{0,1\}$.

The PRNG

$$Z = (z_n)_{n\in\mathbb{N}} \tag{1}$$

based on u is obtained by the following algorithm:

1. Read step by step the letters of u.
2. When you read 0 for the i-th time, copy the i-th symbol from X to the end of the constructed sequence Z.
3. When you read 1 for the i-th time, copy the i-th symbol from Y to the end of the constructed sequence Z.

Of course, it is possible to generalize this construction – using infinite words over a multiliteral alphabet, one can combine more than two PRNGs.

1.1 Lattice Structure

Let $X = (x_n)_{n\in\mathbb{N}}$ be a PRNG whose output is a finite set $M \subset \mathbb{N}$. We say that X has the *lattice structure* if there exists $t \in \mathbb{N}$ such that

$$\{(x_i, x_{i+1}, \ldots, x_{i+t-1}) \mid i \in \mathbb{N}\}$$

is covered by a family of parallel equidistant hyperplanes and at the same time, this family does not cover the whole lattice

$$M^t = \{(a_1, a_2, \ldots, a_t) \mid a_i \in M \text{ for all } i \in \{1, \ldots, t\}\}.$$

It is known that all linear congruential generators have the lattice structure. Recall that a *linear congruential generator* $(x_n)_{n\in\mathbb{N}}$ is given by $a, m, c \in \mathbb{N}$ and defined by the recurrence relation $x_{n+1} = ax_n + c \bmod m$. Let us mention a famous example of a PRNG with a striking lattice structure. For $t = 3$, the set of triples of RANDU, i.e., $\{(x_i, x_{i+1}, x_{i+2}) \mid i \in \mathbb{N}\}$ is covered by only 15 equidistant hyperplanes, see Figure 1.

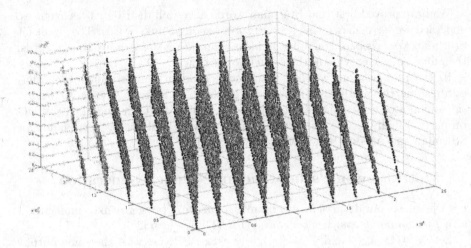

Fig. 1. The triples of RANDU – the linear congruential generator with $a = (2^{16} + 3), m = 2^{31}, c = 0$ – are covered by as few as 15 parallel equidistant planes

1.2 Combinatorial Condition on Absence of the Lattice Structure

Guimond et al. in [2] have shown that PRNGs based on infinite words coding a certain class of cut-and-project sets have no lattice structure. A crucial part of their proof is the following lemma.

Lemma 1.1. *Let Z be the PRNG from (1) based on an aperiodic infinite word. If there exist for any $a, b \in M$ and for any $\ell \in \mathbb{N}$ an ℓ-tuple z such that both za and zb are $(\ell + 1)$-tuples of the sequence Z, then Z does not have the lattice structure.*

We have found the following combinatorial condition on binary infinite words guaranteeing that the assumptions of the previous lemma are met: we say that a binary aperiodic infinite word u over the alphabet $\{0, 1\}$ has *well distributed occurrences* (or has *the WDO property*) if u satisfies for any $m \in \mathbb{N}$ and any factor w of u the following condition. If we denote $i_0, i_1, \ldots$ the occurrences of w in u, then

$$\left\{ \left(|u_0 u_1 \cdots u_{i_j - 1}|_0, |u_0 u_1 \cdots u_{i_j - 1}|_1 \right) \bmod m \mid j \in \mathbb{N} \right\} = \mathbb{Z}_m^2,$$

where mod m is applied elementwise.

See the next section for the definition of aperiodicity, factor occurrences, and the WDO property for general alphabets.

The WDO property for binary words thus ensures no lattice structure for PRNGs defined in (1).

Theorem 1.2. *Let Z be the PRNG from (1) based on a binary aperiodic infinite word having the WDO property. Then Z has no lattice structure.*

We omit the proof of this theorem for the sake of brevity.

Moreover, we have shown that the class of infinite words satisfying the WDO property for binary words is larger than the class described in [2] (see Section 3).

2   Combinatorics on Words and the WDO Property

By A we denote a finite set of symbols called *letters*; the set A is therefore called an *alphabet*. A finite string $w = w_1w_2\ldots w_n$ of letters from A is said to be a *finite word*, its length is denoted by $|w| = n$ and $|w|_a$ denotes the number of occurrences of $a \in A$ contained in w. The empty word, a neutral element for concatenation of finite words, is denoted ε and it is of zero length.

Under an *infinite word* we understand an infinite sequence $u = u_0u_1u_2\ldots$ of letters from A. A finite word w is a *factor* of a word v (finite or infinite) if there exist words p and s such that $v = pws$. If $p = \varepsilon$, then w is said to be a *prefix* of v; if $s = \varepsilon$, then w is a *suffix* of v. The set of factors and prefixes of v are denoted by $\mathrm{Fact}(v)$ and $\mathrm{Pref}(v)$, respectively. If $v = ps$ for finite words v, p, s, then we write $p = vs^{-1}$ and $s = p^{-1}v$.

An infinite word u over the alphabet A is called *eventually periodic* if it is of the form $u = vw^\omega$, where v, w are finite words over A and ω denotes an infinite repetition. An infinite word is called *aperiodic* if it is not eventually periodic.

For any factor w of an infinite word u, every index i such that w is a prefix of the infinite word $u_iu_{i+1}u_{i+2}\ldots$ is called an *occurrence* of w in u.

The *factor complexity* of an infinite word u is a map $\mathcal{C}_u : \mathbb{N} \mapsto \mathbb{N}$ defined by $\mathcal{C}_u(n) :=$ the number of factors of length n contained in u. The factor complexity of eventually periodic words is bounded, while the factor complexity of an aperiodic word u satisfies $\mathcal{C}_u(n) \geq n + 1$ for all $n \in \mathbb{N}$. A *right extension* of a factor w of u over the alphabet A is any letter $a \in A$ such that wa is a factor u. Of course, any factor of u has at least one right extension. A factor w is called *right special* if w has at least two right extensions. Similarly, one can define a *left extension* and a *left special* factor. A factor is *bispecial* if it is both right and left special. An aperiodic word contains right special factors of any length.

The *Parikh vector* of a finite word w over an alphabet $\{0, 1, \ldots, d - 1\}$ is defined as $(|w|_0, |w|_1, \ldots, |w|_{d-1})$. For a finite or infinite word $u = u_0u_1u_2\ldots$, we denote by $\mathrm{Pref}_n u$ the prefix of length n of u, i.e., $\mathrm{Pref}_n u = u_0u_1\ldots u_{n-1}$.

Let us generalize the combinatorial condition on infinite words that guarantees no lattice structure for pseudorandom number generators from binary to multiliteral alphabets.

Definition 2.1 (The WDO property). *We say that an aperiodic infinite word u over the alphabet $\{0, 1, \ldots, d - 1\}$ has* well distributed occurrences *(or has the WDO property) if u satisfies for any $m \in \mathbb{N}$ and any factor w of u the following condition. If we denote $i_0, i_1, \ldots$ the occurrences of w in u, then*

$$\left\{ \left(|u_0u_1\cdots u_{i_j-1}|_0, \ldots, |u_0u_1\cdots u_{i_j-1}|_{d-1} \right) \bmod m \mid j \in \mathbb{N} \right\} = \mathbb{Z}_m^d;$$

that is, the Parikh vectors of $\mathrm{Pref}_{i_j}(u)$ for $j \in \mathbb{N}$, when reduced modulo m, give the whole $\mathbb{Z}_m^d$.

We define the WDO property for aperiodic words since it clearly never holds for periodic ones.

With the above notation, it is easy to see that if a recurrent infinite word u has the WDO property, then for every vector $\mathbf{v} \in \mathbb{Z}_m^d$ there are infinitely many values of j such that the Parikh vector of $\mathrm{Pref}_{i_j}(u)$ is congruent to $\mathbf{v}$ modulo m.

Example 2.2. The Thue-Morse word $t = 0110100110010110\cdots$, which is a fixed point of the morphism $0 \mapsto 01$, $1 \mapsto 10$, does not satisfy the WDO property. Indeed, take $m = 2$ and $w = 00$, then w occurs only in odd positions i_j so that $(|t_0 \cdots t_{i_j-1}|0 + |t_0 \cdots t_{i_j-1}|1) = i_j$ is odd. Thus, e.g., $(|t_0 \cdots t_{i_j-1}|0, |t_0 \cdots t_{i_j-1}|1)$ mod $2 \neq (0,0)$, and hence $\{(|t_0 \cdots t_{i_j-1}|0, |t_0 \cdots t_{i_j-1}|1) \bmod 2 \mid j \in \mathbb{N}\} \neq \mathbb{Z}_2^2$.

Example 2.3. We say that an infinite word u over an alphabet A, $|A| = d$, is *universal* if it contains all finite words over A as its factors. It is easy to see that any universal word satisfies the WDO property. Indeed, for any word $w \in A^*$ and any m there exists a finite word v such that if we denote $i_0, i_1, \ldots, i_k$ the occurrences of w in v, then

$$\left\{ (|\mathrm{Pref}_{i_j} v|0, \ldots, |\mathrm{Pref}_{i_j} v|d-1) \bmod m \mid j \in \{0, 1, \ldots, k\} \right\} = \mathbb{Z}_m^d.$$

Since u is universal, v is a factor of u. Denoting by i an occurrence of v in u, one gets that the positions $i + i_j$ are occurrences of w in u. Hence

$$\left\{ (|\mathrm{Pref}_{i+i_j} u|0, \ldots, |\mathrm{Pref}_{i+i_j} u|d-1) \bmod m \mid j \in \{0, 1, \ldots, k\} \right\} =$$
$$= (|\mathrm{Pref}_i u|0, \ldots, |\mathrm{Pref}_i u|d-1) +$$
$$+ \left\{ (|\mathrm{Pref}_{i_j} v|0, \ldots, |\mathrm{Pref}_{i_j} v|d-1) \bmod m \mid j \in \{0, 1, \ldots, k\} \right\} = \mathbb{Z}_m^d.$$

Therefore, u satisfies the WDO property.

3   Sturmian Words

In this section, we show that Sturmian words have well distributed occurrences.

Definition 3.1. *An aperiodic infinite word u is called* Sturmian *if its factor complexity satisfies $\mathcal{C}_u(n) = n + 1$ for all $n \in \mathbb{N}$.*

So, Sturmian words are by definition binary and they have the lowest possible factor complexity among aperiodic infinite words. Sturmian words admit various types of characterizations of geometric and combinatorial nature. One of such characterizations is via irrational rotations on the unit circle. In [4] Hedlund and Morse showed that each Sturmian word may be realized measure-theoretically by an irrational rotation on the circle. That is, every Sturmian word is obtained by coding the symbolic orbit of a point on the circle of circumference one under a rotation R_α by an irrational angle[1] α, $0 < \alpha < 1$, where the circle is partitioned into two complementary intervals, one of length α and the other of length $1 - \alpha$. And conversely each such coding gives rise to a Sturmian word.

---

[1] Measured by arc length (thus equivalent to $2\pi\alpha$ radians).

Definition 3.2. *The rotation by angle α is the mapping R_α from $[0,1)$ (identified with the unit circle) to itself defined by $R_\alpha(x) = \{x+\alpha\}$, where $\{x\} = x - \lfloor x \rfloor$ is the fractional part of x. Considering a partition of $[0,1)$ into $I_0 = [0, 1-\alpha)$, $I_1 = [1-\alpha, 1)$, define a word*

$$s_{\alpha,\rho}(n) = \begin{cases} 0, & \text{if } R_\alpha^n(\rho) = \{\rho + n\alpha\} \in I_0, \\ 1, & \text{if } R_\alpha^n(\rho) = \{\rho + n\alpha\} \in I_1. \end{cases}$$

One can also define $I_0' = (0, 1-\alpha]$, $I_1' = (1-\alpha, 1]$, the corresponding word is denoted by $s_{\alpha,\rho}'$.

For more information on Sturmian words we refer to [3, Chapter 2].

Theorem 3.3. *Let u be a Sturmian word on $\{0,1\}$. Then u has the WDO property.*

Proof. In the proof we use the definition of Sturmian word via rotation. The main idea is controlling the number of 1's modulo m by taking circle of length m, and controlling the length taking the rotation by $m\alpha$.

For the proof we will use an equivalent reformulation of the theorem:

Let u be a Sturmian word on $\{0,1\}$, for any natural number m and any factor w of u let us denote $i_0, i_1, \ldots$ the occurrences of w in u. Then

$$\left\{ (i_j, |u_0 u_1 \cdots u_{i_j - 1}|_1) \bmod m \mid j \in \mathbb{N} \right\} = \{0, 1, ..., m-1\}^2.$$

That is, we will control the number of 1's and the length instead the number of 0's.

Since a Sturmian word can be defined via rotations by an irrational angle on a unit circle, without loss of generality we may assume that $u = s_{\alpha,\rho}$ for some $0 < \alpha < 1$, $0 \le \rho < 1$, α irrational (see Definition 3.2). Equivalently, we can consider m copies of the circle connected into one circle of length m with m intervals $I_1^i = [i - \alpha, i)$ of length α corresponding to 1. The Sturmian word is obtained by rotation by α on this circle of length m (see Fig. 2).

Namely, we define the rotation $R_{\alpha,m}$ as the mapping from $[0, m)$ (identified with the circle of length m) to itself defined by $R_{\alpha,m}(x) = \{x + \alpha\}_m$, where $\{x\}_m = x - \lfloor x/m \rfloor m$ and for $m = 1$ coincides with the fractional part of x. A partition of $[0, m)$ into $2m$ intervals $I_0^i = [i, i+1-\alpha)$, $I_1^i = [i+1-\alpha, i+1)$, $i = 0, \ldots, m-1$ defines the Sturmian word $u = s_{\alpha,\rho}$:

$$s_{\alpha,\rho}(n) = \begin{cases} 0, & \text{if } R_{\alpha,m}^n(\rho) = \{\rho + n\alpha\} \in I_0^i \text{ for some } i = 0, \ldots, m-1, \\ 1, & \text{if } R_{\alpha,m}^n(\rho) = \{\rho + n\alpha\} \in I_1^i \text{ for some } i = 0, \ldots, m-1. \end{cases}$$

It is well known that any factor $w = w_0 \cdots w_{k-1}$ of u corresponds to an interval I_w in $[0,1)$, so that whenever you start rotating from the interval I_w, you obtain w. Namely, $x \in I_w$ if and only if $x \in I_{w_0}, R_\alpha(x) \in I_{w_1}, \ldots, R_\alpha^{|w|-1}(x) \in I_{w_{|w|-1}}$.

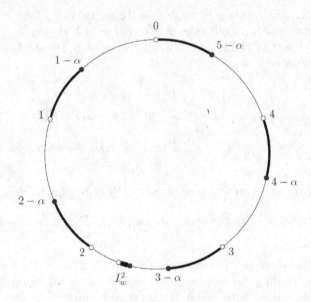

Fig. 2. Illustration to the proof of Theorem 3.3: the example for $m = 5$

Similarly, we can define m intervals corresponding to w in $[0, m)$ (circle of length m), so that if $I_w = [x_1, x_2)$, then $I_w^i = [x_1 + i, x_2 + i)$, $i = 0, \ldots, m - 1$.

Fix a factor w of u, take arbitrary $(j, i) \in \{0, 1, \ldots, m - 1\}^2$. Now we will organize (j, i) among the occurrences of w, i.e., find l such that $u_l \ldots u_{l+|w|-1} = w$, $l \bmod m = j$ and $|\mathrm{Pref}_l u|_1 \bmod m = i$.

Consider rotation $R_{m\alpha, m}(x)$ by $m\alpha$ instead of rotation by α, and start m-rotating from $j\alpha + \rho$. Formally, $R_{m\alpha, m}(x) = \{x + m\alpha\}_m$, where, as above, $\{x\}_m = x - [x/m]m$. This rotation will put us to positions $mk + j$, $k \in \mathbb{N}$ in the Sturmian word: for $a \in \{0, 1\}$ one has $s_{\alpha, \rho}(mk + j) = a$ if $R_{m\alpha, m}^k(j\alpha + \rho) = \{j\alpha + \rho + km\alpha\}_m \in I_a^i$ for some $i = 0, \ldots, m - 1$.

Remark that the points in the orbit of an m-rotation of a point on the m-circle are dense, and hence the rotation comes infinitely often to each interval. So pick k when $j\alpha + mk\alpha + \rho \in I_w^i \subset [i, i + 1)$ (and actually there exist infinitely many such k). Then the length l of the corresponding prefix is equal to $km + j$, and the number of 1's in it is $i + mp$, where p is the number of complete circles you made, i.e., $p = [(j\alpha + mk\alpha + \rho)/m]$. □

Remark 3.4. In the next section we will show that Arnoux-Rauzy words [1], which are natural extensions of Sturmian words to larger alphabets, also satisfy the WDO property. Note that the proof above cannot be generalized to Arnoux-Rauzy words, because it is based on the geometric interpretation of Sturmian words via rotations, while this interpretation does not extend to Arnoux-Rauzy words.

4 Arnoux-Rauzy Words

4.1 Basic Definitions

Definition 4.1. *Let A be a finite alphabet. The* reversal *operator is the operator $\sim: A^* \mapsto A^*$ defined by recurrence in the following way:*

$$\tilde{\varepsilon} = \varepsilon, \quad \widetilde{va} = a\tilde{v}$$

for all $v \in A^*$ and $a \in A$. The fixed points of the reversal operator are called palindromes.

Definition 4.2. *Let $u \in A^*$ be a finite word over the alphabet A. We define the* right palindromic closure *of u, and we denote it by $u^{(+)}$ as the shortest palindrome that has u as a prefix. It is readily verified that if p is the longest palindromic suffix of $u = vp$, then $u^{(+)} = vp\tilde{v}$.*

Definition 4.3. *We call the* iterated (right) palindromic closure *operator the operator ψ recurrently defined by the following rules:*

$$\psi(\varepsilon) = \varepsilon, \quad \psi(va) = (\psi(v)a)^{(+)}$$

for all $v \in A^*$ and $a \in A$. The definition of ψ may be extended to infinite words u over A as $\psi(u) = \lim_n \psi(\mathrm{Pref}_n u)$, i.e., $\psi(u)$ is the infinite word having $\psi(\mathrm{Pref}_n u)$ as its prefix for every $n \in \mathbb{N}$.

Definition 4.4. *Let Δ be an infinite word on the alphabet A such that every letter occurs infinitely often in Δ. The word $c = \psi(\Delta)$ is then called a* characteristic (or standard) Arnoux-Rauzy word *and Δ is called the* directive sequence *of c. An infinite word u is called an* Arnoux-Rauzy word *if it has the same set of factors as a (unique) characteristic Arnoux-Rauzy word, which is called the* characteristic word of u. The directive sequence of an Arnoux-Rauzy word is the directive sequence of its characteristic word.*

Let us also recall the following well-known characterization:

Theorem 4.5. *Let u be an aperiodic infinite word over the alphabet A. Then u is a standard Arnoux-Rauzy word if and only if the following hold:*

1. *$\mathrm{Fact}(u)$ is closed under reversal (that is, if v is a factor of u so is $\tilde{v}$).*
2. *Every left special factor of u is also a prefix.*
3. *If v is a right special factor of u then va is a factor of u for every $a \in A$.*

From the preceding theorem, it can be easily verified that the bispecial factors of a standard Arnoux-Rauzy correspond to its palindromic prefixes (including the empty word), and hence to the iterated palindromic closure of the prefixes of its directive sequence. That is, if

$$\varepsilon = b_0, b_1, b_2, \ldots$$

is the sequence, ordered by length, of bispecial factors of the standard Arnoux-Rauzy word u, $\Delta = \Delta_0\Delta_1 \cdots$ its directive sequence (with $\Delta_i \in A$ for every i), we have $b_{i+1} = (b_i\Delta_i)^{(+)}$.

A direct consequence of this, together with the preceding definitions, is the following statement, which will be used in the sequel.

Lemma 4.6. *Let u be a characteristic Arnoux-Rauzy word and let Δ and $(b_i)_{i\geq 0}$ be defined as above. If Δ_i does not occur in b_i, then $b_{i+1} = b_i\Delta_ib_i$. Otherwise let $j < i$ be the largest integer such that $\Delta_j = \Delta_i$. Then $b_{i+1} = b_ib_j^{-1}b_i$.*

4.2 Parikh Vectors and Arnoux-Rauzy Factors

Where no confusion arises, given an Arnoux-Rauzy word u, we will denote by

$$\varepsilon = b_0, b_1, \ldots, b_n, \ldots$$

the sequence of bispecial factors of u ordered by length and we will set for any $i \in \mathbb{N}$, B_i as the Parikh vector of b_i.

Remark 4.7. By the pigeonhole principle, it is clear that for every $m \in \mathbb{N}$ there exists an integer $N \in \mathbb{N}$ such that, for every $i \geq N$, the set $\{j > i \mid B_j \equiv_m B_i\}$ is infinite. Where no confusion arises and with a slight abuse of notation, fixed m, we will always denote by N the smallest of such integers.

Lemma 4.8. *Let u be a characteristic Arnoux-Rauzy word and let $m \in \mathbb{N}$. Let*

$$\alpha_1 B_{j_1} + \cdots + \alpha_k B_{j_k} \equiv_m \bar{\mathbf{v}} \in \mathbb{Z}_m^d$$

be a linear combination of Parikh vectors such that $\sum_{i=1}^k \alpha_i = 0$, with $j_i \geq N$ and $\alpha_i \in \mathbb{Z}$ for all $i \in \{1, \ldots k\}$. Then, for any $\ell \in \mathbb{N}$, there exists a prefix v of u such that the Parikh vector of v is congruent to $\bar{\mathbf{v}}$ modulo m and vb_ℓ is also a prefix of u.

Proof. Without loss of generality, we can assume $\alpha_1 \geq \alpha_2 \geq \cdots \geq \alpha_k$, hence there exists k' such that

$$\alpha_1 \geq \alpha_{k'} \geq 0 \geq \alpha_{k'+1} \geq \alpha_k.$$

We will prove the result by induction on $\beta = \sum_{j=1}^{k'} \alpha_j$. If $\beta = 0$, trivially, we can take $v = \varepsilon$ and the statement is clearly verified. Let us assume the statement true for all $0 \leq \beta < M$ and let us prove it for $\beta = M$. By the remark preceding this lemma, for every ℓ we can choose $i' > j' > \ell$ such that $B_{j_1} \equiv_m B_{i'}$ and $B_{j_k} \equiv_m B_{j'}$. Since every bispecial factor is a prefix and suffix of all the bigger ones, in particular we have that $b_{j'}$ is a suffix of $b_{i'}$, and b_ℓ is a prefix of $b_{j'}$; this implies that $b_{i'}b_{j'}^{-1}b_\ell$ is actually a prefix of $b_{i'}$. By assumption, the Parikh vector of $b_{i'}b_{j'}^{-1}$ is clearly $B_{i'} - B_{j'} \equiv_m B_{j_1} - B_{j_k}$. Since $\alpha_1 \geq 1$ implies $\alpha_k \leq -1$, we have, by induction hypothesis, that there exists a prefix v of u such that the Parikh vector of v is congruent modulo m to

$$(\alpha_1 - 1)B_{j_1} + \cdots + (\alpha_k + 1)B_{j_k}$$

and $vb_{i'}$ is a prefix of u. Hence $vb_{i'}b_{j'}^{-1}b_\ell$ is also a prefix of u and, by simple computation, the Parikh vector of $vb_{i'}b_{j'}^{-1}$ is congruent modulo m to $\bar{\mathbf{v}}$. $\square$

Definition 4.9. *Let $n \in \mathbb{Z}$. We will say that an integer linear combination of integer vectors is a n-combination if the sum of all the coefficients equals n.*

Lemma 4.10. *Let u be a characteristic Arnoux-Rauzy word and let $n \in \mathbb{N}$. Every n-combination of Parikh vectors of bispecial factors can be expressed as a n-combination of Parikh vectors of arbitrarily large bispecials. In particular, for every $K, M \in \mathbb{N}$, it is possible to find a finite number of integers $\alpha_1, \ldots, \alpha_k$ such that $B_K = \alpha_1 B_{j_1} + \cdots + \alpha_k B_{j_k}$ with $j_i > M$ for every i and $\alpha_1 + \cdots + \alpha_k = 1$.*

Proof. A direct consequence of Lemma 4.6 is that for every i such that Δ_i appears in b_i, we have $B_{i+1} = 2B_i - B_j$, where $j < i$ is the largest such that $\Delta_j = \Delta_i$. This in turn (since every letter in Δ appears infinitely many times from the definition of Arnoux-Rauzy word) implies that *for every* non-negative integer j, there exists a positive k such that $B_j = 2B_{j+k} - B_{j+k+1}$, that is, we can substitute each Parikh vector of a bispecial with a 1-combination of Parikh vectors of strictly larger bispecials. Simply iterating the process, we obtain the statement. $\square$

In the following we will assume the set A to be a finite alphabet of cardinality d. For every set $X \subseteq A^*$ of finite words, we will denote by $\mathrm{PV}(X) \subseteq \mathbb{Z}^d$ the set of Parikh vectors of elements of X and for every $m \in \mathbb{N}$ we will denote by $\mathrm{PV}_m(X) \subseteq \mathbb{Z}_m^d$ the set of elements of $\mathrm{PV}(X)$ reduced modulo m.

Let u be an infinite word over A and let v be a factor of u. We denote by $S_v(u)$ the set of all prefixes of u followed by an occurrence of v. In other words,

$$S_v(u) = \{p \in \mathrm{Pref}(u) \mid pv \in \mathrm{Pref}(u)\}.$$

Definition 4.11. *For any set of finite words $X \subseteq A^*$, we will say that u has the property $\mathcal{P}_X$ (or, for short, that u has $\mathcal{P}_X$) if, for every $m \in \mathbb{N}$ and for every $v \in X$ we have that*

$$\mathrm{PV}_m(S_v(u)) = \mathbb{Z}_m^d.$$

That is to say, for every vector $\mathbf{v} \in \mathbb{Z}_m^d$ there exists a word $w \in S_v(u)$ such that the Parikh vector of w is congruent to $\mathbf{v}$ modulo m.

With this notation, an infinite word u has the WDO property if and only if it has property $\mathcal{P}_{\mathrm{Fact}(u)}$.

Proposition 4.12. *Let u be a characteristic Arnoux-Rauzy word over the d-letter alphabet A. Then u has the property $\mathcal{P}_{\mathrm{Pref}(u)}$.*

Proof. Let us fix an arbitrary $m \in \mathbb{N}$. We want to show that, for every $v \in \mathrm{Pref}(u)$, $\mathrm{PV}_m(S_v(u)) = \mathbb{Z}_m^d$. Let then $\bar{\mathbf{v}} \in \mathbb{Z}^d$ and ℓ be the smallest number such that v is a prefix of b_ℓ. Let $i_1 < i_2 < \cdots < i_d$ be such that Δ_{i_j} does not appear in b_{i_j}, where Δ is the directive word of u. Without loss of generality, we can rearrange the letters so that each Δ_{i_j} is lexicographically smaller than

Δ_{i_j+1}. With this assumption if, for every j, we set $\bar{\mathbf{v}}_j$ as the Parikh vector of b_{i_j+1}, which, by the first part of Lemma 4.6, equals $b_{i_j}\Delta_{i_j}b_{i_j}$, we can find $j-1$ positive integers $\mu_1,\ldots,\mu_{j-1}$ such that $\bar{\mathbf{v}}_j = (\mu_1,\mu_2,\ldots,\mu_{j-1},1,0,\ldots,0)$. It is easy to show, then, that the set $V = \{\bar{\mathbf{v}}_1,\ldots,\bar{\mathbf{v}}_d\}$ generates $\mathbb{Z}^d$, hence there exists an integer n such that $\bar{\mathbf{v}}$ can be expressed as an n-combination of elements of V (which are Parikh vectors of bispecial factors of u). Trivially, then, $\bar{\mathbf{v}} = \bar{\mathbf{v}} - n\bar{\mathbf{0}} = \bar{\mathbf{v}} - nB_0$; thus, it is possible to express $\bar{\mathbf{v}}$ as a 0-combination of Parikh vectors of (by the previous Lemma 4.10) arbitrarily large bispecial factors of u. By Lemma 4.8, then there exists a prefix p of u with Parikh vector $\bar{\mathbf{p}}$ such that $\bar{\mathbf{p}} \equiv_m \bar{\mathbf{v}}$ and pb_ℓ is a prefix of u. Since we picked ℓ such that v is a prefix of b_ℓ, we have that $p \in S_v(u)$. From the arbitrariness of v, $\bar{\mathbf{v}}$ and m, we obtain the statement. $\qquad\square$

As a corollary of Proposition 4.12, we obtain the main result of this section.

Theorem 4.13. *Let u be an Arnoux-Rauzy word over the d-letter alphabet A. Then u has the property $\mathcal{P}_{\mathrm{Fact}(u)}$.*

Proof. Let m be a positive integer and let c be the characteristic word of u. Let v be a factor of u and xvy be the smallest bispecial containing v. By Proposition 4.12, we have that $\mathrm{PV}_m(S_{xv}(c)) = \mathbb{Z}_m^d$ and, since the set is finite, we can find a prefix p of c such that $\mathrm{PV}_m(S_{xv}(p)) = \mathbb{Z}_m^d$. Let w be a prefix of u such that wp is a prefix of u. If $\bar{\mathbf{x}}$ and $\bar{\mathbf{w}}$ are the Parikh vectors of, respectively, x and w, it is easy to see that

$$\bar{\mathbf{w}} + \bar{\mathbf{x}} + \mathrm{PV}(S_{xv}(p)) \subseteq \bar{\mathbf{w}} + \mathrm{PV}(S_v(p)) \subseteq \mathrm{PV}(S_v(u))$$

Since we have chosen p such that $\mathrm{PV}_m(S_{xv}(p)) = \mathbb{Z}_m^d$, we clearly obtain that $\mathrm{PV}_m(S_v(u)) = \mathbb{Z}_m^d$ and hence, by the arbitrariness of v and m, the statement. $\qquad\square$

Remark 4.14. Actually, Theorem 4.13 implies Theorem 3.3.

Remark 4.15. Note the following simple method of obtaining words satisfying the WDO property. Take a word u with the WDO property over an alphabet $\{0,1,\ldots,d-1\}, d > 2$, apply a morphism $\varphi : d-1 \mapsto 0, i \mapsto i$ for $i = 0,\ldots,d-2$, i. e., φ joins two letters into one. It is straightforward that $\varphi(u)$ has WDO property. So, taking Arnoux-Rauzy words and joining some letters, we obtain other words than Sturmian and Arnoux-Rauzy satisfying the WDO property.

Acknowledgements. The first author was supported by the Czech Science Foundation grant GAČR 13-03538S, and thanks L'Oréal Czech Republic for the Fellowship Women in Science. The third author was partially supported by the Italian Ministry of Education (MIUR), under the PRIN 2010–11 project "Automi e Linguaggi Formali: Aspetti Matematici e Applicativi". The fourth author is supported in part by the Academy of Finland under grant 251371 and by Russian Foundation of Basic Research (grants 12-01-00089 and 12-01-00448).

We would like to acknowledge statistical testing of the pseudorandom number generators based on Sturmian and Arnoux-Rauzy words made by Jiří Hladký. He has shown using the Diehard and U01 tests that not only the lattice structure is absent, but also other important properties of PRNGs are improved when LCGs are combined using infinite words having the WDO property.

References

1. Arnoux, P., Rauzy, G.: Représentation géométrique de suites de complexité $2n + 1$. Bull. Soc. Math. France 119, 199–215 (1991)
2. Guimond, L.-S., Patera, J., Patera, J.: Statistical properties and implementation of aperiodic pseudorandom number generators. Applied Numerical Mathematics 46(3-4), 295–318 (2003)
3. Lothaire, M.: Algebraic combinatorics on words. Encyclopedia of Mathematics and its Applications, vol. 90. Cambridge University Press (2002)
4. Morse, M., Hedlund, G.A.: Symbolic Dynamics II: Sturmian trajectories. Amer. J. Math. 62(1), 1–42 (1940)

Generating Discrete Planes with Substitutions

Valérie Berthé[1], Jérémie Bourdon[2], Timo Jolivet[1,3], and Anne Siegel[4]

[1] LIAFA, CNRS, Université Paris Diderot, France
[2] LINA, Université de Nantes, France
[3] FUNDIM, Department of Mathematics, University of Turku, Finland
[4] INRIA, Centre Rennes-Bretagne Atlantique, Dyliss, Rennes, France

Abstract. Given a finite set S of unimodular Pisot substitutions, we provide a method for characterizing the infinite sequences over S that allow to generate a full discrete plane when, starting from a finite seed, we iterate the multidimensional dual substitutions associated with S. We apply our results to study the substitutions associated with the Brun multidimensional continued fraction algorithm.

1 Introduction

The study of Pisot substitutions has been initiated by Rauzy [18] and has led to many developments in several domains, including combinatorics on words, symbolic dynamics, fractal topology and number theory [12,7].

Dual substitutions, introduced by Arnoux and Ito [1] have proven to be a very powerful combinatorial tool in several contexts (see, e.g., [7]). Intuitively, a 3-letter substitution σ acts on broken lines made of translated unit vectors in $\mathbb{Z}^3$, and its dual $\mathbf{E}_1^\star(\sigma)$ acts on 2-dimensional unit faces in $\mathbb{Z}^3$; see Definition 2.4.

A striking fact is that the image by a dual substitution of a discrete plane remains a discrete plane. This link between substitutions and discrete planes leads us to our main concern: given a *finite* patch $\mathcal{V}$ (a *seed*) of a discrete plane, iterating dual substitutions starting from $\mathcal{V}$ yields finite patches of increasing size. When does this procedure generate a *whole* discrete plane?

A finite seed of particular interest is $\mathcal{U} := $ ⬡ (the largest pattern included in every discrete plane, see Remark 2.6). The above question with $\mathcal{V} = \mathcal{U}$ has many equivalent formulations and implications, which constitutes our main motivation for this work, as described in Section 1.1.

Our results Let $\sigma_1^{\mathrm{Brun}}, \sigma_2^{\mathrm{Brun}}, \sigma_3^{\mathrm{Brun}}$ be the substitutions associated with the Brun continued fraction algorithm. In this paper, we obtain in Theorem 5.2:

- The existence of a *finite* seed $\mathcal{V}$ from which iterating $\mathbf{E}_1^\star(\sigma_{i_n}^{\mathrm{Brun}})$ generates a whole discrete plane, for every Brun-admissible sequence $(i_n)_{n \geqslant 0}$.
- A characterization the sequences $(i_n)_{n \geqslant 0}$ for which the seed $\mathcal{V} = \mathcal{U}$ is not sufficient to generate a whole discrete plane when iterating the $\mathbf{E}_1^\star(\sigma_{i_n}^{\mathrm{Brun}})$.

The methods we use are generic and allow the study of other families than the Brun substitutions. Note that the above properties are easy to check for

J. Karhumäki, A. Lepistö, and L. Zamboni (Eds.): WORDS 2013, LNCS 8079, pp. 58–70, 2013.

a given *single* substitution σ [7]. Our main contribution is to extend such results to *infinite* families of substitutions obtained as arbitrary products from a finite set.

1.1   Motivation and Applications

The work presented in this article is motivated by the following consequences (and equivalent formulations) of our results. Establishing these links in detail will be the subject of a forthcoming article.

Multidimensional Sturmian sequences. One-dimensional Sturmian sequences can be defined as the coding (in $\{1,2\}^{\mathbb{Z}}$) of the discretization of a line in the plane. They can also be described as the infinite sequences generated by iterating the substitutions $1 \rightarrow 1, 2 \rightarrow 21$ and $1 \rightarrow 12, 2 \rightarrow 2$ (see [12, Chapter 6]). We generalize this result to two-dimensional Sturmian sequences, that is, discrete planes coded in $\{1,2,3\}^{\mathbb{Z}^2}$. The link between a discrete plane of normal vector $\mathbf{v}$ and substitutions can be made thanks to the multidimensional continued fraction expansion of $\mathbf{v}$ (as it is done for Sturmian sequences with the classical continued fraction algorithm). We use the Brun algorithm for this purpose.

Symbolic dynamics. The subshift associated with a unimodular Pisot substitution σ has pure discrete spectrum if and only if the patches generated by iterating the dual substitution $\mathbf{E}_1^*(\sigma)$ on $\mathcal{U}$ cover balls of arbitrarily large radius [16,7]. The Pisot conjecture states that this is always the case. Our present results allow us to prove this property for some infinite families defined by finite products of substitutions over a finite set. (It remains to prove that, in the case where a whole plane is not generated from $\mathcal{U}$, some arbitrarily large balls are still covered somewhere.)

Topology of Rauzy fractals. The periodic sequences of substitutions that fail to generate a whole plane correspond precisely to the finite products of substitutions whose Rauzy fractal does not contain $\mathbf{0}$ as an interior point (see [6,20]). Moreover, our results imply that the Rauzy fractal associated with a finite product of substitutions is always connected.

Number theory. Generating arbitrarily large patches of a discrete plane allows us to approximate its normal vector. We hence obtain proofs of convergence for the associated multidimensional continued fraction algorithms if the substitutions have been chosen accordingly, see Corollary 5.3.

Generating a whole discrete plane can be seen as an analog of the *finiteness property* in β-numeration (see the *extended (F) property* in [6]). Such properties have already been proved for some infinite families of algebraic numbers (see for example [13]).

We are also able to associate fractal tiles with every real cubic number field, thanks to a result by Paysant-Le-Roux and Dubois [17] and a similar study of the Jacobi-Perron algorithm.

S-adic systems. The study of the dynamical systems and the fractal tiles associated with arbitrary infinite products (*S*-adic sequences) is still at its beginnings. It is for example not completely understood in what cases an *S*-adic sequence can be associated with a fractal tile. Our tools provide a starting point for the study of such systems, as initiated in [8].

1.2   Methods

Ito and Ohtsuki [15] initiated the study of the generation of discrete planes with substitutions, while investigating properties of the Jacobi-Perron algorithm. Their main argument is to prove that some topological annuli are preserved under the image by a substitution, and that these annuli grow to a whole discrete plane when the substitutions are iterated.

We use the same approach in Section 4, but with additional combinatorial restrictions (*strong* coverings) introduced in Section 2.3 that are crucial in order to prove the *annulus property* (the fact that the image of an annulus remains an annulus). We introduce a combinatorial criterion, *Property A* (Definition 4.1), which allows for more systematic proofs.

The algorithmic methods developed in Section 3 (the *generation graph*, Definition 3.1) provide powerful tools to manage the complicated behaviour of the growth of the patterns, without having to deal with numerous cases by hand.

The main steps of our argument are:

1. Choose good substitutions and good patterns for strong coverings. Describe all the possible minimal strongly-covered annuli. (Section 2.2.)
2. Construct generation graphs, both to prove that a first annulus is generated, but also to characterize the sequences that fail to generate whole discrete planes. (Section 3.)
3. Prove that annuli are preserved by substitutions. (Section 4.)

Many of the computational tasks performed in Sections 3 and 4 have been performed using the Sage mathematics software.

1.3   Related Works

The study of the Jacobi-Perron substitutions in this context was initiated in [15]. Arnoux-Rauzy substitutions have been treated in [4] and [5] (for them the seed $\mathcal{U}$ is always enough). The Modified Jacobi-Perron algorithm is studied in [14] and the substitutions associated with the ordered fully subtractive algorithm have been used in [3] for other (discrete geometrical) purposes.

Our work focuses on the case where the coordinates of the normal vector of the discrete plane are linearly independent over $\mathbb{Q}$. The case of rational vectors has been treated by Fernique [11].

Let us note also that depending on the substitutions studied, our techniques can fail to work if the topological features of the generated patterns are too complicated (for example if many holes appear). This is the case for example with the Selmer algorithm (which is described in [19]).

2 Preliminaries

2.1 Discrete Planes and Substitutions

Before defining discrete planes we introduce *faces* $[\mathbf{x}, i]^\star$, which are defined by

$$[\mathbf{x}, 1]^\star = \{\mathbf{x} + \lambda \mathbf{e}_2 + \mu \mathbf{e}_3 : \lambda, \mu \in [0,1]\} = \diamond$$
$$[\mathbf{x}, 2]^\star = \{\mathbf{x} + \lambda \mathbf{e}_1 + \mu \mathbf{e}_3 : \lambda, \mu \in [0,1]\} = \diamond$$
$$[\mathbf{x}, 3]^\star = \{\mathbf{x} + \lambda \mathbf{e}_1 + \mu \mathbf{e}_2 : \lambda, \mu \in [0,1]\} = \diamond$$

where $i \in \{1, 2, 3\}$ is the *type* of $[\mathbf{x}, i]^\star$, and $\mathbf{x} \in \mathbb{Z}^3$ is the *vector* of $[\mathbf{x}, i]^\star$.

Definition 2.1 (Discrete plane). Let $\mathbf{v} \in \mathbb{R}^3_{>0}$. The *discrete plane* $\Gamma_\mathbf{v}$ of *normal vector* $\mathbf{v}$ is the union of faces $[\mathbf{x}, i]^\star$ satisfying $0 \leqslant \langle \mathbf{x}, \mathbf{v} \rangle < \langle \mathbf{e}_i, \mathbf{v} \rangle$.

More intuitively, $\Gamma_\mathbf{v}$ can also be seen as the boundary of the union of the unit cubes with integer coordinates that intersect the lower half-space $\{\mathbf{x} \in \mathbb{R}^3 : \langle \mathbf{x}, \mathbf{v} \rangle < 0\}$.

Remark 2.2. We will often use the arithmetic restrictions of Definition 2.1 in order to simplify the combinatorics of the patterns that appear in a discrete plane of normal vector $\mathbf{v} = (v_1, v_2, v_3)$. For example, if $v_1 \leqslant v_3$ and $v_2 \leqslant v_3$, then $\Gamma_\mathbf{v}$ cannot contain any translate of the two-face pattern $[\mathbf{0}, 1]^\star \cup [(0, 1, 0), 1]^\star = \diamond$ or $[\mathbf{0}, 2]^\star \cup [(0, 0, 1), 2]^\star = \diamond$. If moreover $v_1 \leqslant v_2$, then the pattern $[\mathbf{0}, 1]^\star \cup [(0, 1, 0), 1]^\star = \diamond$ also never appears.

Definition 2.3 (Substitution). Let $\mathcal{A} = \{1, \ldots, n\}$ be a finite set of symbols. A *substitution* is a non-erasing morphism of the free monoid $\mathcal{A}^\star$, *i.e.*, a function $\sigma : \mathcal{A}^\star \to \mathcal{A}^\star$ such that $\sigma(uv) = \sigma(u)\sigma(v)$ for all words $u, v \in \mathcal{A}^\star$, and such that $\sigma(a)$ is non-empty for every $a \in \mathcal{A}$.

The *incidence matrix* $\mathbf{M}_\sigma$ of σ is the matrix of size $n \times n$ defined by $\mathbf{M}_\sigma = (m_{ij})$, where $m_{i,j}$ is the number of occurrences of the letter i in $\sigma(j)$. A substitution σ is *unimodular* if $\det \mathbf{M}_\sigma = \pm 1$.

Definition 2.4 (Dual substitution). Let σ be a unimodular substitution. The *dual substitution* $\mathbf{E}_1^\star(\sigma)$ is defined by

$$\mathbf{E}_1^\star(\sigma)([\mathbf{x}, i]^\star) = \bigcup_{(p,j,s) \in \mathcal{A}^\star \times \mathcal{A} \times \mathcal{A}^\star \,:\, \sigma(j) = pis} [\mathbf{M}_\sigma^{-1}(\mathbf{x} + \ell(s)), j]^\star,$$

where $\ell : w \mapsto (|w|_1, \ldots, |w|_n) \in \mathbb{Z}^3$ is the *abelianization map* and $|w|_i$ denotes the number of occurrences of i in w. We extend the above definition to any union of faces: $\mathbf{E}_1^\star(\sigma)(P_1 \cup P_2) = \mathbf{E}_1^\star(\sigma)(P_1) \cup \mathbf{E}_1^\star(\sigma)(P_2)$.

Note that for every face $[\mathbf{x}, i]^\star$ we have $\mathbf{E}_1^\star(\sigma)([\mathbf{x}, i]^\star) = \mathbf{M}_\sigma^{-1}\mathbf{x} + \mathbf{E}_1^\star([\mathbf{0}, i]^\star)$, which implies the linearity $\mathbf{E}_1^\star(\sigma)$. We also have $\mathbf{E}_1^\star(\sigma \circ \sigma') = \mathbf{E}_1^\star(\sigma') \circ \mathbf{E}_1^\star(\sigma)$ for every unimodular σ and σ' [1]. The next proposition establishes a fundamental link between discrete planes and $\mathbf{E}_1^\star$ maps.

Proposition 2.5 ([1,10]). *Let $\Gamma_\mathbf{v}$ be a discrete plane and σ be a unimodular substitution. We have:*

1. *$\mathbf{E}_1^\star(\sigma)(\Gamma_\mathbf{v})$ is the discrete plane $\Gamma_{{}^t\mathbf{M}_\sigma \mathbf{v}}$.*
2. *If $f, g \in \Gamma_\mathbf{v}$ are distinct, then $\mathbf{E}_1^\star(\sigma)(f) \cap \mathbf{E}_1^\star(\sigma)(g)$ does not contain any face.*

Remark 2.6. The pattern $\mathcal{U} = [\mathbf{0},1]^\star \cup [\mathbf{0},2]^\star \cup [\mathbf{0},3]^\star = $ ⬡ is included in every discrete plane because the coordinates of the normal vector of a discrete plane are assumed to be positive.

2.2   The Brun Algorithm

Let $\mathbf{v} \in \mathbb{R}_{>0}^3$ such that $\mathbf{v} = (v_1, v_2, v_3)$ and $v_1 \leqslant v_2 \leqslant v_3$. The algorithm of Brun [9] is one of the possible natural generalizations of Euclid's algorithm: subtract the second largest component of $\mathbf{v}$ to the largest, and iterate. Here we reorder the coordinates at each step, so that the condition $v_1 \leqslant v_2 \leqslant v_3$ always holds. More formally:

$$\mathbf{v} \mapsto \begin{cases} (v_1, \ v_2, \ v_3 - v_2) & \text{if } v_1 \leqslant v_2 \leqslant v_3 - v_2 \\ (v_1, \ v_3 - v_2, \ v_2) & \text{if } v_1 \leqslant v_3 - v_2 \leqslant v_2 \\ (v_3 - v_2, \ v_1, \ v_2) & \text{if } v_3 - v_2 \leqslant v_1 \leqslant v_2. \end{cases}$$

Iterating this map yields an infinite sequence of vectors $\mathbf{v}_0 = \mathbf{v}, \mathbf{v}_1, \mathbf{v}_2, \dots$ and the algorithm can be rewritten in matrix form: $\mathbf{v}_n = \mathbf{M}_{i_n} \mathbf{v}_{n-1}$ for every $n \geqslant 1$, where

$$\mathbf{M}_1 = \begin{pmatrix} 1 & 0 & 0 \\ 0 & 1 & 0 \\ 0 & -1 & 1 \end{pmatrix} \qquad \mathbf{M}_2 = \begin{pmatrix} 1 & 0 & 0 \\ 0 & -1 & 1 \\ 0 & 1 & 0 \end{pmatrix} \qquad \mathbf{M}_3 = \begin{pmatrix} 0 & -1 & 1 \\ 1 & 0 & 0 \\ 0 & 1 & 0 \end{pmatrix}$$

and $i_n \in \{1, 2, 3\}$. This allows us to define the *Brun expansion* of $\mathbf{v}$ as the infinite sequence $(i_n)_{n \geqslant 1}$ obtained above. It enjoys the following nice property.

Proposition 2.7 ([9]). *The Brun expansion $(i_n)_{n \geqslant 1}$ of $\mathbf{v} \in \mathbb{R}_{>0}^3$ contains infinitely many 3's if and only if $\mathbf{v}$ is totally irrational.*

We now define some substitutions associated with the Brun algorithm.

$$\sigma_1^{\mathsf{Brun}} : \begin{cases} 1 \mapsto 1 \\ 2 \mapsto 2 \\ 3 \mapsto 32 \end{cases} \qquad \sigma_2^{\mathsf{Brun}} : \begin{cases} 1 \mapsto 1 \\ 2 \mapsto 3 \\ 3 \mapsto 23 \end{cases} \qquad \sigma_3^{\mathsf{Brun}} : \begin{cases} 1 \mapsto 2 \\ 2 \mapsto 3 \\ 3 \mapsto 13 \end{cases}$$

and $\Sigma_i^{\mathsf{Brun}} = \mathbf{E}_1^\star(\sigma_i^{\mathsf{Brun}})$. The maps $\Sigma_1^{\mathsf{Brun}}, \Sigma_2^{\mathsf{Brun}}, \Sigma_3^{\mathsf{Brun}}$ are respectively given by

$$
\begin{array}{lll}
[\mathbf{0},1]^\star \mapsto [\mathbf{0},1]^\star & [\mathbf{0},1]^\star \mapsto [\mathbf{0},1]^\star & [\mathbf{0},1]^\star \mapsto [(0,1,0),3]^\star \\
[\mathbf{0},2]^\star \mapsto [\mathbf{0},2]^\star \cup [\mathbf{0},3]^\star & [\mathbf{0},2]^\star \mapsto [(0,1,0),3]^\star & [\mathbf{0},2]^\star \mapsto [\mathbf{0},1]^\star \\
[\mathbf{0},3]^\star \mapsto [(0,1,0),3]^\star & [\mathbf{0},3]^\star \mapsto [\mathbf{0},2]^\star \cup [\mathbf{0},3]^\star & [\mathbf{0},3]^\star \mapsto [\mathbf{0},2]^\star \cup [\mathbf{0},3]^\star
\end{array},
$$

or more graphically

2.3 Coverings and Strong Coverings

We call a *pattern* any finite union of faces. In the definitions below, $\mathcal{L}$ will always denote a set of patterns which is closed by translation of $\mathbb{Z}^3$, so we will define such sets by giving only one element of each translation class. The following set of patterns will be used throughout this article:

$$\mathcal{L}^{\mathsf{Brun}} = \left\{ \text{⬢}, \text{⬠}, \text{◆}, \text{◆}, \text{◇}, \text{◇}, \text{◇}, \text{◆} \right\}.$$

We now introduce $\mathcal{L}$-coverings and strong $\mathcal{L}$-coverings, which are the combinatorial tools we will use in order to prove the annulus property in Section 4.

Definition 2.8 ($\mathcal{L}$-covering). Let $\mathcal{L}$ be a set of patterns. A pattern P is $\mathcal{L}$-*covered* if for all faces $e, f \in P$, there exist patterns $Q_1, \ldots, Q_n \in \mathcal{L}$ such that

1. $e \in Q_1$ and $f \in Q_n$;
2. $Q_k \cap Q_{k+1}$ contains at least one face, for all $k \in \{1, \ldots, n-1\}$;
3. $Q_k \subseteq P$ for all $k \in \{1, \ldots, n\}$.

Proposition 2.9 ([15]). *Let P be an $\mathcal{L}$-covered pattern, Σ be a dual substitution and $\mathcal{L}$ be a set of patterns such that $\Sigma(Q)$ is $\mathcal{L}$-covered for every $Q \in \mathcal{L}$. Then $\Sigma(P)$ is $\mathcal{L}$-covered.*

Definition 2.10 (Strong $\mathcal{L}$-covering). A pattern P is *strongly $\mathcal{L}$-covered* if P is $\mathcal{L}$-covered and if for every pattern $X \subseteq P$ that is edge-connected and consists of two faces, there exists a pattern $Y \in \mathcal{L}$ such that $X \subseteq Y \subseteq P$.

Proposition 2.11 (Brun strong covering). *Let P be an $\mathcal{L}^{\mathsf{Brun}}$-covered pattern such that the patterns ◇, ▯ and ▱ do not occur in P. Then $\Sigma_i^{\mathsf{Brun}}(P)$ is strongly $\mathcal{L}^{\mathsf{Brun}}$-covered for $i \in \{1, 2, 3\}$.*

Proof (Sketch). First, $\Sigma_i^{\mathsf{Brun}}(P)$ is $\mathcal{L}^{\mathsf{Brun}}$-covered thanks to Proposition 2.9, because $\Sigma_i^{\mathsf{Brun}}(Q)$ is $\mathcal{L}^{\mathsf{Brun}}$-covered for every $Q \in \mathcal{L}^{\mathsf{Brun}}$ (there are 24 patterns to check). To prove that $\Sigma_i^{\mathsf{Brun}}(P)$ is *strongly* $\mathcal{L}^{\mathsf{Brun}}$-covered, we can enumerate the preimages by Σ_i of all the two-face connected patterns X to check that there is always a suitable $Y \in \mathcal{L}^{\mathsf{Brun}}$ that satisfies the requirements of Definition 2.10. □

2.4 Minimal Annuli

Definition 2.12 ($\mathcal{L}$-annulus). An $\mathcal{L}$-*annulus* of a pattern P is a pattern A such that A is strongly $\mathcal{L}$-covered and $P \cap \partial(P \cup A) = \varnothing$.

Example 2.13. Let A_1, A_2 and A_3 be defined by

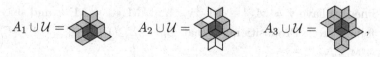

where $\mathcal{U}$ is shown in dark gray and the other faces are the A_i. We have:

- A_1 is not an annulus of $\mathcal{U}$ because it does not satisfy $\mathcal{U} \cap \partial(\mathcal{U} \cup A_1) = \varnothing$ ($\mathcal{U}$ is not well surrounded).
- A_2 is not an $\mathcal{L}^{\mathsf{Brun}}$-annulus of $\mathcal{U}$ because of the two-face pattern $X = $ ⬠ depicted in white: the only pattern in $\mathcal{L}^{\mathsf{Brun}}$ that contains X is $Y = $ ⬡, but it cannot be included in A_2 so A_2 is not strongly $\mathcal{L}^{\mathsf{Brun}}$-covered.
- A_3 is an $\mathcal{L}^{\mathsf{Brun}}$-annulus of $\mathcal{U}$.

Proposition 2.14 (Brun minimal annuli). *Let A be an $\mathcal{L}^{\mathsf{Brun}}$-annulus of $\mathcal{U}$ that is included in a discrete plane of normal vector $\mathbf{v}$ with $v_1 < v_2 < v_3$. Then A contains one of the following two $\mathcal{L}^{\mathsf{Brun}}$-annuli A_1^{Brun} or A_2^{Brun} (shown in light gray) of $\mathcal{U}$ (shown in dark gray):*

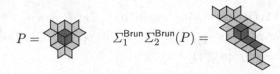

Proof (Sketch). This proposition can be proved by enumerating all the possible surroundings of $\mathcal{U}$ of "thickness 1", and by doing a case analysis on the problematic patterns that appear using the definition of $\mathcal{L}^{\mathsf{Brun}}$. □

Example 2.15. Let P be a pattern equal to the union of $[\mathbf{0}, 3]^{\star} \cup [(1, 0, -1), 2]^{\star} \cup [(0, 1, -1), 1]^{\star}$ (in dark gray) and some other faces in light gray.

$$P = \quad\quad \Sigma_1^{\mathsf{Brun}} \Sigma_2^{\mathsf{Brun}}(P) = \quad\quad$$

The images of the annulus in light gray fail to be annuli. However, the annulus in P is not strongly $\mathcal{L}^{\mathsf{Brun}}$-covered, which shows the need for *strong* coverings if we want the image of an annulus to remain an annulus.

The substitutions above are chosen in such a way that $\mathbf{M}_i = {}^{\mathrm{t}}\mathbf{M}_{\sigma_i^{\mathsf{Brun}}}^{-1}$ for $i \in \{1, 2, 3\}$, which allows us to define the sequence of pattern we will use to generate the discrete plane $\Gamma_{\mathbf{v}}$, as described by the proposition below.

Proposition 2.16. *Let $\mathbf{v} \in \mathbb{R}_{>0}^3$ and $(i_n)_{n \geqslant 1}$ be its Brun expansion. We have $\Sigma_{i_1} \cdots \Sigma_{i_n}(\mathcal{V}) \subseteq \Gamma_{\mathbf{v}}$ for all $n \geqslant 1$, where $\mathcal{V} = \mathcal{U}$, or $\mathcal{V} = \mathcal{U} \cup A_1^{\mathsf{Brun}}$ (if $i_1 \in \{1, 2\}$), or $\mathcal{V} = \mathcal{U} \cup A_2^{\mathsf{Brun}}$ (if $i_1 = 3$).*

Proof. Since we have $\mathbf{v} = \mathbf{M}_{i_1}^{-1} \cdots \mathbf{M}_{i_n}^{-1} \mathbf{v}_n$, and ${}^{\mathrm{t}}\mathbf{M}_{\sigma_{i_n}^{\mathsf{Brun}}} = \mathbf{M}_{i_n}^{-1}$, and since $\mathcal{V} \subseteq \Gamma_{\mathbf{v}_n}$, it follows from Proposition 2.5 that $\Sigma_{i_1} \cdots \Sigma_{i_n}(\mathcal{V}) \subseteq \Sigma_{i_1} \cdots \Sigma_{i_n}(\Gamma_{\mathbf{v}_n}) = \Gamma_{{}^{\mathrm{t}}\mathbf{M}_{\sigma_{i_1}^{\mathsf{Brun}}} \cdots {}^{\mathrm{t}}\mathbf{M}_{\sigma_{i_n}^{\mathsf{Brun}}} \mathbf{v}_n} = \Gamma_{\mathbf{v}}$. □

3   Generation Graphs

We fix the following notation for this section:

- $\Sigma_1, \ldots, \Sigma_k$ are dual substitutions,
- $\mathcal{X}$ and $\mathcal{Y}$ are finite sets of faces,
- $\mathcal{F}$ is an infinite family of faces.

We want to characterize the sequences $(i_1, \ldots, i_n) \in \{1, \ldots, k\}^n$ and the faces $f \in \mathcal{Y}$ such that f *cannot* be reached by iterating $\Sigma_{i_1}, \ldots, \Sigma_{i_n}$ starting from the "seed" $\mathcal{X}$. Our approach below is to recursively track all the possible preimages of the faces in $\mathcal{Y}$, by constructing a *generation graph* providing us with the desired characterization. The set $\mathcal{F}$ is used as a filter, in order to make the generation graph as simple as possible by eliminating some useless faces.

Definition 3.1. The *generation graph* is defined by $\mathcal{G} = \bigcup_{n \in \mathbb{N}} \mathcal{G}_n$ (an increasing union which is not always finite), where $(\mathcal{G}_n)_{n \in \mathbb{N}}$ is the sequence of directed graphs defined by induction as follows.

1. *Initialization.* $\mathcal{G}_0$ has no edges and its set of vertices is $\mathcal{Y}$.
2. *Iteration.* Suppose that $\mathcal{G}_n$ is constructed for some $n \geqslant 0$. Start with $\mathcal{G}_{n+1}$ having the same vertices and edges as $\mathcal{G}_n$. Then, for each vertex f of $\mathcal{G}_n$, for each $i \in \{1, \ldots, k\}$ and for each $g \in \mathcal{F}$ such that $f \in \Sigma_i(g)$, add the vertex g and the edge $g \xrightarrow{i} f$ to $\mathcal{G}_{n+1}$.

Proposition 3.2. *Let $\mathcal{G}$ be the graph defined in Definition 3.1, let $f_0 \in \mathcal{G}$ be a face and let $(i_1, \ldots, i_n) \in \{1, \ldots, k\}^n$. Consider the following two statements.*

1. $f_0 \notin \Sigma_{i_1} \cdots \Sigma_{i_n}(\mathcal{X})$.
2. *There exists a path $f_n \xrightarrow{i_n} \cdots \xrightarrow{i_2} f_1 \xrightarrow{i_1} f_0$ in $\mathcal{G}$ with $f_n \notin \mathcal{X}$.*

We have:

(i) *(1) $\Rightarrow$ (2) if for every $f \in \mathcal{F}$ and every $i \in \{1, \ldots, k\}$, there exists $g \in \mathcal{F}$ such that $f \in \Sigma_i(g)$.*

(ii) *(2) $\Rightarrow$ (1) if $\mathcal{X} = \mathcal{U}$ and if every face of $\mathcal{F}$ belongs to a discrete plane.*

Proof. (i). The assumption in (i) implies that a path $f_n \xrightarrow{i_n} \cdots \xrightarrow{i_2} f_1 \xrightarrow{i_1} f_0$ must exist in $\mathcal{G}$. By (1), we cannot have have $f_n \in \mathcal{X}$, which proves the first implication.

(ii). Let $P = \Sigma_{i_1} \cdots \Sigma_{i_n}(f_n)$, $g \in \mathcal{X}$ and $Q = \Sigma_{i_1} \cdots \Sigma_{i_n}(g)$. By the assumption in (ii), f_n and g must belong to a common discrete plane because $g \in \mathcal{U}$, f_n belongs to a discrete plane and $\mathcal{U}$ is included in every discrete plane. Hence, Proposition 2.5 implies the patterns P and Q do not have any face in common. It follows that $f_0 \notin \Sigma_{i_1} \cdots \Sigma_{i_n}(g)$ for every $g \in \mathcal{X}$.   □

Remark 3.3. Part (i) of Proposition 3.2 will be used to obtaine "positive" results, such as proving that a given seed *always* generate a full discrete plane (see Lemma 3.5, Proposition 5.1 and Theorem 5.2 (1)). Conversely, part (ii) will be used to characterize which sequences do *not* generate a full discrete plane (see Lemma 3.4 and Theorem 5.2 (2)).

Generation graphs for Brun. We now consider substitutions $\Sigma_1^{\mathsf{Brun}}, \Sigma_2^{\mathsf{Brun}}, \Sigma_3^{\mathsf{Brun}}$. We will take the filter $\mathcal{F}^{\mathsf{Brun}}$ to be the set of all the faces f that belong to a discrete plane $\Gamma_{(v_1, v_2, v_3)}$ with $0 < v_1 < v_2 < v_3$. We use Definition 3.1 to compute the following graphs.

- The graph $\mathcal{G}^{\mathsf{Brun}}$ is obtained by starting with $\mathcal{Y} = \mathcal{A}_1^{\mathsf{Brun}} \cup \mathcal{A}_2^{\mathsf{Brun}}$. Its computation stops after two iterations of the algorithm. It has 19 vertices and 47 edges. We will use it below with $\mathcal{X} = \mathcal{U}$.
- The graph $\mathcal{H}^{\mathsf{Brun}}$ is obtained by starting with $\mathcal{Y}$ equal to the set of faces of all the possible minimal $\mathcal{L}^{\mathsf{Brun}}$-annuli of $\mathcal{A}_1^{\mathsf{Brun}}$ and $\mathcal{A}_2^{\mathsf{Brun}}$ (a total of 60 faces). Its computation stops after six iterations of the algorithm. It has 101 vertices and 240 edges. We will use it below with $\mathcal{X} = \mathcal{U} \cup \mathcal{A}_1^{\mathsf{Brun}}$ or $\mathcal{U} \cup \mathcal{A}_2^{\mathsf{Brun}}$.

Lemma 3.4. *The graph $\mathcal{G}^{\mathsf{Brun}}$ verifies (i) and (ii) of Proposition 3.2 with $\mathcal{X} = \mathcal{U}$.*

Lemma 3.5. *The graph $\mathcal{H}^{\mathsf{Brun}}$ verifies item (i) of Proposition 3.2, both with $\mathcal{X} = \mathcal{U} \cup \mathcal{A}_1^{\mathsf{Brun}}$ and $\mathcal{X} = \mathcal{U} \cup \mathcal{A}_2^{\mathsf{Brun}}$.*

Proof. For both lemmas we have to check that the assumption in (i) is satisfied. Let $f \in \mathcal{F}^{\mathsf{Brun}}$ and let $i \in \{1, 2, 3\}$. Because $f \in \mathcal{F}^{\mathsf{Brun}}$, there exists $\mathbf{v} = (v_1, v_2, v_3)$ such that $0 < v_1 < v_2 < v_3$ and $f \in \Gamma_{\mathbf{v}}$. By Proposition 2.5 and by definition of the Brun algorithm (Section 2.2), we have $\Gamma_{\mathbf{v}} = \Sigma_i^{\mathsf{Brun}}(\Gamma_{\mathbf{w}})$, where $\mathbf{w} = {}^t\mathbf{M}_{\sigma_i^{\mathsf{Brun}}}^{-1} \mathbf{v}$. We have $0 < w_1 < w_2 < w_3$, so all the faces of $\Gamma_{\mathbf{w}}$ belong to $\mathcal{F}^{\mathsf{Brun}}$, so there exists a face $g \in \mathcal{F}^{\mathsf{Brun}}$ such that $f \in \Sigma_i(g)$ because $f \in \Gamma_{\mathbf{v}} = \Sigma_i(\Gamma_{\mathbf{w}})$. Finally (for Lemma 3.5 only), the assumptions required in (ii) trivially hold. □

In Section 5 we will need to consider only the infinite paths in $\mathcal{G}^{\mathsf{Brun}}$ and $\mathcal{H}^{\mathsf{Brun}}$ that contain infinitely many edges labelled by 3, and that avoid $\mathcal{X}$. In the case of $\mathcal{H}^{\mathsf{Brun}}$, there turns out to be no such infinite path, which is the key point to prove Proposition 5.1. However $\mathcal{G}^{\mathsf{Brun}}$ is more interesting, and removing all the vertices which are not contained in such a path yields the following graph.

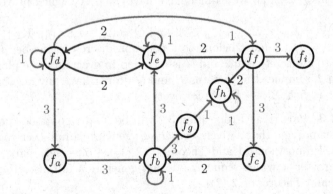

The faces corresponding to the vertices of the graph are

$$f_a = [(1, 1, -1), 1]^\star \qquad f_d = [(-1, 1, 0), 2]^\star \qquad f_g = [(-1, 0, 1), 2]^\star$$
$$f_b = [(1, -1, 1), 3]^\star \qquad f_e = [(-1, 0, 1), 3]^\star \qquad f_h = [(-1, -1, 1), 3]^\star$$
$$f_c = [(1, 1, -1), 2]^\star \qquad f_f = [(-1, 1, 0), 3]^\star \qquad f_i = [(1, 1, -1), 3]^\star.$$

4   The Annulus Property

Definition 4.1 (Property A). Let Σ be a dual substitution and let $\mathcal{L}$ be a set of edge-connected patterns. *Property A holds for Σ with $\mathcal{L}$ if for all faces f, g, f_0, g_0 such that $f \in \Sigma(f_0)$, $g \in \Sigma(g_0)$, $f \cup g$ is connected and $f_0 \cup g_0$ is disconnected, there cannot exist a pattern P and an $\mathcal{L}$-annulus A of P which are included in a common discrete plane Γ such that $f_0 \in P$, $g_0 \notin A \cup P$, and $f_0 \cup g_0 \subseteq \Gamma$ and $f \cup g \subseteq \Sigma(\Gamma)$.*

Proposition 4.2. *Let Σ be a dual substitution and $\mathcal{L}$ be a set of edge-connected patterns such that Property A holds for Σ with $\mathcal{L}$, and such that the image by Σ of every strongly $\mathcal{L}$-covered pattern is strongly $\mathcal{L}$-covered. Let P be a pattern and A be an $\mathcal{L}$-annulus of P, both included in a common discrete plane. Then $\Sigma(A)$ is an $\mathcal{L}$-annulus of $\Sigma(P)$.*

Proof. The pattern A is strongly $\mathcal{L}$-covered because it is an $\mathcal{L}$-annulus, so $\Sigma(A)$ is also strongly $\mathcal{L}$-covered, by assumption. It remains to show that $\Sigma(P) \cap \partial(\Sigma(P) \cup \Sigma(A)) = \varnothing$. Suppose the contrary. This means that there exist faces f, g, f_0, g_0 such that $f \in \Sigma(f_0)$, $g \in \Sigma(g_0)$, $f \cup g$ is connected, and $f_0 \cup g_0$ is disconnected (because $f_0 \in P$ and $g_0 \notin A \cup P$). These are precisely the conditions stated in Property A, so such a situation cannot occur and the proposition holds.   □

Proposition 4.3 (Property A for Brun). *Property A holds for Brun substitutions with $\mathcal{L}^{\mathsf{Brun}}$, when restricted to planes $\Gamma_{(v_1, v_2, v_3)}$ with $v_1 \leqslant v_2 \leqslant v_3$.*

Proof. There are finitely many two-face connected patterns $f \cup g$, so we can enumerate all the faces f, g, f_0, g_0 that satisfy the three conditions of Definition 4.1, for Σ_1^{Brun}, Σ_2^{Brun} and Σ_3^{Brun}. It turns out that there are 9 such possibilities, where the corresponding values for $f_0 \cup g_0$ are shown in the table below.

Σ_1^{Brun}	Σ_2^{Brun}	Σ_3^{Brun}
$[\mathbf{0}, 2]^\star \cup [(0, 1, 0), 1]^\star$	$[\mathbf{0}, 3]^\star \cup [(1, 0, -1), 3]^\star$	$[\mathbf{0}, 3]^\star \cup [(0, 1, -1), 3]^\star$
$[\mathbf{0}, 2]^\star \cup [(1, -1, 0), 2]^\star$	$[\mathbf{0}, 3]^\star \cup [(0, 1, 1), 1]^\star$	$[\mathbf{0}, 3]^\star \cup [(0, 0, 1), 2]^\star$
$[\mathbf{0}, 2]^\star \cup [(0, 1, 1), 1]^\star$	$[\mathbf{0}, 3]^\star \cup [(0, 0, 1), 1]^\star$	$[\mathbf{0}, 3]^\star \cup [(1, 0, 1), 2]^\star$

Let us treat the case $f_0 \cup g_0 = [\mathbf{0}, 2]^\star \cup [(1, -1, 0), 2]^\star$. Suppose that there exists a pattern P and an $\mathcal{L}^{\mathsf{Brun}}$-annulus A of P that is included in a discrete plane such that $f_0 \in P$ and $g_0 \in A$. Because A is an annulus of P, any extension of $f_0 \cup g_0$ within a discrete plane must be of the form ⬛ or ⬛ , where $f_0 \cup g_0$ is shown in light gray and the dark gray faces are included in A.

The first case cannot happen because it contains an occurrence of ▧, which is forbidden since we are restricted to discrete planes with normal vector $\mathbf{v}$ satisfying $v_1 < v_2 < v_3$ (see Remark 2.2). The second case also cannot happen, because A is strongly $\mathcal{L}^{\mathsf{Brun}}$-covered. Indeed, ◪ $\subseteq A$, so there must exist a translation of a pattern of $\mathcal{L}^{\mathsf{Brun}}$ that is included in A and that contains ◪. The only such pattern in $\mathcal{L}^{\mathsf{Brun}}$ is ⬡ (note that ◭ $\notin \mathcal{L}^{\mathsf{Brun}}$). This is impossible because then ⬡ and $f_0 \cup g_0$ overlap, which is a contradiction because $f_0, g_0 \notin A$ and ⬡ $\in A$. The same reasoning applies to the eight other cases. □

5   Main Results

Let P be a pattern that contains $\mathcal{U}$. The *combinatorial radius* of P is the length of the shortest path of faces $f_1, \ldots, f_n$ in P such that: $f_1 \in \mathcal{U}$, the f_i and f_{i+1} are adjacent, and f_n shares an edge with the boundary of P.

Proposition 5.1. *Let $(u_n = u_{n,1} \cdots u_{n,k_n})_{n \geqslant 1}$ be an infinite sequence of words in $\{1,2,3\}^*$ such that the number of 3's in the u_n is strictly increasing. Let $\mathcal{V}$ be equal either $\mathcal{U} \cup \mathcal{A}_1^{\mathsf{Brun}}$ or to $\mathcal{U} \cup \mathcal{A}_2^{\mathsf{Brun}}$. Then the pattern $\Sigma_{u_{n,1}}^{\mathsf{Brun}} \cdots \Sigma_{u_{n,k_n}}^{\mathsf{Brun}}(\mathcal{V})$ has arbitrarily large combinatorial radius when $n \to \infty$.*

Proof. Let R be a positive integer (an arbitrary radius that we want to bound above). We can algorithmically check that, in the graph $\mathcal{H}^{\mathsf{Brun}}$ described in Section 3, there are no infinite paths containing infinitely many 3's that avoid $\mathcal{A}_1^{\mathsf{Brun}} \cup \mathcal{A}_2^{\mathsf{Brun}} \cup \mathcal{U}$. Hence by Lemma 3.5 there exists an integer N such that R annuli are generated from $\mathcal{V}$ by $\Sigma_{u_{N,1}}^{\mathsf{Brun}} \cdots \Sigma_{u_{N,k_N}}^{\mathsf{Brun}}$. By Propositions 4.2 and 4.3, these annuli remain annuli, so the combinatorial radius cannot be less that R. □

Theorem 5.2. *Let $\mathbf{v} \in \mathbb{R}_{>0}^3$ be an ordered totally irrational vector and let $(i_n) \in \{1,2,3\}^{\mathbb{N}}$ be its Brun expansion. We have:*

1. $\bigcup_{n \geqslant 1} \Sigma_{i_1}^{\mathsf{Brun}} \cdots \Sigma_{i_n}^{\mathsf{Brun}}(\mathcal{V}) = \Gamma_{\mathbf{v}}$, *where* $\mathcal{V} = \begin{cases} \mathcal{U} \cup \mathcal{A}_1^{\mathsf{Brun}} & \text{if } i_1 \in \{1,2\}, \\ \mathcal{U} \cup \mathcal{A}_2^{\mathsf{Brun}} & \text{if } i_1 = 3. \end{cases}$

2. $\bigcup_{n \geqslant 1} \Sigma_{i_1}^{\mathsf{Brun}} \cdots \Sigma_{i_n}^{\mathsf{Brun}}(\mathcal{U}) \subsetneq \Gamma_{\mathbf{v}}$ *if and only if there exists $N \geqslant 0$ such that $\bullet \overset{i_N}{\longleftarrow} \bullet \overset{i_{N+1}}{\longleftarrow} \cdots$ is an infinite path in the following graph:*

Proof. Assertion (1) follows from Propositions 2.16 and 5.1, and (2) follows directly from (1), Lemma 3.4 and the description of $\mathcal{G}^{\mathsf{Brun}}$ given in Section 3. □

Some Applications. Theorem 5.2 implies the following for *finite* products of Brun substitutions: for every $\sigma = \sigma_{i_1}^{\mathrm{Brun}} \cdots \sigma_{i_n}^{\mathrm{Brun}}$ such that at least one $i_n = 3$, we have $\bigcup_{n \geqslant 1} \mathbf{E}_1^\star(\sigma)(\mathcal{U}) = \Gamma_{\mathbf{v}}$ if and only if there is no infinite periodic path labelled by $(i_1 \cdots i_n)^\infty$ in the graph above. This has several consequences, as mentioned in Section 1.1. Note that such substitutions σ are always Pisot irreducible [2].

Another application (also mentioned in Section 1.1) is Corollary 5.3 below: the convergence of the Brun algorithm. Indeed, similarly as in the proof of Proposition 2.16, the approximated discrete planes $\Gamma_{\mathbf{w}_n}$ contain patterns of arbitrarily large radius. These patterns are also included in $\Gamma_{\mathbf{v}}$, so the approximated vectors $\mathbf{w}_n$ are constrained and their direction must tend to that of $\mathbf{v}$.

Corollary 5.3. *Let $\mathbf{v} \in \mathbb{R}_{>0}^3$ be an ordered totally irrational vector and let $(i_n) \in \{1, 2, 3\}^{\mathbb{N}}$ be its Brun expansion. Let $\mathbf{w}_n = \mathbf{M}_{i_1}^{-1} \cdots \mathbf{M}_{i_n}^{-1} \cdot (1, 1, 1)$, where the $\mathbf{M}_i$ are the Brun matrices given in Section 2.2. Then, the sequence $(\mathbf{w}_n / \|\mathbf{w}_n\|)_{n \geqslant 1}$ converges to $\mathbf{v} / \|\mathbf{v}\|$ as $n \to \infty$.*

Lastly, note that the above results do not directly imply that iterating substitutions from $\mathcal{U}$ generates patterns containing translations of patterns with arbitrarily large radius. This requires another proof (to be published in a forthcoming article), and is linked with the Pisot conjecture (see Section 1.1).

Acknowledgements. This work was supported by Agence Nationale de la Recherche through project Fractals and Numeration ANR-12-IS01-0002. and project Kidico ANR-2010-BLAN-0205.

References

1. Arnoux, P., Ito, S.: Pisot substitutions and Rauzy fractals. Bull. Belg. Math. Soc. Simon Stevin 8(2), 181–207 (2001)
2. Avila, A., Delecroix, V.: Pisot property for the Brun and fully subtractive algorithms (preprint, 2013)
3. Berthé, V., Jamet, D., Jolivet, T., Provençal, X.: Critical connectedness of thin arithmetical discrete planes. In: Gonzalez-Diaz, R., Jimenez, M.-J., Medrano, B. (eds.) DGCI 2013. LNCS, vol. 7749, pp. 107–118. Springer, Heidelberg (2013)
4. Berthé, V., Jolivet, T., Siegel, A.: Substitutive arnoux-rauzy sequences have pure discrete spectrum. Unif. Distrib. Theory 7(1), 173–197 (2012)
5. Berthé, V., Jolivet, T., Siegel, A.: Connectedness of Rauzy fractals associated with Arnoux-Rauzy substitutions (preprint, 2013)
6. Berthé, V., Siegel, A.: Tilings associated with beta-numeration and substitutions. Integers 5(3), A2, 46 (2005)
7. Berthé, V., Siegel, A., Thuswaldner, J.M.: Substitutions, Rauzy fractals, and tilings. In: Combinatorics, Automata and Number Theory, Encyclopedia of Mathematics and its Applications, vol. 135. Cambridge University Press (2010)
8. Berthé, V., Steiner, W., Thuswaldner, J.M.: Tilings with S-adic Rauzy fractals (preprint, 2013)
9. Brun, V.: Algorithmes euclidiens pour trois et quatre nombres. In: Treizième Congrès des Mathèmaticiens Scandinaves, Tenu à Helsinki, Août 18-23, pp. 45–64 (1957)

10. Fernique, T.: Multidimensional Sturmian sequences and generalized substitutions. Internat. J. Found. Comput. Sci. 17(3), 575–599 (2006)
11. Fernique, T.: Generation and recognition of digital planes using multi-dimensional continued fractions. Pattern Recognition 42(10), 2229–2238 (2009)
12. Fogg, N.P.: Substitutions in dynamics, arithmetics and combinatorics. Lecture Notes in Mathematics, vol. 1794. Springer, Berlin (2002)
13. Frougny, C., Solomyak, B.: Finite beta-expansions. Ergodic Theory Dynam. Systems 12(4), 713–723 (1992)
14. Furukado, M., Ito, S., Yasutomi, S.I.: The condition for the generation of the stepped surfaces in terms of the modified Jacobi-Perron algorithm (preprint, 2013)
15. Ito, S., Ohtsuki, M.: Parallelogram tilings and Jacobi-Perron algorithm. Tokyo J. Math. 17(1), 33–58 (1994)
16. Ito, S., Rao, H.: Atomic surfaces, tilings and coincidence. I. Irreducible case. Israel J. Math. 153, 129–155 (2006)
17. Paysant-Le Roux, R., Dubois, E.: Une application des nombres de Pisot à l'algorithme de Jacobi-Perron. Monatsh. Math. 98(2), 145–155 (1984)
18. Rauzy, G.: Nombres algébriques et substitutions. Bull. Soc. Math. France 110(2), 147–178 (1982)
19. Schweiger, F.: Multidimensional continued fractions. Oxford Science Publications, Oxford University Press (2000)
20. Siegel, A., Thuswaldner, J.M.: Topological properties of Rauzy fractals. Mém. Soc. Math. Fr. (N.S.) (118), 140 (2009)

Convergence and Factor Complexity
for the Arnoux-Rauzy-Poincaré Algorithm

Valérie Berthé and Sebastien Labbé

LIAFA, Université Paris Diderot, Paris 7 - Case 7014, F-75205 Paris Cedex 13
{berthe,sebastien.labbe}@liafa.univ-paris-diderot.fr

Abstract. We introduce a multidimensional continued fraction algorithm based on Arnoux-Rauzy and Poincaré algorithms, and we study its associated S-adic system. An S-adic system is made of infinite words generated by the composition of infinite sequences of substitutions with values in a given finite set of substitutions, together with some restrictions concerning the allowed sequences of substitutions, expressed in terms of a regular language. We prove that these words have a factor complexity $p(n)$ with $\limsup p(n)/n < 3$, which provides a proof for the convergence of the associated algorithm by unique ergodicity.

1 Introduction

Given a vector of frequencies $(f_1, f_2, \cdots, f_d) \in \mathbb{R}^d_+$ (with $\sum f_i = 1$), our goal here is to propose a construction of an infinite word $\mathbf{w}$ over the alphabet $\mathcal{A} = \{1, 2, \cdots, d\}$ such that the frequency of each letter $i \in \mathcal{A}$ exists and is equal to f_i. We also would like the word $\mathbf{w}$ to have particular combinatorial properties, namely a linear factor complexity and a bounded balance. In dimension two, the question is completely answered. The Sturmian words form a well-known family of infinite balanced words having a linear factor complexity ($p(n) = n + 1$). But the situation is more contrasted in higher dimensions.

In [BL11, Lab12], we considered this question under the approach of multidimensional continued fraction algorithms and S-adic systems. Experimentations suggested that Brun multidimensional continued fraction algorithm as well as a fusion of Arnoux-Rauzy and Poincaré algorithms were the two best choices to investigate for such an approach. In this article, we focus on the Arnoux-Rauzy-Poincaré algorithm (a bit better than Brun experimentally), and construct an infinite word for Lebesgue almost each frequency vector $(f_1, f_2, f_3) \in \mathbb{R}^3_+$. We show that such words have a linear factor complexity, namely $p(n + 1) - p(n) \in \{2, 3\}$ for all $n \geq 0$, by describing extensively the life of every bispecial factor, including strong and weak ones which come in pairs (as proved in Lemma 10 below).

More precisely, we introduce an S-adic system associated with a set of 9 substitutions. Three of them are substitutions known under the name of Arnoux-Rauzy substitutions [AR91], and the other six are named Poincaré substitutions after Poincaré algorithm [Nog95]. The execution of the Arnoux-Rauzy-Poincaré algorithm yields restrictions to the allowed infinite sequences of substitutions,

J. Karhumäki, A. Lepistö, and L. Zamboni (Eds.): WORDS 2013, LNCS 8079, pp. 71–82, 2013.
© Springer-Verlag Berlin Heidelberg 2013

expressed in terms of a regular language. We show that we have a bijection (up to a set of zero measure) between infinite words and $\mathbb{R}^3_+$. We show that these words have a factor complexity $p(n)$ that satisfies with $\limsup p(n)/n < 3$. The proof relies on the fact that weak and strong bispecial factors are alternating in the sequence (ordered by increasing length) of non neutral bispecial factors. Then, by using a result of Boshernitzan [Bos85], we deduce the existence of (uniform) frequency of any factor, and thus of the letters. This provides a combinatorial proof of convergence for this multidimensional continued fraction algorithm.

The article is structured as follows. In Section 2, we introduce the Arnoux-Rauzy-Poincaré multidimensional continued fraction algorithm, with its nine associated substitutions, as well as our main result on the factor complexity and on the convergence. In Section 3, we study bispecial factors under Arnoux-Rauzy and Poincaré substitutions with no restriction on the application of substitutions. In Section 4, we prove the result on factor complexity of the associated S-adic system where the language of substitutions is restricted to a regular language defined by a finite automaton.

2   The Arnoux-Rauzy-Poincaré Algorithm

The Arnoux-Rauzy-Poincaré multidimensional continued fraction algorithm belongs to the family of multidimensional continued fraction algorithms defined in terms of triangle maps such as introduced in [Gar01]. It combines the two classical algorithms that are Poincaré algorithm and Arnoux-Rauzy algorithm, which are respectively defined in dimension 3 as follows: Poincaré algorithm acts on a triple of non-negative entries by subtracting the smallest entry to the median and the median to the largest, whereas Arnoux-Rauzy algorithm acts by subtracting the sum of the two smallest entries to the largest, when possible. Our fusion algorithm privilegiates an Arnoux-Rauzy step if possible, otherwise it perfoms a Poincaré step.

We follow here the formalism described in Section 2.1 of [DFG+12]. The Arnoux-Rauzy-Poincaré multidimensional continued fraction algorithm is a fusion algorithm such as introduced in [BL11, Lab12]. It is defined on the 2-simplex

$$\Delta = \{(x_1, x_2, x_3) \in \mathbb{R}^3_+ : x_1 + x_2 + x_3 = 1\}$$

whose vertices are the vectors $\mathbf{e}_1 = (1, 0, 0)^\top$, $\mathbf{e}_2 = (0, 1, 0)^\top$ and $\mathbf{e}_3 = (0, 0, 1)^\top$. In order to partition Δ, we consider the following fifteen matrices:

$$A_1 = \begin{pmatrix} 1&1&1 \\ 0&1&0 \\ 0&0&1 \end{pmatrix}, P_{21} = \begin{pmatrix} 1&1&1 \\ 0&1&1 \\ 0&0&1 \end{pmatrix}, P_{31} = \begin{pmatrix} 1&1&1 \\ 0&1&0 \\ 0&1&1 \end{pmatrix}, H_{21} = \begin{pmatrix} 1&0&0 \\ 0&1&0 \\ 1&0&1 \end{pmatrix}, H_{31} = \begin{pmatrix} 1&0&0 \\ 1&1&0 \\ 0&0&1 \end{pmatrix},$$

$$A_2 = \begin{pmatrix} 1&0&0 \\ 1&1&1 \\ 0&0&1 \end{pmatrix}, P_{12} = \begin{pmatrix} 1&0&1 \\ 1&1&1 \\ 0&0&1 \end{pmatrix}, P_{32} = \begin{pmatrix} 1&0&0 \\ 1&1&1 \\ 1&0&1 \end{pmatrix}, H_{12} = \begin{pmatrix} 1&0&0 \\ 0&1&0 \\ 0&1&1 \end{pmatrix}, H_{32} = \begin{pmatrix} 1&1&0 \\ 0&1&0 \\ 0&0&1 \end{pmatrix},$$

$$A_3 = \begin{pmatrix} 1&0&0 \\ 0&1&0 \\ 1&1&1 \end{pmatrix}, P_{13} = \begin{pmatrix} 1&1&0 \\ 0&1&0 \\ 1&1&1 \end{pmatrix}, P_{23} = \begin{pmatrix} 1&0&0 \\ 1&1&0 \\ 1&1&1 \end{pmatrix}, H_{13} = \begin{pmatrix} 1&0&0 \\ 0&1&1 \\ 0&0&1 \end{pmatrix}, H_{23} = \begin{pmatrix} 1&0&1 \\ 0&1&0 \\ 0&0&1 \end{pmatrix},$$

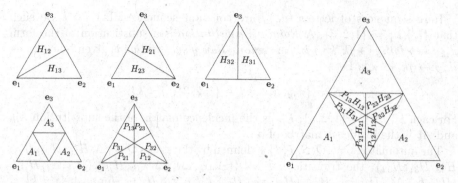

Fig. 1. Left: the three Arnoux-Rauzy matrices, the six Poincaré matrices and the six half triangles. Right: the partition of Arnoux-Rauzy-Poincaré algorithm.

whose column vectors are represented at Figure 1. Then, the column vectors of A_1, A_2, A_3, $P_{31}H_{31}$, $P_{13}H_{13}$, $P_{23}H_{23}$, $P_{32}H_{32}$, $P_{12}H_{12}$ and $P_{21}H_{21}$ describe a disjoint partition of Δ depicted in Figure 1. This partition then allows the definition of the following map:

$$T : \Delta \to \mathbb{R}^3_+$$

$$\mathbf{x} \mapsto \begin{cases} A_k^{-1}\mathbf{x}, & \text{if } \mathbf{x} \in A_k\Delta \text{ (subtract the sum of the two smallest entries} \\ & \text{to the largest),} \\ P_{jk}^{-1}\mathbf{x}, & \text{if } \mathbf{x} \in P_{jk}H_{jk}\Delta \text{ (subtract the smallest entry to the median} \\ & \text{and the median to the largest).} \end{cases}$$

The Arnoux-Rauzy-Poincaré multidimensional continued fractions algorithm is defined as the iteration of the function $\overline{T} : \Delta \to \Delta$, $\mathbf{x} \mapsto \dfrac{T(\mathbf{x})}{||T(\mathbf{x})||}$ with $||\mathbf{x}|| = x_1 + x_2 + x_3$. For each $\mathbf{x}$, it generates a sequence of matrices $(M_n)_n$ with values in the set $\{A_k, P_{jk} \mid j,k \in \{1,2,3\}, j \neq k\}$.

2.1   The Arnoux-Rauzy-Poincaré S-Adic System

We recall below the definition of an S-adic system. For more on S-adic words see [BD13, CN10, DLR13, Ler12]. We say that the infinite word $\mathbf{w} \in \mathcal{A}^\mathbb{N}$ admits an S-adic representation if there exist a finite set S of substitutions defined on the alphabet $\mathcal{A}$, a sequence $s = (\sigma_n)_{n\in\mathbb{N}} \in S^\mathbb{N}$ of substitutions that all belong to S, and $(a_n)_{n\in\mathbb{N}}$ a sequence of letters in $\mathcal{A}$ such that $\mathbf{w} = \lim_{n\to\infty} \sigma_0\sigma_1\cdots\sigma_n(a_n)$. The word $\mathbf{w}$ is said to be S-adic, and the sequence s is called the *directive sequence*. An S-adic system is obtained by adding restrictions on the set of allowed directive sequences $s \in S^\mathbb{N}$: an S-adic system is given by a finite directed strongly connected graph $\mathcal{G}$ labeled by the substitutions in S, with each infinite path giving rise to a directive sequence.

Here sequences of letters $(a_n)_n$ are constant sequences. Let i, j, k be such that $\{i, j, k\} = \{1, 2, 3\}$. A *Poincaré substitution* is a substitution of the form $\pi_{jk} : i \mapsto ijk, j \mapsto jk, k \mapsto k$. An *Arnoux-Rauzy substitution* is given by $\alpha_k : i \mapsto ik, j \mapsto jk, k \mapsto k$. Let

$$\mathcal{S} := \{\pi_{jk}, \alpha_k \mid j, k \in \{1, 2, 3\}, \ j \neq k\}.$$

For each $\{i, j, k\} = \{1, 2, 3\}$, P_{jk} is the incidence matrix of the substitution π_{jk} and A_k is the incidence matrix of α_k.

The automaton $\mathcal{G} = (Q, \mathcal{S}, T, I)$ is defined by the states $Q = \{\Delta, H_{12}, H_{13}, H_{21}, H_{23}, H_{31}, H_{32}\}$, the transitions $T = \{(\Delta, \alpha_k, \Delta), (\Delta, \pi_{jk}, H_{jk}), (H_{jk}, \alpha_j, H_{jk}), (H_{jk}, \alpha_i, \Delta), (H_{jk}, \pi_{ij}, H_{ij}), (H_{jk}, \pi_{ki}, H_{ki}), (H_{jk}, \pi_{ji}, H_{ji}) :$ for each $\{i, j, k\} = \{1, 2, 3\}\} \subset Q \times \mathcal{S} \times Q$ and the initial state $I = \{\Delta\}$ (see Figure 2). We consider the S-adic system associated with the regular language $\mathcal{L}(\mathcal{G})$. This language corresponds to directive sequences $(s_n)_n$ for which the sequence of incidence matrices $(M_{s_n})_n$ is generated by the execution of the Arnoux-Rauzy-Poincaré algorithm.

Proposition 1 (ARP regular language). *The set of directive sequences produced by the Arnoux-Rauzy-Poincaré algorithm is exactly the set of labeled infinite paths starting in Δ in the graph $\mathcal{G}$ illustrated in Figure 2.*

We now state the main theorem. Its proof is given in Section 4. Let us say that $\mathbf{x} \in \Delta$ is *totally irrational* if $x_1, \dot{x}_2, x_3$ are linearly independent over $\mathbb{Q}$.

Theorem 1 (Factor Complexity). *Let $\mathbf{w}$ be an S-adic word generated by the Arnoux-Rauzy-Poincaré algorithm applied to a totally irrational vector $\mathbf{x} \in \Delta$. Then the factor complexity of $\mathbf{w}$ is such that $p(n) \leq 3n+1$, $p(n+1)-p(n) \in \{2, 3\}$ for all $n \geq 0$, and $\limsup_{n \to \infty} \frac{p(n)}{n} < 3$.*

Theorem 2 (Frequencies and Convergence). *Let $\mathbf{w}$ be an S-adic word generated by the Arnoux-Rauzy-Poincaré algorithm applied to a totally irrational*

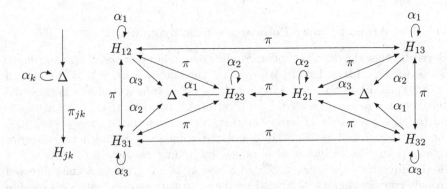

Fig. 2. The deterministic automaton $\mathcal{G}$. To avoid crossing arrows, the initial state Δ is drawn at three places. Also, the indices of π transitions are not written because they are determined by the indices of the arrival state: $\xrightarrow{\pi} H_{jk}$ means $\xrightarrow{\pi_{jk}} H_{jk}$.

vector $\mathbf{x} \in \Delta$. *Then the symbolic dynamical system generated by* $\mathbf{w}$ *is uniquely ergodic, and the frequencies of letters are proved to exist in* $\mathbf{w}$ *and to be equal to the coordinates of* $\mathbf{x}$.

Furthermore, the Arnoux-Rauzy-Poincaré algorithm is a weakly convergent algorithm, that is, for Lebesgue almost every $\mathbf{x} \in \Delta$, *if* $(M_n)_n$ *stands for the sequence of matrices produced by the Arnoux-Rauzy-Poincaré algorithm, then one has* $\cap_n M_0 \cdots M_n(\mathbb{R}_+^3) = \mathbb{R}_+ \mathbf{x}$.

Theorem 2 is a direct consequence of Theorem 1 together with Theorem 1.5 of [Bos85] for the unique ergodicity statement (see also [FM10]). The weak convergence comes from the unique ergodicity. Usual proofs of convergence rely on linear algebra and on the use of the Hilbert projective metric (see e.g. [Sch00]). Let us stress the fact that we provide here a purely combinatorial proof of convergence for a multidimensional continued fraction algorithm.

3   Bispecial Factors under Arnoux-Rauzy and Poincaré Substitutions

3.1   Bispecial Factors and Extension Types

The proof of Theorem 4 requires some preparation. In this section, we follow the notation of [CN10]. Let w be a factor of a recurrent infinite word $\mathbf{u}$. We let $E^+(w) = \{x \in \mathcal{A} \mid wx \in \mathcal{L}(\mathbf{u})\}$ denote the set of right extensions of w in $\mathbf{u}$. The *right valence* $d^+(w) = \operatorname{Card} E^+(w)$ of w (in $\mathbf{u}$) is the number of distinct right extensions of w. *Left extensions* $E^-(w)$ and *left valence* $d^-(w)$ are defined similarly. A factor whose right valence is at least 2 is called *right special*. A factor whose left valence is at least 2 is called *left special*. A factor which is both left and right special is called *bispecial*. The set of bispecial factors of length n are identified by $BS_n(\mathbf{u})$. The *extension type* $E_{\mathbf{u}}(w)$ of a factor w of $\mathbf{u}$ is the set of pairs (a, b) of $\mathcal{A} \times \mathcal{A}$ such that w can be extended in both directions as awb :

$$E_{\mathbf{u}}(w) = \{(a, b) \in \mathcal{A} \times \mathcal{A} \mid awb \in \mathcal{L}(\mathbf{u})\}.$$

We let denote $E_{\mathbf{u}}(w)$ by $E(w)$ when the context is clear. The *bilateral multiplicity* of a factor w is the number

$$m(w) = \operatorname{Card} E(w) - d^-(w) - d^+(w) + 1.$$

A bispecial factor is said *strong* if $m(w) > 0$, *weak* if $m(w) < 0$ and *neutral* if $m(w) = 0$. A bispecial factor whose extension type satisfies

$$E(w) \subseteq (\{a\} \times \mathcal{A}) \cup (\mathcal{A} \times \{b\}) \qquad \text{for a pair of letters} \qquad (a, b) \in E(w) \quad (1)$$

is said *ordinary*. An ordinary bispecial factor is neutral, but the converse is not true for $|\mathcal{A}| > 2$. It is convenient to represent extension type $E(w)$ of a bispecial factor w graphically. Often represented as a bipartite graph, we choose a table representation: a cross ($\times$) is drawn at the intersection of row a and column b if and only if $(a, b) \in E(w)$ (see Figure 3).

	1	2	3
1	×		
2	×		
3	×	×	×

$m(w) = 0$
neutral and ordinary

	1	2	3
1	×		
2		×	
3	×	×	×

$m(w) = 0$
neutral but not ordinary

	1	2	3
1	×		
2			
3		×	

$m(w) = -1$
weak

	1	2	3
1			
2		×	×
3	×	×	×

$m(w) = 1$
strong

Fig. 3. We represent the extension type $E(w)$ of a bispecial factor w by a table. A cross ($\times$) is at the intersection of row a and of column b if and only if $(a, b) \in E(w)$.

Definition 1 (Left equivalence). *Let w and w' be two bispecial factors defined on the alphabet $\mathcal{A}$. We say that their extension types are* left equivalent *if there exists a permutation τ acting on $\mathcal{A}$ such that $E(w') = \{(\tau(a), b) \mid (a, b) \in E(w)\}$.*

Right equivalence is defined similarly. Left equivalence can be interpreted on the table representation of the extension type as follows: one representation can be obtained from the other by a permutation of the rows:

$$E(w) = \begin{array}{c|ccc} & 1 & 2 & 3 \\ \hline 1 & & \times & \\ 2 & & & \\ 3 & \times & \times & \times \end{array} \quad \text{and} \quad E(w') = \begin{array}{c|ccc} & 1 & 2 & 3 \\ \hline 1 & \times & \times & \times \\ 2 & & \times & \\ 3 & & & \end{array}$$

Substitutions considered in this article preserve the first letter and thus preserve the right extensions. Then, the notion of left-equivalence is sufficient for our need. When the extension type of two words are equivalent, they share common properties. In particular, being ordinary, strong or weak is preserved under equivalence.

3.2 Factor Complexity

Let $p(n)$ be the factor complexity function of **w**. The sequences of *finite differences of order 1 and 2* respectively of $p(n)$, that is, $s(n) = p(n+1) - p(n)$ and $b(n) = s(n+1) - s(n)$, are used to show upper bounds for $p(n)$.

Lemma 1. *Suppose $|\mathcal{A}| = 3$. Then, $p(n+1) - p(n) \in \{2, 3\}$ if and only if $\sum_{\ell=0}^{n-1} b(\ell) \in \{0, 1\}$. Also, if the sequence of finite differences of order 2 is such that $(b(\ell))_\ell = 0, \ldots, 0, 1, 0, \ldots, 0, -1, 0, \ldots, 0, 1, 0, \ldots$ then $\sum_{\ell=0}^{n-1} b(\ell) \in \{0, 1\}$.*

Proof. Since $|\mathcal{A}| = 3$, then $p(1) = 3$ and $s(0) = p(1) - p(0) = 3 - 1 = 2$. We have $p(n+1) - p(n) = s(n) = s(0) + \sum_{\ell=0}^{n-1} b(\ell) = 2 + \sum_{\ell=0}^{n-1} b(\ell)$.

Function $b(n)$ is related to the multiplicity of bispecial factors.

Theorem 3. *[CN10, Theorem 4.5.4] Let $\mathbf{u} \in \mathcal{A}^{\mathbb{N}}$ be an infinite recurrent word. Then, for all $n \in \mathbb{N}$: $b(n) = \sum_{w \in BS_n(\mathbf{u})} m(w)$.*

3.3 Synchronization Lemmas

The goal of the next sections is to describe strong and weak bispecial factors. From now on, the alphabet is set to $\mathcal{A} = \{1, 2, 3\}$. The next lemma describes the preimage of a factor under Arnoux-Rauzy (**AR**) and Poincaré (**P**) substitutions.

Lemma 2 (Synchronization). *Let $u \in \mathcal{A}^*$ and w be a factor of $\alpha_k(u)$ for some $\{i, j, k\} = \{1, 2, 3\}$.*

(i) *If w is empty or if the first letter of w is i or j, then there exists a unique $v \in \mathcal{A}^*$ and a unique $s \in \{\varepsilon, i, j\}$ such that $w = \alpha_k(v) \cdot s$.*

(ii) *If the first letter of w is k, then there exists a unique $v \in \mathcal{A}^*$ and a unique $s \in \{\varepsilon, i, j\}$ such that $w = k \cdot \alpha_k(v) \cdot s$.*

Let $u \in \mathcal{A}^*$ and w be a factor of $\pi_{jk}(u)$ for some $\{i, j, k\} = \{1, 2, 3\}$.

(i) *If w is empty or if the first letter of w is i, then there exists a unique $v \in \mathcal{A}^*$ and a unique $s \in \{\varepsilon, i, j, ij\}$ such that $w = \pi_{jk}(v) \cdot s$.*

(ii) *If $w = j$, then there exists a unique $v(= \varepsilon)$ such that $w = j \cdot \pi_{jk}(v)$.*

(iii) *If the first letter of w is j and $|w| > 1$, then there exists a unique $v \in \mathcal{A}^*$ and a unique $s \in \{\varepsilon, i, j, ij\}$ such that $w = jk \cdot \pi_{jk}(v) \cdot s$.*

(iv) *If the first letter of w is k, then there exists a unique $v \in \mathcal{A}^*$ and a unique $s \in \{\varepsilon, i, j, ij\}$ such that $w = k \cdot \pi_{jk}(v) \cdot s$.*

Proof. The sets $\{ik, jk, k\}$ and $\{ijk, jk, k\}$ form a prefix code.

Definition 2 (Antecedent, extended image). *Let $\sigma = \alpha_k$ or $\sigma = \pi_{jk}$, $u \in \mathcal{A}^*$ and w be a factor of $\sigma(u)$. We say that the* antecedent *of w under σ is the unique word v as defined by Lemma 2. If v is the antecedent of a word w, then we say that the word w is an* extended image *of v.*

While the antecedent is unique, a word v may have more than one extended image. For example, $w_1 = 23\pi_{23}(11)1 = 231231231$ and $w_2 = 3\pi_{23}(11)2 = 31231232$ are two distinct extended images of $v = 11$. This is why the situation becomes here quite intricate especiallly for bispecial factors (it happens that strong and weak bispecial words appear in pairs, see Lemma 10 below).

Definition 3 (Bispecial extended image). *We shall say that a* bispecial extended image *w of v under σ is a bispecial word which is an extended image of v under σ.*

3.4 Antecedents and Images of Bispecial Words

Lemma 3 (AR - Bispecial extended image). *Let v be a bispecial factor. There is a unique bispecial extended image $w = k\alpha_k(v)$ of v under α_k.*

Lemma 4 (AR - Antecedent of a bispecial). *Let $u \in \mathcal{A}^*$ and $w \neq \varepsilon$ be a bispecial factor of $\alpha_k(u)$. Let v be the unique antecedent of w under α_k such that $w = k\alpha_k(v)$. Then, v is bispecial and it has the same extension type $E_{\alpha_k(u)}(w) = E_u(v)$ and same multiplicity $m(w) = m(v)$ as w.*

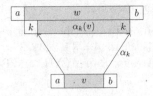

Fig. 4. The preimage of the bispecial word w under α_k

Proof. One checks that $(a,b) \in E(v)$ if and only if $(a,b) \in E(k\alpha_k(v))$ (see Figure 4). Then $E(k\alpha_k(v)) = E(v)$. We deduce that $E^+(k\alpha_k(v)) = E^+(v)$ and $E^-(k\alpha_k(v)) = E^-(v)$. From this we conclude that $m(k\alpha_k(v)) = m(v)$.

Lemma 5 (P - Bispecial extended images). *Let v be a bispecial factor. There are at most two distinct bispecial extended images of v under π_{jk}. They are either $k\pi_{jk}(v)$ or $jk\pi_{jk}(v)$.*

Proof. Let w be a bispecial extended images of v under π_{jk}. Since it is a bispecial factor, it must start with letter j or k and end with letter k. From Lemma 2, $w \in \{jk\pi_{jk}(v), k\pi_{jk}(v)\}$.

Lemma 6 (P - Antecedent of a bispecial). *Let $u \in \mathcal{A}^*$ and $w \neq \varepsilon$ be a bispecial factor of $\pi_{jk}(u)$. Let v be the unique antecedent of w under π_{jk} such that $w = k\pi_{jk}(v)$ or $w = jk\pi_{jk}(v)$. Then, v is bispecial.*

Now we want to describe more precisely under which conditions a bispecial word v has a unique bispecial extended image under Poincaré substitutions and give its extension type. In general, this depends on its left extensions $E^-(v)$. However, if the value of the left valence $d^-(v) = 2$, we deduce the unicity of the bispecial extended image as well as important information on the extension type of the extended image.

Lemma 7 (P - Bispecial extended images in details). *Let v be a bispecial factor.*

(i) *If $d^-(v) = 2$, v admits a unique bispecial extended image $w \in \{k\pi_{jk}(v), jk\pi_{jk}(v)\}$ under π_{jk} and $d^-(w) = 2$. Moreover, the extension types $E(v)$ and $E(w)$ are left equivalent.*

(ii) *If $d^-(v) = 3$, then v admits either one, or two bispecial extended images $w \in \{k\pi_{jk}(v), jk\pi_{jk}(v)\}$ under π_{jk}. In any case, $d^-(w) = 2$ and the two non empty rows of $E(w)$ are obtained by projection of rows of $E(v)$.*

3.5 Life of a Bispecial Factor under Arnoux-Rauzy-Poincaré Substitutions

In this section, the life of a bispecial factor is analyzed more precisely under the application of Arnoux-Rauzy and Poincaré substitutions in the spirit of Section

4.2.2 of [Cas97] where bispecial factors are described under the image of circular morphisms. To achieve this, we need to understand exactly the left extensions which will give information about the multiplicity of the bispecial factors. We denote by $\mathcal{S}_\alpha$, $\mathcal{S}_\pi$, respectively the following sets of substitutions:

$$\mathcal{S}_\alpha = \{\alpha_1, \alpha_2, \alpha_3\}, \ \mathcal{S}_\pi = \{\pi_{12}, \pi_{13}, \pi_{23}, \pi_{21}, \pi_{31}, \pi_{32}\}, \ \text{with } \mathcal{S} = \mathcal{S}_\alpha \cup \mathcal{S}_\pi.$$

Let w be a factor of $\lim_{k\to\infty} \sigma_0\sigma_1\cdots\sigma_k(a_k)$, $a_k \in \mathcal{A}$, where $\sigma_i \in \mathcal{S}$. Let $w_0 = w$ and w_{i+1} be the unique antecedent of w_i under σ_i for $i \geq 0$. If $|w_i| > 0$, then $|w_{i+1}| < |w_i|$, then there exists n such that $w_n = \varepsilon$.

Definition 4 (Age). *The smallest of those integers n is called the* age *of w and is noted* age(w).

Thus, w_1 is the antecedent of w_0 under σ_0 and w_2 is the antecedent of w_1 under σ_1. If $n = \text{age}(w)$, w_n is the antecedent of w_{n-1} under σ_{n-1} and the extension type $E(w_n)$ of $w_n = \varepsilon$ depends on σ_n.

Definition 5 (History, life). *We say that the finite sequence $\sigma_0\sigma_1\cdots\sigma_n$ is the* history *and the sequence $(w_i)_{0\leq i\leq n}$ is the* life *of the bispecial word w.*

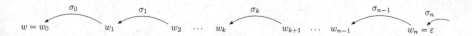

Fig. 5. Life and history of a factor w

Lemma 8. *Let $n \geq 0$ be an integer. Let B_n be the set of all bispecial factors of age n of $\lim_{n\to\infty} \sigma_0\sigma_1\cdots\sigma_n(a_n)$, $a_n \in \mathcal{A}$, where $\sigma_i \in \mathcal{S}$. Then $\text{Card } B_n \leq 2$.*

The life $(w_i)_{0\leq i\leq n}$ of bispecial factors starts as an empty word at $i = n$. The word w_i for $i < n$ is the concatenation of one or two letters and $\sigma_i(w_{i+1})$. These letters depend on the extension type $E(w_{i+1})$ and recursively on the extension type $E(w_n)$ of $w_n = \varepsilon$. Thus, it is important to understand properly what are the possible extension types of the empty word under the application of Arnoux-Rauzy and Poincaré substitutions. Below, the extension type $E(\varepsilon)$ of the empty word considered as a bispecial factor in the language of $\sigma(u)$ is denoted by $E_{\sigma(u)}(\varepsilon)$.

Lemma 9. *Let $\mathbf{u} \in \mathcal{A}^* \cup \mathcal{A}^{\mathbb{N}}$ be such that all letters of $\mathcal{A}$ appear as proper factors of $\mathbf{u}$. Considered as a bispecial factor of the language of the word $\alpha_k(\mathbf{u})$, the empty word ε is ordinary. Considered as a bispecial factor of the language of the word $\pi_{jk}(\mathbf{u})$, the empty word ε is neutral but not ordinary:*

$$E_{\alpha_k(\mathbf{u})}(\varepsilon) = \begin{array}{c|ccc} & i & j & k \\ \hline i & & & \times \\ j & & \times & \\ k & \times & \times & \times \end{array} \quad \text{and} \quad E_{\pi_{jk}(\mathbf{u})}(\varepsilon) = \begin{array}{c|ccc} & i & j & k \\ \hline i & & \times & \\ j & & & \times \\ k & \times & \times & \times \end{array}.$$

In the next lemma, we describe exactly what are the bispecial factors associated with each possible history.

Lemma 10. *Let* $\mathbf{u} = \lim_{n\to\infty} \sigma_0 \sigma_1 \cdots \sigma_n(a_n)$. *Let* w *be a bispecial factor of* $\mathbf{u}$ *such that* $n = \mathrm{age}(w)$ *and* $\lim_{m\to\infty} \sigma_{n+1}\sigma_{n+2}\cdots\sigma_m(a_m)$ *contains all letters of* $\mathcal{A}$ *as proper factors. Let* z *be the other bispecial factor of the same age as* w *if it exists. Then the history* $\sigma_0 \sigma_1 \cdots \sigma_n$ *of* w *determine the left valence, multiplicity and extension type of* w *and* z *according to the following table.*

$\sigma_0\sigma_1\cdots\sigma_n \in$	$d^-(w)$	$m(w)$	ordinary	$d^-(z)$	$m(z)$	ordinary
$\mathcal{S}_\alpha^* \mathcal{S}_\alpha$	3	0	yes			
$\mathcal{S}_\alpha^* \mathcal{S}_\pi$	3	0	no			
$\mathcal{S}^* \pi_{jk}\,\mathcal{S}_\alpha^*\{\alpha_k\}$	2	0	yes			
$\mathcal{S}^* \pi_{jk}\,\mathcal{S}_\alpha^*\{\alpha_i,\alpha_j\}$	2	0	yes	2	0	yes
$\mathcal{S}^* \pi_{jk}\,\mathcal{S}_\alpha^*\{\pi_{ji},\pi_{ki},\pi_{ij},\pi_{kj}\}$	2	0	yes	2	0	yes
$\mathcal{S}^* \pi_{jk}\,\mathcal{S}_\alpha^*\{\pi_{ik},\pi_{jk}\}$	2	+1	no	2	-1	no

Strong and weak bispecial words thus appear in pairs under the application of Poincaré substitutions each time π_{jk} is followed by π_{jk} or π_{ik} for $\{i,j,k\} = \{1,2,3\}$ with possibly some Arnoux-Rauzy substitutions α_k, $k \in \{1,2,3\}$, in between.

4   Proof of Theorem 1

Restricted to the language of the automaton $\mathcal{G}$, illustrated in Figure 2, the history of a strong or weak bispecial factor necessarily contains Arnoux-Rauzy substitutions.

Lemma 11. *Let* $\mathbf{u} = \lim_{n\to\infty} \sigma_0 \sigma_1 \cdots \sigma_n(a_n)$. *Let* w *be a bispecial factor of* $\mathbf{u}$ *such that* $n = \mathrm{age}(w)$ *and* $\lim_{m\to\infty} \sigma_{n+1}\sigma_{n+2}\cdots\sigma_m(a_m)$ *contains all letters of* $\mathcal{A}$ *as proper factors. If* w *is weak or strong and the history of* w *is in the regular language* $\sigma_0\sigma_1\cdots\sigma_n \in \mathcal{L}(\mathcal{G})$, *then*

$$\sigma_0\sigma_1\cdots\sigma_n \in \mathcal{S}^* \pi_{jk}\{\alpha_j\}^* \alpha_i\,\mathcal{S}_\alpha^*\,\{\pi_{ik},\pi_{jk}\}$$

for some $\{i,j,k\} = \{1,2,3\}$.

Lemma 12. *Let* z^+ *and* z^- *be two bispecial factors of a word* u *of the same age* $\mathrm{age}(z^+) = \mathrm{age}(z^-)$. *Suppose that* z^- *is weak and* z^+ *is strong. Then* $|z^+| < |z^-|$.

Lemma 13. *Let* z^- *and* w^+ *be two bispecial factors of a word* u *such that* z^- *is weak and* w^+ *is strong. If* $\mathrm{age}(z^-) < \mathrm{age}(w^+)$, *then* $|z^-| < |w^+|$.

Lemma 14. *Let* z^-, w^+ *and* w^- *be bispecial factors of a word* $\mathbf{u}$ *such that* z^- *is weak,* w^+ *is strong and* w^- *is weak. If* $\mathrm{age}(z^-) < \mathrm{age}(w^+) = \mathrm{age}(w^-)$, *then* $|w^+| - |z^-| > |w^-| - |w^+|$.

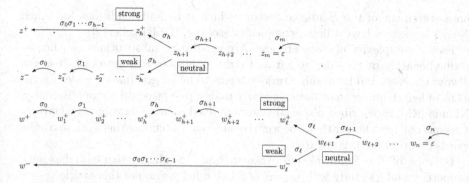

Fig. 6. Lifes of two pairs of strong and weak bispecial factors: z^+, z^- and w^+, w^-

We now have gathered all the elements for giving a proof of Theorem 1. We show that strong and weak bispecial words alternate when the length increases and make use of Lemma 1 (see Figure 6). Note that the notion of alternance was used to prove Theorem 4.11.2 in [CN10, p. 238].

Proof (of Theorem 1). Note first that the assumption on **x**, i.e., **x** is totally irrational, is required for applying Lemma 11 for bispecial factors of all age. The set of bispecial factors of length n contains at most one weak or strong bispecial factor. Indeed, suppose on the contrary that it contains two of them: w and z. They cannot have the same age according to Lemma 12 since this would otherwise imply $|w| \neq |z|$. Also, if one is older, e.g. $age(w) > age(z)$, then $|w| > |z|$ from Lemma 13. Then $b(n) \in \{-1, 0, +1\}$ according to Theorem 3. Finally, it remains to prove that the assumptions of Lemma 1 are satisfied. The first non-zero value of $b(n)$ is $+1$ because strong and weak bispecial factors come in pairs and the strong one is smaller than the weak one from Lemma 12. Moreover, non-zero values are alternating. Indeed, let z^+ and w^+ be two strong bispecial factors such that $age(w^+) > age(z^+)$. Let z^- be the weak bispecial factor such that $age(z^-) = age(z^+)$. From Lemma 12 and Lemma 13, $|z^+| < |z^-| < |w^+|$. Hence, there is always a -1 between two $+1$ in the sequence $(b(n))_{n \geq 0}$. This shows that $p(n+1) - p(n) \in \{2, 3\}$ (Lemma 1), so that $p(n) \leq 3n + 1$ for $n \geq 0$. Moreover, $p(n) < 3n$ for each $n > 0$ since $p(1) = 3$ and $p(2) = 5$. We can show even more. From Lemma 14, the range of consecutive values of 2 for $p(n+1) - p(n)$ is larger than the range of consecutive values of 3 which follows immediately. From this we conclude that $\limsup_{n \to \infty} \frac{p(n)}{n} \leq \frac{5}{2}$.

5 Concluding Remarks

The restriction to the regular language $\mathcal{L}(\mathcal{G})$ is clearly important; there exist examples of S-adic words constructed with the alphabet of substitutions S for which the upper bound of $3n$ is false otherwise. Moreover, a quadratic complexity is even also achievable (fixed point of $\pi_{23}\pi_{13}$). Hence, this gives some more insight on a statement of the S-adic conjecture which is to find conditions for which S-adic sequences have a linear complexity (see e.g. [DLR13, Ler12]).

Factor complexity of Poincaré and Arnoux-Rauzy substitutions can be described exactly by considering left and right extensions of length one. It is not always the case, and Brun substitutions seems to be an example for which extensions of length longer than 1 are necessary to describe bispecial factors. Recently, Klouda [Klo12] described bispecial factors in fixed point of morphisms where extensions of length longer than one were considered. Extending this work to S-adic words deserves further research.

Balance of the Poincaré and Arnoux-Rauzy S-adic system also has nice properties and its study will be part of a extended version of this article.

References

[AR91]   Arnoux, P., Rauzy, G.: Représentation géométrique de suites de complexité 2n+1. Bull. Soc. Math. France 119(2), 199–215 (1991)

[BD13]   Berthé, V., Delecroix, V.: Beyond substitutive dynamical systems: s-adic expansions (preprint, 2013)

[BL11]   Berthé, V., Labbé, S.: Uniformly balanced words with linear complexity and prescribed letter frequencies. In: Proc. 8th Int. Conf. on Words. EPTCS, vol. 63, pp. 44–52. Open Publishing Association (2011)

[Bos85]   Boshernitzan, M.: A unique ergodicity of minimal symbolic flows with linear block growth. J. Analyse Math. 44, 77–96 (1984/1985)

[Cas97]   Cassaigne, J.: Complexité et facteurs spéciaux. Bull. Belg. Math. Soc. Simon Stevin 4(1), 67–88 (1997); Journées Montoises (Mons, 1994)

[CN10]   Cassaigne, J., Nicolas, F.: Factor complexity. In: Combinatorics, Automata and Number Theory. Encyclopedia Math. Appl., vol. 135, pp. 163–247. Cambridge Univ. Press, Cambridge (2010)

[DFG+12] Dasaratha, K., Flapan, L., Garrity, T., Lee, C., Mihaila, C., Neumann-Chun, N., Peluse, S., Stroffregen, M.: Cubic irrationals and periodicity via a family of multi-dimensional continued fraction algorithms. arXiv:1208.4244 (2012)

[DLR13]   Durand, F., Leroy, J., Richomme, G.: Do the Properties of an S-adic Representation Determine Factor Complexity? J. of Int. Seq. 16 (2013)

[FM10]   Ferenczi, S., Monteil, T.: Infinite words with uniform frequencies, and invariant measures. In: Combinatorics, Automata and Number Theory. Encycl. Math. Appl., vol. 135, pp. 373–409. Cambridge Univ. Press (2010)

[Gar01]   Garrity, T.: On periodic sequences for algebraic numbers. J. Number Theory 88(1), 86–103 (2001)

[Klo12]   Klouda, K.: Bispecial factors in circular non-pushy D0L languages. Theoret. Comput. Sci. 445, 63–74 (2012)

[Lab12]   Labbé, S.: Structure des pavages, droites discrètes 3D et combinatoire des mots. PhD thesis, Université du Québec à Montréal (May 2012)

[Ler12]   Leroy, J.: Some improvements of the S-adic conjecture. Adv. in Appl. Math. 48(1), 79–98 (2012)

[Nog95]   Nogueira, A.: The three-dimensional Poincaré continued fraction algorithm. Israel J. Math. 90(1-3), 373–401 (1995)

[Sch00]   Schweiger, F.: Multidimensional continued fractions. Oxford Science Publications. Oxford University Press, Oxford (2000)

The Lexicographic Cross-Section
of the Plactic Monoid Is Regular

Christian Choffrut[1] and Robert Mercaş[2,*]

[1] L.I.A.F.A., Université Paris 7, 2 Pl. Jussieu, 75 251 Paris Cedex, France
Christian.Choffrut@liafa.univ-paris-diderot.fr
[2] Christian-Albrechts-Universität zu Kiel, Institut für Informatik,
D-24098 Kiel, Germany
rgm@informatik.uni-kiel.de

Abstract. The plactic monoid is the quotient of the free monoid by the congruence generated by Knuth's well-celebrated rules. It is well-known that the set of Young tableaux is a cross-section of this congruence which happens to be regular. The main result of this work shows that the set of alphabetically minimal elements in the congruence classes is also regular. We give a full combinatorial characterization of these minimal elements and show that constructing them is as fast as constructing a tableau.

1 Introduction

Young tableaux were introduced in 1900 as combinatorial objects for studying the linear representations of the symmetric group. They can be thought of as Ferrers diagrams filled with the n first nonnegative integers subject to ordering properties along the rows and columns. Allowing arbitrary repetitions of the same integer lead to more general objects, the so-called *semistandard Young tableaux*. Knuth considered them as a possible data structure for sorting but showed that they perform relatively poorly, cf. [10, paragraph 5.1.4.]. Here, we view Young tableaux as representatives of elements of a monoid, called the *plactic monoid* by Lascoux and Schützenberger. The purpose of this work is to study the probably most natural cross-section of this monoid, namely the set of lexicographically minimal elements of each class and to show that this set is regular, i.e., recognizable by a finite automaton.

When a monoid is specified by generators and relators, it is desirable, but not always possible, to have at one's disposal a regular set of representatives. A natural way of selecting a particular element in a congruence class is to pick up the lexicographically minimal element when it exists which is guaranteed when the classes are finite. Examples of such monoids are the trace monoids defined as the quotient of the free monoid by commutation relations of some pairs of the generators, see the classical textbooks [5,11]. For these monoids, there exist two known normal forms of congruence classes. The first one is the Cartier-Foata normal form consisting of the products of successive ordered subalphabets that

* Supported by the Alexander von Humboldt Foundation and DFG grant 582014.

J. Karhumäki, A. Lepistö, and L. Zamboni (Eds.): WORDS 2013, LNCS 8079, pp. 83–94, 2013.

are allowed to occur in the word, [3]. A second normal form is simply defined as the lexicographically minimal element of the class for an arbitrary ordering of the alphabets, [1]. In both cases, the set of representatives is regular. A stronger result would be that *all* regular subsets of the monoid, not only the monoid itself, have a regular cross-section, possibly composed of the minimal representatives. It can be shown that no regular cross-section exists for general trace monoids, which is equivalent to saying that regular subsets of trace monoids are not unambiguous in general.

Extensions of trace monoids considering partial commutations depending on the context were studied in [2]. This paper studies the plactic monoid generated by two elements and, shows that for all regular subsets of this monoid there exists a regular cross-section. In [4] the authors consider "half" of the rules of the plactic monoid and study the closure properties of the regular subsets which possess a regular cross-section.

In the most favorable case, not only the monoid has a regular set of representatives but also the multiplication by a generator, viewed as a binary relation, is recognized by a two tape finite automaton as developed in the theory of automatic groups, [8]. More generally, there is a vast literature on so-called automatic structures consisting of encoding the elements of an algebraic structure by words, and its operations by relations between words, in such a way that all these objects are recognizable by finite automata.

We briefly outline our contribution. In the preliminaries we recall all the material necessary for a good understanding of the results and we put the emphasis on the basic notions of plactic monoid, Young tableaux and so forth, for which we assume the reader has little familiarity. As much as possible we rely not only on formal definitions but also on illustrations through examples since the objects are of geometric nature.

The main result concerns the characterization of the lexicographically minimal words in a congruence class via the notion of P-sequence, see paragraph 3.1. This allows us to draw interesting conclusions such as the fact that the set of lexicographically minimal representatives is regular. As a byproduct we show a property "à la Green": the lexicographically minimal representative and the equivalent Young tableau have the same length distribution of their maximal columns. We also give an upper bound on the complexity for effectively computing this representative. In the last part we show via simple observations why the regularity of the lexicographic cross-section is remarkable: the plactic monoid is not "regularity" friendly. We end the paper with the solution of a problem concerning the relation of conjugacy as an illustration of the type of issues that we think still deserves investigation.

2   Preliminaries

We assume some familiarity of the reader with the first part of these preliminaries which deals with words and free monoids. We try to be more thoroughful in the second part and refer, among the vast literature, to [10] and [12,13] for a more detailed exposition of the theory of the Young tableaux and the plactic monoid.

2.1 Words

Throughout this paper, we consider a finite alphabet Σ consisting of the first nonzero positive integers ordered in the usual way. The elements of the free monoid Σ^* generated by the alphabet are *words*, also called *strings*. The length of a word $u \in \Sigma^*$ is denoted by $|u|$. The *lexicographic ordering* on Σ^* is denoted by $<_{lex}$ and is defined by the condition $u <_{lex} v$ if u is a prefix of v or if $u = xau'$, $v = xbv'$ and $a < b$. Given a string $u \in \Sigma^*$, we denote by $H(u)$ and $T(u)$ respectively its first and last element (H for *head* and T for *tail*). E.g., $H(2615) = 2$ and $T(2615) = 5$. A (concatenation) product of n words $u_1, u_2, \ldots, u_n$ is simply written $u = u_1 u_2 \cdots u_n$. This also holds when the words u_i for $1 \leq i \leq n$ are themselves reduced to a single letter in which case $n = |u|$. This notation is a potential source of ambiguity which should be solved by the context. When we want to decompose each u_i into its letters, we use a double index: $u_i = u_{i,1} u_{i,2} \cdots u_{i,n_i}$, where $n_i = |u_i|$.

We are interested in two special types of words. A *column* is a word with strictly decreasing letters; a *row* is a word with nondecreasing letters (the choice of these terms is standard and justified by the notion of Young tableau, see below). Clearly, every word can be uniquely factored as a product of columns of maximal length (respectively as a product of rows of maximal length). E.g., with 314521 we have respectively three columns 31/4/521 and four rows 3/145/2/1.

Since this work is mainly interested in subsets of words, and more precisely in subsets which are computationally simple, we recall that $X \subseteq \Sigma^*$ is *regular* (or *recognizable*) if it can be recognized by a finite automaton. By Kleene theorem this is equivalent to saying that the subset is *rational*, i.e., that it can be constructed from the single letters by performing finitely many times one of the three operations of set union, set concatenation and Kleene star.

2.2 The Plactic Monoid

The *plactic monoid* is the quotient of the free monoid Σ^* by the congruence generated by the following relations, known as Knuth's rules

$$bac \equiv bca \text{ where } a < b \leq c,$$
$$acb \equiv cab \text{ where } a \leq b < c$$

The simplicity of the rules hides the complexity of the resulting monoid. In particular, it is clearly neither right nor left cancellative. Also, we do not know of any Knuth-Bendix method which would enable us to test equality of two elements of the monoid. Such a verification almost necessarily goes through the construction of the Young tableaux associated with the elements.

We recall the famous *bump rules* which are immediate application of the Knuth relations and on which the construction of the Young tableaux is based.

Lemma 1 (Bump rule for rows). *Let $u \in \Sigma^*$ be a row and let $a < T(u)$. Then $ua \equiv bxay$ where $xby = u$ and b is the leftmost element greater than a.* $\square$

Example 2. $122\underline{3}45 \cdot 2 \equiv 3 \cdot 122\underline{2}45$.

There is a similar rule for columns.

Lemma 3 (Bump rule for columns). *Let $u \in \Sigma^*$ be a column and let $a \leq H(u)$. Then $au \equiv xayb$ where $xby = u$ and b is the least element greater than or equal to a.* □

Example 4. $3 \cdot 54\underline{3}21 \equiv 54\underline{3}21 \cdot 3$, $2 \cdot 54\underline{3}1 \equiv 54\underline{2}1 \cdot 3$ and $5 \cdot \underline{5}4321 \equiv 54321 \cdot \underline{5}$.

2.3 Young Tableaux

The definition of a Young tableau requires the following relation.

Definition 5. *A column u dominates a column v, written $u \succeq v$, if $|u| \geq |v|$ and if $u_{|u|-|v|+i} \leq v_i$ for all $i = 1, 2, \ldots, |v|$.*

This relation is clearly an ordering on the set of columns. There exists a graphical representation of a nonincreasing sequence of columns, namely $v_1 \succeq v_2 \succeq \ldots \succeq v_p$, called a *Young tableau*. Indeed, write each v_j vertically on the first quadrant of the discrete plane with the tail on the horizontal axis with each row left justified. Then each row of the tableau is a sequence of nondecreasing letters.

Example 6. A Young tableau

$$5$$
$$3\ 4\ 5$$
$$1\ 2\ 4\ 5$$

We recall Schensted's algorithm for associating a tableau $Y(u)$ with a word u. The tableau is constructed by reading off from left to right the letters of the word one at a time and by inserting them in the tableau under construction. Given the tableau for u, it suffices to show how to modify it in order to get the tableau for ua, $a \in \Sigma$. If a is greater than or equal to the rightmost letter of the bottom row, just append it to the right of this row. Otherwise, let b denote the element of the bottom row which is bumped out by a, as explained above. Substitute a for b and repeat the procedure by inserting b in the second lowest row of the Young tableau by applying the same rule, and so forth until reaching the top row, if necessary.

				$\leftarrow 5$	5
2 5		2 5	$\leftarrow 3$	2 3	2 3
1 2 3	$\leftarrow 2$	1 2 2		1 2 2	1 2 2
insert 2		insert 3		insert 5	done
bump out 3		bump out 5			

Due to the construction rules, it is clear that the tableau is congruent to the concatenation of its columns from left to right. It is also congruent to the concatenation of its rows from top to bottom.

In the sequel we use the same term "Young tableau" indifferently to denote the above diagram or the $\succeq$-sequence of columns, the context ensuring the notation is not ambiguous.

Dual to Young tableaux are contretableaux. The contretableau occupies the southwest quadrant of the plane. The rows are nonincreasing from right to left and the columns are strictly decreasing from top to bottom. The word is read off from right to left and the insertion rules are dual to those of the tableaux.

Example 7. A Young tableau and its equivalent contretableau

$$
\begin{array}{ll}
5 & \quad 3\,5\,5 \\
4\,5 & \quad 1\,4\,4 \\
3\,3\,4 & \quad 2\,3 \\
1\,2\,2 & \quad 2
\end{array}
$$

The following technical result will be used in the proof of the main theorem.

Proposition 8. *Let u and v be two columns defining a Young tableau, i.e., $u \succeq v$ Let w be a column such that $\mathrm{H}(w) < \mathrm{T}(u)$. Then $uvw \equiv uwv$.*

Proof. Observe that it suffices to prove it in the case where w is a single letter a. The product uv is a Young tableau. Inserting a according to Schensted's rule yields the Young tableau uav.   □

2.4   Cross-Section

We recall that a *cross-section* of an equivalence relation is a set consisting of exactly one element in each class. It is known that Young tableaux, as well as contretableaux, define a cross-section of the plactic monoid, cf. [12, Thm 5.2.5.].

The purpose of this work is to prove that the cross-section of the lexico-graphically minimal representatives, abbreviated as lexicographic cross-section, is regular. For example it is an easy exercise to verify that $1^*(21)^*2^*$ is the lexicographic cross-section over the two letter alphabet. A bit more tedious is to verify that over a three letter alphabet the lexicographic cross-section is $1^*(21)^*(2^* + (31)^*)(321)^*(32)^*3^*$. The case of four letters can still be computed by hand and is again regular which led us to conjecture that this is a general result, but computing the five letter case is rather tedious. On the contrary, the set of lexicographically maximal representatives is not regular from the two-letter plactic monoid on, since it is the set $\{2^n 1^m 2^p \mid 0 \leq n < m \text{ if } p \neq 0\}$.

Clearly the set of Young tableaux provides us with the regular cross-section which is the finite union of all subsets of the form

$$
v_1^* v_2^* \cdots v_p^* \quad \text{with } v_1 \succ v_2 \succ \ldots \succ v_p
$$

This is a special case of the rational cross-section with entropy equal to 0, see [2, Proposition 8]. Actually, this subset lies very low in the hierarchy of rational subsets since it is *local* in the sense that the current state of any input depends on the last $|\Sigma| + 1$ letters. Still we believe it is challenging to ask whether the lexicographic cross-section is also regular.

3   Minimal Representatives

3.1   A Combinatorial Property for Minimal Representatives

The following relation on the set of columns is needed for determining the lexicographically minimal representatives. We write $u \trianglelefteq v$ whenever the following conditions hold

- for all $i = 1, 2, \ldots, \min\{|u|, |v|\}$, the condition $u_i \leq v_i$ holds;
- furthermore, if $|u| < |v|$, then $u_{|u|} \leq v_{|u|+1}$ holds.

The relation $\trianglelefteq$ is not transitive. Indeed, we have $432 \trianglelefteq 43$ and $43 \trianglelefteq 6541$ but the relation $432 \trianglelefteq 6541$ does not hold. However the transitive closure of the relation is an ordering.

Proposition 9. *The transitive closure of $\trianglelefteq$ is antisymmetric.*

Proof. We prove the result by contradiction. Assume there exists an element x and a sequence

$$z_0 \trianglelefteq z_1 \trianglelefteq \ldots \trianglelefteq z_p \tag{1}$$

with $z_0 = z_p = x$, such that for some $0 < i < p$ we have $z_i \neq x$. Furthermore, we assume that p is minimal.

Let $0 < \mu \leq p$ be the greatest integer i such that $|z_j| \geq |z_i|$, for all $0 \leq j \leq p$. If $\mu = p$, then for all $y = z_i$ and for all k with $0 \leq k \leq |x|$, by the definition of $\trianglelefteq$, we have $x_k \leq y_k \leq x_k$ and, thus, x is a prefix of y. Since x has a unique occurrence in the sequence, because of the minimality of its length, x is in particular a proper prefix of z_1, which violates the condition $z_0 \trianglelefteq z_1$. So we must assume $\mu < p$. Set $|z_\mu| = m$. Then, for all $1 \leq i \leq m$, we have

$$x_i \leq z_{\mu,i} \leq z_{\mu+1,i} \leq x_i,$$

thus z_μ is a proper prefix of $z_{\mu+1}$, a contradiction of the relation $z_\mu \trianglelefteq z_{\mu+1}$. □

The characterization of the lexicographically minimal representatives is based on the following notion.

Definition 10. *A sequence of columns $u_1, u_2, \ldots, u_n$ is a P-sequence if it satisfies the condition*

$$u_i \trianglelefteq u_j, \text{ for all } 1 \leq i < j \leq n. \tag{2}$$

The following technical result is crucial in establishing Theorem 12. The proof is routine and consists in applying inductively Proposition 8.

Lemma 11. *Let $u_1, u_2, \ldots, u_n$ be a P-sequence such that $|u_1| \geq |u_i|$ for all $i = 2, \ldots, n$. Then there exists a sequence of columns $w_1, w_2, \ldots, w_n$ satisfying the following conditions*

(1) $|w_1| = |u_2|, |w_2| = |u_3|, \ldots, |w_{n-1}| = |u_n|, |w_n| = |u_1|$

(2) *for all $1 \leq k \leq p$ we have $w_{n,k} = \max\{u_{i,k} \mid i = 1, 2, \ldots, n\}$*

(3) *for all columns x such that $u_1 x$ is still a column we have*

$$u_1 x u_2 \cdots u_n \equiv w_1 w_2 \cdots w_n x$$ □

```
6 7 8 9 10        6 7 8 9 10        6 7 8 9 10         6 7 8 9 10        6 7 8 9 10
5 6 7   9         5 6 7   9         5 6 7   9          5 6   7 9         5 6   7 9
4  6  8      ⟶     4 6   8     →     4 6   8     ⟶      4   6 8     →      4   6 8
3     6           3   6             3   6              3 6               3 6
1                 1                 1                  1                 1
```

Fig. 1. An illustration of Lemma 11

Theorem 12. *Let $u = u_1 u_2 \cdots u_n$ be a factorization of maximal columns. Then, u is lexicographically minimal in its congruence class if and only if the sequence $u_1, u_2, \ldots, u_n$ is a P-sequence.*

Proof. That the condition is necessary in the case $n = 2$ is a consequence of the following.

Lemma 13. *Let u, v be two columns such that uv is not a column.*

(i) *if $v = v'w$ such that $|u| = |v'|$, $u \trianglelefteq v'$ and $H(w) < T(u)$, then $uv \equiv uwv'$.*

(ii) *if $u = u'xby$ and $v = v'a$ such that $|u'| = |v'|$, $u' \trianglelefteq v'$ and $b \le a < T(x)$, then $uv \equiv u'bv'xay$ and $u'bv'xay \lhd uv$.*

Proof. Indeed, the first assertion is a consequence of Proposition 8. Concerning the second assertion we have

$$u'xbyv'a \equiv u'v'xbya \equiv u'v'bxay \equiv u'bv'xay$$

The first and third equivalences are obtained as an application of Proposition 8. The second one is an application of the bump rule on the column xby.   □

We now return to the Theorem and prove the necessity of the condition. Let u be minimal in its class and assume by contradiction, that there exist i, j such that $u_i \not\trianglelefteq u_j$ with $i < j$ and $j - i$ minimal. By previous Lemma we have $j > i+1$.

We first observe that all columns u_k with $i < k < j$ have length less than $\min\{|u_i|, |u_j|\}$. Indeed, consider first the case where there exists a minimal position p such that $u_{i,p} > u_{j,p}$, implying in particular $p \le \min\{|u_i|, |u_j|\}$. Let u_k with $i < k < j$ be a column of length at least p. Then we have $u_{k,p} \ge u_{i,p} > u_{j,p}$, i.e., $u_k \not\trianglelefteq u_j$, contradicting the minimality of $j - i$. In the second case we have $u_{j,p+1} < u_{i,p}$, where $p = |u_i|$. Let u_k with $i < k < j$ be a column with length at least p. Since $u_k \trianglelefteq u_j$, we have either $u_{k,p+1} \le u_{j,p+1}$, thus $u_{k,p+1} < u_{i,p}$, or $u_{k,p} \le u_{j,p+1}$, thus $u_{k,p} < u_{i,p}$ whenever $|u_k| = p$, a contradiction in both cases with the minimality of $j - i$.

Now we shall consider the two causes for the condition $u_i \not\trianglelefteq u_j$ and we will show in both cases that it is possible to replace the factor $u_i u_{i+1} \cdots u_j$ by a factor of the same length but lexicographically smaller.

First we assume that there exists a minimal position p such that $u_{i,p} > u_{j,p}$. We set $u_i = u_i' x$, where u_i' is the prefix of u_i of length $p-1$. Applying Lemma 11 there exists a sequence of columns $w_1, w_2, \ldots, w_n$ such that

$$u_i' y u_{i+1} \cdots u_{j-1} \equiv w_i w_{i+1} \cdots w_{j-1} y \qquad (3)$$

holds for all columns y such that $u_i' y$ is still a column. We apply it first with $y = x$. Because of condition (2) of the lemma the words $w_{j-1}x$ and u_j fail to satisfy $w_{j-1}x \trianglelefteq u_j$, since p is the least integer such that $w_{j-1}x$ and u_j disagree on the letter on position p. Following Lemma 13 we have $w_{j-1}xu_j \equiv w_{j-1}zu_j'$, where $H(z) < H(x)$. Then we have

$$u_i' x u_{i+1} \cdots u_{j-1} u_j \equiv w_i w_{i+1} \cdots w_{j-1} x u_j$$
$$\equiv w_i w_{i+1} \cdots w_{j-1} z u_j' \equiv u_i' z u_{i+1} \cdots u_{j-1} u_j u_j'$$

Because $u_i' z <_{lex} u_i' x$ we obtain a lexicographically smaller representative.

The second possibility is when $|u_i| = p$, $u_{i,\ell} \le u_{j,\ell}$ for all $1 \le \ell \le p$ and $u_{j,p+1} < u_{i,p}$. We still have condition (3) with $u_i' = u_i$. Define $u_j = u_j' u_j''$, where u_j' is the prefix of u_j of length p, and observe that by Lemma 13 the condition $w_{j-1} \trianglelefteq u_j'$ holds. This, via Proposition 8 implies $w_{j-1} u_j \equiv w_{j-1} u_j'' u_j'$. Therefore

$$u_i u_{i+1} \cdots u_{j-1} u_j \equiv w_i w_{i+1} \cdots w_{j-1} u_j$$
$$\equiv w_i w_{i+1} \cdots w_{j-1} u_j'' u_j' \equiv u_i u_j'' u_{i+1} \cdots u_{j-1} u_j'$$

Again $u_i u_j'' <_{lex} u_i u_{i+1}$ and we obtain a lexicographically smaller representative.

In order to prove the sufficiency of the property, we need to define the *packing* operation which associates with every P-sequence a unique equivalent contretableau. We consider a P-sequence represented as a sequence of columns $u_1 \trianglelefteq u_2 \trianglelefteq \ldots \trianglelefteq u_n$. The reader is encouraged to have the example below in mind. The contretableau is obtained by pushing all elements of the columns to the right, along the same row, in order to leave no hole between consecutive elements, in other words to right justify all rows. Then the sufficiency will follow from the fact that every sequence can be packed into an equivalent contretableau and that this correspondence is injective.

$$
\begin{array}{ll}
4\,5\,5\,7\,8 & 4\,5\,5\,7\,8 \\
3 \quad\;\; 5\,6 & \to 3\,5\,6 \\
2 \quad\;\; 5 & \longrightarrow 2\,5 \\
1 & \longrightarrow 1
\end{array}
$$

Fig. 2. A P-sequence and its equivalent contretableau obtained by packing

We first prove that packing yields a contretableau. From the definition of the P-sequence, all rows are nondecreasing and their length is not increasing from top to bottom. Now, denote by $v_1, v_2, \ldots, v_n$ the n sequences obtained by packing. Fix one of them, say v_i, and consider two entries, $v_{i,\ell}$ and $v_{i,k}$ with $\ell < k$. Then there exists $\alpha \le \beta \le i$ such that

$$v_{i,\ell} = u_{\beta,\ell}, v_{i,k} = u_{\alpha,k}$$

Now we have $u_{\beta,\ell} \geq u_{\alpha,\ell} > u_{\alpha,k}$ and therefore $v_{i,\ell} > v_{i,k}$, which proves that the v_i's are columns and the resulting diagram a contretableau.

Given a contretableau, there is a unique way to "unpack" it. Indeed, we construct the rows of the P-sequence one at a time from top to bottom. Assume the r first rows are processed, and consider the $r + 1$-th row. Then the leftmost element of the contretableau, say a, can only go under the leftmost element of the P-sequence under construction, which is greater than a. Such an element exists because in the contretableau a is below a greater element. The second leftmost element of the contretableau, say b, goes below the leftmost element of the P-sequence greater than b, and so forth.

$$
\begin{array}{ccccccccc}
2\ 3\ 4^{\cdot}4 & & 2\ 3\ 4\ 4 & & 2\ 3\ 4\ 4 & & 2\ 3\ 4\ 4 & & 2\ 3\ 4\ 4 \\
1\ 2 & \equiv & 1\ \ 2 & \equiv & 1\ \ \ 2 & \equiv & 1\ \ 2 & \equiv & 1\ 2 \\
1 & & 1 & & 1 & & 1 & & 1
\end{array}
$$

Fig. 3. Packing a P-sequence into a congruent contretableau

It remains to prove that the P-sequence and the contretableau are congruent. However, this is obtained as a repetitive application of Proposition 8, and the proof is completed.   □

Corollary 14. *The minimal representative of a class has the same column length distribution as its Young tableau.*

Proof. Indeed, Young tableaux and contretableaux have the same column length distribution by Greene's invariant Theorem, cf. [9] (this theorem asserts that the sequence, over k, of the maximum sums of lengths of k disjoint columns, is an invariant of the congruence class). The above construction shows that the minimal representative has the same column distribution as its contretableau.   □

3.2   Complexity Issues

Here we consider the effective construction of the minimal representative as a consequence of Theorem 12.

A naive method to obtain the minimal representative in the class of a Young tableau would be to apply the inverse operation of inserting an element in a tableau. More precisely, start from the element in one of the corners of a Young tableau. In Example 6 there are 3 corners all labeled by 5. From one chosen corner on, process the columns from right to left. Substitute the element, say a, on the corner for the element of the column to its left which is the highest element less than or equal to a. If b is this element repeat the process with b instead of a, and next column. This results in pushing elements from column to column, and expelling an element to the left of the Young tableau. This element is a possible first letter of a word in the equivalence class.

$$
\begin{array}{ccc}
 & 5 & 5 \\
3\ 4\ 5 & 4\ 5 & 4\ 5\ 5 \\
(5)\ 1\ 2\ 4\ 5 & (3)\ 1\ 2\ 4\ 5 & (3)\ 1\ 2\ 4
\end{array}
$$

Fig. 4. Extracting a possible first letter from the Young tableau of Example 6

In Example 6, starting from the three corners, from top to bottom, yields 3 possible first letters, namely 5, 3 and 3. The first decomposition is ruled out. At this point we know for sure that the minimal representative starts with the letter 3. However, canceling this letter leads to two nonequivalent Young tableaux and it is not clear whether to compute the next letter from the second or from the third decomposition.

Proposition 15. *Given a word w of length n, there exists an $\mathcal{O}(n^{\frac{3}{2}})$ algorithm which finds the lexicographically minimal representative equivalent to w.*

Proof. Given a word w, construct its contretableau. If n is the length of w, its construction as sketched in paragraph 2.3 has complexity $\mathcal{O}(n^{\frac{3}{2}})$. The unpacking operation is similar to a merge of k arrays, where each array is a row of the contretableau. This costs again $\mathcal{O}(n)$ operations.   □

3.3   Application to the Cross-Section

Consequently we get the main result.

Theorem 16. *The set of alphabetically minimal words of the plactic congruence over an arbitrary finite alphabet is regular.*

Proof. An informal description of the automaton will do. The set of columns define a (suffix) code. Read the word and perform its decomposition into maximal columns. Record all different columns encountered in the order of appearance. If a next column, say u is not the last column recorded, or if it fails to satisfy the condition $v \trianglelefteq u$ with all columns v recorded, stop. Otherwise, put u in the record. If the word can be read off entirely, it is minimal.   □

4   Final Remarks

The purpose of this last section is twofold. The fact that the lexicographic cross-section is regular, is remarkable to the extent that most possible related constructions cannot be recognized by finite memory machines. The second remark concerns an interesting property of yet another classical relation and may be viewed as an invitation to investigate the field further.

4.1   Natural Binary Relations on the Plactic Monoid

None of the following natural binary relations is rational, in the sense that there is no two-tape finite automata recognizing them.

EQUIVALENCE $\{(x, y) \in \Sigma^* \times \Sigma^* \mid x \equiv y\}$

MINIMIZATION $\{(x, y) \in \Sigma^* \times \Sigma^* \mid x \equiv y$ and y is lexicographically minimal$\}$,

MULTIPLICATION for some $a \in \Sigma$,

$$\{(x, y) \in \Sigma^* \times \Sigma^* \mid xa \equiv y \text{ and } x, y \text{ are lexicographically minimal}\}$$

The proof of these claims is a simple exercise if one has in mind Eilenberg's result on length preserving relations that are recognized by two-tape automata, see [7, Thm IX. 6.3].

4.2   The Relation of Conjugacy

We recall that two elements x, y of a monoid are *conjugate*, if there exists an element z such that $xz = yz$ holds, written as $C(x, y)$, and that they are *transposed*, if there exist u, v such that $x = uv$ and $y = vu$, written as $T(x, y)$. It is a simple exercise to verify that the former relation is reflexive and transitive, while the latter is reflexive and symmetric. For free monoids, these relations coincide, see [14]. This is no longer the case for general monoids. The only claim that can be made in all generality is that the transitive closure of the relation of transposition is always included in the conjugacy relation. In the case of the trace monoids equality $C = T^k$ holds where k is the diameter of the graph of noncommutations, [6]. In the present case it is still true that the relation of conjugacy is the transitive closure of the relation of transposition, but we are able to bound the number of compositions by a parameter depending on the size of the alphabet. Consequently, the conjugacy relation is an equivalence relation.

Theorem 17. *The equality* $C = T^{2(k-1)}$ *holds where* $k = |\Sigma|$.

Proof. We prove a stronger result which implies the theorem. Let p be the number of different symbols of an element x of the plactic monoid. We show that $(x, y) \in T^p$ where y is the commutative image of x, i.e., $y = 1^{|x|_1} 2^{|x|_2} \cdots k^{|x|_k}$.

Indeed, let $1 \le a_1 < \cdots < a_p \le k$ be the ordered set of all the different letters occurring in x. Let $\lambda_1 \lambda_2 \cdots \lambda_r$ be the concatenation of the rows of its Young tableau from top to bottom. Clearly we may assume that $r > 1$ since otherwise we are done. All $|x|_1$ occurrences of a_1 are the first letters of row λ_r. Consider the word $w = \lambda_r \lambda_1 \lambda_2 \cdots \lambda_{r-1}$ which is a representative of a conjugate. By Schensted's rules, all $|x|_1$ occurrences of a_1 are followed by all $|x|_2$ occurrences of a_2, and these are the first $|x|_1 + |x|_2$ letters of the bottom row of the Young tableau associated with w. It suffices to carry on this process of putting the last row to the left of the remaining rows at most $p - 1$ times in order to get the result.   □

References

1. Anisimov, A.V., Knuth, D.E.: Inhomogeneous sorting. International Journal of Computer and Information Sciences 8(4), 255–260 (1979)
2. Arnold, A., Kanta, M., Krob, D.: Recognizable subsets of the two letter plactic monoid. Information Processing Letters 64, 53–59 (1997)
3. Cartier, P., Foata, D.: Problèmes combinatoires de commutation et réarrangements. Lecture Notes in Mathematics, vol. 85 (1969)
4. Choffrut, C., Mercaş, R.: Contextual partial commutations. Discrete Mathematics and Theoretical Computer Science 12(4), 59–72 (2010)
5. Diekert, V., Rozenberg, G.: The Book of Traces. World Scientific Publishing Co., Singapore (1995)
6. Duboc, C.: On some equations in free partially commutative monoids. Theoretical Computer Science 46(2-3), 159–174 (1986)
7. Eilenberg, S.: Automata, Languages and Machines, vol. A. Academic Press (1974)
8. Epstein, D.B.A., Cannon, J.W., Holt, D.F., Levy, S.V.F., Paterson, M.S., Thurston, W.P.: Word processing in groups. Jones and Bartlett (1992)
9. Greene, C.: An extension of Schensted's Theorem. Advances in Mathematics 14(2), 254–265 (1974)
10. Knuth, D.E.: The art of computer programming, vol. 3. Addison Wesley (1973)
11. Lallement, G.: Semigroups and Combinatorial Applications. John Wiley & Sons (1979)
12. Lascoux, A., Leclerc, B., Thibon, J.-Y.: The plactic monoid. In: Lothaire, M. (ed.) Algebraic Combinatorics on Words, pp. 144–173. Cambridge University Press (2002)
13. Lascoux, A., Schützenberger, M.-P.: Le monoïde plaxique. In: de Luca, A. (ed.) Non-commutative Structures in Algebra and Geometric Combinatorics, vol. 109, pp. 129–156. C.N.R. (1981)
14. Lentin, A., Schützenberger, M.-P.: A combinatorial problem in the theory of free monoids. In: Bose, R.C., Bowlings, T.E. (eds.) Combinatorial Mathematics, pp. 112–144. North Carolina Press, Chapel Hill (1967)

Suffix Conjugates for a Class of Morphic Subshifts
(Extended Abstract)

James D. Currie, Narad Rampersad, and Kalle Saari

Department of Mathematics and Statistics
University of Winnipeg
515 Portage Avenue
Winnipeg, MB R3B 2E9
Canada
j.currie@uwinnipeg.ca, {narad.rampersad,kasaar2}@gmail.com

Abstract. Let A be a finite alphabet and $f\colon A^* \to A^*$ a morphism with an iterative fixed point $f^\omega(\alpha)$, where $\alpha \in A$. Consider the subshift $(\mathcal{X}, T)$, where $\mathcal{X}$ is the shift orbit closure of $f^\omega(\alpha)$ and $T\colon \mathcal{X} \to \mathcal{X}$ is the shift operation. Let S be a finite alphabet that is in bijective correspondence via a mapping c with the set of nonempty suffixes of the images $f(a)$ for $a \in A$. Let $\mathcal{S} \subset S^{\mathbb{N}}$ be the set of infinite words $\mathbf{s} = (s_n)_{n \geq 0}$ such that $\pi(\mathbf{s}) := c(s_0)f\big(c(s_1)\big)f^2\big(c(s_2)\big)\cdots \in \mathcal{X}$. We show that if f is primitive and $f(A)$ is a suffix code, then there exists a mapping $H\colon \mathcal{S} \to \mathcal{S}$ such that $(\mathcal{S}, H)$ is a topological dynamical system and $\pi\colon (\mathcal{S}, H) \to (\mathcal{X}, T)$ is a conjugacy. We call $(\mathcal{S}, H)$ the *suffix conjugate* of $(\mathcal{X}, T)$. Furthermore, in the special case when f is the Fibonacci or the Thue-Morse morphism, we show that $(\mathcal{S}, T)$ is a sofic shift, that is, the language of $\mathcal{S}$ is regular.

1 Introduction

Let A be a finite alphabet and $f\colon A^* \to A^*$ a morphism with an iterative fixed point $f^\omega(\alpha) = \lim_{n\to\infty} f^n(\alpha)$. Consider the shift orbit closure $\mathcal{X}$ generated by $f^\omega(\alpha)$. If $\mathbf{x} \in \mathcal{X}$, then there exist a letter $a \in A$ and an infinite word $\mathbf{y} \in \mathcal{X}$ such that $\mathbf{x} = sf(\mathbf{y})$, where s is a nonempty suffix of $f(a)$ [4, Lemma 6]. This formula has been observed several times in different contexts, see [6] and the references therein. Since $\mathbf{y} \in \mathcal{X}$, this process can be iterated to generate an expansion

$$\mathbf{x} = s_0 f(s_1) f^2(s_2) \cdots f^n(s_n) \cdots, \tag{1}$$

where each s_n is a nonempty suffix of an image of some letter in A. In general, however, not every sequence $(s_n)_{n\geq 0}$ of suffixes gives rise to an infinite word in $\mathcal{X}$ by means of this kind of expansion. Therefore, in this paper we introduce the set $\mathcal{S}$ that consists of those $(s_n)_{n\geq 0}$ whose expansion (1) is in $\mathcal{X}$. Our goal is then to understand the structure of $\mathcal{S}$. By endowing $\mathcal{S}$ with the usual metric on infinite words, $\mathcal{S}$ becomes a metric space. Furthermore, $\mathcal{S}$ can be associated with a mapping $G\colon \mathcal{S} \to \mathcal{S}$ (see below) giving rise to a topological dynamical system $(\mathcal{S}, G)$ that is an extension of $(\mathcal{X}, f)$; see the discussion around Eq. (4)

J. Karhumäki, A. Lepistö, and L. Zamboni (Eds.): WORDS 2013, LNCS 8079, pp. 95–106, 2013.

However, imposing some further restrictions on f, we obtain a much stronger result: If f is a circular morphism such that $|f^n(a)| \to \infty$ for all $a \in A$ and $f(A)$ is a suffix code, then there exists a mapping $H \colon S \to S$ such that (S, H) and (X, T), where T is the usual shift operation, are conjugates (Theorem 1). We call (S, H) the *suffix conjugate* of (X, T). Since primitive morphisms are circular (i.e., recognizable) by Mossé's theorem [13], primitivity of f together with the suffix code condition suffice for the existence of the suffix conjugate. In particular, both the Fibonacci morphism $\varphi \colon 0 \mapsto 01,\ 1 \mapsto 0$ and the Thue-Morse morphism $\mu \colon 0 \mapsto 01,\ 1 \mapsto 10$ satisfy these conditions, and so the corresponding Fibonacci subshift (X_φ, T) and the Thue-Morse subshift (X_μ, T) have suffix conjugates. In this paper we characterize the language of both subshifts and show that they are regular.

An encoding scheme for X related to ours was considered by Holton and Zamboni [6] and Canterini and Siegel [3], who studied bi-infinite primitive morphic subshifts and essentially used prefixes of images of letters where we use suffixes. Despite of this seemingly insignificant difference, though, we are not aware of any mechanism that would allow transferring results from one encoding scheme to another. See also the work by Shallit [14], who constructed a finite automaton that provides an encoding for the set of infinite overlap-free words.

2   Preliminaries and Generalities

In this paper we will follow the standard notation and terminology of combinatorics on words [10,1] and symbolic dynamics [9,8].

Let A be a finite alphabet and $f \colon A^* \to A^*$ a morphism with an iterative fixed point $f^\omega(\alpha) = \lim_{n \to \infty} f^n(\alpha)$, where $\alpha \in A$. Let X be the shift orbit closure generated by $f^\omega(\alpha)$. Let S' be the set of nonempty suffixes of images of letters under f. Denote $S = \{0, 1, \ldots, |S'| - 1\}$ and let $c \colon S \to S'$ be a bijection. We consider S as a finite alphabet.

If $s = s_0 s_1 \cdots s_n$ with $s_i \in S$, then we denote by $\pi(s)$ the word

$$\pi(s) = c(s_0) f(c(s_1)) f^2(c(s_2)) \cdots f^n(c(s_n)) \in A^*.$$

Then π extends to a mapping $\pi \colon S^{\mathbb{N}} \to A^{\mathbb{N}}$ in a natural way, and so we may define

$$S = \{ \mathbf{s} \in S^{\mathbb{N}} \mid \pi(\mathbf{s}) \in X \}.$$

Our goal in this section is to find sufficient conditions on f so that S can be endowed with dynamics that yields a conjugate to (X, T) via the mapping π. Examples 1 and 2 below show that this task is not trivial. Such sufficient conditions are laid out in Definition 1.

If $\mathbf{x} \in X$ and $\mathbf{s} \in S$ such that $\pi(\mathbf{s}) = \mathbf{x}$, we say that $\mathbf{x}$ is an *expansion* of $\mathbf{s}$.

Lemma 1 (Currie, Rampersad, and Saari [4]). *For every* $\mathbf{x} \in X$, *there exist* $a \in A$, *a non-empty suffix* s *of* $f(a)$, *and an infinite word* $\mathbf{y} \in X$ *such that* $\mathbf{x} = sf(\mathbf{y})$ *and* $a\mathbf{y} \in X$. *Therefore the mapping* $\pi \colon S \to X$ *is surjective.*

Both $A^{\mathbb{N}}$ and $S^{\mathbb{N}}$ are endowed with the usual metric

$$d\big((x_n)_{n\geq 0},(y_n)_{n\geq 0}\big) = \frac{1}{2^n}, \quad \text{where} \quad n = \inf\{\, n \mid x_n \neq y_n \,\},$$

The following lemma is obvious.

Lemma 2. *The mapping* $\pi\colon \mathcal{S} \to \mathcal{X}$ *is continuous.*

We denote the usual shift operation $(x_n)_{n\geq 0} \mapsto (x_{n+1})_{n\geq 0}$ in both spaces $A^{\mathbb{N}}$ and $S^{\mathbb{N}}$ by T. We have $T(\mathcal{X}) \subset \mathcal{X}$ and $f(\mathcal{X}) \subset \mathcal{X}$ by the construction of $\mathcal{X}$, and both T and f are clearly continuous on $\mathcal{X}$, so we have the topological dynamical systems $(\mathcal{X},T)$ and $(\mathcal{X},f)$. Note, however, that in general $T(\mathcal{S})$ is not necessarily a subset of $\mathcal{S}$, as the following example shows.

Example 1. Let $f\colon \{\alpha,a,b\}^* \to \{\alpha,a,b\}^*$ be the morphism $\alpha \mapsto \alpha ab$, $a \mapsto a$, and $b \mapsto ab$. Then

$$f^\omega(\alpha) = \alpha f(b)f^2(b)f^3(b)\cdots \quad \text{and} \quad bf(b)f^2(b)f^3(b)\cdots = babaabaaab\cdots.$$

Since the latter sequence is not in the shift orbit closure $\mathcal{X}$ generated by $f^\omega(\alpha)$, this shows that $\mathcal{S}$ is not closed under T for this particular morphism.

If f is the morphism $0 \mapsto 01$, $1 \mapsto 0$, then f is called the *Fibonacci morphism* and we write $f = \varphi$. The unique fixed point of φ is denoted by **f** and it is called the *Fibonacci word*. The shift orbit closure it generates is denoted by $\mathcal{X}_\varphi$ and pair $(\mathcal{X}_\varphi, T)$ is called the *Fibonacci subshift*.

Similarly, if f is $0 \mapsto 01$, $1 \mapsto 10$, then f is the *Thue-Morse morphism* and we write $f = \mu$. The fixed point $\mu^\omega(0)$ of μ is denoted by **t** and it is called the *Thue-Morse word*. The shift orbit closure generated by **t** is denoted by $\mathcal{X}_\mu$, and the pair $(\mathcal{X}_\mu, T)$ is called the *Thue-Morse subshift*.

Example 2. Let f be the morphism $0 \mapsto 010$, $1 \mapsto 10$. The two fixed points of f generate the Fibonacci subshift. The set of suffixes of $f(0)$ and $f(1)$ is $S' = \{0, 10, 010\}$, and we define a bijection $c\colon \{0,1,2\} \to S'$ by $c(0) = 0$, $c(1) = 10$, and $c(2) = 010$. Then $\pi(01) = \pi(20) = 010010$, and therefore $\pi(01^\omega) = \pi(201^\omega)$. This word equals the Fibonacci word **f** as can be seen by observing that

$$\mathbf{f} = 010\varphi^2(10)\varphi^4(10)\varphi^6(10)\cdots$$

and $010f^n(a) = \varphi^{2n}(a)010$ for all $n \geq 0$ and $a \in \{0,1\}$. This shows that it is possible for two distinct words in $\mathcal{S}$ to have the same expansions.

The following lemma is a straightforward consequence of the definition of π.

Lemma 3. *Let* $\mathbf{s} = s_0 s_1 s_2 \cdots$, *where* $s_i \in S$. *Then*

$$f\big(\pi \circ T(\mathbf{s})\big) = T^{|c(s_0)|}\pi(\mathbf{s}).$$

and

$$\pi(\mathbf{s}) = \pi(s_0 s_1 \cdots s_{n-1})f^n\big(\pi(T^n \mathbf{s})\big). \tag{2}$$

For finite words $x, y \in S^*$, *the above reads* $\pi(xy) = \pi(x)f^{|x|}\big(\pi(y)\big)$.

Note that if $s \in S$ such that $c(s) \in S'$ is a letter, then $f(c(s)) \in S'$. As this connection will be frequently referred to, we define a morphism

$$\lambda \colon S_1^* \to S^* \qquad \text{with} \qquad \lambda(s) = c^{-1}(f(c(s))), \tag{3}$$

where $S_1 \subset S$ consists of those $s \in S$ for which $|c(s)| = 1$. Then in particular, $c(\lambda(s)) = f(c(s))$.

Lemma 4. *Let* $\mathbf{s} = s_0 s_1 \cdots \in \mathcal{S}$ *with* $s_i \in S$, *and write* $\mathbf{x} = \pi(\mathbf{s}) \in \mathcal{X}$. *Let* $r \geq 0$ *be the smallest integer, if it exists, such that* $|c(s_r)| \geq 2$ *and write* $c(s_r) = au$, *where* $a \in A$ *and* $u \in A^+$. *Then* $f(\mathbf{x}) = \pi(\mathbf{t})$, *where* $\mathbf{t} = t_0 t_1 \cdots \in \mathcal{S}$ *satisfies*

- $t_i = \lambda(s_i)$ *for* $i = 0, 1, \ldots, r-1$,
- $t_r = c^{-1}(f(a))$,
- $t_{r+1} = c^{-1}(u)$, *and*
- $t_i = s_{i-1}$ *for* $i \geq r+2$.

If each of $c(s_i)$ *is a letter, then* $f(\mathbf{x}) = \pi(\mathbf{t})$, *where*

$$\mathbf{t} = \lambda(s_0)\lambda(s_1) \cdots \lambda(s_n) \cdots .$$

Proof. Suppose r exists. The identity $\mathbf{x} = \pi(\mathbf{s})$ says that

$$\mathbf{x} = c(s_0) f(c(s_1)) \cdots f^{r-1}(c(s_{r-1})) f^r(c(s_r)) f^{r+1}(c(s_{r+1})) \cdots$$

Therefore, by denoting $f(c(s_i)) = \hat{s}_i \in S'$ for $i = 0, 1, \ldots, r-1$, we see that

$$\begin{aligned}
f(\mathbf{x}) &= f(c(s_0)) f^2(c(s_1)) \cdots f^r(c(s_{r-1})) f^{r+1}(c(s_r)) f^{r+2}(c(s_{r+1})) \cdots \\
&= \hat{s}_0 f(\hat{s}_1) \cdots f^{r-1}(\hat{s}_{r-1}) f^{r+1}(au) f^{r+2}(c(s_{r+1})) \cdots \\
&= \hat{s}_0 f(\hat{s}_1) \cdots f^{r-1}(\hat{s}_{r-1}) f^r(f(a)) f^{r+1}(u) f^{r+2}(c(s_{r+1})) \cdots \\
&= c(t_0) f(c(t_1)) f^2(c(t_2)) \cdots ,
\end{aligned}$$

where the t_i's are as in the statement of the lemma. The case when r does not exist is a special case of the above.

Let $\mathbf{s} \in \mathcal{S}$ and $\mathbf{t} \in \mathcal{S}$ be defined as in the previous lemma. This defines a mapping $G \colon \mathcal{S} \to \mathcal{S}$ for which $G(\mathbf{s}) = \mathbf{t}$, which is obviously continuous. Thus we have a topological dynamical system $(\mathcal{S}, G)$. Furthermore, by the definition of G, we have

$$f \circ \pi = \pi \circ G. \tag{4}$$

Therefore $\pi \colon (\mathcal{S}, G) \to (\mathcal{X}, f)$ is a factor map because π is surjective by Lemma 1 and continuous by Lemma 2. We can get a more concise definition for G if we extend the domain of λ defined in (3) to S as follows. If $s \in S \setminus S_1$, then $f(c(s)) = au$ with $a \in A$ and $u \in A^+$, and we define

$$\lambda(s) = c^{-1}(f(a)) c^{-1}(u). \tag{5}$$

Then we have, for all $\mathbf{s} \in \mathcal{S}$,

$$G(\mathbf{s}) = \begin{cases} \lambda(ps)\mathbf{t} & \text{if } \mathbf{s} = pst \text{ with } p \in S_1^* \text{ and } s \in S \setminus S_1 \\ \lambda(\mathbf{s}) & \text{if } \mathbf{s} \in S_1^{\mathbb{N}}. \end{cases} \tag{6}$$

We got this far without imposing any restrictions on f, but now we have to introduce some further concepts.

If $\mathcal{Y}$ is a shift orbit closure of some infinite word $\mathbf{x}$, then the set of finite factors of $\mathbf{x}$ is called the *language* of $\mathcal{Y}$ or $\mathbf{x}$ and denoted by $\mathcal{L}(\mathcal{Y})$ or by $\mathcal{L}(\mathbf{x})$.

If x is a finite word and y a finite or infinite word and x is a factor of y, we will express this by writing $x \subset y$. This handy notation has been used before at least in [5].

A key property we would like our morphism f to have is *circularity*, which has various formulations and is also called *recognizability*. We use the formulation of Cassaigne [2] and Klouda [7]; see also [11,8]. The morphism f whose fixed point generates the shift orbit closure $\mathcal{X}$ is called *circular on* $\mathcal{L}(\mathcal{X})$ if f is injective on $\mathcal{L}(\mathcal{X})$ and there exists a *synchronization delay* $\ell \geq 1$ such that if $w \in \mathcal{L}(\mathcal{X})$ and $|w| \geq \ell$, then it has a *synchronizing point* (w_1, w_2) satisfying the following two conditions: First, $w = w_1 w_2$. Second,

$$\forall v_1, v_2 \in A^* \left[v_1 w v_2 \in f(\mathcal{L}(\mathcal{X})) \implies v_1 w_1 \in f(\mathcal{L}(\mathcal{X})) \quad \text{and} \quad w_2 v_2 \in f(\mathcal{L}(\mathcal{X})) \right].$$

A well-known result due to Mossé [13] (see also [8]) says that a primitive morphism with an aperiodic fixed point is circular (or *recognizable*).

Definition 1. *We write $f \in \mathcal{N}$ to indicate that $f: A^* \to A^*$ with an iterative fixed point $f^\omega(\alpha)$ has the following properties.*

(i) f is circular on the language of $f^\omega(\alpha)$;
(ii) the set $f(A)$ is a suffix code; i.e., no image of a letter is a suffix of another;
(iii) each letter $a \in A$ is growing; i.e., $|f^n(a)| \to \infty$ as $n \to \infty$.

In particular, if f is primitive and $f^\omega(\alpha)$ aperiodic, then f is circular by Mossé's theorem, and if in addition $f(A)$ is a suffix code, then $f \in \mathcal{N}$. Therefore both the Fibonacci morphism φ and the Thue-Morse morphism μ are in $\mathcal{N}$.

In Example 1 we saw that, in general, $\mathcal{S}$ is not necessarily closed under the shift map T for general morphism f. The next lemma shows, however, that if $f \in \mathcal{N}$, this problem does not arise.

Lemma 5. *If $f \in \mathcal{N}$, then $T(\mathcal{S}) \subseteq \mathcal{S}$. Thus $(\mathcal{S}, T)$ is a subshift.*

Proof. Let $\mathbf{s} = s_0 s_1 \cdots \in \mathcal{S}$; then $\pi(\mathbf{s}) \in \mathcal{X}$. Equation (2) says that $\pi(\mathbf{s}) = c(s_0) f(\pi(T\mathbf{s}))$, and so $f(\pi(T\mathbf{s})) \in \mathcal{X}$. Suppose that $\pi(T\mathbf{s}) \notin \mathcal{X}$.

Since $f \in \mathcal{N}$, it is circular. Let $\ell \geq 1$ be a synchronization delay for f. Note that $f^{n-1}(s_n)$ occurs both in $\pi(T\mathbf{s})$ and in $f^\omega(\alpha)$ for every $n \geq 1$. Since also $|f^{n-1}(s_n)| \to \infty$ as $n \to \infty$ because $f \in \mathcal{N}$, it follows that there are arbitrarily long words in $\mathcal{L}(\mathcal{X})$ that occur in infinitely many positions in $\pi(T\mathbf{s})$. Therefore there exists a word $zy \subset \pi(T\mathbf{s})$ such that z is not in $\mathcal{L}(\mathcal{X})$, $y \in \mathcal{L}(\mathcal{X})$, and $|y| \geq \ell$.

Next, consider the word $f(zy) \subset f(\pi(T\mathbf{s}))$. Since $f(y) \in \mathcal{L}(\mathcal{X})$ and $|f(y)| \geq \ell$, the word $f(y)$ has a synchronizing point (w_1, w_2). In particular, since $y \in \mathcal{L}(\mathcal{X})$, there exists y_1, y_2 for which $y = y_1 y_2$, $f(y_1) = w_1$, and $f(y_2) = w_2$. On the other hand, $f(zy) \in \mathcal{L}(\mathcal{X})$ implies that we can write $f^\omega(\alpha) = put\mathbf{x}$ such that $f(zy) \subset f(ut)$ and $f(y) \subset f(t)$. Thus there exists t_1, t_2 such that $t = t_1 t_2$, the word w_1 is a suffix of $f(t_1)$, and w_2 is a prefix of $f(t_2)$. Thus $f(y_1)$ is a suffix of $f(t_1)$. Since $f(A)$ is a suffix code and f is injective, it follows that y_1 is a suffix of t_1, and furthermore that zy_1 is a suffix of ut_1. But then $z \in \mathcal{L}(\mathcal{X})$ contradicting the choice of z. Therefore $\pi(T\mathbf{s}) \in \mathcal{X}$ and so $T\mathbf{s} \in \mathcal{S}$.

Lemma 6. *If $f \in \mathcal{N}$, then the mapping $\pi \colon \mathcal{S} \to \mathcal{X}$ is injective.*

Proof. For every $u, v \in A^*$ and $\mathbf{x}, \mathbf{y} \in \mathcal{X}$, we have that $uf(\mathbf{x}) = vf(\mathbf{y})$ implies $u = v$ and $\mathbf{x} = \mathbf{y}$. This follows from the circularity and suffix code property of f. (See also the proof of Lemma 5.) Therefore if $\mathbf{s}, \mathbf{s}' \in \mathcal{S}$ and $\pi(\mathbf{s}) = \pi(\mathbf{s}')$, then Lemma 3 gives

$$c(s_0) f\big(\pi(T\mathbf{s})\big) = c(s_0') f\big(\pi(T\mathbf{s}')\big),$$

so that $c(s_0) = c(s_0')$ and $\pi(T\mathbf{s}) = \pi(T\mathbf{s}')$. Thus $s_0 = s_0'$, and since $T\mathbf{s}, T\mathbf{s}' \in \mathcal{S}$ by Lemma 5, we can repeat the argument obtaining $s_1 = s_1'$, $s_2 = s_2'$, ... Therefore $\mathbf{s} = \mathbf{s}'$.

Now we are ready to define the desired dynamics on $\mathcal{S}$.

Theorem 1. *Suppose that $f \in \mathcal{N}$. Let $H \colon \mathcal{S} \to \mathcal{S}$ be the mapping given by $H = T \circ G$. Then $\pi \circ H = T \circ \pi$ and so $\pi \colon (\mathcal{S}, H) \to (\mathcal{X}, T)$ is a conjugacy.*

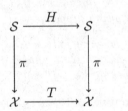

Proof. Observe first that $H(\mathcal{S}) \subset \mathcal{S}$ by Lemma 5, so the definition of H is sound. The mapping π is surjective by Lemma 1 and injective by Lemma 6, so it is a bijection. Furthermore π is continuous by Lemma 2. Finally, let us verify $\pi \circ H = T \circ \pi$. Let $\mathbf{s} = s_0 s_1 \cdots \in \mathcal{S}$ with $s_i \in \mathcal{S}$. If $|c(s_0)| \geq 2$, then we leave it to the reader to check that, by denoting $c(s_0) = au$ with $a \in A$, we have

$$\pi \circ H(\mathbf{s}) = \pi \circ T \circ G(\mathbf{s}) = uf\big(c(s_1)\big) f^2\big(c(s_2)\big) \cdots = T \circ \pi(\mathbf{s}).$$

If $|c(s_0)| = 1$, then it is readily seen that $T \circ G(\mathbf{s}) = G \circ T(\mathbf{s})$. Using this, Equation (4), and Lemma 3 in this order gives

$$\pi \circ H(\mathbf{s}) = \pi \circ T \circ G(\mathbf{s}) = \pi \circ G \circ T(\mathbf{s}) = f \circ \pi \circ T(\mathbf{s}) = T^{|c_0|} \circ \pi(\mathbf{s}) = T \circ \pi(\mathbf{s}),$$

and the proof is complete.

The rest of this section is devoted to developing a few results for understanding the language of S. They will be needed in the next sections that deal with the suffix conjugates of the Fibonacci and the Thue-Morse subshifts.

If u is a finite nonempty word, we denote by $u^\flat$ and $^\triangleleft u$ the words obtained from u by deleting its last and first letter, respectively.

If a finite word u is not in $\mathcal{L}(\mathcal{X})$, then u is called a *forbidden word* of $\mathcal{X}$. If both $^\triangleleft u$ and $u^\flat$ are in $\mathcal{L}(\mathcal{X})$, then u is a *minimal forbidden word* of $\mathcal{X}$. There is a connection between the minimal forbidden words and the so-called bispecial factors of an infinite word. See a precise formulation of this in [12] and examples in Sections 3 and 4.

We say that a word $u \in S^*$ is a *cover* of a word $v \in A^*$ if $v \subset \pi(u)$. Furthermore, we say that the cover u is *minimal* if $v \not\subset \pi(u^\flat)$ and $v \not\subset f(\pi(^\triangleleft u))$. The latter expression comes from the identity $\pi(u) = c(u_0)f(\pi(^\triangleleft u))$, where u_0 is the first letter of u, given by Lemma 3.

Let $\mathcal{C}$ be the set of minimal covers of the minimal forbidden factors of $\mathcal{X}$.

Lemma 7. *Suppose $f \in \mathcal{N}$. Let $\mathbf{s} \in S^{\mathbb{N}}$. Then $\mathbf{s} \notin S$ if and only if $\mathbf{s}$ has a factor in $\mathcal{C}$.*

Proof. Suppose that $\mathbf{s}$ has a factor in $\mathcal{C}$, so that $\mathbf{s} = pt\mathbf{s}'$ with $t \in \mathcal{C}$. If $\mathbf{s} \in S$, then $T^{|p|}\mathbf{s} = t\mathbf{s}' \in S$ by Lemma 5. But $\pi(t\mathbf{s}')$ has prefix $\pi(t)$, in which a forbidden word occurs by the definition of $\mathcal{C}$, a contradiction.

Conversely, suppose that $\mathbf{s} \notin S$. Then $\pi(\mathbf{s}) \notin \mathcal{X}$, so there exists a minimal forbidden word v_0 of $\mathcal{X}$ occurring in $\pi(\mathbf{s})$. Let u_0 be the shortest prefix of $\mathbf{s}$ such that $v_0 \subset \pi(u_0)$. Then either u_0 is a minimal cover of v_0 or $v_0 \subset f(\pi(^\triangleleft u_0))$. In the former case we are done, so suppose the latter case holds. Then $v_0 \subset f(\pi(T\mathbf{s}))$ and so $\pi(T\mathbf{s})$ has a factor v_1 such that $v_0 \subset f(v_1)$ and $|v_1| \leq |v_0|$. Since $f(\mathcal{L}) \subset \mathcal{L}$, it follows that v_1 is a forbidden word of $\mathcal{X}$; by taking a factor of v_1 if necessary, we may assume v_1 is also minimal. Let u_1 be the shortest prefix of $T\mathbf{s}$ such that $v_1 \subset \pi(u_1)$. Then either u_1 is a minimal cover of v_1 or $v_1 \subset f(\pi(^\triangleleft u_1))$. In the former case $u_1 \in \mathcal{C}$ and so $\mathbf{s}$ has a factor u_1 in $\mathcal{C}$. In the latter case $v_1 \subset f(\pi(T^2\mathbf{s}))$, and we continue the process. This generates a sequence $v_0, v_1, \ldots$ of minimal forbidden words of $\mathcal{X}$ such that $v_n \subset f(\pi(T^{n+1}\mathbf{s}))$, $v_{n+1} \subset f(v_n)$, and $|v_{n+1}| \leq |v_n|$. Each letter $a \in A$ is growing because $f \in \mathcal{N}$, and therefore the words v_n are pairwise distinct. Thus the length restriction on the v_n's implies that the sequence $v_0, v_1, \ldots$ is finite with a last element, say, v_k. The fact that there is no element v_{k+1} means that $T^{k+1}\mathbf{s}$ has a prefix u_k that is a minimal cover of v_k. Since $u_k \in \mathcal{C}$ then occurs also in $\mathbf{s}$, we are done.

Theorem 2. *Suppose that $f \in \mathcal{N}$ and that the set $\mathcal{C}$ of minimal covers of minimal forbidden words is a regular language. Then the language of S is regular. In particular, (S, T) is a sofic subshift.*

Proof. Since $\mathcal{C}$ is regular, so is the complement $S^* \setminus S^*\mathcal{C}S^*$, which we denote by L_0. Let M_0 be the minimal DFA accepting L_0. Modify M_0 by removing the states from which there are no arbitrarily long directed walks to accepting states.

Remove also the corresponding edges and denote the obtained NFA by M. We claim that the language $\mathcal{L}(\mathcal{S})$ of $\mathcal{S}$ is the language $L(M)$ recognized by M.

If $w \in \mathcal{L}(\mathcal{S})$, then w is in $S^* \setminus S^*CS^*$ by Lemma 7, so that it is accepted by M_0. Furthermore, since w has arbitrarily long extensions to the right that are also in $\mathcal{L}(\mathcal{S})$, each accepted by M_0 of course, it follows that w is accepted by M. Conversely, by the construction of M, if $w \in L(M)$, then there exists an infinite walk on the graph of M whose label contains w. The label of this infinite path is in $\mathcal{S}$.

3 The Suffix Conjugate of the Fibonacci Subshift

Recall the Fibonacci morphism φ for which $0 \mapsto 01$ and $1 \mapsto 0$, the Fibonacci word $\mathbf{f} = \varphi^\omega(0)$, and the Fibonacci subshift $(\mathcal{X}_\varphi, T)$. The suffix conjugate $(\mathcal{S}_\varphi, H_\varphi)$ of the Fibonacci subshift is guaranteed to exist by Theorem 1. The goal of this section is to give a characterization for $\mathcal{S}_\varphi$ and H_φ, and it will be achieved in Theorem 3.

The set of suffixes of φ is $S' = \{0, 1, 01\}$, and we define a bijection c between $S = \{0, 1, 2\}$ and S' as $c(0) = 0$, $c(1) = 1$, and $c(2) = 01$. In this case we have $\mathcal{S}_\varphi \subset \{0, 1, 2\}^\mathbb{N}$.

We will now continue by finding a characterization for the set $\mathcal{C}_\varphi$ of minimal covers of minimal forbidden words of the Fibonacci subshift.

Denote $f_n = \varphi^{n-1}(0)$ for all $n \geq 1$, so that in particular $f_1 = 0$ and $f_2 = 01$. For $n \geq 2$, we let p_n be the word defined by the relation $f_n = p_n ab$, where $ab \in \{01, 10\}$. Then $p_2 = \varepsilon$ and $p_3 = 0$. The words p_n are known as the *bispecial factors* of the Fibonacci word, and they possess the following well-known and easily established properties:

– For all $n \geq 2$, we have

$$f_n f_{n-1} = p_{n+1} ab \qquad \text{and} \qquad f_{n-1} f_n = p_{n+1} ba, \qquad (7)$$

where $ab = 10$ for even n and $ab = 01$ for odd n.
– For all $n \geq 2$, we have $\varphi(p_n)0 = p_{n+1}$.

The minimal forbidden words of the Fibonacci word $\mathbf{f}$ can be expressed in terms of the bispecial factors p_n as follows [12]. For every $n \geq 2$, write

$$d_n = \begin{cases} 1p_n1 & \text{for } n \text{ even,} \\ 0p_n0 & \text{for } n \text{ odd.} \end{cases}$$

Then a word is a minimal forbidden word of $\mathbf{f}$ if and only if it equals d_n for some $n \geq 2$. The first few d_n's are 11, 000, and 10101.

Lemma 8. *We have $d_3 = \pi(01)0$ and $d_4 = \pi(10)01$. For all $n \geq 0$, we have*

$$\pi(021^{2n}2) = d_{2n+5}1 \qquad \text{and} \qquad \pi(121^{2n+1}2) = d_{2n+6}0$$

Lemma 9. *The forbidden word $d_2 = 11$ does not have covers. The minimal covers of d_3 are the words in $01(0 + 1 + 2)$. The minimal covers of d_4 are the words in $(1 + 2)0(0 + 1 + 2)$. For other forbidden words, we have the following. Let $n \geq 0$.*

(i) The minimal covers of d_{2n+5} are

$$021^{2n}(2 + 00 + 01 + 02).\tag{8}$$

(ii) The minimal covers of d_{2n+6} are

$$(1 + 2)21^{2n+1}(2 + 00 + 01 + 02).$$

Theorem 3. *The language $\mathcal{L}(\mathcal{S}_\varphi)$ of the suffix conjugate $(\mathcal{S}_\varphi, H_\varphi)$ of the Fibonacci subshift $(\mathcal{X}_\varphi, T)$ is regular. An infinite word $\mathbf{s} \in S^{\mathbb{N}}$ is in $\mathcal{S}_\varphi$ if and only if it is the label of an infinite walk on the graph depicted in Fig. 1b. The mapping $H_\varphi \colon \mathcal{S}_\varphi \to \mathcal{S}_\varphi$ is given by*

$$H_\varphi(\mathbf{s}) = \begin{cases} \mathbf{1t} & \text{if } \mathbf{s} = \mathbf{2t}; \\ \lambda(\mathbf{t}) & \text{if } \mathbf{s} = a\mathbf{t} \text{ with } a \in \{0, 1\} \text{ and } \mathbf{t} \in \{0, 1\}^{\mathbb{N}}; \\ \lambda(x)\mathbf{21t} & \text{if } \mathbf{s} = ax\mathbf{2t} \text{ with } a \in \{0, 1\}, x \in \{0, 1\}^*, \end{cases}$$

where λ is the morphism given by $\lambda(1) = 0$, $\lambda(0) = 2$, and $\lambda(2) = 21$.

We say that an infinite word $\mathbf{x}$ is the *positive orbit* of $\mathbf{z}$ if $T^n(\mathbf{z}) = \mathbf{x}$ for some $n > 0$ and that $\mathbf{x}$ is the *negative orbit* of $\mathbf{z}$ if $T^n(\mathbf{x}) = \mathbf{z}$ for some $n > 0$.

Since $\mathbf{f} = 01\varphi(1)\varphi^2(1)\cdots$, we have $\mathbf{f} = \pi(21^\omega)$. Thus using Theorem 3,

$$T^2(\mathbf{f}) = T^2 \circ \pi(21^\omega) = \pi \circ H^2(21^\omega) = \pi(0^\omega).$$

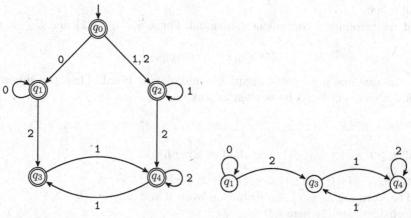

(a) An NFA accepting the language of $\mathcal{L}(\mathcal{S}_\varphi)$.

(b) A graph for the sequences in $\mathcal{S}_\varphi$.

Fig. 1. The suffix conjugate of the Fibonacci subshift

The next result shows that $T^2(\mathbf{f})$ acts as a divider in the shift orbit of the Fibonacci word. We omit the proof here.

Theorem 4. *Let* $\mathbf{s} \in \mathcal{S}_\varphi$. *Then*

(i) $\pi(\mathbf{s})$ *is in the positive orbit of* $T^2(\mathbf{f})$ *if and only if* $\mathbf{s}$ *has a suffix* 2^ω.
(ii) $\pi(\mathbf{s})$ *is in the negative orbit of* $T^2(\mathbf{f})$ *if and only if* $\mathbf{s}$ *has a suffix* 1^ω.

4   The Suffix Conjugate of the Thue-Morse Subshift

Let μ be the Thue-Morse morphism $0 \mapsto 01$, $1 \mapsto 10$, $\mathbf{t} = \mu^\omega(0)$ the Thue-Morse word. Denoting the shift orbit closure of $\mathbf{t}$ by $\mathcal{X}_\mu$, the Thue-Morse subshift is $(\mathcal{X}_\mu, T)$. In this section we will characterize its suffix conjugate $(\mathcal{S}_\mu, H_\mu)$ defined in Theorem 1.

Here the set of suffixes is $S' = \{0, 1, 01, 10\}$ and $S = \{0, 1, 2, 3\}$, and we let c be the bijection between S and S' given by

$$c(0) = 0, \qquad c(1) = 1, \qquad c(2) = 01, \qquad c(3) = 10.$$

The structure of the minimal forbidden words of the Thue-Morse word is well-known [12,15]. They are exactly the words 000, 111,

$$0\mu^{2n}(010)0, \qquad 0\mu^{2n}(101)0, \qquad 1\mu^{2n}(010)1, \qquad 1\mu^{2n}(101)1$$

and

$$1\mu^{2n+1}(010)0, \qquad 1\mu^{2n+1}(101)0, \qquad 0\mu^{2n+1}(010)1, \qquad 0\mu^{2n+1}(101)1$$

for all $n \geq 0$.

Let us introduce a convenient shorthand. For $x, y, z \in \{0, 1\}$ and $k \geq 0$, we write

$$\gamma(k, x, y, z) = x\mu^k(y\bar{y}y)z.$$

Here the overline notation $\bar{\ast}$ swaps 0's and 1's, as usual. Then the minimal forbidden words of $\mathbf{t}$ can be written as xxx and

$$\gamma(2n, x, x, x), \quad \gamma(2n, x, \bar{x}, x), \quad \gamma(2n+1, x, x, \bar{x}), \quad \gamma(2n+1, x, \bar{x}, \bar{x}), \qquad (9)$$

for all $n \geq 0$ and $x \in \{0, 1\}$, and the following holds:

- We have $\mu\big(\gamma(k, x, y, z)\big) = x\gamma(k+1, \bar{x}, y, z)\bar{z}$.
- The word $\gamma(k, x, y, z)$ is a forbidden word if and only if $\gamma(k-1, \bar{x}, y, z)$ is a forbidden word, where $k \geq 1$.

The mapping λ defined in (3) and (5) in the current case is

$$\lambda(0) = 2, \qquad \lambda(1) = 3, \qquad \lambda(2) = 21, \qquad \lambda(3) = 30.$$

Lemma 10. *Let $x \in \{0,1\}$. The forbidden words xxx and $\gamma(0,x,x,x)$ do not have covers. For other forbidden words, we have the following.*

(i) The minimal covers of $\gamma(0,x,\overline{x},x)$ are in

$$\bigl(x + \lambda(\overline{x})\bigr)\overline{x}\bigl(\overline{x} + \lambda(\overline{x})\bigr) \qquad and \qquad \lambda(x)x\bigl(x + \lambda(x)\bigr).$$

(ii) The minimal covers of $\gamma(1,x,x,\overline{x})$ are in

$$\bigl(x + \lambda(\overline{x})\bigr)x\overline{x}\bigl(\overline{x} + \lambda(\overline{x})\bigr) \qquad and \qquad \bigl(x + \lambda(\overline{x})\bigr)\lambda(x)\bigl(x + \lambda(x)\bigr).$$

(iii) The minimal covers of $\gamma(1,x,\overline{x},\overline{x})$ are in

$$\bigl(x + \lambda(\overline{x})\bigr)\overline{x}x\bigl(\overline{x} + \lambda(\overline{x})\bigr) \qquad and \qquad \bigl(x + \lambda(\overline{x})\bigr)\overline{x}\lambda(x).$$

Lemma 11. *Let $x,y \in \{0,1\}$ and $k \geq 2$. A word is a minimal cover of $\gamma(k,x,y,y)$ if and only if it is in*

$$\bigl(x + \lambda(\overline{x})\bigr)\lambda(y)\overline{y}^{k-2}\lambda(\overline{y})\bigl(y + \lambda(y)\bigr). \tag{10}$$

A word is a minimal cover of $\gamma(k,x,y,\overline{y})$ if and only if it is in

$$\bigl(x + \lambda(\overline{x})\bigr)\lambda(y)\overline{y}^{k-2}\left[\lambda(\overline{y})\bigl(\overline{y} + \lambda(\overline{y})\bigr) + \overline{y}\bigl(y + \lambda(y)\bigr)\right]. \tag{11}$$

Theorem 5. *The language $\mathcal{L}(\mathcal{S}_\mu)$ of the suffix conjugate $(\mathcal{S}_\mu, H_\mu)$ of the Thue-Morse subshift $(\mathcal{X}_\mu, T)$ is regular. An infinite word $\mathbf{s} \in S^{\mathbb{N}}$ is in $\mathcal{S}_\mu$ if and only if it is the label of an infinite walk on the graph depicted in Fig. 2. The mapping $H_\mu\colon \mathcal{S}_\mu \to \mathcal{S}_\mu$ is given by*

$$H_\mu(\mathbf{s}) = \begin{cases} 1\mathbf{t} & \text{if } \mathbf{s} = 2\mathbf{t}; \\ 0\mathbf{t} & \text{if } \mathbf{s} = 3\mathbf{t}; \\ \lambda(\mathbf{t}) & \text{if } \mathbf{s} = a\mathbf{t} \text{ with } a \in \{0,1\} \text{ and } \mathbf{t} \in \{0,1\}^{\mathbb{N}}; \\ \lambda(x)21\mathbf{t} & \text{if } \mathbf{s} = ax2\mathbf{t} \text{ with } a \in \{0,1\}, \, x \in \{0,1\}^*; \\ \lambda(x)30\mathbf{t} & \text{if } \mathbf{s} = ax3\mathbf{t} \text{ with } a \in \{0,1\}, \, x \in \{0,1\}^*, \end{cases}$$

where λ is the morphism given by $\lambda(0) = 2$, $\lambda(1) = 3$, $\lambda(2) = 21$, and $\lambda(3) = 30$.

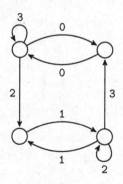

Fig. 2. The suffix conjugate of the Thue-Morse subshift

References

1. Allouche, J.-P., Shallit, J.: Automatic sequences: Theory, Applications, and Generalizations. Cambridge University Press (2003)
2. Cassaigne, J.: An algorithm to test if a given circular HD0L-language avoids a pattern. In: Information Processing 1994, Hamburg. IFIP Trans. A Comput. Sci. Tech., vol. I, A-51, pp. 459–464. North-Holland, Amsterdam (1994)
3. Canterini, V., Siegel, A.: Automate des préfixes-suffixes associé à une substitution primitive. J. Théorie Nombres Bordeaux 13, 353–369 (2001)
4. Currie, J.D., Rampersad, N., Saari, K.: Extremal words in the shift orbit closure of a morphic sequence. In: Béal, M.-P., Carton, O. (eds.) DLT 2013. LNCS, vol. 7907, pp. 143–154. Springer, Heidelberg (2013), preprint available at http://arxiv.org/abs/1301.4972
5. Holton, C., Zamboni, L.Q.: Descendants of primitive substitutions. Theory Comput. Systems 32, 133–157 (1999)
6. Holton, C., Zamboni, L.Q.: Directed graphs and substitutions. Theory Comput. Systems 34, 545–564 (2001)
7. Klouda, K.: Bispecial factors in circular non-pushy D0L languages. Theoret. Comput. Sci. 445, 63–74 (2012)
8. Kůrka, P.: Topological and Symbolic Dynamics. Société Mathématique de France, Paris (2003)
9. Lind, D., Marcus, B.: An introduction to symbolic dynamics and coding. Cambridge University Press (1995)
10. Lothaire, M.: Algebraic Combinatorics on Words. Encyclopedia of Mathematics and its Applications, vol. 90, Cambridge University Press, Cambridge (2002)
11. Mignosi, F., Séébold, P.: If a D0L language is k-power free then it is circular. In: Lingas, A., Carlsson, S., Karlsson, R. (eds.) ICALP 1993. LNCS, vol. 700, pp. 507–518. Springer, Heidelberg (1993)
12. Mignosi, F., Restivo, A., Sciortino, M.: Words and forbidden factors. Theoret. Comput. Sci. 273, 99–117 (2002)
13. Mossé, B.: Puissances de mots et reconnaissabilité des points fixes d'une substitution. Theoret. Comput. Sci. 99, 327–334 (1992)
14. Shallit, J.: Fife's theorem revisited. In: Mauri, G., Leporati, A. (eds.) DLT 2011. LNCS, vol. 6795, pp. 397–405. Springer, Heidelberg (2011)
15. Shur, A.: Combinatorial complexity of rational languages. Discr. Anal. and Oper. Research, Ser. 1 12(2), 78–99 (2005) (in Russian)

Periodicity Forcing Words*

Joel D. Day[1],**, Daniel Reidenbach[1], and Johannes C. Schneider[2]

[1] Department of Computer Science, Loughborough University,
Loughborough, Leicestershire, LE11 3TU, UK
J.Day-10@student.lboro.ac.uk,
D.Reidenbach@lboro.ac.uk
[2] DIaLOGIKa GmbH, Pascalschacht 1,
66125 Saarbrücken, Germany
johannes.schneider@dialogika.de

Abstract. The Dual Post Correspondence Problem asks, for a given word α, if there exists a non-periodic morphism g and an arbitrary morphism h such that $g(\alpha) = h(\alpha)$. Thus α satisfies the Dual PCP if and only if it belongs to a non-trivial equality set. Words which do not satisfy the Dual PCP are called *periodicity forcing*, and are important to the study of word equations, equality sets and ambiguity of morphisms. In this paper, a 'prime' subset of periodicity forcing words is presented. It is shown that when combined with a particular type of morphism it generates exactly the full set of periodicity forcing words. Furthermore, it is shown that there exist examples of periodicity forcing words which contain any given factor/prefix/suffix. Finally, an alternative class of mechanisms for generating periodicity forcing words is developed, resulting in a class of examples which contrast those known already.

Keywords: Equality sets, Morphisms, Dual Post Correspondence Problem, Periodicity forcing sets, Periodicity forcing words, Ambiguity of morphisms.

1 Introduction

The Dual Post Correspondence Problem (Dual PCP) is a decidable variation of the famous Post Correspondence Problem (see Post [10]). It was introduced by Culik II and Karhumäki in [1], where the authors make progress towards a characterisation of binary equality sets. A word is said to satisfy the Dual PCP if it belongs to an equality set $E(g, h)$ for two morphisms g, h where at least one morphism is non-periodic. For example, the word abba belongs to $E(g, h)$ where $g(\mathsf{a}) := \mathsf{aba}$, $g(\mathsf{b}) := \mathsf{b}$, $h(\mathsf{a}) := \mathsf{a}$, and $h(\mathsf{b}) := \mathsf{bab}$. Thus abba satisfies the Dual PCP; in other words, it is a non-trivial *equality word*. In contrast, the word abaab does not satisfy the Dual PCP, but this claim is much harder to verify.

---

* This work was supported by the London Mathematical Society, grant SC7-1112-02.
** Corresponding author.

J. Karhumäki, A. Lepistö, and L. Zamboni (Eds.): WORDS 2013, LNCS 8079, pp. 107–118, 2013.
© Springer-Verlag Berlin Heidelberg 2013

In this paper, words which do not satisfy the Dual PCP (often referred to as *periodicity forcing words*) are examined. Periodicity forcing words are of immediate importance to the study of equality sets, since they are words which do not belong to any non-trivial equality set. As a result, they can be viewed as being opposite to equality words. Furthermore, they are strongly related to the studies of word equations and of the ambiguity of morphisms.

Due to both the original research by Culik II and Karhumäki [1], and from more recent research into equality sets (e. g., Holub [5], Hadravova, Holub [4]) and word equations (e. g., Czeizler et al. [2], Karhumäki, Petre [7]), quite a lot is known about the binary case. Much less, however, is known about the general case. One reason for this is that although the Dual PCP is known to be decidable (due to Makanin's algorithm [9], as shown by Culik II and Karhumäki [1]) deciding on whether a word is periodicity forcing can be a particularly intricate task, and becomes even more so as the alphabet size increases. In [3], we overcome this problem by employing the use of morphisms to generate periodicity forcing words over arbitrary alphabets.

In Sect. 3 of the present paper, we explore the structure of the set of periodicity forcing words (DPCP⁻) in relation to morphisms. Specifically, a 'prime' subset of DPCP⁻ is considered from which all periodicity forcing words may be generated using a specific type of morphism, characterised in [3]. In Sect. 4, it is shown that there exist periodicity forcing words with arbitrary factors, providing a level of generality not yet achieved. Finally, in light of the results on 'prime' periodicity forcing words, some alternative approaches to generating periodicity forcing words (specifically over large alphabets) are investigated.

2   Notation and Preliminary Results

Let $\mathbb{N} = \{1, 2, ...\}$ be the set of natural numbers, and let $\mathbb{N}_0 := \mathbb{N} \cup \{0\}$. The set $\mathbb{N}$ is used as an infinite alphabet of symbols, and words over $\mathbb{N}$ are referred to as *patterns*. The symbols occurring in a pattern are called *variables*, and the set of variables occurring in a pattern α is denoted by $\mathrm{var}(\alpha)$. Symbols from words which are not patterns (referred to as letters) are indicated using typewriter font (e. g., $\Sigma := \{\mathtt{a}, \mathtt{b}, \mathtt{c}...\}$).

For an alphabet $\Sigma := \{a_1, a_2, ..., a_n\}$ and a word $u \in \Sigma^*$, the *Parikh vector*, written $\mathrm{P}(u)$, is the vector $(|u|_{a_1}, |u|_{a_2}, ..., |u|_{a_n})$. The result of dividing the Parikh vector by the greatest common divisor of its components is called the *basic Parikh vector*. A word u is *primitive* if it is not a repetition of a shorter word (i. e., $u = v^n$ implies $n = 1$). Otherwise it is *imprimitive*. A word $u \in \Sigma^*$ is *ratio-imprimitive* if there exist words $v, w \in \Sigma^+$ such that $u = vw$ and u, v share the same basic Parikh vector. Otherwise, it is *ratio-primitive*.

A *morphism* $h : A^* \to B^*$ is a mapping which is compatible with concatenation (meaning $h(uv) = h(u) \cdot h(v)$ for any words $u, v \in A^*$). Thus, although a morphism maps words in A^* to words in B^*, it is fully defined once it is specified for each individual symbol in A. The composition of two morphisms $g : A^* \to B^*$ and $h : B^* \to C^*$ is the morphism $g \circ h : A^* \to C^*$, given by $g \circ h(x) = g(h(x))$ for every $x \in A$.

A morphism $g : A^* \to B^*$ is *periodic* if there exists a word $w \in B^*$ such that for every $x \in A$, $g(x) \in \{w\}^*$. Given another morphism $h : A^* \to B^*$, g and h are said to be *distinct* if there exists an $x \in A$ such that $g(x) \neq h(x)$. If, for some word $\alpha \in A^+$, $g(\alpha) = h(\alpha)$, then g and h are said to *agree* on α. A *renaming* of a word $u \in \{a_1, a_2, ..., a_n\}^+$ is the word $\sigma(u)$ where $\sigma : \{a_1, a_2, ... , a_n\}^* \to \{b_1, b_2, ... , b_n\}^*$ is a morphism given by $\sigma(a_i) = b_i$, and where $b_1, b_2, ..., b_n$ are distinct letters. If $\{a_1, a_2, ... a_n\} \cap \{b_1, b_2, ... , b_n\} = \emptyset$, then the renaming is said to be *strict*. On the other hand, if $a_i \in \{b_1, b_2, ..., b_n\}$ for $1 \leq i \leq n$, then $\sigma(u)$ is a *permutation* of u. For sets Δ and $V \subset \Delta$, the morphism $\pi_V : \Delta^* \to V^*$, given by $\pi_V(x) = x$ if $x \in V$ and $\pi_V(x) = \varepsilon$ otherwise, is called a *projection*.

A set of patterns is *periodicity forcing if*, whenever two morphisms agree on every pattern in the set, they are periodic. A set of patterns T is said to be a *test set* of another set of patterns S if any two morphisms which agree on every pattern in T also agree on every pattern in S. Note that this means any test set of a periodicity forcing set must also be periodicity forcing.

A morphism σ is said to be *ambiguous* with respect to a pattern α if there exists another morphism τ such that $\sigma(\alpha) = \tau(\alpha)$ and σ, τ are distinct. It is convenient to refer to the following set: DPCP $:= \{\alpha \in \mathbb{N}^+ \mid$ there exists a non-periodic morphism σ and an arbitrary morphism τ such that $\sigma(\alpha) = \tau(\alpha)\}$. Note that this implies the complement DPCP⁻ is exactly the set of periodicity forcing words.

For a set of unknowns Δ, a word equation is an equation $\alpha = \beta$ for some words α, $\beta \in \Delta^+$. It is non-trivial if $\alpha \neq \beta$. For a given alphabet Σ, solutions to the word equation are morphisms $\sigma : \Delta^* \to \Sigma^*$ such that $\sigma(\alpha)$ and $\sigma(\beta)$ are equal. Unless otherwise specified, Δ is usually a set of variables, while Σ is a set of letters. As a result, word equations equate patterns, and their solutions map to terminal words (words which are not patterns). The following is a well known and important result on word equations.

Lemma 1 (Lothaire [8]). *Non-trivial word equations in two unknowns have only periodic solutions.*

One consequence of Lemma 1 which provides a particularly useful tool is that if two words u and v commute (i.e., $uv = vu$), then u and v (and therefore also uv) share a primitive root. Similarly, an arbitrarily large set of words $\{u_1, u_2, ..., u_n\}$ is said to commute if $u_1, u_2, ..., u_n$ all share the same primitive root.

In our investigation into the use of morphisms to generate periodicity forcing words in [3], we provide the following criterion.

Lemma 2 ([3]). *Let Δ_1, Δ_2 be sets of variables. Let $\varphi : \Delta_1^* \to \Delta_2^*$ be a morphism such that for every $x \in \Delta_2$, there exists a $y \in \Delta_1$ such that $x \in \mathrm{var}(\varphi(y))$, and*

(i) *for every non-periodic morphism $\sigma : \Delta_2^* \to \{\mathsf{a}, \mathsf{b}\}^*$, $\sigma \circ \varphi$ is non-periodic, and*
(ii) *for all distinct morphisms σ, $\tau : \Delta_2^* \to \{\mathsf{a}, \mathsf{b}\}^*$, where at least one is non-periodic, $\sigma \circ \varphi$ and $\tau \circ \varphi$ are distinct.*

Then for any $\alpha \notin$ DPCP with $\mathrm{var}(\alpha) = \Delta_1$, $\varphi(\alpha) \notin$ DPCP.

Characterisations of morphisms which satisfy conditions (i) and (ii) of Lemma 2 are given in the following propositions respectively.

Proposition 3 ([3]). *Let Δ_1 and Δ_2 be sets of variables, let $\varphi : \Delta_1^* \to \Delta_2^*$ be a morphism, and let $\beta_i := \varphi(i)$ for every $i \in \Delta_1$. The morphism φ satisfies Condition (i) of Lemma 2 if and only if, for every non-periodic morphism $\sigma : \Delta_2^* \to \{a, b\}^*$,*

(i) *there are at least two patterns β_i such that $\sigma(\beta_i) \neq \varepsilon$, and*
(ii) *there do not exist $k_1, k_2, ..., k_n \in \mathbb{N}$ such that*

$$\sigma(\gamma_1)^{k_1} = \sigma(\gamma_2)^{k_2} = \cdots = \sigma(\gamma_n)^{k_n} \tag{1}$$

where $\{\gamma_1, \gamma_2, ..., \gamma_n\}$ is the set of all patterns β_i such that $\sigma(\beta_i) \neq \varepsilon$.

Proposition 4 ([3]). *Let Δ_1, Δ_2 be sets of variables, and let $\varphi : \Delta_1^* \to \Delta_2^*$ be a morphism. For every $i \in \Delta_1$, let $\beta_i := \varphi(i)$. The morphism φ satisfies Condition (ii) of Lemma 2 if and only if $\{\beta_1, \beta_2, ..., \beta_n\}$ is a periodicity forcing set.*

3   A 'Prime' Generating Subset of DPCP⁻

In this section, the structure of the set DPCP⁻, with respect to morphisms, is investigated. Specifically, DPCP⁻ is partitioned according to whether, for a given pattern α, there exists a morphism φ, and a second pattern $\beta \notin$ DPCP, such that $\alpha = \varphi(\beta)$.[1] This condition is clearly trivial if β is permitted to be a renaming of α, so only morphisms which alter the structure of β are considered. Furthermore, the Dual PCP is trivial for unary alphabets, so only patterns α and β over non-unary alphabets are considered. This partition allows DPCP⁻ to be represented as chains of patterns. It can be inferred directly from the constructions given in [3] that every periodicity forcing word is a pre-image of another, meaning these chains are infinite in one direction. In Proposition 9 below, it is shown that there exist patterns for which there does not exist a non-trivial pre-image in DPCP⁻ and therefore that some chains terminate. More generally, it can be shown that DPCP⁻ is spanned by one-sided infinite chains of this type, and thus that there exists a (strict) subset of DPCP⁻ from which all periodicity forcing words can be generated using the morphisms characterised in [3].

The proofs rely on a lower bound on the size of periodicity forcing words (relative to the number of variables), achieved by developing a strong sufficient condition for a pattern to be contained in DPCP. To do this, morphisms of the following form are considered.

$$\sigma(x) := \begin{cases} a^{p_y} \, ba^{q_y} & \text{if } x = y, \text{ and} \\ a^{r_x} & \text{otherwise,} \end{cases}$$

---

[1] It is worth noting that a characterisation of such morphisms φ is given in [3] (Theorem 14).

for some fixed variable y, where p_x, q_y, r_y are numbers depending on the variables x and y respectively. Clearly two morphisms σ_1 and σ_2 of this type agree on a pattern α if and only if the number of occurrences of **a** coincide between each occurrence of **b**. Thus the agreement of the two morphisms can be determined by solving a system of linear Diophantine equations. In the case that $n < |\operatorname{var}(\alpha)|$, it is possible to show that such a system always permits a non-trivial solution – meaning the two morphisms are distinct. Furthermore, it is clear that they are non-periodic, so it is possible to conclude the following.

Proposition 5. *Let α be a pattern, and let $n := |\operatorname{var}(\alpha)|$. Suppose that $|\alpha|_x < n$ for some $x \in \operatorname{var}(\alpha)$. Then $\alpha \in \text{DPCP}$.*

It follows that, for a periodicity forcing word with n letters, each letter must occur at least n times, implying the next corollary which provides a lower bound on the length of the shortest periodicity forcing word with n letters.

Corollary 6. *Let $\alpha \notin \text{DPCP}$, and let $n := |\operatorname{var}(\alpha)|$. Then $|\alpha| \geq n^2$.*

Since periodicity forcing words can be obtained as concatenations of words in a particular type of periodicity forcing set (see Sect. 5), it is possible to infer a corresponding upper bound from results in [6]. The authors provide a concise test set (containing at most $5n$ words, each of length n) for the set S_n consisting of all permutations of the word $x_1 \cdot x_2 \cdots x_n$. Although it is stated in [6] that S_n itself is not periodicity forcing, it can be verified using results from [6] and [1] that the augmented set $S_n' := S_n \cup \{x_1 \cdot x_1 \cdot x_2 \cdot x_2 \cdots x_n \cdot x_n\}$ is. Given a test set T_n for S_n, a test set for S_n' is clearly $T_n \cup \{x_1 \cdot x_1 \cdot x_2 \cdot x_2 \cdots x_n \cdot x_n\}$. Thus there exists a test set for S_n' containing at most $5n$ words of length n and one word of length $2n$. The periodicity forcing word resulting from concatenating these words is at most $5n^2 + 2n$ letters long.

Proposition 7. *Let α_n be a shortest pattern not in DPCP such that $|\operatorname{var}(\alpha)| = n$. Then $n^2 \leq |\alpha| \leq 5n^2 + 2n$.*

The above bounds not only demonstrate the growth of periodicity forcing words with respect to alphabet size, but also provide an indication of how restrictive the set $\text{DPCP}^{\neg}$ is. Furthermore, the lower bound is particularly useful when considering the following.

Definition 8. *Let $\alpha \notin \text{DPCP}$ be a pattern with $|\operatorname{var}(\alpha)| \geq 2$. Then α is said to be a* prime element of $\text{DPCP}^{\neg}$ *(or simply* prime*) if for every pattern $\beta \notin \text{DPCP}$ with $|\operatorname{var}(\beta)| > 1$, and every morphism $\varphi : \operatorname{var}(\beta)^* \to \operatorname{var}(\alpha)^*$, $\varphi(\beta) = \alpha$ implies φ is a renaming morphism.*

Showing that a pattern satisfies Definition 8 is a highly non-trivial task, since all morphisms must be accounted for with respect to every pattern $\beta \notin \text{DPCP}$. However, due to Proposition 5, it is possible to provide an example. Specifically, it is possible to conclude that $1 \cdot 2 \cdot 1 \cdot 1 \cdot 2$ is a prime element of $\text{DPCP}^{\neg}$, since any pre-image β must contain a variable x such that $|\beta|_x \leq 2$. By Proposition 5, this excludes the possibility that $|\operatorname{var}(\beta)| \geq 3$, and reduces the candidates for β to a finite number of patterns which may be checked individually with little effort. This demonstrates that it is possible to produce chains of periodicity forcing words which terminate in exactly one direction (i.e., they are not bi-infinite).

Proposition 9. *Prime elements of* DPCP⁻ *exist.*

It is possible to generalise the reasoning behind Proposition 9, and show that each periodicity forcing word is either prime, or may be obtained from a prime periodicity forcing word using morphisms. This results in a structure comprised of one-sided infinite chains which spans exactly the set DPCP⁻.

Theorem 10. *Let S be the set of all prime elements of* DPCP⁻. *Let $\alpha \notin$* DPCP *with $|\operatorname{var}(\alpha)| \geq 2$. Then either $\alpha \in S$, or there exists $\beta \in S$ and a non-trivial morphism φ such that $\varphi(\beta) = \alpha$.*

Thus, there exists a non-trivial subset of DPCP⁻ whose elements, when combined with the morphisms characterised in [3], generate the set DPCP⁻. Moreover, it is not difficult to see that the conditions for satisfying Definition 8 are very restrictive, and therefore one can expect such a subset to be much smaller than the original set.

4   Patterns in DPCP⁻ with Arbitrary Factors

One particular consequence of the research on periodicity forcing words in [3] is that there exist periodicity forcing sets which include any given pattern α – it is sufficient to simply include a pattern $\beta \notin$ DPCP where $\operatorname{var}(\beta) = \operatorname{var}(\alpha)$. By constructing these sets such that they satisfy the conditions for Proposition 3, it is possible to provide a morphism φ which satisfies Lemma 2 such that $\varphi(\alpha)$ contains an arbitrary given factor β for some $\alpha \notin$ DPCP. Thus a level of generality previously not achieved is reached: that there exist periodicity forcing words with arbitrary factors. It is worth noting that due to the properties of morphisms, the construction may be altered with little effort to guarantee that β appears as a prefix or suffix.

Proposition 3 is addressed in the following proposition, which demonstrates that the conditions may always be satisfied. The task is somewhat simplified by using patterns with the same Parikh vector, since any morphism σ either maps all, or none of them to the empty word. The result is also relevant to Theorem 19, confirming that such a construction always exists.

Proposition 11. *Let α_0 be a pattern, and let $n := \lceil \log_2(|\operatorname{var}(\alpha_0)|)\rceil$. There exist patterns $\alpha_1, \alpha_2, ..., \alpha_n$ with $\mathrm{P}(\alpha_0) = \mathrm{P}(\alpha_1) = \cdots = \mathrm{P}(\alpha_n)$ such that for any $k_0, k_1, ..., k_n \in \mathbb{N}$, the system of word equations*

$$\alpha_0{}^{k_0} = \alpha_1{}^{k_1} = \cdots = \alpha_n{}^{k_n}$$

has only periodic solutions.

It is now possible to show that there exists a pattern not in DPCP which has an arbitrary pattern β as a factor. This is achieved as follows. Let β_1 be a pattern not in DPCP such that $\mathrm{var}(\beta_1) = \mathrm{var}(\beta)$. In accordance with Proposition 11, construct the patterns $\beta_2, \ldots, \beta_n$, and consider the morphism $\varphi : \{1, 2, \ldots, n+1\}^* \to \mathrm{var}(\beta)^*$ given by $\varphi(i) := \beta_i$ for $1 \leq i \leq n$, and $\varphi(n+1) = \beta$. Since $\beta_1 \notin$ DPCP, and $\mathrm{var}(\beta_1) = \mathrm{var}(\beta_i) = \mathrm{var}(\beta)$ for $1 \leq i \leq n$, the set $\{\varphi(x) \mid 1 \leq x \leq n+1\}$ is periodicity forcing, so by Proposition 4, φ satisfies Condition (ii) of Lemma 2. By construction, φ also satisfies Condition (i). Let $\alpha \notin$ DPCP be a pattern such that $\mathrm{var}(\alpha) = \{1, 2, \ldots n+1\}$. By Lemma 2, $\varphi(\alpha) \notin$ DPCP. It is clear that β appears as a factor of $\varphi(\alpha)$. It is therefore possible to formulate the following theorem.

Theorem 12. *For any pattern $\beta \in \mathbb{N}^+$, there exists a pattern $\alpha \notin$ DPCP such that β is a factor of α.*

Example 13 demonstrates how such a morphism may be constructed. Note that the patterns $\beta_2, \ldots \beta_n$ are constructed around β, rather than β_1. This is simply to keep example more compact, and it is not difficult to see why the correctness is unaffected. In a similar way, the patterns can be 'swapped' around to guarantee that β appears as a prefix or suffix of $\varphi(\alpha)$.

Example 13. Let $\beta := 1 \cdot 1 \cdot 2 \cdot 3$, let $\beta_2 := 2 \cdot 3 \cdot 1 \cdot 1$, and let $\beta_3 := 3 \cdot 1 \cdot 1 \cdot 2$. Let $\beta_1 := 1 \cdot 2 \cdot 1 \cdot 1 \cdot 2 \cdot 1 \cdot 3 \cdot 1 \cdot 1 \cdot 3 \cdot 2 \cdot 1 \cdot 1 \cdot 2 \cdot 1 \cdot 1 \cdot 2 \cdot 1 \cdot 1 \cdot 2 \cdot 1 \cdot 2 \cdot 1 \cdot 1 \cdot 2 \cdot 1 \cdot 3 \cdot 1 \cdot 1 \cdot 3 \cdot 2 \cdot 1 \cdot 1 \cdot 2 \cdot 1$. By [3] (Proposition 32), $\beta_1 \notin$ DPCP. Thus, by Proposition 4, the morphism $\varphi : \{1, 2, 3, 4\}^* \to \{1, 2, 3\}^*$ given by $\varphi(i) := \beta_i$ for $1 \leq i \leq 3$ and $\varphi(4) := \beta$ satisfies Condition (ii) of Lemma 2.

Condition (i) is now considered. Let $\sigma : \{1, 2, 3\}^* \to \{\mathtt{a}, \mathtt{b}\}^*$ be a non-periodic morphism. Note that, since $\mathrm{var}(\beta) = \mathrm{var}(\beta_1) = \mathrm{var}(\beta_2) = \mathrm{var}(\beta_3)$, $\sigma(\gamma) \neq \varepsilon$ for every $\gamma \in \{\beta, \beta_1, \beta_2, \beta_3\}$. Let $k_1, k_2, k_3, k_4 \in \mathbb{N}$ and consider the equation

$$\sigma(\beta_1)^{k_1} = \sigma(\beta_2)^{k_2} = \sigma(\beta_3)^{k_3} = \sigma(\beta)^{k_4}. \tag{2}$$

Clearly, this is only satisfied if

$$\sigma(2 \cdot 3 \cdot 1 \cdot 1)^{k_2} = \sigma(3 \cdot 1 \cdot 1 \cdot 2)^{k_3} = \sigma(1 \cdot 1 \cdot 2 \cdot 3)^{k_4},$$

and therefore

$$\sigma(1 \cdot 1 \cdot 2 \cdot 3) = \sigma(2 \cdot 3 \cdot 1 \cdot 1) = \sigma(3 \cdot 1 \cdot 1 \cdot 2).$$

Assume that (2), and therefore the subsequent systems of equations, are satisfied. This implies that

$$\sigma(311)\sigma(2) = \sigma(2)\sigma(311)$$
$$= \sigma(11)\sigma(23) = \sigma(23)\sigma(11)$$
$$= \sigma(112)\sigma(3) = \sigma(3)\sigma(112)$$

and therefore by Lemma 1 $\sigma(1)$, $\sigma(2)$, $\sigma(3)$ share a primitive root. Thus σ is periodic. This is a contradiction; there does not exist a non-periodic morphism

σ such that (2) is satisfied. By Proposition 3, φ therefore satisfies Condition (i) of Lemma 2. Thus, for any pattern $\alpha \notin$ DPCP with var$(\alpha) = \{1, 2, 3, 4\}$, $\varphi(\alpha) \notin$ DPCP, and β is a factor of $\varphi(\alpha)$.

5 An Alternative Means of Finding Patterns Not in DPCP

While Theorem 10 provides motivation for the further study of morphisms in the context of DPCP⁻, it also demonstrates the need to identify periodicity forcing words by other means. In [1], Culik II and Karhumäki show that this may be done using periodicity forcing sets. Indeed, patterns not in DPCP are essentially periodicity forcing sets with a cardinality of 1. However, it is generally easier to construct periodicity forcing sets with higher cardinalities, as more patterns results in a more restricted class of (pairs of) morphisms which agree on every pattern. This is precisely the reason why the morphisms approach is useful (see Proposition 4).

It follows from the properties of morphisms that the agreement of two morphisms on a ratio-imprimitive pattern can be reduced to the agreement of those morphisms on a set of two (or more) smaller patterns. The following lemma establishes this relationship formally, providing a characterisation of when a ratio-imprimitive pattern is in DPCP.

Lemma 14. *Let $\alpha = \beta_1 \cdot \beta_2 \cdot ... \cdot \beta_n$ be a pattern such that $\beta_1, \beta_2, ..., \beta_n$ share a basic Parikh vector. Then $\alpha \notin$ DPCP if and only if $\{\beta_1, \beta_2, ..., \beta_n\}$ is a periodicity forcing set.*

For patterns with a higher element of ratio-imprimitivity (i.e., those which have many different prefixes with the same basic Parikh vector as the whole pattern), larger values of n can be taken. This results in a larger potential simplification gained by applying Lemma 14. While this does restrict the range of patterns to which this approach may be applied, it is worth noting that any concatenation of all the patterns $\beta_1, \beta_2, ..., \beta_n$ is also not be in DPCP. This means that relatively rich classes of patterns can be established with any single set of factors. Expressing the same result using morphisms demonstrates more clearly this trade-off. The following proposition gives a criterion for a morphism $\varphi : \Delta_1{}^* \to \Delta_2{}^*$ which maps any pattern α with var$(\alpha) = \Delta_1$ to a pattern not in DPCP.

Proposition 15. *Let Δ_1, Δ_2 be sets of variables, and let $\varphi : \Delta_1{}^* \to \Delta_2{}^*$ be a morphism. For every $i \in \Delta_1$, let $\beta_i := \varphi(i)$. If $\{\beta_i \mid i \in \Delta_1\}$ is a periodicity forcing set, and $\beta_1, \beta_2, ... \beta_n$ share the same basic Parikh vector, then $\varphi(\alpha) \notin$ DPCP for any pattern α satisfying var$(\alpha) = \Delta_1$.*

While the set of patterns to which morphisms satisfying Proposition 15 can be applied is much larger than for morphisms satisfying Lemma 2, the images are more restricted. The result is a contrasting class of examples of patterns not in

DPCP. The characterisation given in Lemma 14 shows that periodicity forcing sets of patterns with the same basic Parikh vectors are very closely related to sets of ratio-imprimitive patterns not in DPCP. Indeed, every ratio-imprimitive pattern not in DPCP can be decomposed into a unique periodicity forcing set of ratio-primitive patterns with the same basic Parikh vectors, and for every such set, there exists a unique corresponding set of ratio-imprimitive patterns not in DPCP, obtained by concatenating every pattern in the set at least once.

It is therefore appropriate to simply investigate periodicity forcing sets of ratio-primitive patterns with equal basic Parikh vectors, since such sets automatically yield sets of patterns not in DPCP. While it is not difficult to construct periodicity forcing sets for any set of variables, generating sets of patterns with equal basic Parikh vectors present more of a challenge. Similarly to the morphisms approach studied in [3] and Sect. 3, the following techniques produce periodicity forcing words by building on the existing knowledge in the two variable case. Strong sufficient conditions are known for a set of patterns over two variables to be periodicity forcing (see Holub [5]), so they are generally not difficult to produce. Lemma 16 provides a conveniently concise example to use as a starting point.

Lemma 16 (Culik II, Karhumäki [1]). *The set* $\{1\cdot2, 1\cdot1\cdot2\cdot2\}$ *is periodicity forcing.*

The advantage of starting with a smaller periodicity forcing set is that strict conditions can already be imposed on factors of the larger patterns. It is not difficult to see that for any periodicity forcing set $\Pi := \{\beta_1, \beta_2, \ldots, \beta_n\}$, and any morphism $\varphi : (\mathrm{var}(\beta_1) \cup \cdots \cup \mathrm{var}(\beta_n))^* \to \mathbb{N}^*$, the set $\varphi(\Pi) := \{\varphi(\beta_1), \varphi(\beta_2), \ldots, \varphi(\beta_n)\}$ is periodicity forcing with respect to each factor $\varphi(x)$, where $x \in \mathrm{var}(\beta_1) \cup \mathrm{var}(\beta_2) \cup \cdots \cup \mathrm{var}(\beta_n)$. Specifically, for each pair of morphisms σ, τ which agree on $\varphi(\Pi)$, at least one of the following cases needs to be satisfied:

(i) There exists a primitive word w such that, for every $x \in \mathrm{var}(\beta_1) \cup \mathrm{var}(\beta_2) \cup \cdots \cup \mathrm{var}(\beta_n)$, $\sigma(\varphi(x)) \in \{w\}^*$ and $\tau(\varphi(x)) \in \{w\}^*$.
(ii) For every $x \in \mathrm{var}(\beta_1) \cup \mathrm{var}(\beta_2) \cup \cdots \cup \mathrm{var}(\beta_n)$, $\sigma(\varphi(x)) = \tau(\varphi(x))$.

This can be verified by contradiction: assuming that neither condition holds, the morphisms $\sigma \circ \varphi$ and $\tau \circ \varphi$ are evidence that $\{\beta_1, \beta_2, \ldots \beta_n\}$ is not a periodicity forcing set. It can therefore be more efficient to generate new periodicity forcing sets from existing ones, by substituting individual variables for patterns as this considerably restricts the morphisms σ, τ which need to be accounted for.

The first case is, generally speaking, the more difficult – and is addressed in the following two lemmas, which provide a tool for exploiting the 'partial' periodicity of two morphisms, and extending it to guarantee their total periodicity. This is achieved by introducing patterns which are formed by 'splitting' a pattern which has a periodicity constraint on it.

Lemma 17. *Let w, u, v be words, and let k_1, k_2, k_3, $k_4 \in \mathbb{N}_0$ with $k_2 \geq 1$. If*

$$w^{k_1} \cdot u \cdot w^{k_2} \cdot v \cdot w^{k_3} = w^{k_4}$$

then u, v, and w commute.

Lemma 18. *Let w be a primitive word, and let u, u', v, v' be non-empty words such that $u \cdot v = u' \cdot v' = w$. Then for any k_1, k_2, k_3, $k_4 \in \mathbb{N}_0$ and any q_1, $q_2 \in \mathbb{N}$, the equation*

$$w^{k_1} \cdot u \cdot w^{q_1} \cdot v \cdot w^{k_2} = w^{k_3} \cdot u' \cdot w^{q_2} \cdot v' \cdot w^{k_4} \tag{3}$$

only has solutions if $k_1 = k_3$, $k_2 = k_4$, $q_1 = q_2$, $u = u'$ and $v = v'$.

It is now easier to formulate methods for generating larger periodicity sets from smaller ones, allowing for the preservation of the property of having patterns with the same basic Parikh vector. The following method relies on 'splitting' one variable y into two (so each occurrence of y becomes, e.g., $y_1 y_2$) in each pattern. New patterns are then introduced to 'force' the periodicity of y_1 and y_2. Although the theorem appears very technical, it is relatively simple to apply, as example 20 shows.

Theorem 19. *Let $\Delta := \{x_1, x_2, ..., x_n\}$ be a set of variables, and let $y \notin \Delta$ be a variable. Let $\Pi := \{\alpha_1, \alpha_2, ..., \alpha_m\}$ be a periodicity forcing set such that $\bigcup_{i=1}^{m} \text{var}(\alpha_m) = \Delta$. Let $\varphi : \Delta^* \to (\Delta \cup \{y\})^*$ be the morphism given by $\varphi(x_n) := x_n \cdot y$ and $\varphi(x_i) := x_i$ for $1 \leq i < n$. Let $t \in \mathbb{N}$, and for $1 \leq i \leq t$, let $\beta_i := x_n \cdot \gamma_i \cdot y$ for some pattern γ_i. Let $\beta_{t+1} = x_1 \cdot x_1 \cdot x_2 \cdot x_2 \cdots x_n \cdot x_n \cdot y \cdot y$. If*

   (i) γ_1, γ_2, ..., γ_t are patterns such that $\text{var}(\gamma_1) = \text{var}(\gamma_2) = \cdots = \text{var}(\gamma_t) = \Delta \backslash \{x_n\}$,

   (ii) for any k_1, k_2, ..., $k_q \in \mathbb{N}$, the series of word equations $\gamma_1^{k_1} = \gamma_2^{k_2} = \cdots = \gamma_t^{k_t}$ has only periodic solutions,

then the set $\{\varphi(\alpha_1), \varphi(\alpha_2), ..., \varphi(\alpha_m), \beta_1, \beta_2, ..., \beta_{t+1}\}$ is periodicity forcing.

Example 20. Let $\Pi := \{1 \cdot 2, 1 \cdot 1 \cdot 2 \cdot 2\}$. It is established in Lemma 16 that Π is a periodicity forcing set. Let $\varphi : \{1, 2\}^* \to \{1, 2, 3\}^*$ be the morphism given by $\varphi(1) := 1$ and $\varphi(2) := 2 \cdot 3$. Consider the set $\Pi' := \{\varphi(1 \cdot 2), \varphi(1 \cdot 1 \cdot 2 \cdot 2), \beta_1, \beta_2\}$ where $\beta_1 := 2 \cdot 1 \cdot 3$ and $\beta_2 := 1 \cdot 1 \cdot 2 \cdot 2 \cdot 3 \cdot 3$. It follows from the fact that Π is a periodicity forcing set that, for any two morphisms σ, $\tau : \{1, 2, 3\}^* \to \{a, b\}^*$, if σ and τ agree on every pattern in Π', then

(1) $\sigma(1)$, $\tau(1)$, $\sigma(2 \cdot 3)$, $\tau(2 \cdot 3)$ commute, or
(2) $\sigma(1) = \tau(1)$ and $\sigma(2 \cdot 3) = \tau(2 \cdot 3)$.

Assume the first case is true. It follows from Lemmas 17 and 18 that if σ and τ agree on $2 \cdot 1 \cdot 3$, they must be periodic. Assume that the second case is true. Then if σ and τ agree on $1 \cdot 1 \cdot 2 \cdot 2 \cdot 3 \cdot 3$, they must agree on $2 \cdot 2 \cdot 3 \cdot 3$. They also agree on $2 \cdot 3$, and $\{2 \cdot 3, 2 \cdot 2 \cdot 3 \cdot 3\}$ is a periodicity forcing set. Thus if σ and τ are distinct, they must be periodic over $\{2, 3\}$. Furthermore, if they agree on $2 \cdot 1 \cdot 3$, then since $\sigma(1) = \tau(1) = u$ for some word $u \in \{a, b\}^*$,

$$\sigma(2) \cdot u \cdot \sigma(3) = \tau(2) \cdot u \cdot \tau(3).$$

If σ and τ are periodic over $\{2, 3\}$, there exist k_1, k_2, k_3, $k_4 \in \mathbb{N}_0$ and a primitive word $w \in \{a, b\}^*$ such that $\sigma(2) = w^{k_1}$, $\sigma(3) = w^{k_2}$, $\tau(2) = w^{k_3}$ and $\tau(3) = w^{k_4}$. Thus

$$w^{k_1} \cdot u \cdot w^{k_2} = w^{k_3} \cdot u \cdot w^{k_4}$$

which is a non-trivial equation in two unknowns unless $k_1 = k_3$ and $k_2 = k_4$, in which case σ and τ are not distinct. Therefore by Lemma 1, $u \in \{w\}^*$. Consequently, if two distinct morphisms agree on every pattern in Π', they are periodic, so Π' is a periodicity forcing set.

An alternative to splitting variables in the patterns of a periodicity forcing set is to generate a set of patterns obtained by inserting a new variable repeatedly into occurrences of a single pattern not in DPCP. It is relatively simple to establish a set of patterns with the same basic Parikh vectors in this way. The next results demonstrate how it can be shown that such a set is also periodicity forcing. The following definition is given to provide a notation for inserting a new variable x at a specified place in a pattern α.

Definition 21. *Let α be a pattern and let $x \in \text{var}(\alpha)$ be a variable. Let $\text{pre}_x(\alpha)$ be the prefix of α up to, and including the first occurrence of x. Let $\text{suf}_x(\alpha)$ be the suffix of α starting after (not including) the first occurrence of x.*

Note that $\text{pre}_x(\alpha) \cdot \text{suf}_x(\alpha) = \alpha$, so the pattern $\text{pre}_x(\alpha) \cdot y \cdot \text{suf}_x(\alpha)$ is the pattern obtained by inserting the variable y into the pattern α directly after the first occurrence of x. Again, knowledge of existing periodicity forcing sets is used to impose the required conditions. For clarity, a specific example (from Lemma 16) is used; however, any periodicity forcing set of patterns with two variables would be suitable.

Theorem 22. *Let $\alpha \notin$ DPCP and let $x \notin \text{var}(\alpha)$. Then the set $\Pi := \{x \cdot \alpha, x \cdot x \cdot \alpha \cdot \alpha\} \cup \{\text{pre}_y(\alpha) \cdot x \cdot \text{suf}_y(\alpha) \mid y \in \text{var}(\alpha)\}$ is periodicity forcing.*

It is clear that the patterns generated in the style of Theorem 22 have the pattern α^k as a sub-pattern, where $k := |\text{var}(\alpha)| + 3$. Thus there exists a non-trivial morphism φ and a pattern $\beta \notin$ DPCP such that $\varphi(\beta) = \alpha^k$.

Proposition 23. *Let $\alpha = \beta^k$ for some pattern β and number $k \geq |\text{var}(\alpha)| + 3$. Then α is not a prime element of DPCP⁻.*

This is an interesting result since the properties associated with the Dual PCP are, due to the nature of morphisms, generally consistent for powers of the same word. It can also be interpreted that, as a result, the majority of periodicity forcing words are not prime.

6 Conclusion

Section 3 introduces a prime subset of DPCP⁻, allowing the set to be described as chains of morphic images. It is shown that this subset is non-empty, and thus that DPCP⁻ can be exactly generated by the set of prime periodicity forcing words. In Section 4, a construction is given for periodicity forcing words containing any given factor/prefix/suffix. This not only produces a rich class of new examples, but demonstrates a previously unknown level of generality within the seemingly very restrictive set. Motivated by the study of the prime periodicity forcing words introduced earlier, Section 5 examines alternative methods for generating periodicity forcing words. The results give examples of periodicity forcing words which contrast those known so far, and provide further insights into the prime words considered earlier in the paper. As a by-product of results from this paper and existing literature, tight bounds on the length of the shortest periodicity forcing word over a given alphabet can be given.

Acknowledgements. The authors wish to thank the anonymous referees for their helpful remarks and suggestions which have provided a useful additional reference and a construction which has produced a stronger form of Proposition 7.

References

1. Culik II, K., Karhumäki, J.: On the equality sets for homomorphisms on free monoids with two generators. Theoretical Informatics and Applications (RAIRO) 14, 349–369 (1980)
2. Czeizler, E., Holub, S., Karhumäki, J., Laine, M.: Intricacies of simple word equations: An example. International Journal of Foundations of Computer Science 18, 1167–1175 (2007)
3. Day, J.D., Reidenbach, D., Schneider, J.C.: On the Dual Post Correspondence problem. In: Béal, M.-P., Carton, O. (eds.) DLT 2013. LNCS, vol. 7907, pp. 167–178. Springer, Heidelberg (2013)
4. Hadravova, J., Holub, S.: Large simple binary equality words. International Journal of Foundations of Computer Science 23, 1385–1403 (2012)
5. Holub, S.: Binary equality sets are generated by two words. Journal of Algebra 259, 1–42 (2003)
6. Holub, S., Kortelainen, J.: Linear size test sets for certain commutative languages. Theoretical Informatics and Applications (RAIRO) 35, 453–475 (2001)
7. Karhumäki, J., Petre, E.: On some special equations on words. Technical Report 584, Turku Centre for Computer Science, TUCS (2003)
8. Lothaire, M.: Combinatorics on Words. Addison-Wesley, Reading (1983)
9. Makanin, G.S.: The problem of solvability of equations in a free semi-group. Soviet Mathematics Doklady 18, 330–334 (1977)
10. Post, E.L.: A variant of a recursively unsolvable problem. Bulletin of the American Mathematical Society 52, 264–268 (1946)

Balancedness of Arnoux-Rauzy and Brun Words

Vincent Delecroix[1], Tomáš Hejda[2,3], and Wolfgang Steiner[3]

[1] Institut de Mathématiques de Jussieu, CNRS UMR 7586,
Université Paris Diderot – Paris 7, Case 7012, 75205 Paris Cedex 13, France
delecroix@math.jussieu.fr
[2] Department of Mathematics and Doppler Institute, FNSPE,
Czech Technical University in Prague, Czech Republic
tohecz@gmail.com
[3] LIAFA, CNRS UMR 7089, Université Paris Diderot – Paris 7,
Case 7014, 75205 Paris Cedex 13, France
steiner@liafa.univ-paris-diderot.fr

Abstract. We study balancedness properties of words given by the Arnoux-Rauzy and Brun multi-dimensional continued fraction algorithms. We show that almost all Brun words on 3 letters and Arnoux-Rauzy words over arbitrary alphabets are finitely balanced; in particular, boundedness of the strong partial quotients implies balancedness. On the other hand, we provide examples of unbalanced Brun words on 3 letters.

1 Introduction

It is well known that Sturmian words are exactly the 1-balanced aperiodic words on 2 letters. Standard Sturmian words can be characterized in the following way: Each standard Sturmian word $\omega \in \{1,2\}^{\mathbb{N}}$ is the image of a standard Sturmian word by the substitution $\alpha_1 : 1 \mapsto 1, 2 \mapsto 12$, or $\alpha_2 : 1 \mapsto 21, 2 \mapsto 2$; it has thus an '$S$-adic representation' $\omega = \alpha_1^{a_1} \alpha_2^{a_2} \alpha_1^{a_3} \alpha_2^{a_4} \cdots$ (with $S = \{\alpha_1, \alpha_2\}$). Moreover, $[0; a_1, a_2, \ldots]$ is the continued fraction expansion of f_2/f_1, where f_i denotes the frequency of the letter i in ω; e.g., the Fibonacci word is $\omega = \alpha_1 \alpha_2 \alpha_1 \alpha_2 \cdots$, with $[0; 1, 1, \ldots]$ being the golden mean. For details, we refer to [17, Chapter 2] and [15, Chapter 6]. Since each Sturmian word has the same language as a standard Sturmian word, it is sufficient to study the standard ones for all properties that depend only on the language, such as balancedness.

Many different generalizations of Sturmian words to larger alphabets can be found in the literature; see e.g. [5]. We are interested in words that are provided by multi-dimensional continued fraction algorithms and the corresponding substitutions; see [6]. Since 1-balancedness is a strong restriction [16,19], we are interested in finite balancedness of words given by the Arnoux-Rauzy and Brun continued fraction algorithms; see Sections 2 and 3 for precise definitions.

The prototype of an Arnoux-Rauzy word is the Tribonacci word, which is 2-balanced [18]. However, we know from [13] that there are Arnoux-Rauzy words (on 3 letters) that are not finitely balanced; see also [12]. In [7], it was shown that Arnoux-Rauzy words are finitely balanced if the 'weak partial quotients' are

J. Karhumäki, A. Lepistö, and L. Zamboni (Eds.): WORDS 2013, LNCS 8079, pp. 119–131, 2013.
© Springer-Verlag Berlin Heidelberg 2013

bounded, and that a large class of Arnoux-Rauzy words are 2-balanced. Here, we show that the set of finitely balanced Arnoux-Rauzy words has full measure (with respect to a suitably chosen measure on Arnoux-Rauzy words), and contains the words with bounded 'strong partial quotients' (in arbitrary dimension). Note however that, for $d \geq 3$, Arnoux-Rauzy words are defined only for a set of slopes of zero Lebesgue measure that form the the so-called Rauzy gasket [3].

The Brun algorithm has the advantage over Arnoux-Rauzy that it is defined for all directions in $\mathbb{R}_+^d$. To our knowledge, the balancedness of words associated to the Brun algorithm has not been studied yet. We show that almost all Brun words on 3 letters are finitely balanced; in particular, this holds for words with bounded 'strong partial quotients'. We also exhibit Brun words (on 3 letters) that are not finitely balanced. Note that, for fixed points of substitutions, an exact criterion for balancedness is provided by [1].

2   Notation

Let $\mathcal{A} = \{1, 2, \ldots, d\}$ be a finite alphabet and $\mathcal{A}^*$ be the free monoid over $\mathcal{A}$ (with the concatenation as product). Let $|w|$ be the length of a word $w \in \mathcal{A}^*$ and $|w|_j$ the number of occurrences of the letter $j \in \mathcal{A}$ in w. A pair of words $u, v \in \mathcal{A}^*$ with $|u| = |v|$, is C-balanced if

$$-C \leq |u|_j - |v|_j \leq C \quad \text{for all } j \in \mathcal{A}.$$

A *factor* of an infinite word $\omega = (\omega_n)_{n \in \mathbb{N}} \in \mathcal{A}^{\mathbb{N}}$ is a finite word of the form $\omega_{[k,\ell)} = \omega_k \omega_{k+1} \cdots \omega_{\ell-1}$. An infinite word ω is C-*balanced* if each pair of factors u, v of ω with $|u| = |v|$ is C-balanced; ω is *finitely balanced* if it is C-balanced for some $C \in \mathbb{N}$. The *balance* of an infinite word ω is the smallest number $B(\omega)$ such that ω is $B(\omega)$-balanced, with $B(\omega) = \infty$ if ω is not finitely balanced.

The *frequency* f_i of a letter $i \in \mathcal{A}$ in $\omega = (\omega_n)_{n \in \mathbb{N}} \in \mathcal{A}^{\mathbb{N}}$ is $\lim_{n \to \infty} |\omega_{[0,n)}|_i / n$, if the limit exists. It is easy to see that the frequency of each letter exists when ω is finitely balanced (see [10]).

A *substitution* σ over $\mathcal{A}$ is an endomorphism of $\mathcal{A}^*$. Its *incidence matrix* is the square matrix $M_\sigma = (|\sigma(j)|_i)_{i,j \in \mathcal{A}} \in \mathbb{N}^{d \times d}$ (with $\mathbb{N} = \{0, 1, 2, \ldots\}$). The map

$$\ell: \ \mathcal{A}^* \to \mathbb{N}^d, \ w \mapsto {}^t(|w|_1, |w|_2, \ldots, |w|_d)$$

is called the *abelianization map*. Note that $\ell(\sigma(w)) = M_\sigma \ell(w)$ for all $w \in \mathcal{A}^*$.

Let $(\sigma_n)_{n \in \mathbb{N}}$ be a sequence of substitutions over the alphabet $\mathcal{A}$. To keep notation concise, we set $M_n = M_{\sigma_n}$ for $n \in \mathbb{N}$ and denote products of consecutive substitutions and their incidence matrices by $\sigma_{[k,\ell)} = \sigma_k \sigma_{k+1} \cdots \sigma_{\ell-1}$ and $M_{[k,\ell)} = M_k M_{k+1} \cdots M_{\ell-1}$ respectively. A word $\omega \in \mathcal{A}^{\mathbb{N}}$ is a *limit word* of $(\sigma_n)_{n \in \mathbb{N}}$ if there is a sequence $(\omega^{(n)})_{n \in \mathbb{N}}$ with

$$\omega^{(0)} = \omega, \quad \omega^{(n)} = \sigma_n(\omega^{(n+1)}) \quad \text{for all } n \in \mathbb{N},$$

where the substitutions σ_n are extended naturally to infinite words. The word ω is called an S-*adic word* with *directive sequence* $(\sigma_n)_{n \in \mathbb{N}}$ and $S = \{\sigma_n : n \in \mathbb{N}\}$.

Given a directive sequence $(\sigma_n)_{n\in\mathbb{N}}$, we can define different generalizations of partial quotients. The sequence of *weak partial quotients* is the sequence of positive integers $(a_n)_{n\in\mathbb{N}}$ such that $\sigma_0\sigma_1\cdots = \sigma_{A_0}^{a_0}\sigma_{A_1}^{a_1}\cdots$, with $A_n = \sum_{k=0}^{n-1} a_k$ and $\sigma_{A_n} = \cdots = \sigma_{A_{n+1}-1} \neq \sigma_{A_{n+1}}$ for all $n \in \mathbb{N}$. The notion of strong partial quotients refers to the time we need to reach a positive (or at least primitive) matrix in the product of incidence matrices. A good precise definition of them probably depends on S and the intended use, but properties like being bounded should hold simultaneously for all suitable definitions. In this paper, we say that the *strong partial quotients are bounded by h* if $M_{[n,n+h)}$ is primitive for all $n \in \mathbb{N}$.

3   Arnoux-Rauzy and Brun Words

We are interested in this paper in two S-adic systems that arise naturally from multi-dimensional continued fraction algorithms. The set of *Arnoux-Rauzy substitutions* over d letters is $S_{\mathrm{AR}} = \{\alpha_i : i \in \mathcal{A}\}$ with

$$\alpha_i : \ i \mapsto i, \ j \mapsto ij \text{ for } j \in \mathcal{A} \setminus \{i\}.$$

For each directive sequence $(\sigma_n)_{n\in\mathbb{N}} = (\alpha_{i_n})_{n\in\mathbb{N}} \in S_{\mathrm{AR}}^{\mathbb{N}}$, the words $\sigma_{[0,n)}(i_n)$ are nested prefixes of the limit word ω. If the directive sequence contains infinitely many occurrences of each substitution α_i, $i \in \mathcal{A}$, the unique limit word ω is called a *standard Arnoux-Rauzy word*. Any word that has the same language (and thus the same balancedness properties) as a standard Arnoux-Rauzy word is called Arnoux-Rauzy word. The *Tribonacci word* is the Arnoux-Rauzy word on 3-letters with periodic directive sequence $\alpha_1\alpha_2\alpha_3\alpha_1\alpha_2\alpha_3\cdots$; it satisfies

$$\omega = 1213121121312121312112131213121121312121312112131211213121121 \cdots$$

and is known to be 2-balanced [18].

A set of *Brun substitutions* was defined in [9] to provide a connection between stepped planes and the Brun algorithm. Here, we consider the set of substitutions $S_{\mathrm{Br}} = \{\beta_{ij} : i \in \mathcal{A}, j \in \mathcal{A} \setminus \{i\}\}$ over d letters, with

$$\beta_{ij} : \ j \mapsto ij, \ k \mapsto k \text{ for } k \in \mathcal{A} \setminus \{j\},$$

that corresponds to the additive version of this algorithm. An S_{Br}-adic word is called a *Brun word* if its directive sequence $(\sigma_n)_{n\in\mathbb{N}}$ satisfies

$$\sigma_n\sigma_{n+1} \in \{\beta_{ij}\beta_{ij} : i \in \mathcal{A}, j \in \mathcal{A} \setminus \{i\}\}$$
$$\cup \{\beta_{ij}\beta_{jk} : i \in \mathcal{A}, j \in \mathcal{A} \setminus \{i\}, k \in \mathcal{A} \setminus \{j\}\} \quad \text{for all } n \in \mathbb{N} \quad (1)$$

and for each $i \in \mathcal{A}$ there is $j \in \mathcal{A}$ such that β_{ij} occurs infinitely often in $(\sigma_n)_{n\in\mathbb{N}}$. E.g., the Brun word with periodic directive sequence $\beta_{12}\beta_{23}\beta_{31}\beta_{12}\beta_{23}\beta_{31}\cdots$ is

$$\omega = 12311212312311231121231121231231121231231123112311212312 \cdots.$$

Recall that the Brun algorithm [11] subtracts at each step the second largest coordinate from the largest coordinate. It is given by the transformations

$$T_{ij} : \ D_{ij} \to \mathbb{R}_+^d, \ \mathbf{f} \mapsto M_{\beta_{ij}}^{-1}\mathbf{f}/\|M_{\beta_{ij}}^{-1}\mathbf{f}\|_1,$$

where $D_{ij} \subset \mathbb{R}_+^d$ is the set of vectors $\mathbf{f} = {}^t(f_1, \ldots, f_d)$ such that $f_i \geq f_j$ are the two largest components of $\mathbf{f}$; here, $\mathbb{R}_+ = [0, \infty)$. A sequence $(i_0, j_0)(i_1, j_1)$ $(i_2, j_2) \cdots$ is a Brun representation of $\mathbf{f} \in \mathbb{R}_+^d$ if

$$T_{i_{k-1}j_{k-1}} \cdots T_{i_1 j_1} T_{i_0 j_0}(\mathbf{f}) \in D_{i_k j_k} \quad \text{for all} \quad k \in \mathbb{N}.$$

Given a Brun word ω with directive sequence $\beta_{i_0 j_0} \beta_{i_1 j_1} \beta_{i_2 j_2} \cdots$, we get that $(i_0, j_0)(i_1, j_1)(i_2, j_2) \cdots$ is a Brun representation of the vector of frequencies of ω.

In the Arnoux-Rauzy algorithm, all but one coordinates are subtracted from the largest coordinate, which is assumed to be larger than the sum of the other coordinates. Here, we have transformations $T_i : D_i \to \mathbb{R}_+^d$ with $D_i \subset \mathbb{R}_+^d$ being the set of vectors $\mathbf{f} = {}^t(f_1, \ldots, f_d)$ such that $f_i \geq \sum_{j \in \mathcal{A} \setminus \{i\}} f_j$.

The following two lemmas translate the fact that these two algorithms converge and show that the frequency vector $\mathbf{f} = \mathbf{f}(\omega)$ of the limit word of a directive sequence $(\sigma_n)_{n \in \mathbb{N}}$ is given by the limit cone

$$\mathbb{R}_+ \mathbf{f} = \bigcap_{n \in \mathbb{N}} M_{[0,n)} \mathbb{R}_+^d. \tag{2}$$

Moreover, because of the relation with the continued fraction algorithms, two distinct standard Arnoux-Rauzy words and two distinct standard Brun words respectively have different frequency vectors.

Lemma 1. *Each Brun word on 3 letters has letter frequencies.*

Proof. Let $(\sigma_n)_{n \in \mathbb{N}} \in S_{\text{Br}}^{\mathbb{N}}$ be a directive sequence of a Brun word on 3 letters, M_n the associated incidence matrices, and $\mathbf{f} \in \bigcap_{n \in \mathbb{N}} M_{[0,n)} \mathbb{R}_+^d$. From [4], we know that there is a sequence of matrices $(\tilde{M}_n)_{n \in \mathbb{N}}$ such that $\| {}^t(\tilde{M}_{[0,n)}) \|_\infty \leq 1$,

$${}^t(\tilde{M}_{[0,n)}) \, \mathbf{x} = {}^t(M_{[0,n)}) \, \mathbf{x} \quad \text{for all} \quad \mathbf{x} \in \mathbf{f}^\perp, \; n \in \mathbb{N}, \tag{3}$$

where $\mathbf{f}^\perp$ denotes the hyperplane orthogonal to $\mathbf{f}$; see also Section 6.

For each $\mathbf{v} \in \mathbf{f}^\perp$ with $\|\mathbf{v}\|_\infty = 1$, we have

$$\left| \left\langle \mathbf{v}, \frac{M_{[0,n)} \, \mathbf{e}_i}{\|M_{[0,n)} \, \mathbf{e}_i\|_1} \right\rangle \right| = \left| \left\langle {}^t(\tilde{M}_{[0,n)}) \, \mathbf{v}, \frac{\mathbf{e}_i}{\|M_{[0,n)} \, \mathbf{e}_i\|_1} \right\rangle \right| \leq \frac{1}{\|M_{[0,n)} \, \mathbf{e}_i\|_1}$$

for each unit vector $\mathbf{e}_i$, $i \in \mathcal{A}$. Since $\min_{i \in \mathcal{A}} \|M_{[0,n)} \, \mathbf{e}_i\|_1 \to \infty$ for each directive sequence of a Brun word, the cone $M_{[0,n)} \mathbb{R}_+^d$ tends to the line $\mathbb{R}_+ \mathbf{f}$, i.e., (2) holds. From (2), it is standard to prove that $\mathbf{f}$ is the frequency vector of ω; see [8]. □

The proof of Lemma 1 could be adapted to Arnoux-Rauzy words because the incidence matrix of an Arnoux-Rauzy substitution is similar to a matrix given by the fully subtractive algorithm, which was studied in [4]. However, we prefer using the results of [4] in a different way in the proof of the following lemma.

Lemma 2. *Each Arnoux-Rauzy word (on $d \geq 2$ letters) has letter frequencies.*

Proof. Let $(\sigma_n)_{n \in \mathbb{N}} = (\alpha_{i_n})_{n \in \mathbb{N}}$ be the directive sequence of an Arnoux-Rauzy word and $\mathbf{f} \in \bigcap_{n \in \mathbb{N}} M_{[0,n)} \mathbb{R}_+^d$ with $\|\mathbf{f}\|_1 = 1$. We know from the results on the fully subtractive algorithm in [4] that there is a sequence of matrices $(\tilde{M}_n)_{n \in \mathbb{N}}$ such that $\|\tilde{M}_{[0,n)}\|_\infty \leq 1$ and

$$\tilde{M}_{[0,n)}\, \mathbf{x} = M_{[0,n)}\, \mathbf{x} \quad \text{for all} \quad \mathbf{x} \in (M_{[0,n)})^{-1} \mathbf{1}^\perp, \ n \in \mathbb{N}, \tag{4}$$

where $\mathbf{1} = {}^t(1, \ldots, 1)$; see also Section 5.

Denote by π_n be the projection along $(M_{[0,n)})^{-1}\mathbf{f}$ onto $(M_{[0,n)})^{-1}\mathbf{1}^\perp$. Then

$$\|\pi_0 \, M_{[0,n)}\, \boldsymbol{\ell}(i_n)\|_\infty = \|M_{[0,n)}\, \pi_n\, \boldsymbol{\ell}(i_n)\|_\infty = \|\tilde{M}_{[0,n)}\, \pi_n\, \boldsymbol{\ell}(i_n)\|_\infty \leq \|\pi_n\, \boldsymbol{\ell}(i_n)\|_\infty.$$

Since $(M_{[0,n)})^{-1}\mathbf{f} \in M_n \mathbb{R}_+^d$, the i_n-th coordinate of $(M_{[0,n)})^{-1}\mathbf{f}$ is larger than or equal to (the sum of) the other coordinates, thus $\|\pi_n\, \boldsymbol{\ell}(i_n)\|_\infty \leq \|\boldsymbol{\ell}(i_n)\|_\infty = 1$.

Following Dumont and Thomas [14], each prefix $\omega_{[0,k)}$ of ω can be written as

$$\omega_{[0,k)} = \sigma_{[0,m-1)}(p_{m-1})\, \sigma_{[0,m-2)}(p_{m-2}) \cdots \sigma_{[0,1)}(p_1)\, p_0,$$

with a sequence of words $(p_n)_{0 \leq n < m}$ defined in the following way. Let $m = m(k) \in \mathbb{N}$ be minimal such that $|\sigma_{[0,m)}(i_m)| > k$. Then there is a unique prefix p_{m-1} of $\sigma_{m-1}(i_m)$ such that

$$|\sigma_{[0,m-1)}(p_{m-1})| \leq k < |\sigma_{[0,m-1)}(p_{m-1}a_{m-1})|,$$

with $a_{m-1} \in \mathcal{A}$ being the letter following p_{m-1} in $\sigma_{m-1}(i_m)$. Inductively, we obtain for $0 \leq n < m$ unique $p_n \in \mathcal{A}^*$ and $a_n \in \mathcal{A}$ such that

$$|\sigma_{[0,n)}(p_n)| \leq k - \sum_{j=n+1}^{m-1} |\sigma_{[0,j)}(p_j)| < |\sigma_{[0,n)}(p_n a_n)|$$

and $p_n a_n$ is a prefix of $|\sigma_n(a_{n+1})|$, with $a_m = i_m$. We thus have

$$\boldsymbol{\ell}(\omega_{[0,k)}) = \sum_{n=0}^{m-1} \boldsymbol{\ell}(\sigma_{[0,n)}(p_n)) = \sum_{n=0}^{m-1} \pi_0\, M_{[0,n)}\, \boldsymbol{\ell}(p_n).$$

By the definition of the Arnoux-Rauzy substitutions, p_n is either empty or equal to i_n, thus

$$\|\pi_0\, \boldsymbol{\ell}(\omega_{[0,k)})\|_\infty \leq \sum_{n=0}^{m-1} \|\pi_0\, M_{[0,n)}\, \boldsymbol{\ell}(i_n)\|_\infty \leq m.$$

Since $m(k)/\|\boldsymbol{\ell}(\omega_{[0,k)})\|_\infty \to 0$ as $k \to \infty$, the direction of $\boldsymbol{\ell}(\omega_{[0,k)})$ converges to that of $\mathbf{f}$, thus $\mathbf{f}$ is the frequency vector of ω. $\qquad\square$

4   Discrepancy and Balancedness

Let ω be an infinite word with frequency vector $\mathbf{f} = {}^t(f_1, f_2, \ldots, f_d)$, and denote by π be the projection along $\mathbf{f}$ onto $\mathbf{1}^\perp$. It is easily written down in coordinates:

$$\pi\, \boldsymbol{\ell}(w) = {}^t(|w|_1 - |w|\, f_1, \ |w|_2 - |w|\, f_2, \ \ldots, \ |w|_d - |w|\, f_d).$$

Note that the so called Rauzy fractal is the closure of $\{\pi\,\ell(\omega_{[0,n)}) : n \in \mathbb{N}\}$, which is the projection of the vertices of the broken line associated with ω.

More generally, for a function $\phi : \mathcal{A} \to \mathbb{R}$, we consider the Birkhoff sums

$$S_n(\phi, \omega) = \phi(\omega_0) + \phi(\omega_1) + \cdots + \phi(\omega_{n-1}).$$

Remark that, if χ_i denotes the characteristic function of a letter $i \in \mathcal{A}$, then $S_n(\chi_i, \omega) = |\omega_{[0,n)}|_i$, and the coordinates of $\pi\,\ell(\omega_{[0,n)})$ are $S_n(\chi_i - f_i, \omega)$. The ϕ-discrepancy of ω is $\Delta(\phi, \omega) = \sup_{n \in \mathbb{N}} |S_n(\phi, \omega)|$. We set

$$\Delta(\omega) = \max_{i \in \mathcal{A}} \Delta(\chi_i - f_i, \omega) = \sup_{n \in \mathbb{N}} \|\pi\,\ell(\omega_{[0,n)})\|_\infty,$$

and say that ω has *finite discrepancy* if $\Delta(\omega) < \infty$. The following result from [1, Proposition 7 and Remark 8] establishes a link between balance and discrepancy.

Lemma 3. *We have $\Delta(\omega) \le B(\omega) \le 4\Delta(\omega)$.*

For many words, balancedness can be shown using the following proposition.

Proposition 1. *Let ω be an Arnoux-Rauzy or Brun word with directive sequence $(\sigma_n)_{n \in \mathbb{N}}$. For each sequence of matrices $(\tilde{M}_n)_{n \in \mathbb{N}}$ satisfying (3), we have*

$$\Delta(\omega) \le \sum_{n=0}^{\infty} \left\| {}^t(\tilde{M}_{[0,n)}) \right\|_\infty.$$

For each sequence of matrices $(\tilde{M}_n)_{n \in \mathbb{N}}$ satisfying (4), we have

$$\Delta(\omega) \le \sum_{n=0}^{\infty} \left\| \tilde{M}_{[0,n)} \right\|_\infty.$$

Proof. The first statement follows from

$$\Delta(\chi_i - f_i, \omega) = \sup_{k \in \mathbb{N}} \left| \langle \mathbf{e}_i - f_i\,\mathbf{1}, \ell(\omega_{[0,k)}) \rangle \right| \le \sum_{n=0}^{\infty} \left| \langle \mathbf{e}_i - f_i\,\mathbf{1}, M_{[0,n)}\,\ell(i_n) \rangle \right|$$

$$= \sum_{n=0}^{\infty} \left| \langle {}^t(\tilde{M}_{[0,n)})\,(\mathbf{e}_i - f_i\,\mathbf{1}), \ell(i_n) \rangle \right| \le \sum_{n=0}^{\infty} \left\| {}^t(\tilde{M}_{[0,n)}) \right\|_\infty,$$

where we have used the Dumont-Thomas representations in the first inequality (see the proof of Lemma 2), the fact that $\mathbf{e}_i - f_i\,\mathbf{1} \in \mathbf{f}^\perp$ in the second equality and $\|\mathbf{e}_i - f_i\,\mathbf{1}\|_\infty \le 1$ in the last inequality. The proof of the second statement runs along the lines of the proof of Lemma 2, where we can replace α_{i_n} by $\beta_{i_n j_n}$. $\square$

5   Contractivity of Arnoux-Rauzy Matrices

Now we study the contractivity of Arnoux-Rauzy matrices on certain hyperplanes, quantifying the approach in [4]. For a directive sequence $(\sigma_n)_{n \in \mathbb{N}}$, let

$$\mathbf{v}^{(n)} = {}^t\big(v_1^{(n)}, v_2^{(n)}, \ldots, v_d^{(n)}\big) = \frac{{}^t(M_{[0,n)})\,\mathbf{1}}{\|{}^t(M_{[0,n)})\,\mathbf{1}\|_1} \qquad (n \in \mathbb{N}).$$

Lemma 4. *Let ω be an Arnoux-Rauzy word with directive sequence $(\alpha_{i_n})_{n \in \mathbb{N}}$. Then $\|\mathbf{v}^{(n)}\|_\infty < \frac{1}{d-1}$ for all $n \in \mathbb{N}$. If moreover $\{i_n, i_{n+1}, \dots, i_{n+h-1}\} = \mathcal{A}$, $h \in \mathbb{N}$, then $\|\mathbf{v}^{(n+h)}\|_\infty < \frac{2^h-1}{2^h(d-1)}$.*

Proof. First note that $\|\mathbf{v}^{(0)}\|_\infty = \frac{1}{d}$. Assume now that $\|\mathbf{v}^{(n)}\|_\infty < \frac{1}{d-1}$, and let w.l.o.g. $i_n = 1$. Then the simplex $\{\mathbf{x} \in \mathbb{R}^d : \|\mathbf{x}\|_1 = 1, \|\mathbf{x}\|_\infty \le \frac{1}{d-1}\}$ is mapped by ${}^t M_n$ (after normalizing) to the simplex spanned by ${}^t(0, \frac{1}{d-1}, \dots, \frac{1}{d-1})$, ${}^t(\frac{1}{2(d-1)}, \frac{1}{2(d-1)}, \frac{1}{d-1}, \dots, \frac{1}{d-1})$, $\dots$, ${}^t(\frac{1}{2(d-1)}, \frac{1}{d-1}, \dots, \frac{1}{d-1}, \frac{1}{2(d-1)})$. This shows that $\|\mathbf{v}^{(n+1)}\|_\infty < \frac{1}{d-1}$ and that $v_{i_n}^{(n+1)} < \frac{1}{2(d-1)}$. Similar considerations show that $v_{i_n}^{(n+h)} < \frac{2^h-1}{2^h(d-1)}$ for all $h \ge 1$. If $\{i_n, i_{n+1}, \dots, i_{n+h-1}\} = \mathcal{A}$, then we obtain that $v_j^{(n+h)} < \frac{2^h-1}{2^h(d-1)}$ for all $j \in \mathcal{A}$. $\square$

Lemma 5. *Let ω be an Arnoux-Rauzy word with directive sequence $(\alpha_{i_n})_{n \in \mathbb{N}}$. Then there is a sequence of matrices $(\tilde{M}_n)_{n \in \mathbb{N}}$ satisfying (4) with*

$$\left\| {}^t\tilde{M}_n \, \mathbf{e}_{i_n} \right\|_1 = d - \|\mathbf{v}^{(n+1)}\|_\infty^{-1} < 1$$

and ${}^t\tilde{M}_n \, \mathbf{e}_j = \mathbf{e}_j$ for all $j \in \mathcal{A} \setminus \{i_n\}$, $n \in \mathbb{N}$.

Proof. For each $n \in \mathbb{N}$, let $\tilde{M}_n$ be the matrix with i_n-th row equal to ${}^t\mathbf{1} - \frac{{}^t\mathbf{v}^{(n+1)}}{\|\mathbf{v}^{(n+1)}\|_\infty}$ and j-th row ${}^t\mathbf{e}_j$ for all $j \in \mathcal{A}\setminus\{i_n\}$. Then $\left\| {}^t\tilde{M}_n \, \mathbf{e}_{i_n} \right\|_1 = d - \|\mathbf{v}^{(n+1)}\|_\infty^{-1}$ and ${}^t\tilde{M}_n \, \mathbf{e}_j = \mathbf{e}_j$ for all $j \in \mathcal{A} \setminus \{i_n\}$, with $\|\mathbf{v}^{(n+1)}\|_\infty^{-1} > d - 1$ by Lemma 4. Since adding a multiple of ${}^t\mathbf{v}^{(n+1)}$ to a row of M_n does not change $M_n\mathbf{x}$ for $\mathbf{x} \in (\mathbf{v}^{(n+1)})^\perp$, we have $\tilde{M}_n\mathbf{x} = M_n\mathbf{x}$ for all $\mathbf{x} \in (\mathbf{v}^{(n+1)})^\perp$. Using that $M_n(\mathbf{v}^{(n+1)})^\perp = (\mathbf{v}^{(n)})^\perp$, we obtain inductively that (4) holds, which proves the lemma. $\square$

Lemma 6. *Let ω be an Arnoux-Rauzy word with directive sequence $(\alpha_{i_n})_{n \in \mathbb{N}}$ and $(\tilde{M}_n)_{n \in \mathbb{N}}$ as in Lemma 5. If $\{i_k, i_{k+1}, \dots, i_{\ell-1}\} = \mathcal{A}$ and there is $h \in \mathbb{N}$ such that $\{i_{n-h+1}, i_{n-h+2}, \dots, i_n\} = \mathcal{A}$ for all $n \in [k, \ell)$, then*

$$\|\tilde{M}_{[k,\ell)}\|_\infty < \frac{2^h - d}{2^h - 1}.$$

Proof. Let $j \in \mathcal{A}$ and let $m \in [k, \ell)$ be minimal such that $i_m = j$. Then

$$\left\| {}^t(\tilde{M}_{[k,\ell)}) \, \mathbf{e}_j \right\|_1 \le \left\| {}^t(\tilde{M}_{[m+1,\ell)}) \right\|_1 \left\| {}^t(\tilde{M}_{[k,m+1)}) \, \mathbf{e}_j \right\|_1 \le \left\| {}^t\tilde{M}_m \, \mathbf{e}_j \right\|_1 < \frac{2^h - d}{2^h - 1},$$

where we have used that, for all $n \in [k, \ell)$ by Lemmas 4 and 5, $\|{}^t\tilde{M}_n\| \le 1$, ${}^t\tilde{M}_n \, \mathbf{e}_j = \mathbf{e}_j$ for all $j \in \mathcal{A} \setminus \{i_n\}$, and $\|{}^t\tilde{M}_n \mathbf{e}_{i_n}\|_1 < \frac{2^h-d}{2^h-1}$. This shows that $\|\tilde{M}_{[k,\ell)}\|_\infty = \|{}^t(\tilde{M}_{[k,\ell)})\|_1 < \frac{2^h-d}{2^h-1}$. $\square$

Theorem 1. *Let $h \in \mathbb{N}$. There is a constant $C(h)$ such that each Arnoux-Rauzy word with strong partial quotients bounded by h, i.e., with directive sequence $(\alpha_{i_n})_{n \in \mathbb{N}}$ satisfying $\{i_n, \dots, i_{n+h-1}\} = \mathcal{A}$ for all $n \in \mathbb{N}$, is $C(h)$-balanced.*

Proof. By Lemma 6, there is a sequence $(\tilde{M}_n)_{n\in\mathbb{N}}$ satisfying (4) such that $\|\tilde{M}_{[n,n+h)}\|_\infty < \frac{2^h-d}{2^h-1}$ for all $n \geq h-1$, thus $\|\tilde{M}_{[0,n)}\|_\infty = \mathcal{O}\big(\big(\frac{2^h-d}{2^h-1}\big)^{n/h}\big)$, hence $\sum_{n=0}^{\infty} \|\tilde{M}_{[0,n)}\|_\infty$ is bounded. Lemma 3 and Proposition 1 conclude the proof.   □

6   Contractivity of 3-Dimensional Brun Matrices

For Brun words (over 3 letters), we follow a similar strategy as for Arnoux-Rauzy words. For a Brun word ω with directive sequence $(\psi_{i_n,j_n})_{n\in\mathbb{N}}$, let $(k_n)_{n\in\mathbb{N}}$ be the sequence of letters defined by $\{i_n, j_n, k_n\} = \mathcal{A}$, and let

$$\mathbf{f}^{(n)} = {}^t\big(f_1^{(n)}, f_2^{(n)}, \ldots, f_d^{(n)}\big) = \frac{(M_{[0,n)})^{-1}\mathbf{f}}{\|(M_{[0,n)})^{-1}\mathbf{f}\|_1}$$

be the frequency vector of $\omega^{(n)}$. Moreover, let $(F_n)_{n\in\mathbb{N}}$ be the sequence of Fibonacci numbers defined by $F_0 = 1$, $F_1 = 2$, $F_n = F_{n-1} + F_{n-2}$ for all $n \geq 2$.

Lemma 7. *Let* ω *be a Brun word over* 3 *letters with directive sequence* $(\beta_{i_n,j_n})_{n\in\mathbb{N}}$. *Then* $f_{i_n}^{(n-h)} \geq \frac{1}{F_{h+1}+1}$ *for all* $h \leq n$. *If* $\{i_n, i_{n+1}, \ldots, i_{n+h-1}\} = \mathcal{A}$ *for all* $n \in \mathbb{N}$, *then we have* $(f_{j_n}^{(n)} - f_{k_n}^{(n)})/f_{i_n}^{(n)} \geq \frac{1}{F_h}$ *for all* $n \in \mathbb{N}$.

Proof. Since $f_{i_n}^{(n)} \geq f_j^{(n)}$ for all $j \in \mathcal{A}$, we have $f_{i_n}^{(n)} \geq 1/3$, and it is easily checked that the minimum for $f_{i_n}^{(n-h)}$ is attained when $\mathbf{f}^{(n)} = (1/3, 1/3, 1/3)$ and $i_{n-h} \cdots i_{n-1}$ is an alternating sequence of j_n and k_n. In this case, we have $f_{i_n}^{(n-h)} = 1$, $f_{i_{n-h}}^{(n-h)} = F_h$, and $f_{i_{n-h+1}}^{(n-h)} = F_{h-1}$, thus $f_{i_n}^{(n-h)} = \frac{1}{F_{h+1}+1}$.

Let now, w.l.o.g. $i_n = 1$, $j_n = 2$, and assume that $\{1,3\} \subset \{i_{n+2}, \ldots, i_{n+h}\}$. Then $\mathbf{f}^{(n+1)}$ lies in the quadrangle with corners $\big(\frac{1}{3}, \frac{1}{3}, \frac{1}{3}\big)$, $\big(\frac{F_h}{2(F_h+1)}, \frac{F_h}{2(F_h+1)}, \frac{1}{F_h+1}\big)$, $\big(\frac{1}{F_h+1}, \frac{F_h-1}{F_h+1}, \frac{1}{F_h+1}\big)$, and $\big(\frac{1}{F_h+1}, \frac{F_h}{2(F_h+1)}, \frac{F_h}{2(F_h+1)}\big)$. Therefore, $\mathbf{f}^{(n)}$ lies in the quadrangle with corners $\big(\frac{1}{2}, \frac{1}{4}, \frac{1}{4}\big)$, $\big(\frac{2F_h}{3F_h+2}, \frac{F_h}{3F_h+2}, \frac{2}{3F_h+2}\big)$, $\big(\frac{1}{2}, \frac{F_h-1}{2F_h}, \frac{1}{2F_h}\big)$, and $\big(\frac{F_h+2}{3F_h+2}, \frac{F_h}{3F_h+2}, \frac{F_h}{3F_h+2}\big)$. In particular, note that $f_1^{(n)} - f_2^{(n)} \geq \frac{1}{2F_h}$.

Assume now that $i_{n-1} = 3$. (The situation is similar if $i_{n-1}, \ldots, i_{n-\ell+1}$ are alternatingly 2 and 1, and $i_{n-\ell} = 3$.) Then $(f_1^{(n-1)} - f_2^{(n-1)})/f_1^{(n-1)}$ is minimal when $\mathbf{f}^{(n)} = \big(\frac{1}{2}, \frac{F_h-1}{2F_h}, \frac{1}{2F_h}\big)$, which implies that $\mathbf{f}^{(n-1)} = \big(\frac{1}{3}, \frac{F_h-1}{3F_h}, \frac{F_h+1}{3F_h}\big)$, thus $(f_1^{(n-1)} - f_2^{(n-1)})/f_1^{(n-1)} \geq \frac{1}{F_h}$. A study of several cases shows that this is a lower bound for $(f_{j_n}^{(n)} - f_{k_n}^{(n)})/f_{i_n}^{(n)}$ when $\{i_n, i_{n+1}, \ldots, i_{n+h-1}\} = \mathcal{A}$ for all $n \in \mathbb{N}$.   □

Lemma 8. *Let* ω *be a Brun word with directive sequence* $(\beta_{i_n,j_n})_{n\in\mathbb{N}}$. *Then there is a sequence of matrices* $(\tilde{M}_n)_{n\in\mathbb{N}}$ *satisfying* (3) *with*

$$\|\tilde{M}_n \mathbf{e}_{i_n}\|_1 = 1 - \frac{f_{j_n}^{(n)} - f_{k_n}^{(n)}}{f_{i_n}^{(n)}} \leq 1$$

and $\tilde{M}_n \mathbf{e}_j = \mathbf{e}_j$ *for all* $j \in \mathcal{A} \setminus \{i_n\}$, $n \in \mathbb{N}$.

Proof. For each $n \in \mathbb{N}$, let $\tilde{M}_n$ be the matrix built from M_n by subtracting $\mathbf{f}^{(n)}/f_{i_n}^{(n)}$ from the i_n-th column. Then

$$\left\|\tilde{M}_n \mathbf{e}_{i_n}\right\|_1 = \left(1 - \frac{f_{i_n}^{(n)}}{f_{i_n}^{(n)}}\right) + \left(1 - \frac{f_{j_n}^{(n)}}{f_{i_n}^{(n)}}\right) + \frac{f_{k_n}^{(n)}}{f_{i_n}^{(n)}} = 1 - \frac{f_{j_n}^{(n)} - f_{k_n}^{(n)}}{f_{i_n}^{(n)}},$$

and ${}^t\tilde{M}_n \mathbf{e}_j = \mathbf{e}_j$ for all $j \in \mathcal{A} \setminus \{i_n\}$. Since adding a multiple of $\mathbf{f}^{(n)}$ to a column of M_n does not change ${}^t M_n \mathbf{x}$ for $\mathbf{x} \in (\mathbf{f}^{(n)})^\perp$, we have $\tilde{M}_n \mathbf{x} = M_n \mathbf{x}$ for all $\mathbf{x} \in (\mathbf{f}^{(n)})^\perp$. Using that ${}^t M_n (\mathbf{f}^{(n)})^\perp = (\mathbf{f}^{(n+1)})^\perp$, we obtain inductively that (3) holds, which proves the lemma. $\qquad\square$

Theorem 2. *Let $h \in \mathbb{N}$. There is a constant $C(h)$ such that each Brun word over 3 letters with strong partial quotients bounded by h, i.e., with directive sequence $(\beta_{i_n j_n})_{n \in \mathbb{N}}$ satisfying $\{i_n, \ldots, i_{n+h-1}\} = \{1, 2, 3\}$ for all $n \in \mathbb{N}$, is $C(h)$-balanced.*

Proof. The proof runs along the same lines as that of Theorem 1. Here, Lemma 8 implies that $\left\|{}^t(\tilde{M}_{[n,n+h)})\right\|_\infty \leq \frac{1}{F_h}$ for all $n \in \mathbb{N}$, similarly to Lemma 6, thus $\left\|{}^t(\tilde{M}_{[0,n)})\right\|_\infty = \mathcal{O}(F_h^{-n/h})$. Lemma 3 and Proposition 1 conclude the proof. $\qquad\square$

7 Balancedness of Almost All Words

We use here the results of [4] on Lyapunov exponents to prove that for almost all directive sequences for Brun or Arnoux-Rauzy algorithms, the associated infinite words have finite balances. Here, we define cylinders for both algorithms as follows: given a finite word w, we denote by $[w]$ the set of frequency vectors for which the continued fraction expansion starts by w.

Theorem 3. *Let μ be an ergodic invariant probability measure for the Arnoux-Rauzy algorithm (on d letters) such that $\mu([w]) > 0$ for the cylinder corresponding to a word $w_0 w_1 \cdots w_{n-1} \in \mathcal{A}^*$ with $\{w_0, w_1, \ldots, w_{n-1}\} = \mathcal{A}$. Then, for μ-almost every $\mathbf{f}$ in the Rauzy gasket, the Arnoux-Rauzy word $\omega_{\mathrm{AR}}(\mathbf{f})$ is finitely balanced.*

Let μ be an ergodic invariant probability measure for the Brun algorithm on 3 letters such that $\mu([w]) > 0$ for the cylinder corresponding to a word $w = (i_0, j_0) \cdots (i_{n-1}, j_{n-1})$ with $\{j_0, j_1, \ldots, j_{n-1}\} = \{1, 2, 3\}$. Then, for μ-almost every $\mathbf{f}$, the Brun word $\omega_{\mathrm{Br}}(\mathbf{f})$ is finitely balanced.

Proof. From [4], we know that the second Lyapunov exponent of the cocycle $M_{[0,n)}$ is negative and hence $\|{}^t(M_{[0,n)}) \mathbf{v}\|$ decays exponentially fast for μ-almost every $\mathbf{f}$ and all $\mathbf{v} \in \mathbf{f}^\perp$. By Proposition 1, this implies that $\omega_{\mathrm{AR}}(\mathbf{f})$ and $\omega_{\mathrm{Br}}(\mathbf{f})$ respectively are finitely balanced. $\qquad\square$

The Brun algorithm admits an invariant ergodic probability measure absolutely continuous with respect to Lebesgue [2]. Therefore, we have the following corollary of Theorem 3.

Corollary 1. *For Lebesgue almost all frequency vectors* $\mathbf{f} \in \mathbb{R}^3$, *the Brun word* $\omega_{\mathrm{Br}}(\mathbf{f})$ *is finitely balanced.*

8   Imbalances in Brun Sequences

Similarly to the construction of unbalanced Arnoux-Rauzy words (over 3 letters) in [13], we construct now unbalanced Brun words for $d = 3$. First, for any sequence $(\sigma_n)_{n\in\mathbb{N}}$ satisfying (1), define a sequence $(\tilde{\sigma}_n)_{n\in\mathbb{N}}$ as follows:

$$\tilde{\sigma}_0 = \zeta_1 \quad \text{and} \quad \tilde{\sigma}_n = \begin{cases} \zeta_1 : 1 \mapsto 1, 2 \mapsto 2, 3 \mapsto 23, & \text{if } \sigma_{n-1}\sigma_n = \beta_{ij}\beta_{ij}, \\ \zeta_2 : 1 \mapsto 1, 2 \mapsto 3, 3 \mapsto 32, & \text{if } \sigma_{n-1}\sigma_n = \beta_{ij}\beta_{ji}, \\ \zeta_3 : 1 \mapsto 2, 2 \mapsto 3, 3 \mapsto 31, & \text{if } \sigma_{n-1}\sigma_n = \beta_{ij}\beta_{jk}, \end{cases}$$

see Figure 1. If ω and $\tilde{\omega}$ have the directive sequences $(\sigma_n)_{n\in\mathbb{N}}$ and $(\tilde{\sigma}_n)_{n\in\mathbb{N}}$ respectively, then ω and $\tilde{\omega}$ differ only by a bijective letter-to-letter morphism, which does not influence the balance properties. The proofs of the following results will be given by the end of this section.

Proposition 2. *Let* $C \in \mathbb{N}$ *and let*

$$\omega = \underbrace{\zeta_1^{C-1}\zeta_2\zeta_1\zeta_3^2\zeta_1}_{=\tau_{C-1}} \underbrace{\zeta_1^{C-2}\zeta_2\zeta_1\zeta_3^2\zeta_1}_{=\tau_{C-2}} \cdots \underbrace{\zeta_1\zeta_2\zeta_1\zeta_3^2\zeta_1}_{=\tau_1} \underbrace{\zeta_2\zeta_1\zeta_3^2\zeta_1}_{=\tau_0}(\omega')$$

for some $\omega' \in \{1,2,3\}^{\mathbb{N}}$ *containing the letters 1 and 3. Then* ω *is not* C*-balanced.*

Notice that the segment $\zeta_1^k\zeta_2\zeta_1\zeta_3^2\zeta_1\,\zeta_1^{k-1}\zeta_2\zeta_1\zeta_3^2\zeta_1$ in $(\tilde{\sigma}_n)_{n\in\mathbb{N}}$ comes from the segment $\beta_{ij}^k\beta_{ji}^2\beta_{ik}\beta_{kj}^2\,\beta_{kj}^{k-1}\beta_{jk}^2\beta_{ki}\beta_{ij}^2$ in $(\sigma_n)_{n\in\mathbb{N}}$. Therefore, there exist directive sequences where each substitution β_{ij} occurs with gaps that are bounded by $2C + 5$.

The proposition shows that for any C there are uncountably many Brun words that are not C-balanced. Moreover, there are also uncountably many Brun words that are not finitely balanced.

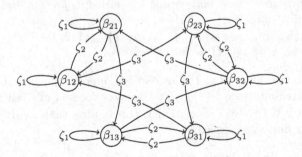

Fig. 1. Relation between the directive sequences of ω and $\tilde{\omega}$. If we follow the directive seqence of ω on the nodes, then we read the directive sequence of $\tilde{\omega}$ on the edges.

Theorem 4. *Let $(c_k)_{k \in \mathbb{N}}$ be a sequence of natural numbers such that*

$$c_k > 12\sqrt{3}\, 3^{N(c_0)+N(c_1)+\cdots+N(c_{k-1})} k \quad \text{for all} \quad k \in \mathbb{N},$$

with $N(c) = c(c+1)/2 + 3c$. Let $\rho_c = \tau_{c-1}\tau_{c-2}\cdots\tau_1\tau_0$, with τ_j as in Proposition 2. Then the Brun word with directive sequence $\rho_{c_0}\rho_{c_1}\cdots$ is not finitely balanced.

To prove these statements, we will use techniques that are typical for finding imbalances in S-adic sequences. Let $u, v \in \mathcal{A}^*$. Then we put $\boldsymbol{\Delta}_{u,v} = \boldsymbol{\ell}(u) - \boldsymbol{\ell}(v)$. For any substitution σ, we clearly have

$$\boldsymbol{\Delta}_{\sigma(u),\sigma(v)} = M_\sigma \boldsymbol{\Delta}_{u,v}, \tag{5}$$

and consequently:

Lemma 9. *Let σ be a substitution over the alphabet $\mathcal{A}$ such that the images of all letters under σ start with the same letter $a \in \mathcal{A}$. Let u, v be non-empty factors of a word $\omega \in \mathcal{A}^{\mathbb{N}}$. Then $\sigma(\omega)$ contains factors u', v' with $\boldsymbol{\Delta}' = \boldsymbol{\Delta}_{u',v'} = M_\sigma \boldsymbol{\Delta} + p\, \mathbf{e}_a$ for all $p \in \{0, \pm 1, \pm 2\}$.*

Proof (of Proposition 2). Consider a pair of words u, v, with $\boldsymbol{\Delta}_{u,v} = {}^t(q+1, -q, -1)$. Then, using (5) and applying Lemma 9 with the substitution $\zeta_3^2 : 1 \mapsto 3, 2 \mapsto 31, 3 \mapsto 312$, we obtain the following chain of $\boldsymbol{\Delta}$'s:

$$\begin{pmatrix} q+1 \\ -q \\ -1 \end{pmatrix} \xrightarrow{\zeta_1} \begin{pmatrix} q+1 \\ -q-1 \\ -1 \end{pmatrix} \xrightarrow[p=2]{\zeta_3^2} \begin{pmatrix} -q-2 \\ -1 \\ 1 \end{pmatrix} \xrightarrow{\zeta_2\zeta_1} \begin{pmatrix} q-2 \\ 1 \\ 1 \end{pmatrix} \xrightarrow{\zeta_1^q} \begin{pmatrix} -(q+2) \\ q+1 \\ 1 \end{pmatrix},$$

and by symmetry ${}^t(-q-1, q, 1) \xrightarrow{\tau_q} {}^t(q-2, -q-1, -1)$.

ting from the pair of factors $1, 3$ of ω', we have the chain

$$\begin{pmatrix} 1 \\ 0 \\ -1 \end{pmatrix} \xrightarrow{\tau_0} \begin{pmatrix} -2 \\ 1 \\ 1 \end{pmatrix} \to \cdots \to \pm \begin{pmatrix} -C \\ C-1 \\ 1 \end{pmatrix} \xrightarrow{\tau_{C-1}} \pm \begin{pmatrix} C+1 \\ -C \\ -1 \end{pmatrix}.$$

The last vector sums to zero, therefore it corresponds to factors u, v of ω such that $|u| = |v|$ and $\big||u|_1 - |v|_1\big| = C + 1$. $\qquad\square$

Lemma 10. *Let ω be a Brun word and let $C, N \in \mathbb{N}$ be such that $\omega^{(N)}$ is not $(12\sqrt{3}\, 3^N C)$-balanced. Then ω is not C-balanced.*

Proof. We will only sketch the proof. According to Lemma 3, there is a prefix u of $\omega^{(N)}$ such that $\|\pi_N \mathbf{x}\|_\infty > \frac{1}{4} 12\sqrt{3}\, 3^N C$, where $\mathbf{x} = \boldsymbol{\ell}(u)$ and π_N is the projection along the frequency vector $\mathbf{f}^{(N)}$ of $\omega^{(N)}$ onto $\mathbf{1}^\perp$. Then the frequency vector of ω is $\mathbf{f} = M_{[0,N)} \mathbf{f}^{(N)}$, and $M_{[0,N)} \mathbf{x}$ is the abelianization of a prefix of ω.

Let γ be the angle between the vectors $\mathbf{f}^{(N)}$ and $\mathbf{x}$. Then it can be verified that applying M_n divides the angle between two non-negative vectors by at most 3, thus the angle between $\mathbf{f}$ and $\mathbf{x}$ is at least $\gamma/3^N$. Since the matrices M_n are of the form identity matrix + non-negative matrix, and the vector $\mathbf{x}$ is non-negative, we get that $\|\mathbf{x}\|_2 \geq \|\mathbf{x}^{(N)}\|_2$. Therefore the (orthogonal) distance δ of the point $\mathbf{x}$ from the line $\mathbb{R}\mathbf{f}$ is at least $1/3^N$ times the distance of $\mathbf{x}$ from $\mathbb{R}\mathbf{f}^{(N)}$, which is at least $\frac{1}{\sqrt{3}}\|\pi_N \mathbf{x}\|_2$. Altogether, $\delta \geq \frac{1}{\sqrt{3}\cdot 3^N}\|\pi_N \mathbf{x}\|_2 \geq \frac{1}{3\cdot 3^N}\|\pi_N \mathbf{x}\|_\infty > 3C$.

Finally, $\|\pi M_{[0,N)} \mathbf{x}\|_\infty \geq \frac{1}{\sqrt{3}}\|\pi M_{[0,N)} \mathbf{x}\|_2 \geq \frac{1}{3}\delta > C$, which means according to Lemma 3 that ω is not C-balanced. $\square$

Proof (of Theorem 4). The Brun word with directive sequence $\rho_{c_k}\rho_{c_{k+1}}\rho_{c_{k+1}} \cdots$ is not $N(c_k)$-balanced according to Proposition 2. Lemma 10 therefore gives that ω is not k-balanced. $\square$

Acknowledgements. The authors are very grateful to Valérie Berthé, Timo Jolivet, and Sébastien Labbé for many fruitful discussions.

This work was supported by the Grant Agency of the Czech Technical University in Prague grant SGS11/162/OHK4/3T/14, Czech Science Foundation grant 13-03538S, and the ANR/FWF project "FAN – Fractals and Numeration" (ANR-12-IS01-0002, FWF grant I1136).

References

1. Adamczewski, B.: Balances for fixed points of primitive substitutions. Theoret. Comput. Sci. 307(1), 47–75 (2003)
2. Arnoux, P., Nogueira, A.: Mesures de Gauss pour des algorithmes de fractions continues multidimensionnelles. Ann. Sci. École Norm. Sup. (4) 26(6), 645–664 (1993)
3. Arnoux, P., Starosta, Š.: The Rauzy gasket. In: Barral, J., Seuret, S. (eds.) Further Developments in Fractals and Related Fields. Trends in Mathematics. Springer (2013)
4. Avila, A., Delecroix, V.: Pisot property for Brun and fully subtractive algorithm (preprint, 2013)
5. Balková, L., Pelantová, E., Starosta, Š.: Sturmian jungle (or garden?) on multi-literal alphabets. RAIRO – Theoretical Informatics and Applications 44, 443–470 (2010)
6. Berthé, V.: Multidimensional Euclidean algorithms, numeration and substitutions. Integers 11B(A2), 1–34 (2011)
7. Berthé, V., Cassaigne, J., Steiner, W.: Balance properties of Arnoux-Rauzy words. To appear in Internat. J. Algebra Comput. (2013)
8. Berthé, V., Delecroix, V.: Beyond substitutive dynamical systems: S-adic expansions (preprint, 2013)
9. Berthé, V., Fernique, T.: Brun expansions of stepped surfaces. Discrete Math. 311(7), 521–543 (2011)
10. Berthé, V., Tijdeman, R.: Balance properties of multi-dimensional words. Theoret. Comput. Sci. 273(1-2), 197–224 (2002), WORDS (Rouen, 1999)
11. Brun, V.: Algorithmes euclidiens pour trois et quatre nombres. In: Treizième Congrès des Mathèmaticiens Scandinaves, Tenu à Helsinki, Août 18-23, pp. 45–64. Mercators Tryckeri, Helsinki (1957, 1958)

12. Cassaigne, J., Ferenczi, S., Messaoudi, A.: Weak mixing and eigenvalues for Arnoux-Rauzy sequences. Ann. Inst. Fourier (Grenoble) 58(6), 1983–2005 (2008)
13. Cassaigne, J., Ferenczi, S., Zamboni, L.Q.: Imbalances in Arnoux-Rauzy sequences. Ann. Inst. Fourier (Grenoble) 50(4), 1265–1276 (2000)
14. Dumont, J.M., Thomas, A.: Systèmes de numération et fonctions fractales relatifs aux substitutions. Theoret. Comput. Sci. 65(2), 153–169 (1989)
15. Fogg, N.P.: Substitutions in dynamics, arithmetics and combinatorics. Lecture Notes in Mathematics, vol. 1794. Springer, Berlin (2002), Berthé, V., Ferenczi, S., Mauduit, C., Siegel, A. (eds.)
16. Hubert, P.: Suites équilibrées. Theoret. Comput. Sci. 242(1-2), 91–108 (2000)
17. Lothaire, M.: Algebraic combinatorics on words. Encyclopedia of Mathematics and its Applications, vol. 90. Cambridge University Press, Cambridge (2002)
18. Richomme, G., Saari, K., Zamboni, L.Q.: Balance and abelian complexity of the Tribonacci word. Adv. in Appl. Math. 45(2), 212–231 (2010)
19. Vuillon, L.: Balanced words. Bull. Belg. Math. Soc. Simon Stevin 10(suppl.) (2003)

Open and Closed Prefixes of Sturmian Words

Alessandro De Luca[1] and Gabriele Fici[2]

[1] DIETI, Università di Napoli Federico II, Italy
alessandro.deluca@unina.it
[2] Dipartimento di Matematica e Informatica, Università di Palermo, Italy
gabriele.fici@unipa.it

Abstract. A word is closed if it contains a proper factor that occurs both as a prefix and as a suffix but does not have internal occurrences, otherwise it is open. We deal with the sequence of open and closed prefixes of Sturmian words and prove that this sequence characterizes every finite or infinite Sturmian word up to isomorphisms of the alphabet. We then characterize the combinatorial structure of the sequence of open and closed prefixes of standard Sturmian words. We prove that every standard Sturmian word, after swapping its first letter, can be written as an infinite product of squares of reversed standard words.

1 Introduction

In a recent paper with M. Bucci [1], the authors dealt with trapezoidal words, also with respect to the property of being *closed* (also known as periodic-like [2]) or open. Factors of Sturmian words are the most notable example of trapezoidal words, and in fact the last section of [1] showed the sequence of open and closed prefixes of the Fibonacci word, a famous characteristic Sturmian word.

In this paper we build upon such results, investigating the sequence of open and closed prefixes of Sturmian words in general, and in particular in the standard case. More precisely, we prove that the sequence $oc(w)$ of open and closed prefixes of a word w (i.e., the sequence whose n-th element is 1 if the prefix of length n of w is closed, or 0 if it is open) characterizes every (finite or infinite) Sturmian word, up to isomorphisms of the alphabet.

In [1], we investigated the structure of the sequence $oc(F)$ of the Fibonacci word. We proved that the lengths of the runs (maximal subsequences of consecutive equal elements) in $oc(F)$ form the doubled Fibonacci sequence. We prove in this paper that this doubling property holds for every standard Sturmian word, and describe the sequence $oc(w)$ of a standard Sturmian word w in terms of the *semicentral* prefixes of w, which are the prefixes of the form $u_n xyu_n$, where x, y are letters and $u_n xy$ is an element of the standard sequence of w. As a consequence, we show that the word $ba^{-1}w$, obtained from a standard Sturmian word w starting with letter a by swapping its first letter, can be written as the infinite product of the words $(u_n^{-1}u_{n+1})^2$, $n \geq 0$. Since the words $u_n^{-1}u_{n+1}$ are reversals of standard words, this induces an infinite factorization of $ba^{-1}w$ in squares of reversed standard words.

J. Karhumäki, A. Lepistö, and L. Zamboni (Eds.): WORDS 2013, LNCS 8079, pp. 132–142, 2013.

Finally, we show how the sequence of open and closed prefixes of a standard Sturmian word of slope α is related to the continued fraction expansion of α.

2   Open and Closed Words

Let us begin with some notation and basic definitions; for those not included below, we refer the reader to [1] and [3].

Let $\Sigma = \{a, b\}$ be a 2-letter alphabet. Let Σ^* and $\widehat{\Sigma}^*$ stand respectively for the free monoid and the free group generated by Σ. Their elements are called *words* over Σ. The *length* of a word w is denoted by $|w|$. The *empty word*, denoted by ε, is the unique word of length zero and is the neutral element of Σ^* and $\widehat{\Sigma}^*$.

A *prefix* (resp. a *suffix*) of a word w is any word u such that $w = uz$ (resp. $w = zu$) for some word z. A *factor* of w is a prefix of a suffix (or, equivalently, a suffix of a prefix) of w. An *occurrence* of a factor u in w is a factorization $w = vuz$. An occurrence of u is *internal* if both v and z are non-empty. The set of prefixes, suffixes and factors of the word w are denoted by $Pref(w)$, $Suff(w)$ and $Fact(w)$, respectively. From the definitions, we have that ε is a prefix, a suffix and a factor of any word. A *border* of a word w is any word in $Pref(w) \cap Suff(w)$ different from w.

A factor v of a word w is *left special in w* (resp. *right special in w*) if av and bv are factors of w (resp. va and vb are factors of w). A *bispecial factor* of w is a factor that is both left and right special.

The word $\widetilde{w}$ obtained by reading w from right to left is called the *reversal* (or *mirror image*) of w. A *palindrome* is a word w such that $\widetilde{w} = w$. In particular, the empty word is a palindrome.

We recall the definitions of open and closed word given in [4]:

Definition 1. *A word w is* closed *if and only if it is empty or has a factor $v \neq w$ occurring exactly twice in w, as a prefix and as a suffix of w (with no internal occurrences). A word that is not closed is called* open.

The word aba is closed, since its factor a appears only as a prefix and as a suffix. The word $abaa$, on the contrary, is not closed. Note that for any letter $a \in \Sigma$ and for any $n > 0$, the word a^n is closed, a^{n-1} being a factor occurring only as a prefix and as a suffix in it (this includes the special case of single letters, for which $n = 1$ and $a^{n-1} = \varepsilon$).

More generally, any word that is a power of a shorter word is closed. Indeed, suppose that $w = v^n$ for a non-empty v and $n > 1$. Without loss of generality, we can suppose that v is not a power itself. If v^{n-1} has an internal occurrence in w, then there exists a proper prefix u of v such that $uv = vu$, and it is a basic result in Combinatorics on Words that two words commute if and only if they are powers of a same shorter word, in contradiction with our hypothesis on v.

Remark 2. The notion of closed word is equivalent to that of *periodic-like* word [2]. A word w is periodic-like if its longest repeated prefix is not right special.

The notion of closed word is also closely related to the concept of *complete return* to a factor, as considered in [5]. A complete return to the factor u in a word w is any factor of w having exactly two occurrences of u, one as a prefix and one as a suffix. Hence, w is closed if and only if it is a complete return to one of its factors; such a factor is clearly both the longest repeated prefix and the longest repeated suffix of w (i.e., the longest border of w).

Remark 3. Let w be a non-empty word over Σ. The following characterizations of closed words follow easily from the definition:

1. the longest repeated prefix (resp. suffix) of w does not have internal occurrences in w, i.e., occurs in w only as a prefix and as a suffix;
2. the longest repeated prefix (resp. suffix) of w is not a right (resp. left) special factor of w;
3. w has a border that does not have internal occurrences in w;
4. the longest border of w does not have internal occurrences in w.

Obviously, the negations of the previous properties characterizate open words. In the rest of the paper we will use these characterizations freely and without explicit mention to this remark.

We conclude this section with two lemmas on right extensions.

Lemma 4. *Let w be a non-empty word over Σ. Then there exists at most one letter $x \in \Sigma$ such that wx is closed.*

Proof. Suppose by contradiction that there exist $a, b \in \Sigma$ such that both wa and wb are closed. Let va and $v'b$ be the longest borders of wa and wb, respectively. Since va and $v'b$ are prefixes of w, one has that one is a prefix of the other. Suppose that va is shorter than $v'b$. But then va has an internal occurrence in wa (that appearing as a prefix of the suffix v') against the hypothesis that wa is closed.   □

When w is closed, then exactly one such extension is closed. More precisely, we have the following (see also [2, Prop. 4]):

Lemma 5. *Let w be a closed word. Then wx, $x \in \Sigma$, is closed if and only if wx has the same period of w.*

Proof. Let w be a closed word and v its longest border; in particular, v is the longest repeated prefix of w. Let x be the letter following the occurrence of v as a prefix of w. Clearly, wx is has the same period as w, and it is closed as its border vx cannot have internal occurrences. Conversely, if $y \neq x$ is a letter, then wy has a different period and it is open as its longest repeated prefix v is right special.   □

For more details on open and closed words and related results see [1,2,4,6,7].

3   Open and Closed Prefixes of Sturmian Words

Let Σ^ω be the set of (right) infinite words over Σ, indexed by $\mathbb{N}_0$. An element of Σ^ω is a *Sturmian word* if it contains exactly $n+1$ distinct factors of length n, for every $n \geq 0$. A famous example of Sturmian word is the Fibonacci word

$$F = abaababaabaababaababa \cdots$$

If w is a Sturmian word, then aw or bw is also a Sturmian word. A Sturmian word w is *standard* (or *characteristic*) if aw and bw are both Sturmian words. The Fibonacci word is an example of standard Sturmian word. In the next section, we will deal specifically with standard Sturmian words. Here, we focus on finite factors of Sturmian words, called *finite Sturmian words*. Actually, finite Sturmian words are precisely the elements of Σ^* verifying the following balance property: for any $u, v \in Fact(w)$ such that $|u| = |v|$ one has $||u|_a - |v|_a| \leq 1$ (or, equivalently, $||u|_b - |v|_b| \leq 1$).

We let St denote the set of finite Sturmian words. The language St is factorial (i.e., if $w = uv \in St$, then $u, v \in St$) and extendible (i.e., for every $w \in St$ there exist letters $x, y \in \Sigma$ such that $xwy \in St$).

We recall the following definitions given in [8].

Definition 6. *A word $w \in \Sigma^*$ is a left special (resp. right special) Sturmian word if $aw, bw \in St$ (resp. if $wa, wb \in St$). A bispecial Sturmian word is a Sturmian word that is both left special and right special.*

For example, the word $w = ab$ is a bispecial Sturmian word, since aw, bw, wa and wb are all Sturmian. This example also shows that a bispecial Sturmian word is not necessarily a bispecial factor of some Sturmian word (see [9] for more details on bispecial Sturmian words).

Remark 7. It is known that if w is a left special Sturmian word, then w is a prefix of a standard Sturmian word, and the left special factors of w are prefixes of w. Symmetrically, if w is a right special Sturmian word, then the right special factors of w are suffixes of w.

We now define the sequence of open and closed prefixes of a word.

Definition 8. *Let w be a finite or infinite word over Σ. We define the sequence $oc(w)$ as the sequence whose n-th element is 1 if the prefix of length n of w is closed, or 0 otherwise.*

For example, if $w = abaaab$, then $oc(w) = 101001$.

In this section, we prove the following:

Theorem 9. *Every (finite or infinite) Sturmian word w is uniquely determined, up to isomorphisms of the alphabet Σ, by its sequence of open and closed prefixes $oc(w)$.*

We need some intermediate lemmas.

Lemma 10. *Let w be a right special Sturmian word and u its longest repeated prefix. Then u is a suffix of w.*

Proof. If w is closed, the claim follows from the definition of closed word. If w is open, then u is right special in w, and by Remark 7, u is a suffix of w.   □

Lemma 11. *Let w be a right special Sturmian word. Then wa or wb is closed.*

Proof. Let u be the longest repeated prefix of w and x the letter following the occurrence of u as a prefix of w. By Lemma 10, u is a suffix of w. Clearly, the longest repeated prefix of wx is ux, which is also a suffix of wx and cannot have internal occurrences in wx otherwise the longest repeated prefix of w would not be u. Therefore, wx is closed.   □

So, by Lemmas 4 and 11, if w is a right special Sturmian word, then one of wa and wb is closed and the other is open. This implies that the sequence of open and closed prefixes of a (finite or infinite) Sturmian word characterizes it up to exchange of letters. The proof of Theorem 9 is therefore complete.

4   Standard Sturmian Words

In this section, we deal with the sequence of open and closed prefixes of standard Sturmian words. In [1] a characterization of the sequence $oc(F)$ of open and closed prefixes of the Fibonacci word F was given.

Let us begin by recalling some definitions and basic results about standard Sturmian words. For more details, the reader can see [10] or [3].

Let α be an irrational number such that $0 < \alpha < 1$, and let $[0; d_0 + 1, d_1, \ldots]$ be the continued fraction expansion of α. The sequence of words defined by $s_{-1} = b$, $s_0 = a$ and $s_{n+1} = s_n^{d_n} s_{n-1}$ for $n \geq 0$, converges to the infinite word w_α, called the *standard Sturmian word of slope α*. The sequence of words s_n is called the *standard sequence* of w_α.

Note that w_α starts with letter b if and only if $\alpha > 1/2$, i.e., if and only if $d_0 = 0$. In this case, $[0; d_1 + 1, d_2, \ldots]$ is the continued fraction expansion of $1 - \alpha$, and $w_{1-\alpha}$ is the word obtained from w_α by exchanging a's and b's. Hence, without loss of generality, we will suppose in the rest of the paper that w starts with letter a, i.e., that $d_0 > 0$.

For every $n \geq -1$, one has

$$s_n = u_n xy, \tag{1}$$

for x, y letters such that $xy = ab$ if n is odd or ba if n is even. Indeed, the sequence $(u_n)_{n \geq -1}$ can be defined by: $u_{-1} = a^{-1}$, $u_0 = b^{-1}$, and, for every $n \geq 1$,

$$u_{n+1} = (u_n xy)^{d_n} u_{n-1}, \tag{2}$$

where x, y are as in (1).

Example 12. The Fibonacci word F is the standard Sturmian word of slope $(3 - \sqrt{5})/2$, whose continued fraction expansion is $[0; 2, 1, 1, 1, \ldots]$, so that $d_n = 1$ for every $n \geq 0$. Therefore, the standard sequence of the Fibonacci word F is the sequence defined by: $f_{-1} = b$, $f_0 = a$, $f_{n+1} = f_n f_{n-1}$ for $n \geq 0$. This sequence is also called the sequence of *Fibonacci finite words*.

Definition 13. *A standard word is a finite word belonging to some standard sequence. A central word is a word $u \in \Sigma^*$ such that uxy is a standard word, for letters $x, y \in \Sigma$.*

It is known that every central word is a palindrome. Actually, central words play a central role in the combinatorics of Sturmian words and have several combinatorial characterizations (see [10] for a survey). For example, a word over Σ is central if and only if it is a palindromic bispecial Sturmian word.

Remark 14. Let $(s_n)_{n \geq -1}$ be a standard sequence. It follows by the definition that for every $k \geq 0$ and $n \geq -1$, the word $s_{n+1}^k s_n$ is a standard word. In particular, for every $n \geq -1$, the word $s_{n+1} s_n = u_{n+1} yx u_n xy$ is a standard word. Therefore, for every $n \geq -1$, we have that

$$u_n xy u_{n+1} = u_{n+1} yx u_n \tag{3}$$

is a central word.

The following lemma is a well known result (cf. [11]).

Lemma 15. *Let w be a standard Sturmian word and $(s_n)_{n \geq -1}$ its standard sequence. Then:*

1. *A standard word v is a prefix of w if and only if $v = s_n^k s_{n-1}$, for some $n \geq 0$ and $k \leq d_n$.*
2. *A central word u is a prefix of w if and only if $u = (u_n xy)^k u_{n-1}$, for some $n \geq 0$, $0 < k \leq d_n$, and distinct letters $x, y \in \Sigma$ such that $xy = ab$ if n is odd or ba if n is even.*

Note that $(u_n xy)^{d_n+1} u_{n-1}$ is a central prefix of w, but this does not contradict the previous lemma since, by (2), $(u_n xy)^{d_n+1} u_{n-1} = u_{n+1} yx u_n$.

Recall that a *semicentral word* (see [1]) is a word in which the longest repeated prefix, the longest repeated suffix, the longest left special factor and the longest right special factor all coincide. It is known that a word v is semicentral if and only if $v = uxyu$ for a central word u and distinct letters $x, y \in \Sigma$. Moreover, xuy is a factor of $uxyu$ and thus semicentral words are open, while central words are closed.

Proposition 16. *The semicentral prefixes of w are precisely the words of the form $u_n xy u_n$, $n \geq 1$, where x, y and u_n are as in (1).*

Proof. Since u_n is a central word, the word $u_n xy u_n$ is a semicentral word by definition, and it is a prefix of $u_n xy u_{n+1} = u_{n+1} yx u_n$, which in turn is a prefix of w by Lemma 15.

Conversely, assume that w has a prefix of the form $u\xi\eta u$ for a central word u and distinct letters $\xi, \eta \in \Sigma$. From Lemma 15 and (1), we have that

$$u\xi\eta u = (u_n xy)^k u_{n-1} \cdot \xi\eta \cdot (u_n xy)^k u_{n-1},$$

for some $n \geq 1$, $k \leq d_n$, and distinct letters $x, y \in \Sigma$ such that $xy = ab$ if n is odd or ba if n is even. In particular, this implies that $\xi\eta = yx$.

If $k = d_n$, then $u = u_{n+1} yx u_{n+1}$, and we are done. So, suppose by contradiction that $k < d_n$. Now, on the one hand we have that $(u_n xy)^{k+1} u_{n-1} yx$ is a prefix of w by Lemma 15, and so $(u_n xy)^{k+1} u_{n-1}$ is followed by yx as a prefix of w; on the other hand we have

$$
\begin{aligned}
u\xi\eta u &= (u_n xy)^k u_{n-1} \cdot yx \cdot (u_n xy)^k u_{n-1} \\
&= (u_n xy)^k \cdot u_{n-1} yx u_n xy \cdot (u_n xy)^{k-1} u_{n-1} \\
&= (u_n xy)^k \cdot u_n xy u_{n-1} xy \cdot (u_n xy)^{k-1} u_{n-1} \\
&= (u_n xy)^{k+1} \cdot u_{n-1} xy \cdot (u_n xy)^{k-1} u_{n-1},
\end{aligned}
$$

so that $(u_n xy)^{k+1} u_{n-1}$ is followed by xy as a prefix of w, a contradiction. □

The next theorem shows the behavior of the runs of open and closed prefixes in w by determining the structure of the last elements of the runs.

Theorem 17. *Let vx, $x \in \Sigma$, be a prefix of w. Then:*

1. *v is open and vx is closed if and only if there exists $n \geq 1$ such that $v = u_n xy u_n$;*
2. *v is closed and vx is open if and only if there exists $n \geq 0$ such that $v = u_n xy u_{n+1} = u_{n+1} yx u_n$.*

Proof. 1. If $v = u_n xy u_{n+1} = u_{n+1} yx u_n$, then v is semicentral and therefore open. The word vx is closed since its longest repeated prefix $u_n x$ occurs only as a prefix and as a suffix in it.

Conversely, let vx be a closed prefix of w such that v is open, and let ux be the longest repeated suffix of vx. Since vx is closed, ux does not have internal occurrences in vx. Since u is the longest repeated prefix of v (suppose the longest repeated prefix of v is a z longer than u, then vx, which is a prefix of z, would be repeated in v and hence in vx, contradiction) and v is open, u must have an internal occurrence in v followed by a letter $y \neq x$. Symmetrically, if ξ is the letter preceding the occurrence of u as a suffix of v, since u is the longest repeated suffix of v one has that u has an internal occurrence in v preceded by a letter $\eta \neq \xi$. Thus u is left and right special in w. Moreover, u is the longest special factor in v. Indeed, if u' is a left special factor of v, then u must be a prefix of u'. But ux cannot appear in v since vx is closed, and if uy was a left special factor of v, it would be a prefix of v. Symmetrically, u is the longest right special factor in v. Thus v is semicentral, and the claim follows from Proposition 16.

2. If $v = u_n xy u_{n+1} = u_{n+1} yx u_n$, then v is a central word and therefore it is closed. Its longest repeated prefix is u_{n+1}. The longest repeated prefix of

vx is either a^{d_0-1} (if $n = 0$) or $u_n x$ (if $n > 0$); in both cases, it has an internal occurrence as a prefix of the suffix $u_{n+1}x$. Therefore, vx is open.

Conversely, suppose that vx is any open prefix of w such that v is closed. If $vx = a^{d_0}b$, then $v = u_0 xy u_1 = u_1 yx u_0$ and we are done. Otherwise, by 1), there exists $n \geq 1$ such that $|u_n \xi y u_n| < |v| < |u_{n+1} y \xi u_{n+1}|$, where $\{\xi, y\} = \{a, b\}$. We know that $u_n \xi y u_{n+1}$ is closed and $u_n \xi y u_{n+1} \xi$ is open; it follows $v = u_n \xi y u_{n+1} = u_n xy u_{n+1}$, as otherwise there should be in w a semicentral prefix strictly between $u_n xy u_n$ and $u_{n+1} yx u_{n+1}$. $\qquad\qquad\square$

Note that, for every $n \geq 1$, one has:

$$u_{n+1} yx u_{n+1} = u_{n+1} yx u_n (u_n^{-1} u_{n+1})$$
$$= u_n xy u_{n+1} (u_n^{-1} u_{n+1})$$
$$= u_n xy u_n (u_n^{-1} u_{n+1})^2.$$

Therefore, starting from an (open) semi-central prefix $u_n xy u_n$, one has a run of closed prefixes, up to the prefix $u_n xy u_{n+1} = u_{n+1} yx u_n = u_n xy u_n (u_n^{-1} u_{n+1})$, followed by a run of the same length of open prefixes, up to the prefix $u_{n+1} yx u_{n+1} = u_{n+1} yx u_n (u_n^{-1} u_{n+1}) = u_n xy u_n (u_n^{-1} u_{n+1})^2$. See Table 1 for an illustration.

In Table 2, we show the first elements of the sequence $oc(w)$ for a standard Sturmian word $w = aabaabaaabaabaa \cdots$ of slope $\alpha = [0; 3, 2, 1, \ldots]$, i.e., with $d_0 = d_1 = 2$ and $d_2 = 1$. One can notice that the runs of closed prefixes are followed by runs of the same length of open prefixes.

The words $u_n^{-1} u_{n+1}$ are reversals of standard words, for every $n \geq 1$. Indeed, let $r_n = \widetilde{s_n}$ for every $n \geq -1$, so that $r_{-1} = b$, $r_0 = a$, and $r_{n+1} = r_{n-1} r_n^{d_n}$ for $n \geq 0$. Since by (1) $s_n = u_n xy$ and $s_{n+1} = u_{n+1} yx$, one has $r_n = yx u_n$ and $r_{n+1} = xy u_{n+1}$, and therefore, by (3),

$$u_n r_{n+1} = u_{n+1} r_n. \qquad\qquad (4)$$

Table 1. The structure of the prefixes of a standard Sturmian word $w = aabaabaaabaabaa \cdots$ with respect to the u_n prefixes. Here $d_0 = d_1 = 2$ and $d_2 = 1$.

prefix of w	open/closed	example
$u_n xy u_n$	open	$aaba$
$u_n xy u_n x$	closed	$aabaa$
$u_n xy u_n xy$	closed	$aabaab$
$\cdots$	$\cdots$	$\cdots$
$u_n xy u_{n+1} = u_{n+1} yx u_n$	closed	$aabaabaa$
$u_{n+1} yx u_n y$	open	$aabaabaaa$
$u_{n+1} yx u_n yx$	open	$aabaabaaab$
$\cdots$	$\cdots$	$\cdots$
$u_{n+1} yx u_{n+1}$	open	$aabaabaaabaa$
$u_{n+1} yx u_{n+1} y$	closed	$aabaabaaabaab$

Table 2. The sequence $oc(w)$ of open and closed prefixes for the word $w = aabaabaaabaabaa\cdots$

n	1	2	3	4	5	6	7	8	9	10	11	12	13	14	15
w	a	a	b	a	a	b	a	a	a	b	a	a	b	a	a
$oc(w)$	1	1	0	0	1	1	1	1	0	0	0	0	1	1	1

Multiplying (4) on the left by u_n^{-1} and on the right by r_n^{-1}, one obtains

$$r_{n+1} r_n^{-1} = u_n^{-1} u_{n+1}. \tag{5}$$

Since $r_{n+1} = r_{n-1} r_n^{d_n}$, one has that $r_{n+1} r_n^{-1} = r_{n-1} r_n^{d_n-1}$, and therefore $r_{n+1} r_n^{-1}$ is the reversal of a standard word. By (5), $u_n^{-1} u_{n+1}$ is the reversal of a standard word.

Now, note that for $n = 0$, one has $u_0 x y u_1 = u_1 y x u_0 = a^{d_0}$ and $(u_0^{-1} u_1) = ba^{d_0-1}$. Thus, we have the following:

Theorem 18. *Let w be the standard Sturmian word of slope α, with $0 < \alpha < 1/2$, and let $[0; d_0+1, d_1, \ldots]$, with $d_0 > 0$, be the continued fraction expansion of α. The word $ba^{-1}w$ obtained from w by swapping the first letter can be written as an infinite product of squares of reversed standard words in the following way:*

$$ba^{-1}w = \prod_{n \geq 0} (u_n^{-1} u_{n+1})^2,$$

where $(u_n)_{n \geq -1}$ is the sequence defined in (1).

In other words, one can write

$$w = a^{d_0} ba^{d_0-1} \prod_{n \geq 1} (u_n^{-1} u_{n+1})^2.$$

Example 19. Take the Fibonacci word. Then, $u_1 = \varepsilon$, $u_2 = a$, $u_3 = aba$, $u_4 = abaaba$, $u_5 = abaababaaba$, etc. So, $u_1^{-1} u_2 = a$, $u_2^{-1} u_3 = ba$, $u_3^{-1} u_4 = aba$, $u_4^{-1} u_5 = baaba$, etc. Indeed, $u_n^{-1} u_{n+1}$ is the reversal of the Fibonacci finite word f_{n-1}. By Theorem 18, we have:

$$F = ab \prod_{n \geq 1} (u_n^{-1} u_{n+1})^2$$

$$= ab \prod_{n \geq 0} (\widetilde{f_n})^2$$

$$= ab \cdot (a \cdot a)(ba \cdot ba)(aba \cdot aba)(baaba \cdot baaba) \cdots$$

i.e., F can be obtained by concatenating ab and the squares of the reversals of the Fibonacci finite words f_n starting from $n = 0$.

Note that F can also be obtained by concatenating the reversals of the Fibonacci finite words f_n starting from $n = 0$:

$$F = \prod_{n \geq 0} \widetilde{f_n}$$

$$= a \cdot ba \cdot aba \cdot baaba \cdot ababaaba \cdots$$

and also by concatenating ab and the Fibonacci finite words f_n starting from $n = 0$:

$$F = ab \prod_{n \geq 0} f_n$$

$$= ab \cdot a \cdot ab \cdot aba \cdot abaab \cdot abaababa \cdots$$

One can also characterize the sequence of open and closed prefixes of a standard Sturmian word w in terms of the directive sequence of w.

Recall that the *continuants* of an integer sequence $(a_n)_{n \geq 0}$ are defined as $K[\ ] = 1$, $K[a_0] = a_0$, and, for every $n \geq 1$,

$$K[a_0, \ldots, a_n] = a_n K[a_0, \ldots, a_{n-1}] + K[a_0, \ldots, a_{n-2}].$$

Continuants are related to continued fractions, as the n-th convergent of $[a_0; a_1, a_2, \ldots]$ is equal to $K[a_0, \ldots, a_n] / K[a_1, \ldots, a_n]$.

Let w be a standard Sturmian word and $(s_n)_{n \geq -1}$ its standard sequence. Since $|s_{-1}| = |s_0| = 1$ and, for every $n \geq 1$, $|s_{n+1}| = d_n |s_n| + |s_{n-1}|$, then one has, by definition, that for every $n \geq 0$

$$|s_n| = K[1, d_0, \ldots, d_{n-1}].$$

For more details on the relationships between continuants and Sturmian words see [12].

By Theorems 17 and 18, all prefixes up to a^{d_0} are closed; then all prefixes from $a^{d_0}b$ till $a^{d_0}ba^{d_0-1}$ are open, then closed up to $a^{d_0}ba^{d_0-1} \cdot u_1^{-1}u_2$, open again up to $a^{d_0}ba^{d_0-1} \cdot (u_1^{-1}u_2)^2$, and so on. Thus, the lengths of the successive runs of closed and open prefixes are: d_0, d_0, $|u_2| - |u_1|$, $|u_2| - |u_1|$, $|u_3| - |u_2|$, $|u_3| - |u_2|$, etc. Since $d_0 = K[1, d_0 - 1]$ and, for every $n \geq 1$,

$$|u_{n+1}| - |u_n| = |s_{n+1}| - |s_n| = (d_n - 1)|s_n| + |s_{n-1}|$$
$$= K[1, d_0, \ldots, d_{n-1}, d_n - 1],$$

we have the following:

Corollary 20. *Let w and α be as in the previous theorem and let, for every $n \geq 0$, $k_n = K[1, d_0, \ldots, d_{n-1}, d_n - 1]$. Then*

$$oc(w) = \prod_{n \geq 0} 1^{k_n} 0^{k_n}.$$

Acknowledgments. We thank an anonymous referee for helpful comments that led us to add the formula in Corollary 20 to this final version. We also acknowledge the support of the PRIN 2010/2011 project "Automi e Linguaggi Formali: Aspetti Matematici e Applicativi" of the Italian Ministry of Education (MIUR).

References

1. Bucci, M., De Luca, A., Fici, G.: Enumeration and Structure of Trapezoidal Words. Theoretical Computer Science 468, 12–22 (2013)
2. Carpi, A., de Luca, A.: Periodic-like words, periodicity and boxes. Acta Informatica 37, 597–618 (2001)
3. Lothaire, M.: Algebraic Combinatorics on Words. Encyclopedia of Mathematics and its Applications. Cambridge Univ. Press, New York (2002)
4. Fici, G.: A Classification of Trapezoidal Words. In: 8th International Conference on Words, WORDS 2011. Electronic Proceedings in Theoretical Computer Science, vol. 63, pp. 129–137 (2011)
5. Glen, A., Justin, J., Widmer, S., Zamboni, L.Q.: Palindromic richness. European J. Combin. 30, 510–531 (2009)
6. Bucci, M., de Luca, A., De Luca, A.: Rich and Periodic-Like Words. In: Diekert, V., Nowotka, D. (eds.) DLT 2009. LNCS, vol. 5583, pp. 145–155. Springer, Heidelberg (2009)
7. Fici, G., Lipták, Z.: Words with the Smallest Number of Closed Factors. In: 14th Mons Days of Theoretical Computer Science (2012)
8. de Luca, A., Mignosi, F.: Some combinatorial properties of Sturmian words. Theoret. Comput. Sci. 136, 361–385 (1994)
9. Fici, G.: A Characterization of Bispecial Sturmian Words. In: Rovan, B., Sassone, V., Widmayer, P. (eds.) MFCS 2012. LNCS, vol. 7464, pp. 383–394. Springer, Heidelberg (2012)
10. Berstel, J.: Sturmian and episturmian words. In: Bozapalidis, S., Rahonis, G. (eds.) CAI 2007. LNCS, vol. 4728, pp. 23–47. Springer, Heidelberg (2007)
11. Fischler, S.: Palindromic prefixes and episturmian words. J. Combin. Theory Ser. A 113, 1281–1304 (2006)
12. de Luca, A.: Some extremal properties of the Fibonacci word. Internat. J. Algebra Comput. (to appear)

Finitely Generated Ideal Languages
and Synchronizing Automata

Vladimir V. Gusev, Marina I. Maslennikova, and Elena V. Pribavkina

Ural Federal University, Ekaterinburg, Russia
{vl.gusev,maslennikova.marina}@gmail.com,
elena.pribavkina@usu.ru

Abstract. We study representations of ideal languages by means of strongly connected synchronizing automata. For every finitely generated ideal language L we construct such an automaton with at most 2^n states, where n is the maximal length of words in L. Our constructions are based on the De Bruijn graph.

Keywords: ideal language, synchronizing automaton, synchronizing word, reset complexity.

1 Introduction

Let $\mathscr{A} = \langle Q, \Sigma, \delta \rangle$ be a *deterministic finite automaton* (DFA for short), where Q is the *state set*, Σ stands for the *input alphabet*, and $\delta : Q \times \Sigma \to Q$ is the *transition function* defining an action of the letters in Σ on Q. When δ is clear from the context, we will write $q \cdot w$ instead of $\delta(q, w)$ for $q \in Q$ and $w \in \Sigma^*$.

A DFA $\mathscr{A} = \langle Q, \Sigma, \delta \rangle$ is called *synchronizing* if there exists a word $w \in \Sigma^*$ which leaves the automaton in unique state no matter at which state in Q it is applied: $q \cdot w = q' \cdot w$ for all $q, q' \in Q$. Any word w with such property is said to be *synchronizing* (or *reset*) word for the DFA $\mathscr{A}$. For the last 50 years synchronizing automata received a great deal of attention. For a brief introduction to the theory of synchronizing automata we refer the reader to the recent surveys [9, 10].

In the present paper we focus on language theoretic aspects of the theory of synchronizing automata. We denote by $\mathrm{Syn}(\mathscr{A})$ the language of synchronizing words for a given automaton $\mathscr{A}$. It is well known that $\mathrm{Syn}(\mathscr{A})$ is regular [10]. Furthermore, it is an *ideal* in Σ^*, i.e. $\mathrm{Syn}(\mathscr{A}) = \Sigma^* \mathrm{Syn}(\mathscr{A})\Sigma^*$. In what follows we will assume considered ideal languages to be regular. On the other hand, every ideal language L serves as the language of synchronizing words for some automaton. For instance, the minimal automaton recognizing L is synchronized exactly by L [4]. Thus, synchronizing automata can be considered as a special representation of an ideal language. Effectiveness of such representation was addressed in [4]. The *reset complexity* $rc(L)$ of an ideal language L is the minimal possible number of states in a synchronizing automaton $\mathscr{A}$ such that $\mathrm{Syn}(\mathscr{A}) = L$. Every such automaton $\mathscr{A}$ is called *minimal synchronizing automaton* (for brevity, MSA). Let $sc(L)$ be the number of states in the minimal automaton recognizing

J. Karhumäki, A. Lepistö, and L. Zamboni (Eds.): WORDS 2013, LNCS 8079, pp. 143–153, 2013.
© Springer-Verlag Berlin Heidelberg 2013

L. Then for every ideal language L we have $rc(L) \leq sc(L)$. Moreover, there are languages L_n for every $n \geq 3$ such that $rc(L_n) = n$ and $sc(L_n) = 2^n - n$, see [4]. Thus, representation of an ideal language by means of a synchronizing automaton can be exponentially more succinct than "traditional" representation via minimal automaton. However, no reasonable algorithm is known for computing an MSA of a given language. One of the obstacles is that an MSA is not uniquely defined. For instance, there is a language with at least two different MSA's: one of them is strongly connected, another one has a sink state [4]. Therefore, some refinement of the notion of MSA seems to be necessary. Another important observation is the following: minimal synchronizing automata for the aforementioned languages L_n are strongly connected. Thus, one may expect that there is always a strongly connected MSA for an ideal language. In the present paper we show that it is not the case. Moreover, the smallest strongly connected automaton with a language L as the language of synchronizing words may be exponentially larger than a minimal synchronizing automaton of L.

Another source of motivation for studying representations of ideal languages by means of synchronizing automata comes from the famous Černý conjecture. In 1964 Černý conjectured that every synchronizing automaton with n states possesses a synchronizing word of length at most $(n - 1)^2$. Despite intensive efforts of researchers this conjecture still remains open. We can restate the Černý conjecture in terms of reset complexity as follows: if ℓ is the minimal length of words in an ideal language L then $rc(L) \geq \sqrt{\ell} + 1$. Thus, we hope that deeper understanding of reset complexity will bring us new ideas to resolve this long standing conjecture. It is well known that the Černý conjecture holds true whenever it holds true for strongly connected automata. In this regard an interesting related question was posed in [2]: does every ideal language serve as the language of synchronizing words for some strongly connected automaton? For instance, if the answer is negative then there is a way to simplify formal language statement of the Černý conjecture. Unfortunately, it is not the case. Recently Reiss and Rodaro [8] for every ideal language L (over an alphabet with at least two letters) presented a strongly connected automaton $\mathscr{A}$ such that $Syn(\mathscr{A}) = L$. Their proof is non-trivial and technical. In the present paper we give simple constructive proof of the fact that every finitely generated ideal language L, i.e. $L = \Sigma^* S \Sigma^*$ for some finite set S, serves as the language of synchronizing words for some strongly connected automaton. (The study of synchronizing automata whose language of synchronizing words is a finitely generated ideal was initiated in papers [6, 7].) Our constructions reveal interesting connections with classical objects from combinatorics on words.

2   Algorithms and Automata Constructions

Let Σ be a finite alphabet with $|\Sigma| > 1$. Let L be a finitely generated ideal language over Σ, i.e. $L = \Sigma^* S \Sigma^*$, where S is a finite set of words. In this section we construct a strongly connected synchronizing automaton for which $L = \Sigma^* S \Sigma^*$.

First recall some standard definitions and fix notation. A word u is a *factor* (*prefix, suffix*) of a word w, if $w = xuy$ ($w = uy$, $w = xu$ respectively) for some $x, y \in \Sigma^*$. By $Fact(w)$ we denote the set of all factors of w. The ith letter of the word w is denoted by $w[i]$. The factor $w[i]w[i+1] \cdots w[j]$ is denoted by $w[i..j]$. By Σ^n ($\Sigma^{\leq n}$, $\Sigma^{\geq n}$) we denote the set of all words over Σ of length n (at most n, at least n respectively).

Note, that if a word $s \in S$ is a factor of some other word $t \in S$, then the word t may be deleted from the set S without affecting the ideal language, generated by S. Thus, we may assume, that the set S is *anti-factorial*, i.e. no word in S is a factor of another word in S.

2.1   Ideal Language Generated by Σ^n

Theorem 1. *Let $\Sigma = \{a, b\}$. There is unique up to isomorphism strongly connected synchronizing automaton $\mathscr{B}$ such that $\mathrm{Syn}(\mathscr{B}) = \Sigma^{\geq n}$.*

Proof. Consider De Bruijn graph for the words of length n. Recall that the vertices of this graph are the words of length n, and there is a directed edge from the vertex u to the vertex v, if $u = xs$ and $v = sy$ for some $s \in \Sigma^{n-1}$, $x, y \in \Sigma$. By labeling each edge $e = (u, v)$ by the last letter of v we obtain De Bruijn automaton. Its state set is $Q = \Sigma^n$, and transition function is defined in the following way: $xs \cdot y = sy$ for $s \in \Sigma^{n-1}$, $x, y \in \Sigma$. De Bruijn automaton is known to be strongly connected. Thus it remains to verify that $\mathrm{Syn}(\mathscr{B}) = \Sigma^{\geq n}$. It is easy to see that for an arbitrary word u of length at most n we have $Q \cdot u = \Sigma^{n-|u|}u$. Hence for any word w of length n we have $|Q \cdot w| = 1$, and for any word u of length less than n we have $|Q \cdot u| > 1$. So, $\mathrm{Syn}(\mathscr{B}) = \Sigma^{\geq n}$.

Let $\mathscr{C} = \langle Q, \Sigma, \delta \rangle$ be a strongly connected synchronizing DFA such that $\mathrm{Syn}(\mathscr{C}) = \Sigma^{\geq n}$. Let us prove that $|Q| \leq 2^n$. Strong connectivity implies $Q \cdot a \cup Q \cdot b = Q$. By induction it is easy to see that $Q = \bigcup_{|w|=k} Q \cdot w$. In particular, we have $Q = \bigcup_{|w|=n} Q \cdot w$. Thus, $|Q| = |\bigcup_{|w|=n} Q \cdot w| \leq \sum_{|w|=n} |Q \cdot w| = 2^n$. The last equality follows from the fact that every word of length n synchronizes $\mathscr{C}$, so each $Q \cdot w$ is a singleton. For the converse inequality $2^n \leq |Q|$ consider the DFA $\mathscr{C}_a$, obtained from $\mathscr{C}$ by removing all transitions corresponding to the action of b in $\mathscr{C}$. The word a^n synchronizes $\mathscr{C}$, so $\mathscr{C}_a$ contains no cycles but unique loop. So the automaton $\mathscr{C}_a$ has a tree-like structure as it is shown on Fig.1. Denote by s the state of $\mathscr{C}$ such that $s \cdot a = s$. The state s is called *root* of the tree, and the states $p_1, p_2, \ldots, p_k$ having no incoming transitions labeled by a are called *leaves* of the tree. The *height* $h(p_i)$ of a vertex p_i is the length of the path from p_i to the root s. The height of the tree $h(\mathscr{C}_a)$ is the maximal height of its leaves. We have $h(\mathscr{C}_a) = n$. Indeed, if $h(\mathscr{C}_a) = h < n$, then we would have $Q \cdot a^h = \{s\}$, meaning that $a^h \in \mathrm{Syn}(\mathscr{C})$, which is impossible.

Consider the set of leaves $H = Q \setminus Q \cdot a = \{p_1, p_2, ..., p_k\}$. Since the DFA $\mathscr{C}$ is strongly connected, for each state p_ℓ in H there exists a state q_ℓ such that $q_\ell \cdot b = p_\ell$. Thus $H \subseteq Q \cdot b$. We show that H is exactly $Q \cdot b$, meaning that $Q \cdot a \cap Q \cdot b = \varnothing$. Take a leaf of height n. Without loss of generality suppose it is p_1. Let q_1 be such that $q_1 \cdot b = p_1$. The word ba^{n-1} is synchronizing, so

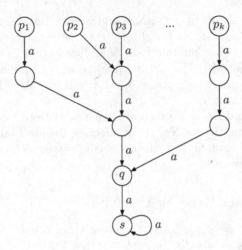

Fig. 1. The action of a in $\mathscr{C}$

$Q \cdot ba^{n-1} = \{q\}$ for some $q \in Q$. We have $q_1 \cdot ba^{n-1} = q$, and $q \cdot a = s$ (see Fig.1). Suppose there is $\overline{p} \in Q \cdot a \cap Q \cdot b$. Then there is a state $\overline{q}$ such that $\overline{q} \cdot b = \overline{p}$. Since $\overline{p}$ is not a leaf, we have $h(\overline{p}) < n$. Then $\overline{q} \cdot ba^{n-1} = \overline{p} \cdot a^{n-1} = s \neq q$. A contradiction. Hence $H = Q \cdot b$. Furthermore, the height of any leaf of $\mathscr{C}_a$ is exactly n. To see this assume that there exists a state p_m such that $h(p_m) < n$, i.e. $p_m \cdot a^{\ell} = s$, for some $\ell < n$. Then the word ba^{n-1} is not synchronizing. Indeed, take a state q_m such that $q_m \cdot b = p_m$. We have $q_m \cdot ba^{n-1} = p_m \cdot a^{n-1} = s \neq q$.

Consider an arbitrary state $p \in Q \cdot a$. Let $\delta^{-1}(p, u) = \{p' \in Q \mid p' : u = p\}$. We prove that $|\delta^{-1}(p, a)| \geq 2$ for each $p \in Q \cdot a$. For the root s we have $\{s, q\} \subseteq \delta^{-1}(s, a)$, thus, $|\delta^{-1}(s, a)| \geq 2$. Let p be an arbitrary state in $Q \cdot a$. Then p is not a leaf. Strong connectivity of $\mathscr{C}$ implies that there exists a state $\overline{p}$ and a word $w \in \Sigma^n$ with $w[n] = a$ such that $\overline{p} \cdot w = p$. Since w is synchronizing, we have $Q \cdot w = \{p\}$. Consider the word $w[1..n-1]$ that does not synchronize $\mathscr{C}$. Then $|Q \cdot w[1..n-1]| \geq 2$. However, $(Q \cdot w[1..n-1]) \cdot w[n] = p$. And we obtain the inequality $|\delta^{-1}(p, a)| \geq 2$. Denote $H_0 = \{q\}$ and construct sets $H_i = \delta^{-1}(H_{i-1}, a)$ for $1 \leq i \leq n-1$. We have $|H_i| \geq 2^i$ for all $1 \leq i \leq n-1$. Then $\mathscr{C}$ possesses at least $1 + 1 + 2 + 4 + \ldots + 2^{n-1} = 2^n$ states.

Thus we have $|Q| = 2^n$. Moreover, $Q = \cup_{|w|=n} Q \cdot w$. It means that with each state q of Q we can associate the word w of length n such that $Q \cdot w = \{q\}$. It is clear that it gives us the desired isomorphism between $\mathscr{C}$ and $\mathscr{B}$. $\qquad \square$

Remark 1. In case $\Sigma = \{a, b\} \cup \Delta$, where $\Delta \neq \varnothing$, we consider De Bruijn automaton constructed for the binary alphabet $\{a, b\}$ and put the action of each letter in Δ to be the same as the action of the letter a. It is clear that the language of synchronizing words of the modified De Bruijn automaton coincides with $\Sigma^{\geq n}$.

The Theorem implies that the minimal DFA recognizing an ideal language L can be exponentially smaller than a strongly connected MSA $\mathscr{B}$ with $Syn(\mathscr{B}) = L$.

2.2   Ideal Language Generated by a Set of Words of Fixed Length

Theorem 2. *Let $U \subsetneq \Sigma^n$. There is a strongly connected synchronizing automaton $\mathscr{B}_U$ with 2^n states such that $\mathrm{Syn}(\mathscr{B}_U) = \Sigma^* U \Sigma^*$.*

Proof. We modify the De Bruijn automaton $\mathscr{B}$ from the section 2.1 to obtain the desired automaton $\mathscr{B}_U$. First of all it is convenient to view the states of the automaton $\mathscr{B}$ not as the words of length n, but as pairs (x, u), where $x \in \Sigma$ and $u \in \Sigma^{n-1}$. Then by the definition of the transitions in $\mathscr{B}$ we have

$$(x, u) \xrightarrow{y} (z, v) \Leftrightarrow uy = zv \tag{1}$$

For a word uy which is not in U, we modify the corresponding transition given by (1) in the following way. If $uy \notin U \cup \{a^n, b^n\}$ we put

$$(x, u) \xrightarrow{y} (x, v), \tag{2}$$

where v is defined by (1).

If $uy = a^n \notin U$ ($uy = b^n \notin U$ respectively) we put

$$(a, a^{n-1}) \xrightarrow{a} (b, a^{n-1}), \quad ((b, b^{n-1}) \xrightarrow{b} (a, b^{n-1}) \text{ respectively}). \tag{3}$$

The other transitions remain unchanged. The obtained automaton is denoted by $\mathscr{B}_U$. The examples of the automaton $\mathscr{B}$ and the corresponding modified automaton $\mathscr{B}_U$ for $U = \{aaa, abb, bab\}$ are shown on Fig.2 and Fig.3 respectively. We prove that the automaton $\mathscr{B}_U$ satisfies the statement of the proposition. First we show that $\mathscr{B}_U$ is strongly connected. For this purpose we prove that all the states are reachable from the state (a, a^{n-1}), and the state (a, a^{n-1}) is reachable from all states.

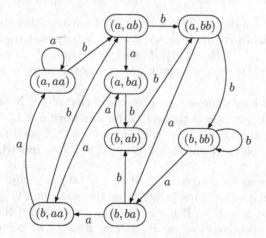

Fig. 2. De Bruijn automaton for $n = 3$

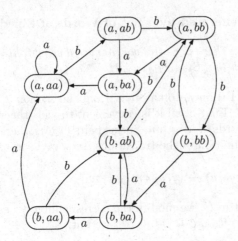

Fig. 3. Automaton $\mathscr{B}_U$ for $U = \{aaa, abb, bab\}$

First we show that a state (a, u) is reachable from (a, a^{n-1}) for any $u \in \Sigma^{n-1}$. If $u = a^{n-1}$, the claim obviously holds. Hence we may assume $u = a^k b\hat{u}$, where $k \geq 0$, $\hat{u} \in \Sigma^{n-k-2}$. By the definition of transitions in $\mathscr{B}_U$ we have

$$(a, a^{n-1}) \xrightarrow{b} (a, a^{n-2}b) \xrightarrow{\hat{u}[1]} (a, a^{n-3}b\hat{u}[1]) \xrightarrow{\hat{u}[2]} \cdots \xrightarrow{\hat{u}[n-k-3]}$$

$$(a, a^{k+1}b\hat{u}[1..n-k-3]) \xrightarrow{\hat{u}[n-k-2]} (a, a^k b\hat{u}[1..n-k-2]) = (a, u).$$

Symmetrically any state (b, u) is reachable from the state (b, b^{n-1}). The latter state is reachable from (a, b^{n-1}). Thus the state (b, u) is reachable also from (a, a^{n-1}):

$$(a, a^{n-1}) \rightsquigarrow (a, b^{n-1}) \xrightarrow{b} (b, b^{n-1}) \rightsquigarrow (b, u).$$

Now we show that the state (a, a^{n-1}) is reachable from any other state. Apply the word a^{n-1} to an arbitrary state (x, u). By the definition of transitions we have $(x, u) \cdot a^{n-1} \in \{(a, a^{n-1}), (b, a^{n-1})\}$. If $(x, u) \cdot a^{n-1} = (a, a^{n-1})$ we are done. If $(x, u) \cdot a^{n-1} = (b, a^{n-1})$, then we apply once more the letter a and obtain $(x, u) \cdot a^n = (a, a^{n-1})$.

Thus the constructed automaton $\mathscr{B}_U$ is strongly connected. Next we show that $\mathrm{Syn}(\mathscr{B}_U) = \Sigma^* U \Sigma^*$. It is easy to see that for any word $u \in \Sigma^{n-1}$ we have $Q \cdot u \subseteq \{(a, u), (b, u)\}$, and $Q \cdot u \cap Q \cdot v = \varnothing$ for $u, v \in \Sigma^{n-1}$ such that $u \neq v$. Thus $Q \supseteq \bigcup_{|u|=n-1} Q \cdot u$. Next we check that $Q = \bigcup_{|u|=n-1} Q \cdot u$. Indeed, if $a^n \in U$ we have $(a, a^{n-1}) \xrightarrow{u} (a, u)$ for all $u \in \Sigma^{n-1}$. If $a^n \notin U$ take any word $u \in \Sigma^{n-1}$. If $u = a^{n-1}$ then u maps the state (a, a^{n-1}) or the state (b, a^{n-1}) to (a, u). Let us assume now that $u = a^k b\hat{u}$. If k is even (odd, respectively) then u maps (a, a^{n-1}) $((b, a^{n-1})$, respectively) to (a, u). So any state (a, u) belongs to the set $\bigcup_{|u|=n-1} Q \cdot u$. Symmetrically any state (b, u) belongs to the latter set. Hence

$Q = \bigcup\limits_{|u|=n-1} Q \cdot u$. Since $|Q| = 2^n$, if there is a synchronizing word u of length $n-1$, we would have $2^n = |Q| = \left|\ \bigcup\limits_{|u|=n-1} Q \cdot u\right| < 2^n$, which is a contradiction.

Thus, none of the words of length $n-1$ is synchronizing. Consider an arbitrary word w of length n and factorize it as $w = uy$ with $u \in \Sigma^{n-1}$ and $y \in \Sigma$. We have $Q \cdot u = \{(a, u), (b, u)\}$. If $w \in U$, then the corresponding transitions from the states (a, u) and (b, u) were not changed, and we have $Q \cdot uy = \{(z, v)\}$, where $uy = zv$, so w is synchronizing. If $w \notin U$, then $Q \cdot uy = \{(a, v), (b, v)\}$, so $w \notin \mathrm{Syn}(\mathscr{B}_U)$. $\qquad\square$

2.3   Ideal Languages Generated by a Finite Set of Words

Theorem 3. *Let S be finite and anti-factorial set of words in Σ^+. There is a strongly connected synchronizing automaton $\mathscr{C}_S$ such that $\mathrm{Syn}(\mathscr{C}_S) = \Sigma^* S \Sigma^*$. This automaton has at most 2^n states, where $n = \max\{|s| \mid s \in S\}$.*

Proof. Let $T = \{w \in \Sigma^n \mid \exists s \in S, s \in Fact(w)\}$. First we construct the automaton $\mathscr{B}_T$ as described in the previous proposition. In that proposition the states of $\mathscr{B}_T$ were viewed as pairs (x, u) with $x \in \Sigma$, $u \in \Sigma^{n-1}$. Here it will be convenient to view the states as the words xu of length n (as it was in the initial De Bruijn automaton). Note, that since S is anti-factorial, every state in T can be uniquely factorized as usv such that $s \in S$, $u, v \in \Sigma^*$ and sv does not contain factors in S except s. In what follows we will use this unique representation without stating it explicitly.

Next we define an equivalence relation $\simeq$ on the set of states of this automaton (i.e. on words of length n) in the following way. Let $w, w' \in T$. We have $w \simeq w'$ iff $w = usv$ and $w' = u'sv$, where $s \in S$, $u, u', v \in \Sigma^*$. On the set $\Sigma^n \setminus T$ the relation $\simeq$ is defined trivially, i.e. for $w, w' \in \Sigma^n \setminus T$ we have $w \simeq w'$ iff $w = w'$. It is easy to see that $\simeq$ is indeed an equivalence relation on Σ^n. In fact, $\simeq$ is a congruence on the set of states of the automaton $\mathscr{B}_T$. Let us check that for any $x \in \Sigma$ and any $w, w' \in \Sigma^n$ $w \simeq w'$ implies $w \cdot x \simeq w' \cdot x$. If $w, w' \in \Sigma^n \setminus T$, then $w = w'$ and we are done. If $w, w' \in T$, then $w = usv$, $w' = u'sv$. If $u = u' = \varepsilon$, then $w = w'$, and there is nothing to prove. So we may assume, that $u, u' \neq \varepsilon$. Then $usv \cdot x = tsvx$ and $u'sv \cdot x = t'svx$ for some $t, t' \in \Sigma^*$. Since the obtained two words have the same suffixes, containing a word in S, they are equivalent. So we can consider the factor automaton $\mathscr{B}_T / \simeq$, whose states are the equivalence classes of $\simeq$, and the transition function is induced from the initial automaton. Let us denote by $[sv]$ the equivalence class of a word $usv \in T$, and by $[u]$ the equivalence class of a word $u \notin T$. We claim, that $\mathscr{C}_S = \mathscr{B}_T / \simeq$. In other words, the constructed automaton is strongly connected, and $\mathrm{Syn}(\mathscr{B}_T / \simeq) = \Sigma^* S \Sigma^*$. The first property holds trivially, since a factor automaton of a strongly connected automaton is strongly connected.

For any $w \in \Sigma^*$ and $s \in S$ previously in $\mathscr{B}_T$ we had $w \cdot s = us$, where $u \in \Sigma^*$. Since S is anti-factorial, in $\mathscr{B}_T / \simeq$ we have $[w] \cdot s = [s]$, so any $s \in S$ is synchronizing for the automaton $\mathscr{B}_T / \simeq$. Now let t be a synchronizing word, so there is a state $[w]$ such that for any state $[w']$ we have $[w'] \cdot t = [w]$. If $[w]$ is a

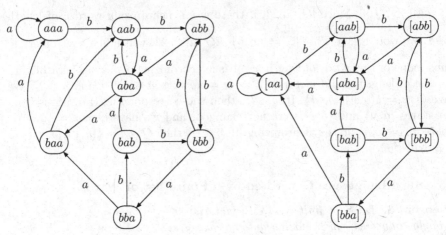

Fig. 4. Automata $\mathscr{B}_T$ and $\mathscr{B}_T/\simeq$ for $T = \{aaa, aab, baa, aba\}$

one-element class, then the word t was synchronizing for the initial automaton $\mathscr{B}_T$, so t contains some word in S as a factor, i.e. $t \in \Sigma^* S \Sigma^*$. Consider the case when $[w]$ is a class consisting of elements $u_1 sv, u_2 sv, \ldots, u_k sv, k > 1$. Note that in this case $u_i \neq \varepsilon$ for each $i = 1, \ldots, k$. This means that $t = usv$ for some $u \in \Sigma^*$, thus, also in this case $t \in \Sigma^* S \Sigma^*$. □

Let us complete this section with an example. Take $S = \{a^2, aba\}$ and $\Sigma = \{a, b\}$. Let us construct the corresponding set $T = \{a^3, a^2b, ba^2, aba\}$. We next build the DFA $\mathscr{B}_T$. The resulting automaton is shown on the left side of Fig.4.

By the definition of $\simeq$ the class $[aa]$ includes states aaa and baa. The other classes are one-element classess. The resulting automaton $\mathscr{B}_T/\simeq$ is shown on the right side of Fig.4

2.4   Ideal Languages Generated by Two Words

Let $S = \{u, v\} \subseteq \Sigma^+$ and let $|u| = n$, $|v| = m$. Again we suppose that S is anti-factorial. In most cases we can construct a strongly connected automaton $\mathscr{D}_{u,v}$ which has $n+m$ states such that $\mathrm{Syn}(\mathscr{D}_{u,v}) = \Sigma^*(u+v)\Sigma^*$, thus improving the construction from the previous section. For simplicity we state and prove our result only for the case of a binary alphabet, although the same argument works in general.

Let $\Sigma = \{a, b\}$. We assume that $u \in \Sigma^n \setminus \{ab^{n-1}, a^{n-1}b, ba^{n-1}, b^{n-1}a\}$, and $v \in \Sigma^m \setminus \{ab^{m-1}, a^{m-1}b, ba^{m-1}, b^{m-1}a\}$. Such a restriction follows from the fact that the minimal automaton of the language $\Sigma^* w \Sigma^*$ after deleting its sink state is strongly connected if and only if $w \notin \{ab^{n-1}, a^{n-1}b, ba^{n-1}, b^{n-1}a\}$. This fact was proved in [3]. We use it as the basis for the construction of the required automaton $\mathscr{D}_{u,v}$. Nevertheless in some cases the proposed construction still works. For instance, the construction gives rise to a strongly connected automaton in case $u = a^n$ and $v = ba^{m-1}$, where $m \leq n$.

Theorem 4. *Let* $\Sigma = \{a, b\}$, *and let* $u \in \Sigma^n \setminus \{ab^{n-1}, a^{n-1}b, ba^{n-1}, b^{n-1}a\}$, $v \in$ $\Sigma^m \setminus \{ab^{m-1}, a^{m-1}b, ba^{m-1}, b^{m-1}a\}$. *There is a strongly connected synchronizing automaton* $\mathscr{D}_{u,v}$ *having* $n + m$ *states such that* $\mathrm{Syn}(\mathscr{D}_{u,v}) = \Sigma^*(u + v)\Sigma^*$.

Proof. In order to obtain $\mathscr{D}_{u,v}$ we combine the minimal automata for the languages $\Sigma^*u\Sigma^*$ and $\Sigma^*v\Sigma^*$. For a letter $x \in \{a, b\}$ by $\bar{x}$ we denote its *complementary* letter, i.e. $\bar{a} = b$, and $\bar{b} = a$. Recall the construction of the minimal automaton recognizing the language $\Sigma^*w\Sigma^*$, where $w \in \Sigma^+$. It is well-known that this automaton has $|w| + 1$ states. We enumerate the states of this automaton by the prefixes of the word w so that the state $w[1..i]$ maps to the state $w[1..i+1]$ under the action of the letter $w[i+1]$ for all i, $0 \le i < k$. The other letter $\overline{w[i+1]}$ sends the state $w[1..i]$ to state p such that p is the maximal prefix of w that appears in $w[1..i+1]$ as a suffix. The state w is the sink state of the automaton. The initial state is ε and the unique final state is w, see Fig.5 (the transitions labeled by complementary letters $\overline{w[i]}$ are not shown).

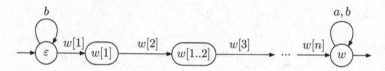

Fig. 5. The minimal DFA $\mathscr{A}_w$

Construct minimal automata $\mathscr{A}_u$ and $\mathscr{A}_v$. Denote by $\mathscr{A}'_u$ the automaton obtained from $\mathscr{A}_u$ by deleting the sink state and the transition from $u[1..n-1]$ labeled by $u[n]$. Denote by $\mathscr{A}'_v$ the corresponding automaton for v. Define the action of letters $u[n]$ and $v[m]$ on states $u[1..n-1]$ and $v[1..m-1]$ as follows. Denote by p the state in $\mathscr{A}'_u$ corresponding to the maximal prefix of u that appears in v as a suffix. Denote by s the state in $\mathscr{A}'_v$ corresponding to the maximal prefix of v that appears in u as a suffix. We put $u[1..n-1].u[n] = s$ and $v[1..m-1].v[m] = p$. Denote the resulting automaton by $\mathscr{D}_{u,v}$ and prove that it satisfies the desired properties. Figures 6,7,8 illustrate the construction for $u = abaab$ and $v = babab$.

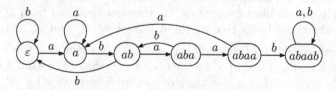

Fig. 6. The minimal DFA recognizing $\Sigma^*abaab\Sigma^*$

The following claim is rather easy to see. The explicit proof can be found in [3].

Claim. If $w \in \Sigma^n \setminus \{a^{n-1}b, ab^{n-1}, b^{n-1}a, ba^{n-1}\}$, then the automaton $\mathscr{A}'_w$ is strongly connected.

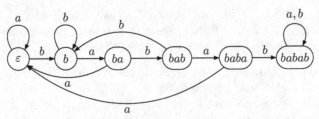

Fig. 7. The minimal DFA recognizing $\Sigma^* babab \Sigma^*$

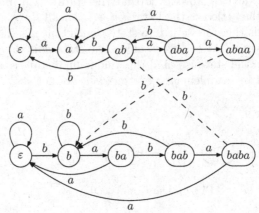

Fig. 8. The DFA $\mathscr{D}_{u,v}$

By the Claim automata $\mathscr{A}'_u$ and $\mathscr{A}'_v$ are strongly connected. By the definition of the action of letters $u[n]$ and $v[m]$ on states $u[1..n-1]$ and $v[1..m-1]$, the resulting automaton $\mathscr{D}_{u,v}$ is also strongly connected.

Now we are going to verify that $u, v \in \mathrm{Syn}(\mathscr{D}_{u,v})$. The state set of $\mathscr{D}_{u,v}$ is the union of the state set of $\mathscr{A}'_u$ (denoted by Q^u), and the state set of $\mathscr{A}'_v$ (denoted by Q^v). To avoid confusion when necessary we will use the upper indices u and v for the states in Q^u and Q^v respectively. Let w be an arbitrary word. We claim that $\varepsilon^u \cdot w = r$, where r is the maximal prefix of u that is a suffix of w or the maximal prefix of v which is a suffix of w. Let us consider the path from ε^u to r. As long as we do not use modified transitions, i.e. the ones that lead from Q^u to Q^v or vice versa, the claim holds true by the definition of $\mathscr{A}'_u$ and $\mathscr{A}'_v$. Suppose now that the path contains a transition $u[1..n-1] \xrightarrow{u[n]} s$ and $\varepsilon^u \cdot w' = u[1..n-1]$, where w' is a prefix of w. Let s' be the maximal prefix of the word v which is a suffix of $w'u[n]$. Note that $w'u[n]$ has u as a suffix. Therefore $|s'| < |u|$, otherwise u is a factor of v. Since $|s'| < |u|$ we have $s' = s$. Similar reasoning applies in case of transition $v[1..m-1] \xrightarrow{v[m]} p$. Therefore, the claim holds true. It is not hard to see that also $\varepsilon^v \cdot w = r'$, where r' is the maximal prefix of either u or v which is a suffix of w.

Now we are ready to show that u is a synchronizing word for $\mathscr{D}_{u,v}$. By the definition of $\mathscr{D}_{u,v}$ we have $\varepsilon^u \cdot u = s$. Let us consider an arbitrary state $t \in Q^u$.

Let $\varepsilon^u . tu = r$. Note that the maximal prefix of the word u which is a suffix of tu is equal to u. Then by the claim r is a prefix of v. Since u is not a factor of v we have $|r| < |u|$. Thus, $r = s$ due to maximality. Since $\varepsilon^u . t = t$ we have $t . u = s$. Thus, $Q^u . u = \{s\}$. Arguing in the same way for the state ε^v we get $Q^v . u = \{s\}$. So, u is synchronizing. Analogously, one can show that v is synchronizing.

To complete the proof it remains to verify that each word from the set $\mathrm{Syn}(\mathscr{D}_{u,v})$ contains u or v as a factor. Take $w \in \mathrm{Syn}(\mathscr{D}_{u,v})$ and a state $r \in Q^u$. If $r . w \in Q^u$, then w maps all states in the component Q^v into the same state. In particular, $\varepsilon^v . w \in Q^u$. Thus v appears in w as a factor. Analogously if $r . w \in Q^v$, the word u appears as a factor in w. So we have proved that $\mathrm{Syn}(\mathscr{D}_{u,v}) = \Sigma^*(u + v)\Sigma^*$. $\qquad\qquad\qquad\square$

Acknowledgement. The authors acknowledge support from the Presidential Programm for young researchers, grant MK-266.2012.1, and from the Russian Foundation for Basic research, grant 13-01-00852.

References

1. Černý, J.: Poznámka k homogénnym eksperimentom s konečnými automatami. Mat.-Fyz. Cas. Slovensk. Akad. Vied. 14, 208–216 (1964)
2. Gusev, V.V., Maslennikova, M.I., Pribavkina, E.V.: Principal ideal languages and synchronizing automata. In: Halava, V., Karhumäki, J., Matiyasevich, Y. (eds.) Proc. of the Second Russian Finnish Symposium on Discrete Mathematics. TUCS Lecture Notes, pp. 79–84 (2012)
3. Gusev, V.V., Maslennikova, M.I., Pribavkina, E.V.: Principal Ideal languages and synchronizing automata (April 2013), http://arxiv.org/abs/1304.3307
4. Maslennikova, M.I.: Reset Complexity of Ideal Languages. In: Bieliková, M., Friedrich, G., Gottlob, G., Katzenbeisser, S., Špánek, R., Turán, G. (eds.) Proc. Int. Conf. SOFSEM 2012, vol. II, pp. 33–44. Institute of Computer Science Academy of Sciences of the Czech Republic (2012)
5. Perrin, D.: Finite automata. In: van Leewen, J. (ed.) Handbook of Theoretical Computer Science, pp. 1–57. Elsevier, B. (1990)
6. Pribavkina, E., Rodaro, E.: Synchronizing automata with finitely many minimal synchronizing words. Inf. and Comput. 209(3), 568–579 (2011)
7. Pribavkina, E.V., Rodaro, E.: Recognizing synchronizing automata with finitely many minimal synchronizing words is PSPACE-complete. In: Löwe, B., Normann, D., Soskov, I., Soskova, A. (eds.) CiE 2011. LNCS, vol. 6735, pp. 230–238. Springer, Heidelberg (2011)
8. Reis, R., Rodaro, E.: Regular Ideal Languages and Synchronizing Automata. In: Karhumäki, J., Lepistö, A., Zamboni, L. (eds.) WORDS 2013. LNCS, vol. 8079, pp. 205–216. Springer, Heidelberg (2013)
9. Sandberg, S.: Homing and synchronizing sequences. In: Broy, M., Jonsson, B., Katoen, J.-P., Leucker, M., Pretschner, A. (eds.) Model-Based Testing of Reactive Systems. LNCS, vol. 3472, pp. 5–33. Springer, Heidelberg (2005)
10. Volkov, M.V.: Synchronizing automata and the Černý conjecture. In: Martín-Vide, C., Otto, F., Fernau, H. (eds.) LATA 2008. LNCS, vol. 5196, pp. 11–27. Springer, Heidelberg (2008)

A Note on Square-Free Shuffles of Words

Tero Harju

Department of Mathematics
University of Turku, Finland
harju@utu.fi

Abstract. We consider shuffles of words. It is first shown that there are infinite square-free words w over a four-letter alphabet such that w is a perfect shuffle of two square-free words u and v. Then we show that there exists an infinite square-free word u on three letters such that u can be shuffled with itself to produce another infinite square-free word. The proof of the latter result is constructive on finite factors, and it relies on a computer program for checking square-freeness of longer words.

1 Introduction

The operation of shuffle and the study of repetition in words are both popular items in combinatorics on words. These topics where combined, e.g., by Prodinger and Urbanek [10] in 1979 while they considered squares in shuffles of two words; see also Currie and Rampersad [5] and Rampersad [11].

Recently shuffling of words were considered by Charlier et al. [3] in the case of self-shuffling, i.e., where shuffling is applied to an infinite word w with itself to obtain the original word w. In [3] a short and elegant proof is given for the fact that the Fibonacci word can be self-shuffled, and a longer and more difficult proof is provided for the self-shuffling property of the Thue-Morse.

In this paper we consider finite and infinite square-free ternary words w that can be obtained by shuffling a word u by itself: $(u, u) \mapsto w$. Here we do not consider self-shuffling since we do allow the words u and w to be different. We show that there exists an infinite square-free word u on three letters such that u can be shuffled with itself to produce infinite square-free word.

2 Preliminaries

Let
$$\Sigma_n = \{0, 1, \ldots, n-1\}$$
be a fixed alphabet of n letters. We mostly need the alphabets Σ_n for $2, 3$ and 4.

In general, let u_0 and u_1 be two words over an arbitrary alphabet Σ and let $\beta \in \Sigma_2^*$ be a binary word of length $|u_0| + |u_1|$, called a *conducting sequence*, such that the number of letters $i \in \Sigma_2$ in β is equal to the length $|u_i|$. While forming the shuffle of u_0 and u_1, at step i the sequence β will choose the first

J. Karhumäki, A. Lepistö, and L. Zamboni (Eds.): WORDS 2013, LNCS 8079, pp. 154–160, 2013.

unused letter from u_0 if $\beta(i) = 0$ and from u_1 if $\beta(i) = 1$. In other words, we let $w = \beta[u_0, u_1]$ be the *shuffled word* of (u_0, u_1) *conducted by* β: The ith letter $w(i)$ of w becomes defined by

$$w(i) = u_{\beta(i)}(j) \quad \text{where } j = |\{k \mid \beta(k) = \beta(i) \text{ for } k = 1, 2, \ldots, i\}| \,.$$

The length of w is $|\beta|$. The shuffled word of a single word u conducted by a sequence β with itself is denoted simply by $\beta[u]$.

The above definitions can be extended to infinite words $u, v \in \Sigma^{\mathbb{N}}$ in a natural way. In this case, $\beta[u, v] \in \Sigma^{\mathbb{N}}$ is an infinite word obtained by shuffling u and v conducted by the sequence $\beta \in \Sigma_2^{\mathbb{N}}$, where one requires that β contains infinitely many occurrences of both 0 and 1. Again, if u is an infinite word, then $\beta[u]$ denotes $\beta[u, u]$.

A finite or infinite word w over Σ is *square-free* if it does not contain any factors $u^2 = uu$ for nonempty words u. Axel Thue showed a hundred years ago that there are infinite square-free words over ternary alphabets. One example, see Lothaire [9] or Hall [7], is obtained by iterating the *Hall morphism*

$$\tau(0) = 012, \quad \tau(1) = 02, \quad \tau(2) = 1$$

starting from the word 0. The iteration gives a square-free word

$$t = 01202101210201202102012012 \cdots . \tag{1}$$

3   Perfect Shuffles

Given two words u and v of the same length n their *perfect shuffle* is $\beta[u, v]$ where $\beta = (01)^n$. Clearly every word $w \in \Sigma_n^*$ is obtained as the perfect shuffle $\beta[u, v]$ unique words $u, v \in \Sigma_n^*$, and every infinite word is a perfect shuffle of two infinite words.

Example 1. For all square-free ternary words $u, v \in \Sigma_3^*$ of length ≥ 3, their perfect shuffle $\beta[u, v]$ is not square-free. Indeed, let without restriction $u = 01a_3 \cdots$ and $v = b_1 b_2 b_3 \cdots$, and thus $\beta[u, v] = 0b_1 1b_2 a_3 b_3 \cdots$. To avoid squares in u, v and in $\beta[u, v]$, we must have $b_1 = 2$ and then $b_2 = 0$, and so $a_3 = 2$. Finally, $b_3 = 1$, and $\beta[u, v]$ starts with the square 021021; a contradiction.   □

On the other hand, for four letters we have

Theorem 1. *There exist infinite square-free words* $w = \beta[u, v] \in \Sigma_4^{\mathbb{N}}$ *obtained as a perfect shuffle of two square-free words* u *and* v.

Proof. Dean [6] showed that there are infinite square-free words $u \in \Sigma_4^{\mathbb{N}}$ over the four letter alphabet that are *reduced* in the free group of two generators, i.e., u avoids the four factors $02, 20, 13$ and 31 (where 0 and 2 are inverses of each other, and 1 and 3 are inverses of each other). Given such a word u, let u' be its *dual word* obtained by interchanging 0 and 2, and interchanging 1 and 3 in all positions. For instance, if $u = 010301210$ then $u' = 232123032$.

We claim that for any reduced square-free word u, the perfect shuffle $w = \beta[u, u']$ is also square-free. Indeed, let $u = a_1 a_2 \cdots a_n$ and $u' = b_1 b_2 \cdots b_n$, where a_i and b_i are inverses of each other. Suppose that w contains a square vv.

Suppose first that $|v|$ is even. If v begins with a_i, $v = a_k b_k \cdots a_m b_m = a_{m+1} b_{m+1} \cdots a_{2m-k+1} b_{2m-k+1}$, then clearly $(a_k a_{k+1} \cdots a_m)^2$ would be a square in u. Similarly, if $v = b_k a_{k+1} \cdots b_m a_{m+1} = b_{m+1} a_{m+1} \cdots b_{2m-k+1} a_{2m-k+1}$, then $(b_k b_{k+1} \cdots b_m)^2$ would be a square in u'; a contradiction.

Assume thus that $|v|$ is odd. If $v = a_k b_k \cdots a_m = b_m a_{m+1} \cdots a_r b_r$, then $a_k = b_m$ is the inverse of b_k, and $b_k = a_{m+1}$. But a_m is the inverse of b_m, and hence $a_m = b_k = a_{m+1}$ leads to a contradiction, since $a_m a_{m+1}$ is a factor of u, and u was supposed to be square-free. The other case where $|v|$ is odd and begins with a b_k is similar. $\qquad\square$

4   Shuffling a Single Square-Free Word

In this section we study the words $\beta[u]$ that are obtained by shuffling a single word, and the conducting sequence β can be arbitrary binary word.

Example 2. A shuffled word $w = \beta[u]$ can be obtained in more than one way from a single word u using different conducting sequences. To see this, let, e.g., $u = 012102010212$ and choose

$$\beta_1 = 00000000000011111111101111$$
$$\beta_2 = 00000011010010011101111.$$

Then $\beta_1[u] = 01210201021012102012020212 = \beta_2[u]$. $\qquad\square$

After some preliminaries and examples around the problem we shall prove the following theorem.

Theorem 2. *There exists an infinite square-free word u on three letters and a conducting sequence $\beta \in \Sigma_2^{\mathbb{N}}$ such that $\beta[u]$ is square-free.*

A morphism $h\colon \Sigma^* \to \Delta^*$ is said to be *uniform* if, for all $a, b \in \Sigma$, $|h(a)| = |h(b)|$. Also, a morphism h is *square-free*, if it preserves square-freeness of words, i.e., if $v \in \Sigma^*$ is square-free, then so is the image $h(v) \in \Delta^*$.

The following result is due to Crochemore [4] improving a result of Bean et al. [1]; see also Berstel [2].

Theorem 3. *A morphism $h\colon \Sigma^* \to \Delta^*$ is square-free if it preserves square-freeness of words of length*

$$\max\left(3, \left\lceil \frac{M-3}{m} + 1 \right\rceil\right),$$

where $M = \max(|h(a)| : a \in \Sigma)$ and $m = \min(|h(a)| : a \in \Sigma)$.

In particular, a uniform morphism $h\colon \Sigma^* \to \Delta^*$ is square-free if it preserves square-freeness of words of length 3.

Example 3. The shuffled word $\beta[u]$ can be square-free even if u is not so. For instance, if $u = (012)^2$ then the following shuffled words are square-free:

$$\beta_0[u] = 012010212012, \text{ where } \beta_0 = 000001011111$$
$$\beta_1[u] = 010201210212, \text{ where } \beta_1 = 001001101011$$
$$\beta_2[u] = 010210120212, \text{ where } \beta_2 = 001010011011.$$ □

Proof of Theorem 2. We observe first that if β_1 and β_2 are conducting sequences with β_1 finite in length and containing equally many 0's and 1's, then

$$\beta_1\beta_2[u] = \beta_1[u_1]\beta_2[u_2] \text{ where } u = u_1u_2 \text{ such that } 2 \cdot |u_1| = |\beta_1|. \quad (2)$$

The words to be shuffled will be the images of the uniform morphism $\rho: \Sigma_4^* \to \Sigma_3^*$ that is defined by

$$\rho(0) = 010210120212$$
$$\rho(1) = 012101202102$$
$$\rho(2) = 012102010212$$
$$\rho(3) = 012102120102.$$

The images $\rho(i)$ are of length 12 and they are all square-free, but *the morphism ρ is not square-free*. Indeed, the images of the words $12, 20$ and 30 contain squares. For instance, $\rho(20) = 01210 \cdot (201021)^2 \cdot 0120212$. For this reason, we need a morphism α that will fix this problem. It will be defined below.

Each of the words $\rho(i)$, for $i = 0, 1, 2, 3$, can be shuffled to obtain a square-free word $\sigma(i) = \beta_i[\rho(i)]$ as seen in Table 1.

Next, let the uniform morphism $\alpha: \Sigma_3^* \to \Sigma_4^*$ be defined by

$$\alpha(0) = 1013$$
$$\alpha(1) = 1023$$
$$\alpha(2) = 1032.$$

Notice that, for any word $w \in \Sigma_3^*$, the image $\alpha(w)$ avoids the 'forbidden' words $12, 20$ or 30 as a factor. Also, the word 10 occurs in $\alpha(w)$ only as a prefix of each $\alpha(a)$ for $a \in \Sigma_3$. It is then easy to prove, and it also follows by applying Theorem 3, that the morphism α is square-free.

Table 1. Square-free words $\sigma(i) = \beta_i[\rho(i)]$ of length 24. The column on the right shows the conducting sequences.

$$\sigma(0) = 010210120102120210120212, \quad \beta_0 = 000000001100001111111111$$
$$\sigma(1) = 012101202101210201202102, \quad \beta_1 = 000000000011110011111111$$
$$\sigma(2) = 012102010210120120120212, \quad \beta_2 = 000000110100100111101111$$
$$\sigma(3) = 012102120102101202120102, \quad \beta_3 = 000000001101001011111111.$$

Finally, we combine the above morphisms to obtain $B, S\colon \Sigma_3^* \to \Sigma_3^*$ by letting

$$B(i) = \rho\alpha(i)$$
$$S(i) = \sigma\alpha(i)$$

for $i = 1, 2, 3$. The images of the words $B(i)$ are:

$B(0)$ =012101202102010210120212012101202102012102120102
$B(1)$ =012101202102010210120212012101202010212012102120102
$B(2)$ =012101202102010210120212012101202120102012102010212.

The lengths of these words are 48. The images of the shuffled words are of length 96:

$S(0)$ =012101202101210201202102010210120102120210120212012101
·120210121020120210201210212010210120212010102

$S(1)$ =012101202101210201202102010210120102120210120212012101
·201021012102012021201210212010210120212010102

$S(2)$ =012101202101210201202102010210120102120210120212012101
·212010210120212010201210201021012102010120212.

Now, Theorem 3 and a computer check verify that the morphisms B and S are square-free. Hence if $w = i_1 i_2 \cdots$ is an infinite square-free ternary word in $\Sigma_3^{\mathbb{N}}$, then both $B(w)$ and $S(w)$ are square-free. By the constructions of B and S, we have

$$S(i) = \sigma\alpha(i) = \beta_{\alpha(i)}[\rho\alpha(i)] = \beta_{\alpha(i)}[B(i)] \text{ for each } i \in \Sigma_3. \qquad (3)$$

Then

$$S(w) = S(i_1)S(i_2)\cdots = \beta_{\alpha(i_1)}[B(i_1)]\beta_{\alpha(i_2)}[B(i_2)]\cdots,$$

and inductively using (2), we find that $\beta = \beta_{\alpha(i_1)}\beta_{\alpha(i_2)}\cdots$ is a conducting sequence such that $S(w) = \beta[B(w)]$. This proves Theorem 2. $\square$

We also observe that the words $B(0), B(1)$ and $B(2)$ have equally many, 16, of the letters, and therefore these words are Abelian equivalent.

Corollary 1. *There exist infinite square-free ternary words that are Abelian periodic.*

A simpler solution to Corollary 1 was given in [8], where an infinite square-free ternary word was constructed that has Abelian period equal to three.

5   Open Questions

Problem 1. Which square-free words u can be shuffled to obtain a square-free word $w = \beta[u]$?

Problem 2. Which words u can be shuffled to a unique square-free word $\beta[u]$?

Problem 3. Which words w can be obtained in more than one way from a single word u using different conducting sequences?

Example 4. The same square-free word can be shuffled to produce different square-free words; see Table 2. As one can see there $u = 01021201$ gives rise to three square-free words $\beta_i(u)$, but, e.g., $u = 01201021$ gives rise to a single one. The rest of the square-free words of length eight with prefix 01 do not shuffle to any square-free word.   □

Example 5. Square-free words w that are shuffles of $w = \beta[u]$ of square-free u seem to be relatively few compared to the number of all square-free words. Also, the number of different square-free words u for which there exists β such that $\beta[u]$ is square-free is much lower. Table 3 gives values for small lengths of w.   □

The converse of Problem 1 reads as follows.

Problem 4. Which square-free words w are shuffles of square-free words: $w = \beta[u]$?

Problem 5. For each $n \geq 3$, does there exist a square-free word u of length n such that $\beta[u]$ is square-free for some β?

The next question involves self-shuffling.

Problem 6. Does there exist an infinite square-free word w such that $w = \beta[w]$ for some infinite β?

Note that the Hall word t is an infinite Lyndon word, and thus, by [3] it is not self shuffled.

Table 2. Square-free words u with a prefix 01 of length 8 having a square-free shuffle $\beta[u]$. (Missing items for u mean that they are the same as in the above line).

Word u	Shuffled $\beta[u]$	Conducting β
01021201	0102120102012101	0000001111011011
	0102120102101201	0000001111100111
	0102101201021201	0000011000111111
01201021	0102101201020121	0010100111001011
01202101	0120210120102101	0000001110011111
	0120102101202101	0001100000111111
	0102012101202101	0010010000111111
01202102	0102120210201202	0010110001101011
01202120	0120210201202120	0000001001111111
01210120	0121012010210120	0000000110111111
01210201	0121020102101201	0000001101110111
	0120102012101201	0001000011110111
	0120102101210201	0001000100111111

Table 3. The table gives the numbers of ternary square-free $w = \beta[u]$ of length L where u is square-free of length $L/2$. The column for u gives the number of different square-free words of length $L/2$ that can be shuffled to obtain a square-free word of length L.

L	square-free	$\beta[u]$	u	L	square-free	$\beta[u]$	u
4	18	0	0	6	42	0	0
8	78	12	6	10	144	30	12
12	264	24	18	14	456	42	30
16	798	78	42	18	1392	138	36
20	2388	228	54	22	4146	396	138
24	7032	588	168	26	11892	1008	234

Example 6. According to [3], no infinite aperiodic Lyndon word can be self shuffled. Finite square-free Lyndon words can be shuffled to obtain other square-free Lyndon words. For this, consider $u = 01202102$. It can be shuffled to obtain $w = 0102120210201202$ by using the conducting sequence $\beta = 0010111110010100$. Note, however, that $w < u$ in the lexicographic ordering.   □

References

1. Bean, D.R., Ehrenfeucht, A., McNulty, G.F.: Avoidable patterns in strings of symbols. Pacific J. Math. 85(2), 261–294 (1979)
2. Berstel, J.: Some recent results on squarefree words. In: Fontet, M., Mehlhorn, K. (eds.) STACS 1984. LNCS, vol. 166, pp. 14–25. Springer, Heidelberg (1984)
3. Charlier, É., Kamae, T., Puzynina, S., Zamboni, L.Q.: Self-shuffling words. arXiv:1302.3844 (2013)
4. Crochemore, M.: Sharp characterizations of squarefree morphisms. Theoret. Comput. Sci. 18(2), 221–226 (1982)
5. Currie, J., Rampersad, N.: Cubefree words with many squares. DMTCS 12(3), 29–34 (2010)
6. Dean, R.A.: A sequence without repeats on x, x^{-1}, y, y^{-1}. Amer. Math. Monthly 72, 383–385 (1965)
7. Hall Jr., M.: Generators and relations in groups—The Burnside problem. In: Lectures on Modern Mathematics, vol. II, pp. 42–92. Wiley, New York (1964)
8. Harju, T.: Square-free words obtained from prefixes by permutations. Theoret. Comput. Sci. 429, 128–133 (2012)
9. Lothaire, M.: Combinatorics on words. Cambridge Mathematical Library. Cambridge University Press, Cambridge (1997)
10. Prodinger, P., Urbanek, F.J.: Infinite 0-1-sequences without long adjacent identical blocks. Discrete Math. 28, 277–289 (1979)
11. Rampersad, N.: Infinite sequences and pattern avoidance. Master's thesis, University of Waterloo (2003)

Strongly k-Abelian Repetitions*

Mari Huova and Aleksi Saarela

Department of Mathematics and Statistics & TUCS
University of Turku, Finland
{mahuov,amsaar}@utu.fi

Abstract. We consider with a new point of view the notion of nth powers in connection with the k-abelian equivalence of words. For a fixed natural number k, words u and v are k-abelian equivalent if every factor of length at most k occurs in u as many times as in v. The usual abelian equivalence coincides with 1-abelian equivalence. Usually k-abelian squares are defined as words w for which there exist non-empty k-abelian equivalent words u and v such that $w = uv$. The new way to consider k-abelian nth powers is to say that a word is *strongly k-abelian nth power* if it is k-abelian equivalent to an nth power. We prove that strongly k-abelian nth powers are not avoidable on any alphabet for any numbers k and n. In the abelian case this is easy, but for $k > 1$ the proof is not trivial.

Keywords: k-abelian equivalence, nth powers, avoidability.

1 Introduction

In combinatorics on words the theory of avoidability is one of the oldest and most studied topics. Axel Thue, who proved at the beginning of 20th century the existence of an infinite binary cube-free word and an infinite square-free ternary word, can be referred to as the initiator of this area[12,13]. Corresponding avoidability questions for *abelian equality*, the commutative variant of equality where only the number of each letter counts and not their order, have been studied since late 1960s. Dekking [3] has proved that the optimal value for the size of the alphabet where abelian cubes are avoidable is three. The problem of the minimal size of the alphabet in which abelian squares can be avoided was an open question for a long time until the optimal value, four, was found by Keränen [8].

Lately, new variants of the avoidability problems have been introduced by defining repetitions via *k-abelian equivalence*, see e.q. [4]. This new equivalence relation, where $k \geq 1$ is a natural number, lies properly in between equality and abelian equality. The obvious modifications of the above Thue's problems ask for what are the smallest alphabets where k-abelian squares and cubes can be avoided. It is known that for $k \geq 3$ k-abelian cubes can be avoided over a binary alphabet [10]. In a case of square-freeness it is known that 2-abelian squares

---

* Supported by the Academy of Finland under grant 257857.

J. Karhumäki, A. Lepistö, and L. Zamboni (Eds.): WORDS 2013, LNCS 8079, pp. 161–168, 2013.

can not be avoided over a ternary alphabet but for large enough values of k avoidability is achieved [4,6]. In [5] it is shown that k-abelian square-free word cannot be obtained by iterating a single prefix preserving morphism.

In this note we consider abelian and k-abelian avoidability with a new perspective. We say that a word w is *a strongly abelian nth power* if it is abelian equivalent to a word which is a usual nth power, i.e., concatenation of n equivalent words. Now if an abelian equivalence class contains a word which is a usual nth power then all the words in this equivalence class are strongly abelian nth powers. So we consider the word more like a representative of its equivalence class than a single word. Corresponding notion of *a strongly k-abelian nth power* can be introduced similarly. We prove that every infinite word contains strongly k-abelian nth powers for all values of k and n.

2   Preliminaries

For the basic terminology of words as well as avoidability we refer to [9] and [2]. Here we define only our basic notions for this note.

Definition 1. *Let $k \geq 1$ be a natural number. We say that words u and v in Σ^+ are k-abelian equivalent, in symbols $u \sim_k v$, if*

1. *$pref_{k-1}(u) = pref_{k-1}(v)$ and $suf_{k-1}(u) = suf_{k-1}(v)$, and*
2. *for all $w \in \Sigma^k$, the number of occurrences of w in u and v coincide, i.e. $|u|_w = |v|_w$.*
3. *Different words of length at most k are not k-abelian equivalent.*

The k-abelian equivalence is like a sharpening of abelian equivalence and for the value $k = 1$ these define the same equivalence relation. For more about this notion, see [7]. In fact, k-abelian equivalence is a congruence of words, i.e. an equivalence relation R such that $uvRu'v'$ whenever uRu' and vRv'. We are interested in the products of words which are k-abelian equivalent but we will first define squares for all congruences R. Higher powers can be defined analogously.

If u, v are congruent words, then their product uv is an R-*square*. This definition has been used in the study of abelian and k-abelian repetition-freeness. In this article, however, we concentrate on another definition:

Definition 2. *A word w is a strongly R-square if it is congruent to a square of some non-empty word v, i.e. $wRvv$.*

For example, $aabb$ is not an abelian square because aa and bb are not abelian equivalent, but it is a strongly abelian square because it is abelian equivalent to $(ab)^2$.

Square-freeness in partially commutative monoids was studied by Carpi and De Luca in [1]. Their approach to square-freeness is similar but not identical to the one in this paper. Another interesting related concept is that of approximate squares, which can be defined as words of the form uv, where the Hamming distance of u and v is "small enough" (this definition is analogous to the definition of R-squares), or equivalently as words w such that the Hamming distance of w and some square is "small enough" (this definition is analogous to the definition of strongly R-squares). The avoidability of approximate squares has been studied by Ochem, Rampersad and Shallit [11].

Lemma 3. *A word is a strongly R-square if and only if it is congruent to an R-square.*

Proof. The "only if" direction is clear. If w is congruent to an R-square, say $wRuv$ and uRv, then $wRuu$, because uRv implies $uvRuu$ (here the assumption that R is not just an equivalence relation but a congruence is used). $\qquad\square$

It could be said that strongly R-squares take the concept of squares farther away from words and closer to the monoid defined by R.

Let us now state the definitions of strongly abelian and k-abelian nth powers for any $n \geq 1$.

Definition 4. *A word w is a strongly abelian nth power if it is abelian equivalent to a word which is an nth power.*

Definition 5. *A word w is a strongly k-abelian nth power if it is k-abelian equivalent to a word which is an nth power.*

The basic problem we are considering is avoidability of strongly abelian and strongly k-abelian nth powers. We prove that, for all k and n, they are unavoidable on all finite alphabets.

3 Unavoidability of Strongly Abelian and k-Abelian n-Powers

First we show that in abelian case it is easy to see that there does not exist infinite word which would avoid a strongly abelian nth power. Recall that two words are abelian equivalent if and only if they have the same Parikh vectors. Parikh vector p is a function from the set of words over m-letter alphabet $\{a_1, a_2, \ldots, a_m\}$ to the set of m-dimensional vectors over natural numbers, where $p(w) = (|w|_{a_1}, |w|_{a_2}, \ldots, |w|_{a_m})$.

Theorem 6. *Let Σ be an alphabet and let $n \geq 2$. Every infinite word $w \in \Sigma^\omega$ contains a non-empty factor that is abelian equivalent to an nth power.*

Proof. A word is abelian equivalent to an nth power if and only if its Parikh vector is zero modulo n. The number of different Parikh vectors modulo n is finite, so w has two prefixes u and uv such that their Parikh vectors are the same modulo n. Then the Parikh vector of v is zero modulo n, so v is abelian equivalent to an nth power. $\qquad\square$

Theorem 6 can be generalized for k-abelian equivalence, but this is not trivial. One important difference between abelian and k-abelian equivalence is that if a vector with non-negative elements is given, then a word having that Parikh vector can be constructed, but if for every $t \in \Sigma^k$ a non-negative number n_t is given, then there need not exist a word u such that $|u|_t = n_t$ for all t (see Example 10).

Perhaps the biggest difficulty in generalizing Theorem 6 lies in finding an analogous version of the fact that a word is abelian equivalent to an nth power if and only if its Parikh vector is zero modulo n. On the one direction we have:

Lemma 7. *If a word v of length at least $k - 1$ is k-abelian equivalent to an nth power, then*

$$|v|_t + |\operatorname{suf}_{k-1}(v)\operatorname{pref}_{k-1}(v)|_t \equiv 0 \pmod{n} \tag{1}$$

for all $t \in \Sigma^k$.

Proof. Let v be k-abelian equivalent to u^n. Then

$$|v|_t + |\operatorname{suf}_{k-1}(v)\operatorname{pref}_{k-1}(v)|_t = |v\operatorname{pref}_{k-1}(v)|_t$$
$$= |u^n\operatorname{pref}_{k-1}(v)|_t = |u^n\operatorname{pref}_{k-1}(u^n)|_t = n|u\operatorname{pref}_{k-1}(u^n)|_t \equiv 0 \pmod{n}$$

for all $t \in \Sigma^k$. $\qquad\square$

The converse does not hold. For example, $v = babbbbab$ satisfies (1) for $n = 2$ and $k = 3$ but it is not 3-abelian equivalent to any square. However, the converse does hold if $|v|_t$ is either large enough or zero for every t. This is formulated precisely in Lemma 11. To prove this we need the following definitions and Lemma 8. These were used in [7] to estimate the number of k-abelian equivalence classes.

Let $s_1, s_2 \in \Sigma^{k-1}$ and let

$$S(s_1, s_2, n) = \Sigma^n \cap s_1\Sigma^* \cap \Sigma^*s_2$$

be the set of words of length n that start with s_1 and end with s_2. For every word $u \in S(s_1, s_2, n)$ we can define a function

$$f_u : \Sigma^k \to \{0, \ldots, n - k + 1\}, \quad f_u(t) = |u|_t.$$

If $u, v \in S(s_1, s_2, n)$, then $u \sim_k v$ if and only if $f_u = f_v$.

If a function $f : \Sigma^k \to \mathbb{N}_0$ is given, then a directed multigraph G_f can be defined as follows:

- The set of vertices is Σ^{k-1}.
- If $t = s_1a = bs_2$, where $a, b \in \Sigma$, then there are $f(t)$ edges from s_1 to s_2.

If $f = f_u$, then this multigraph is related to the Rauzy graph of u.

As stated above, the following lemma was proved in [7]. The proof is simple, so it is repeated here for completeness. Here $\deg^-$ denotes the indegree and $\deg^+$ the outdegree of a vertex in G_f.

Lemma 8. *For a function $f : \Sigma^k \to \mathbb{N}_0$ and words $s_1, s_2 \in \Sigma^{k-1}$, the following are equivalent:*

(i) *there is a number n and a word $u \in S(s_1, s_2, n)$ such that $f = f_u$,*
(ii) *there is an Eulerian path from s_1 to s_2 in G_f,*
(iii) *the underlying graph of G_f is connected, except possibly for some isolated vertices, and $\deg^-(s) = \deg^+(s)$ for every vertex s, except that if $s_1 \neq s_2$, then $\deg^-(s_1) = \deg^+(s_1) - 1$ and $\deg^-(s_2) = \deg^+(s_2) + 1$,*
(iv) *the underlying graph of G_f is connected, except possibly for some isolated vertices, and*

$$\sum_{a \in \Sigma} f(as) = \sum_{a \in \Sigma} f(sa) + c_s$$

for all $s \in \Sigma^{k-1}$, where

$$c_s = \begin{cases} -1, & \text{if } s = s_1 \neq s_2, \\ 1, & \text{if } s = s_2 \neq s_1, \\ 0, & \text{otherwise.} \end{cases}$$

Proof. (i) $\Leftrightarrow$ (ii): $u = a_1 \ldots a_n \in S(s_1, s_2, n)$ and $f = f_u$ if and only if

$$s_1 = a_1 \ldots a_{k-1} \to a_2 \ldots a_k \to \cdots \to a_{n-k+2} \ldots a_n = s_2$$

is an Eulerian path in G_f.

(ii) $\Leftrightarrow$ (iii): This is well known.

(iii) $\Leftrightarrow$ (iv): (iv) is just a reformulation of (iii) in terms of the function f. $\square$

Example 9. Let $k = 3$ and consider the word $u = aaabaab$. The multigraph G_{f_u} is

The word u corresponds to the Eulerian path

$$aa \to aa \to ab \to ba \to aa \to ab.$$

There is also another Eulerian path from aa to ab:

$$aa \to ab \to ba \to aa \to aa \to ab.$$

This corresponds to the word $aabaaab$, which is 3-abelian equivalent to u.

Example 10. We consider some functions $f : \{a, b\}^2 \to \mathbb{N}_0$.

If $f(aa) = f(bb) = 1$ and $f(t) = 0$ otherwise, then the underlying graph of G_f is not connected, so there does not exist a word u such that $f = f_u$.

If $f(ab) = 2$ and $f(t) = 0$ otherwise, then the indegree of a in G_f is zero but the outdegree is two, so there does not exist a word u such that $f = f_u$.

Lemma 11. *If*

$$|v|_t + |\mathrm{suf}_{k-1}(v)\mathrm{pref}_{k-1}(v)|_t \equiv 0 \pmod{n} \tag{2}$$

and either $|v|_t > (n-1)(k-1)$ *or* $|v|_t = 0$ *for all* $t \in \Sigma^k$, *then* v *is* k-*abelian equivalent to an* nth *power.*

Proof. Let $s_1 = \mathrm{pref}_{k-1}(v)$ and $s_2 = \mathrm{suf}_{k-1}(v)$. By Lemma 8,

$$\sum_{a \in \Sigma} f_v(as) = \sum_{a \in \Sigma} f_v(sa) + c_s \quad \text{and} \quad \sum_{a \in \Sigma} f_{s_2 s_1}(as) = \sum_{a \in \Sigma} f_{s_2 s_1}(sa) - c_s \tag{3}$$

for all $s \in \Sigma^{k-1}$, where

$$c_s = \begin{cases} -1, & \text{if } s = s_1 \neq s_2, \\ 1, & \text{if } s = s_2 \neq s_1, \\ 0, & \text{otherwise.} \end{cases}$$

By (2), a function $f : \Sigma^k \to \mathbb{N}_0$ can be defined by

$$f(t) = \frac{f_v(t) - (n-1)f_{s_2 s_1}(t)}{n}.$$

By (3),

$$\sum_{a \in \Sigma} f(as) = \sum_{a \in \Sigma} f(sa) + c_s$$

for all $s \in \Sigma^{k-1}$. If $f_v(t) > 0$, then

$$f_v(t) = |v|_t > (n-1)(k-1) \geq (n-1)f_{s_2 s_1}(t)$$

and thus $f(t) > 0$. This means that since the underlying graph of G_{f_v} is connected, also the underlying graph of G_f must be connected. By Lemma 8, there is a word $u \in S(s_1, s_2, |u|)$ such that $f = f_u$. Then u^n begins with s_1 and ends with s_2 and

$$|u^n|_t = n|u|_t + (n-1)|s_2 s_1|_t = nf(t) + (n-1)f_{s_2 s_1}(t) = f_v(t) = |v|_t$$

for all $t \in \Sigma^k$, so u^n is k-abelian equivalent to v.   □

Now we are ready to express the main result of strongly k-abelian avoidability.

Theorem 12. *Let* Σ *be an alphabet and let* $k, n \geq 2$. *Every infinite word* $w \in \Sigma^\omega$ *contains a non-empty factor that is* k-*abelian equivalent to an* nth *power.*

Proof. For a prefix u of w, consider the pair $(f_u \bmod n, \mathrm{suf}_{k-1}(u))$. The number of different pairs is finite, so w has infinitely many prefixes $u_1, u_2, \ldots$ such that their pairs are the same. Let i be such that no factor of length k appearing only finitely many times in w appears after u_i. Let $j > i$ be such that if $u_j = u_i v$, then every other factor of length k appears at least $(n-1)(k-1)$ times in v. Then

$$|v|_t + |\text{suf}_{k-1}(v)\text{pref}_{k-1}(v)|_t = |\text{suf}_{k-1}(v)v|_t = |\text{suf}_{k-1}(u_i)v|_t$$
$$= |u_i v|_t - |u_i|_t = f_{u_j}(t) - f_{u_i}(t) \equiv 0 \pmod{n}$$

for all $t \in \Sigma^k$. Thus v satisfies the conditions of Lemma 11 and v is k-abelian equivalent to an nth power. $\qquad\square$

4   Further Questions

Some further questions that might be asked on strongly k-abelian powers are:

- How many k-abelian equivalence classes of words of length l contain an nth power?
- How many words there are in those equivalence classes, i.e. how many words of length l are strongly k-abelian nth powers?
- What is the length of the longest word avoiding strongly k-abelian nth powers?
- How many words avoid strongly k-abelian nth powers?

The answers depend on k, n, l and the size of the alphabet. The analysis of these questions is outside the scope of this extended abstract, but a few remarks can be made.

First, it is easy to prove that two squares uu and vv are k-abelian equivalent if and only if u and v are. Thus the number of k-abelian equivalence classes of words of length $2l$ containing a square is the number of k-abelian equivalence classes of words of length l. This number has been estimated in [7] and is polynomial with respect to l.

Second, some of the equivalence classes contain exponentially many words. For example, a word on the alphabet $\{a, b\}$ is 2-abelian equivalent to $(a^m(ab)^m)^2$ if and only if it has the same length, begins with a, ends with b, contains no two consecutive b's and contains $2m$ b's. The number of such words is exponential with respect to m.

Example 13. In $\{a, b\}^{12}$ there are

- 64 squares,
- 168 2-abelian squares,
- 924 abelian squares,
- 1024 strongly 2-abelian squares,
- 2048 strongly abelian squares,
- 4096 words.

Those 1024 strongly 2-abelian squares belong to 32 different equivalence classes and strongly abelian squares belong to 7 different equivalence classes. Representatives for each of these seven classes over a binary alphabet are as follows: $a^{12}, a^{10}b^2, a^8b^4, a^6b^6, a^4b^8, a^2b^{10}, b^{12}$.

5   Conclusion

We have shown that for $k, n \geq 2$ every infinite word contains a non-empty factor which is strongly abelian nth power as well as a non-empty factor which is strongly k-abelian nth power. As is known, usual abelian nth powers can be avoided depending on the value of n and the size of the alphabet. Corresponding results are also known for k-abelian powers. Other questions arising from the notion of strongly k-abelian equivalence are, for example, counting the number of words of length l that contain strongly k-abelian nth powers, or counting the number of strongly k-abelian nth powers of length l.

References

1. Carpi, A., De Luca, A.: Square-free words on partially commutative free monoids. Information Processing Letters 22(3), 125–131 (1986)
2. Choffrut, C., Karhumäki, J.: Combinatorics of words. In: Rozenberg, G., Salomaa, A. (eds.) Handbook of Formal Languages, vol. 1, pp. 329–438. Springer, Heidelberg (1997)
3. Dekking, F.M.: Strongly non-repetitive sequences and progression-free sets. J. Combin. Theory Ser. A 27(2), 181–185 (1979)
4. Huova, M., Karhumäki, J., Saarela, A., Saari, K.: Local squares, periodicity and finite automata. In: Calude, C.S., Rozenberg, G., Salomaa, A. (eds.) Rainbow of Computer Science. LNCS, vol. 6570, pp. 90–101. Springer, Heidelberg (2011)
5. Huova, M., Karhumäki, J.: On the unavoidability of k-abelian squares in pure morphic words. Journal of Integer Sequences 16, article 13.2.9 (2013)
6. Huova, M.: Existence of an infinite ternary 64-abelian square-free word. Special Issue of the Journal RAIRO - Theoretical Informatics and Applications dedicated to "Journees Montoises d'Informatique Theorique 2012" (submitted)
7. Karhumäki, J., Saarela, A., Zamboni, L.: On a generalization of Abelian equivalence and complexity of infinite words (submitted), arXiv preprint at http://arxiv.org/abs/1301.5104
8. Keränen, V.: Abelian squares are avoidable on 4 letters. In: Kuich, W. (ed.) ICALP 1992. LNCS, vol. 623, pp. 41–52. Springer, Heidelberg (1992)
9. Lothaire, M.: Combinatorics on words. Addison-Wesley, Reading (1983)
10. Mercaş, R., Saarela, A.: 3-abelian cubes are avoidable on binary alphabets. In: Béal, M.-P., Carton, O. (eds.) DLT 2013. LNCS, vol. 7907, pp. 374–383. Springer, Heidelberg (2013)
11. Ochem, P., Rampersad, N., Shallit, J.: Avoiding approximate squares. International Journal of Foundations of Computer Science 19(3), 633–648 (2008)
12. Thue, A.: Über unendliche Zeichenreihen. Norske vid. Selsk. Skr. Mat. Nat. Kl. 7, 1–22 (1906)
13. Thue, A.: Über die gegenseitige Lage gleicher Teile gewisser Zeichenreihen. Norske vid. Selsk. Skr. Mat. Nat. Kl. 1, 1–67 (1912)

Similarity Relations and Repetition-Freeness

Tomi Kärki[1,2]

[1] Department of Teacher Education
University of Turku, PO Box 175, 26101 Rauma, Finland
[2] Department of Mathematics,
University of Turku, 20014 Turku, Finland

Abstract. A similarity relation is a relation on words of equal length induced by a symmetric and reflexive relation on letters. The aim of this article is to give an overview of the results concerning repetition-freeness in connection with similarity relations. We consider so called chain relations, cyclic relations and partial words, which can be seen as a special case of similarity relations. As a new result, we prove that local 3^+-repetitions can be avoided in binary partial words and the local avoidability index of $\mathring{R}$-cubes is five, where $\mathring{R}$ is a relation such that the graph of the relation is a cycle.

1 Introduction

Combinatorics on words contains a huge variety of results on pattern avoidance (see [8]), the case of repetition-freeness being one of the most important and most deeply studied. Let $|u|$ denote the length of the word u. For a rational number k, a word w is a *repetition of order k* if w is a prefix of length $k \cdot |u|$ of the infinite catenation $u^\omega = uuu\cdots$ for some non-empty word u. *Squares* are repetitions of order $k = 2$ and *cubes* are repetitions of order $k = 3$. A word w is said to be k-*free* if it does not contain a repetition of order k, i.e., the word w *avoids* such repetitions. Moreover, the word w is said to be k^+-*free* if, it is k'-free for any $k' > k$, i.e., it avoids any repetition of order k' greater than k. A repetition of order k (resp. k^+) is said to be n-*avoidable*, if there exists an infinite k-free (resp. k^+-free) word over an n-letter alphabet. The *avoidability index* of a repetition is the smallest n such that the repetition is n-avoidable.

The most classical results of repetition freeness can be found in the seminal papers of Thue [20,21]. At the beginning of the 20th century, Thue showed that there exists an infinite word over a 3-letter alphabet which does not contain any square. Moreover, he constructed an infinite binary word t which does not contain any overlap $uvuvu$ for a word v and a non-empty word u. This celebrated word is nowadays called the Thue-Morse word, which has many surprising and remarkable properties; see [1].

Many generalizations have been considered. For example, for an integer $k \geq 2$, an *abelian repetition of order k* is a nonempty word $u_1 \cdots u_k$ such that all factors u_i, $1 \leq i \leq k$, are permutations of each other. The question of avoiding abelian squares was raised by Erdös in 1961 [10]. Dekking showed in 1979 that

J. Karhumäki, A. Lepistö, and L. Zamboni (Eds.): WORDS 2013, LNCS 8079, pp. 169–180, 2013.

abelian repetitions of order at least four are 2-avoidable and abelian cubes are 3-avoidable (but not 2-avoidable) [9]. Finally in 1992, Keränen showed that the avoidablity index of abelian squares is four [16]. A more recent generalization based on the Hamming distance was introduced by Krieger, Ochem, Rampersad and Shallit in [17], where they considered c-*approximate* and α-*similar squares*. A word uv with $|u| = |v|$ is a c-approximate square, if u and v differ on at most c positions, and an α-similar square if the ratio between the number of positions u and v agree on and the length of u is at least α.

Abelian repetitions and approximate squares are repetitions where the consecutive factors are not equal but similar. Another generalization of repetition of this kind has been studied in connection with *partial words*, i.e., words with 'do not know'-symbols ◇ called *holes*. Partial words were invented by Berstel and Boasson in 1999 [2] and the topic has been intensively studied in the recent years; see [3]. A *completion* of a partial word is a full word where the holes are replaced by other letters. Two partial words are *compatible* if they have a common completion. For any integer $k \geq 2$, a partial word is a repetition of order k if it is of the form $u_1 \cdots u_k$ where the words u_i are pairwise compatible. In other words, $u_1 \cdots u_k$ can be transformed into a full word u^k by a suitable replacement of holes. Repetition freeness in partial words has been considered in several articles (see e.g. [4,6,7,13,14,19]).

Repetitions in partial words are a special case of repetitions in connection with similarity relations. The compatibility of the factors u_i in a repetition $u_1 \cdots u_k$ in a partial word can be replaced by another similarity relation between the factors. A *similarity relation* introduced by Halava, Harju and Kärki in [11] is a relation on words of equal length induced by a reflexive and symmetric relation on letters. For example, if s is related to f, then the words *sun* and *fun* are considered similar. In addition to the compatibility relation $R_\uparrow$ of partial words, repetition-freeness has also been consider in the case of cyclic relations $\mathring{R}$ and chain relations $\overline{R}$ in [15], where the avoidability indices of squares and overlaps were discovered.

In this article, we give an overview of the results concerning avoidability of repetitions in connection with chain relations, cyclic relations and partial words. There are two types of relational repetitions and therefore also two types of relational avoidability indices, namely global and local. As a new result, we consider the local avoidability indices of repetitions of order 3^+. These repetitions can be avoided in binary partial words. Moreover, it follows that in the case of chain relations this avoidability index is three and in the case of cyclic relations the index is four. Moreover, we show that local $\mathring{R}$-cubes are 5-avoidable but not 4-avoidable. A summary of the results is given in Table 1 at the end of this article.

2   Similarity Relations

Let $\mathcal{A}$ be an alphabet. The set of all finite words $\mathcal{A}^*$ is a free monoid under the operation of concatenation. The set of non-empty finite words is denoted by $\mathcal{A}^+$ and the set of all (right) infinite words is denoted by $\mathcal{A}^\omega$. A binary relation R on a set X is subset of the cartesian product $X \times X$. If two elements x and y are related, i.e., $(x, y) \in R$, we may write $x\,R\,y$. The identity relation is denoted by ι.

Definition 1. *A relation R is called a* similarity relation *on words over $\mathcal{A}$ if it is a submonoid of $\mathcal{A}^* \times \mathcal{A}^*$ generated by a reflexive and symmetric relation $R_\mathcal{A} \subseteq \mathcal{A} \times \mathcal{A}$ on letters. The relation $R_\mathcal{A}$ is called the* generating relation *of R. Words u and v satisfying $u\,R\,v$ are said to be* similar *or, more precisely, R-similar.*

In other words, a similarity relation is a "letter-to-letter" compatibility relation on words of equal length. Since a similarity relation R is induced by its restriction $R_\mathcal{A}$ on letters, it can be represented by listing all pairs $\{a, b\}$ $(a \neq b)$ such that $a\,R\,b$. We use the notation

$$R = \langle \{r_1, \ldots, r_n\} \rangle,$$

where $r_i = (a_i, b_i) \in \mathcal{A} \times \mathcal{A}$ for $i = 1, 2, \ldots, n$, to denote that R is the similarity relation generated by the symmetric closure of $\iota_\mathcal{A} \cup \{r_1, \ldots, r_n\}$. Moreover, the similarity relation R can be represented by a graph G_R, where the set of vertices is the alphabet $\mathcal{A}$ and there is an edge between two different letters a and b if $a\,R\,b$.

As mentioned in the introduction, the compatibility relation of partial words is one example of a similarity relation. A partial word over an alphabet $\mathcal{A}$ can be represented as a word over the extended alphabet $\mathcal{A}_\diamond = \mathcal{A} \cup \{\diamond\}$, where $\diamond$ does not belong to $\mathcal{A}$. The letter $\diamond$ is a *hole*, i.e., a 'do not know'-symbol which may correspond to any letter of the alphabet $\mathcal{A}$. Two partial words $u = u_1 \cdots u_n$ and $v = v_1 \cdots v_n$, where $u_i, v_i \in \mathcal{A}$ for $1 \leq i \leq n$, are said to be *compatible* if $u_i = v_i$ whenever both u_i and v_i are not holes. In this case, there exists a full word over $\mathcal{A}$ which is a *completion* of both partial words u and v, i.e., it is obtained from these partial words by replacing the holes with suitable letters. Let us define

$$R_\uparrow = \langle \{(\diamond, a) \mid a \in \mathcal{A}\} \rangle. \tag{1}$$

The compatibility relation of partial words over $\mathcal{A}$ corresponds to the similarity relation $R_\uparrow$ on the extended alphabet $\mathcal{A}_\diamond$ [11]. As an example, a graph of the similarity relation $R_\uparrow$ on the alphabet $\{0, 1, 2, 3, 4, 5, \diamond\}$ is depicted in Figure 1.

Example 1. Consider partial words over the alphabet $\{a, b, c, \diamond\}$. Let

$$u = u_1 \cdots u_5 = a\diamond cb\diamond \quad \text{and} \quad v = v_1 \cdots v_5 = \diamond bcb\diamond \;.$$

These two partial words are compatible, since $u_3 u_4 = cb = v_3 v_4$ and in all other positions there is a hole either in u or in v. Hence, the words u and v are $R_\uparrow$-similar. Since the last letter of both u and v is a hole, these partial words have three common completions: $abcba$, $abcbb$ and $abcbc$. The word $w = w_1 \cdots w_5 = b\diamond cba$ is not $R_\uparrow$-similar with u because $(u_1, w_1) = (a, b) \notin R_\uparrow$. On the other hand, we have $v\,R_\uparrow\,w$.

In this paper we consider also two other types of similarity relations which both have a special and quite simple and natural structure. Without loss of generality, we fix an n-letter alphabet to be $\mathcal{A}_n = \{0, 1, \ldots, n-1\}$.

Definition 2. *For $n \geq 2$, the chain relation $\overline{R}_n$ is a similarity relation on $\mathcal{A}_n^*$ defined by*

$$\overline{R}_n = \langle \{(i, i+1) \mid i = 0, 1, \ldots, n-2\} \rangle \tag{2}$$

and the cyclic relation $\mathring{R}_n$ is a similarity relation on $\mathcal{A}_n^*$ defined by

$$\mathring{R}_n = \langle \{(i, i+1) \mid i = 0, 1, \ldots, n-2\} \cup \{(n-1, 0)\} \rangle. \tag{3}$$

In other words, all consecutive integers are related in the chain relation and in the cyclic relation also the largest integer is related to zero. For example, the words 543210 and 432105 are $\mathring{R}_6$-similar but not $\overline{R}_6$-similar, since the last letters 5 and 0 are not $\overline{R}_6$-compatible. The graphs of the similarity relations $\overline{R}_6$ and $\mathring{R}_6$ are depicted in Figure 1. If the considered alphabet is clear from the context, we may simply denote $\overline{R}$ and $\mathring{R}$.

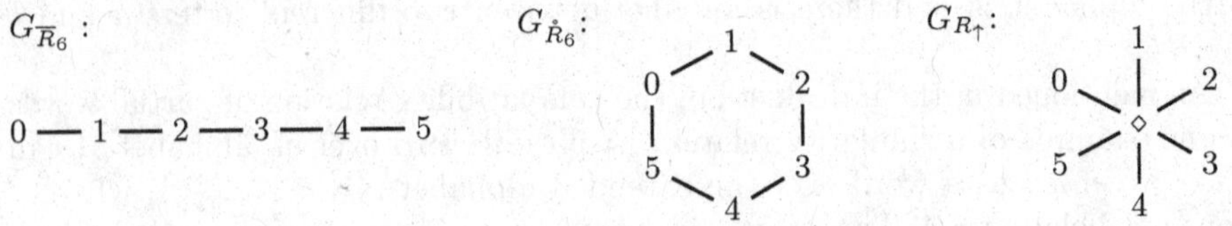

Fig. 1. The graphs $G_{\overline{R}_6}$ and $G_{\mathring{R}_6}$ and $G_{R_\uparrow}$ in $\mathcal{A}_6 \cup \{\diamond\}$

3   Relational Repetition-Freeness

Let us first defined what are relational repetitions in the context of similarity relations. As in the repetitions of partial words, the consecutive factors of an R-repetition are not necessarily equal but R-similar.

Definition 3. *Let R be a similarity relation on $\mathcal{A}$ and let $\mathrm{pref}_\ell(w)$ denote the prefix of length ℓ of a word w.*

- *A word $w \in \mathcal{A}^+$ is a global R-repetition of order k if it can be written in the form $u_1 \cdots u_m u'$ where the words u_i are pairwise R-similar, $u'\, R\, \mathrm{pref}_{|u'|}(u_i)$ for every $i = 1, 2, \ldots, m$ and $k = |w|/|u_i|$.*
- *A word $w \in \mathcal{A}^+$ is a local R-repetition of order k if $w = u_1 \cdots u_m u'$ where $u_i\, R\, u_{i+1}$ for $i = 1, 2, \ldots, m-1$, $u'\, R\, \mathrm{pref}_{|u'|}(u_m)$ and $k = |w|/|u_i|$.*
- *A word $w \in \mathcal{A}^+$ is globally (resp. locally) (R, k)-free if it does not contain any global (resp. local) R-repetitions of order k.*
- *A word $w \in \mathcal{A}^+$ is globally (resp. locally) (R, k^+)-free if it does not contain any global (resp. local) R-repetitions of order $\ell > k$.*

The terminology in the definition above comes from the two different relational periods introduced in [12]. A word $w = w_1 \cdots w_n$, $w_i \in \mathcal{A}$ has a *global R-period* p if $i \equiv j \pmod{p}$ implies $w_i R w_j$ for every $i, j \in \{1, 2, \ldots, n\}$. It has a *local R-period* p if $w_i R w_{i+p}$ for $i = 1, 2, \ldots, n - p$. Hence, a global (resp. local) R-repetition $u_1 \cdots u_m u'$ has a global (resp. local) R-period $|u_i|$. Note that in the literature of partial words the global period is sometimes called a *strong* period and the local period is called a *weak* period. Therefore, instead of global and local overlaps, the terms *strong overlap* and *weak overlap* have been used; see, e.g., [5].

An R-repetition of order 2 is called an *R-square*. A *local R-overlap* is a word of the form $uu'vv'w$, where $u R v$, $u' R v'$ and $v R w$. In this case, there are two R-similar overlapping words $uu'v$ and $vv'w$ and the word $uu'vv'w$ has a local R-period $|uu'|$. A *global R-overlap* is a local R-overlap $uu'vv'w$ such that also $u R w$. Hence, this word has a global R-period $|uu'|$. An $\overline{R}$-overlap is called a *chain overlap* and an $\mathring{R}$-overlap is called a *cyclic overlap*. An R-repetition of order 3 is a called an *R-cube*.

Example 2. Let $u_1 = 002$, $u_2 = 102$ and $u' = 2$. The word $u = u_1 u_2 u' = 0021022$ is a local $\overline{R}_3$-repetition of order $\frac{7}{3}$, since $u_1 \, \overline{R}_3 \, u_2$ and $u' \overline{R}_3 \, \mathrm{pref}_1(u_2) = 1$. However, u is not a global $\overline{R}_3$-repetition, since $u' = 2$ and $\mathrm{pref}_1(u_1) = 0$ are not $\overline{R}_3$-similar. If the relation $\overline{R}_3$ is replaced by $\mathring{R}_3$, all letters are related to each other and u is a global and local $\mathring{R}_3$-repetition of order $\frac{7}{3}$.

Avoidability of relational repetitions was consider in [15] mainly in the case of chain relations and cyclic relations. Note that if the alphabet is large enough, one can find three letters which are not $\overline{R}$-similar or $\mathring{R}$-similar with each other. Hence, writing any infinite square-free ternary word using these three letters, one constructs an $(\overline{R}, 2)$-free word or an $(\mathring{R}, 2)$-free word. In the case of partial words this kind of "trivial" avoidability was prevented by considering partial words which do contain holes, preferably, infinitely many holes [13,14], and even words which stay repetition-free after an arbitrary insertion of holes were considered [4]. Similarly, the $(\overline{R}, k)$-freeness and the $(\mathring{R}, k)$-freeness were studied in [15] in infinite words where each letter of the alphabet occurs infinitely often.

Definition 4

- Let R be the chain relation $\overline{R}$ or the cyclic relation $\mathring{R}$. An R-repetition of order k is globally (resp. locally) n-avoidable if there exists an infinite word w over the alphabet $\mathcal{A}_n$ such that each letter of the alphabet $\mathcal{A}_n$ occurs infinitely many times in w and w is globally (resp. locally) (R_n, k)-free.
- An $R_\uparrow$-repetition of order k is globally (resp. locally) n-avoidable if there exists an infinite word w over the alphabet $\mathcal{A}_n \cup \{\diamond\}$ such that each letter of the alphabet $\mathcal{A}_n \cup \{\diamond\}$ occurs infinitely many times in w and w is globally (resp. locally) $(R_\uparrow, k)$-free.

Definition 5. Let R be the chain relation $\overline{R}$, the cyclic relation $\mathring{R}$ or the relation $R_\uparrow$.

- *The* global avoidability index $\gamma(R, k)$ *is the minimal* n *(if it exists) such that* R-*repetitions of order* k *are globally* n-*avoidable.*
- *The* local avoidability index $\lambda(R, k)$ *is the minimal* n *(if it exists) such that* R-*repetitions of order* k *are locally* n-*avoidable.*

The indices $\gamma(R, k^+)$ and $\lambda(R, k^+)$ are defined as above by replacing k by k^+. Since a global R-repetition of order k is a local R-repetition of order k, any locally (R, k)-free word is also globally (R, k)-free. Hence, we have

$$\gamma(R, k) \leq \lambda(R, k) \ .$$

For $k > 1$, we have

$$\lambda(\overline{R}, k) \geq \gamma(\overline{R}, k) \geq 3, \quad \lambda(\mathring{R}, k) \geq \gamma(\mathring{R}, k) \geq 4, \quad \lambda(R_\uparrow, k) \geq \gamma(R_\uparrow, k) \geq 2, \quad (4)$$

since in $\mathcal{A}_2$ all letters are $\overline{R}_2$-similar, in $\mathcal{A}_3$ all letters are $\mathring{R}_3$-similar and in $\mathcal{A}_1 \cup \{\diamond\}$ all letters are $R_\uparrow$-similar.

Also, note that if R-repetitions of order k are n-avoidable for $R = \overline{R}$, $R = \mathring{R}$ or $R = R_\uparrow$, then they are also $(n + 1)$-avoidable. Namely, if an (R, k)-free word contains infinitely many occurrences of each letter in $\mathcal{A}_n$, we may construct a new infinite word by replacing, for example, every other occurrence of the letter $n - 1$ by the new letter n. This new word contains infinitely many occurrences of each letter in $\mathcal{A}_{n+1}$ and the words is still (R, k)-free.

4   Square-Freeness and Overlap-Freeness

Squares cannot be avoided in partial words since every word containing holes contains also at least one of the *trivial squares* $a\diamond$ or $\diamond a$, where a is a letter. Hence, the avoidability indices $\gamma(R_\uparrow, 2)$ and $\lambda(R_\uparrow, 2)$ do not exist. However, we may avoid larger squares. Namely, over a three-letter alphabet there exist uncountably many partial words with an infinite number of holes such that the only square factors are the trivial ones [13]; see also [4].

Theorem 1. *There exists uncountably many infinite words with an infinite number of holes over a three-letter alphabet such that they do not contain any squares other than the trivial ones.*

Using the terminology of Blanchet-Sadri et al. [7], an occurrence of a pattern is *non-trivial* if none of its variables is substituted by a hole. Otherwise, the occurrence is *trivial*. Thus, trivial squares are trivial occurrences of the pattern $\alpha\alpha$ and, by the result mentioned above, *the non-trivial avoidability index* of squares is 3. We may also consider partial words which stay k-free after replacing arbitrary occurrences of letters by holes under the restriction that two holes must always be separated by at least two letters. Blanchet-Sadri et al. constructed an infinite word over an 8-letter alphabet that remains non-trivially square-free even after this kind of insertion of holes, and they showed that the alphabet size eight is optimal [4].

A partial word is an overlap if any of its completions is an overlap $xyxyx$. These overlaps are global $R_\uparrow$-repetitions and the overlap-freeness of partial words means global $(R_\uparrow, 2^+)$-freeness in our terminology. Halava et al. showed that an infinite overlap-free binary partial word is either full or of the form $\diamond w$ or $x\diamond w$, where w is an infinite full word and x is a letter. There are infinitely many overlap-free words of each type [14]; see also [4]. Hence, it is impossible to build a globally $(R_\uparrow, 2^+)$-free infinite binary partial word with infinitely many holes, which implies

$$\gamma(R_\uparrow, 2^+) > 2. \tag{5}$$

However, there exist infinitely many binary partial words containing infinitely many holes but no factor having a completion of the form $xyxyx$ where the length of x is at least 2; see [14].

On the other hand, Blanchet-Sadri et al. [4] have shown that there exist infinitely many overlap-free partial words with infinitely many holes over a three-letter alphabet. Indeed, this is a consequence of Theorem 1. Namely, a ternary infinite word w with an infinite number of holes that does not contain any other squares than the trivial ones cannot contain any factors which have a completion $xyxyx$ where $|xy| \geq 2$. Moreover, if w contains a factor that has a completion xxx where x is a letter, then the factor must be of the form $x\diamond x$ and there must be a square $x\diamond xy$ in w. This is a contradiction. Hence, overlaps in partial words are 3-avoidable and by (5) this gives us the following theorem.

Theorem 2. *The global avoidability index of overlaps in partial words is*

$$\gamma(R_\uparrow, 2^+) = 3 \ .$$

The minimal alphabet size for avoiding overlaps after an arbitrary insertion of holes under the restriction that two holes must always be separated by at least two letters was proved to be five [5]. Moreover, Blanchet-Sadri et al. have showed that the non-trivial avoidability index for all binary patterns is the same as in the case of full words [7].

Since a partial word $x\diamond y$ where x and y are letters is a local $R_\uparrow$-cube, it is not possible to avoid local cubes or local overlaps in partial words over any alphabet. Hence, the avoidability index $\lambda(R_\uparrow, 2^+)$ does not exist.

The avoidability indices of squares and overlaps in the case of chain relations and cyclic relations were solved in [15].

Theorem 3. *Let $\overline{R}$ be a chain relation and $\mathring{R}$ be a cyclic relation. We have the following avoidability indices:*

$$\gamma(\overline{R}, 2) = \lambda(\overline{R}, 2) = 6, \quad \gamma(\mathring{R}, 2) = \lambda(\mathring{R}, 2) = 7,$$
$$\gamma(\overline{R}, 2^+) = \lambda(\overline{R}, 2^+) = 4, \quad \gamma(\mathring{R}, 2^+) = \lambda(\mathring{R}, 2^+) = 5.$$

In the proofs of the results above, repetition-free infinite words are often generated by iterating morphisms. A morphism $\varphi\colon \mathcal{A}^* \to \mathcal{A}^*$ is said to be *prolongable* on a letter a if $\varphi(a) = aw$ for some word $w \in \mathcal{A}^+$ such that $\varphi^n(w)$ is non-empty for all integers $n \geq 1$. By definition, $\varphi^n(a)$ is a prefix of $\varphi^{n+1}(a)$ for all integers $n \geq 0$ and the sequence $(\varphi^n(a))_{n \geq 0}$ converges to the unique infinite word generated by φ,

$$\varphi^\omega(a) := \lim_{n \to \infty} \varphi^n(a) = aw\varphi(w)\varphi^2(w)\cdots.$$

This infinite word is a fixed point of φ, i.e., $\varphi(\varphi^\omega(a)) = \varphi^\omega(a)$.

In [15] the *Leech word* was modified in order to prove that there exists an $(\overline{R}, 2)$-free infinite word containing every letter of $\mathcal{A}_6$ infinitely many times. A Leech word is a ternary infinite word

$$\Lambda := \varphi^\omega(a) = abcbacbcabcbabcacbacabcacbcabacbabcabacbca\cdots,$$

generated by iterating the morphism $\varphi\colon \{a,b,c\}^* \to \{a,b,c\}^*$ defined by $a \mapsto abcbacbcabcba$, $b \mapsto bcacbacabcacb$, $c \mapsto cabacbabcabac$. The words Λ is known to be square-free [18]. In order to show that cyclic squares are 7-avoidable, the square-free word $\mu^\omega(a)$ of Thue [20] was mapped in [15] with a 6-uniform morphism $\nu\colon \{a,b,c\}^* \to \mathcal{A}_7^*$. The morphism $\mu\colon \{a,b,c\}^* \to \{a,b,c\}^*$ is defined by $a \mapsto abc$, $b \mapsto ac$, $c \mapsto b$.

The overlap-freeness results of [15] are based on the celebrated Thue-Morse word $t = \tau^\omega(a)$, where $\tau\colon \{a,b\}^* \to \{a,b\}^*$ is defined by $a \mapsto ab$, $b \mapsto ba$. In the case of global and local $(\overline{R}, 2^+)$-freeness, the letter a is replaced by 0 and the letter b is replaced by 3. Then, by arbitrarily replacing factors 303 by 313 and factors 030 by 020, a locally $\overline{R}_4$-overlap-free infinite word is constructed. The construction of a locally $\mathring{R}_5$-overlap-free infinite word in [15] is quite involved. The Thue-Morse word is used to recursively define an infinite word $\hat{t}$ such that the Thue-Morse word is divided into blocks of different size and these blocks are mapped with ten different codings σ_i, i.e., letter-to-letter morphism. The beginning of this word is

$$\hat{t} = \sigma_0(ab)\sigma_1(ba)\sigma_2(baab)\sigma_3(baababba)\sigma_4(baababbaabbabaab)\cdots.$$

5   Cube-Freeness and 3^+-Freeness

The first results of repetition-freeness of partial words were proved by Manea and Mercaş in 2007 [19]. In particular, they proved the following theorem.

Theorem 4. *There exist infinitely many cube-free infinite partial words over a binary alphabet containing an infinite number of holes.*

Moreover, they proved that there exists an infinite word over a four-letter alphabet such that the word stays cube-free after an arbitrary insertion of holes under the restriction that two holes must always be separated by at least two letters. Over a ternary alphabet, it is impossible to construct such infinite words.

In Theorem 4, the cube-freeness of partial words means the global $(R_\uparrow, 3)$-freeness. As mentioned above, for any letters x and y, the word $x \diamond y$ is a local $R_\uparrow$-cube and therefore the local avoidability index $\lambda(R_\uparrow, 3)$ does not exist. As a consequence of Theorem 4, we have the following result.

Theorem 5. *For any $k \geq 3$, we have*

$$\gamma(R_\uparrow, k) = 2, \quad \gamma(\overline{R}, k) = 3 \quad and \quad \gamma(\mathring{R}, k) = 4 .$$

Proof. By (4) and Theorem 4, the global avoidability index of $R_\uparrow$-repetitions of order $k \geq 3$ is $\gamma(R_\uparrow, k) = 2$. Since in a chain relation $\overline{R}_3$ the letter 1 is related to both 0 and 2, it corresponds to a hole in the alphabet $\{0, 2\} \cup \{\diamond\}$. Hence, Theorem 4 says that cubes are globally avoidable in this alphabet and, by (4), we have $\gamma(\overline{R}, k) = 3$ for any $k \geq 3$.

Next, let us consider the relation $\mathring{R}_4$. Let w be an infinite globally $(\overline{R}, 3)$-free word over the alphabet $\mathcal{A}_3$. Let $\hat{w}$ be a word obtained from w by replacing every other occurrence of 1 by 3. Assume that $\hat{w}$ contains a global $\mathring{R}$-cube u. Since both 3 and 1 are related to the letters 0 and 2, it means that by replacing the occurrences of 3 in u again by 1, we obtain a factor which is a global $\overline{R}$-cube in w. This is a contradiction. Hence, every letter of $\mathcal{A}_4$ occurs in $\hat{w}$ infinitely many times and the word is globally $(\mathring{R}, 3)$-free. By (4), we conclude $\gamma(\mathring{R}, k) = 4$ for $k \geq 3$.

Let us next consider local $\overline{R}$-cubes and $\mathring{R}$-cubes.

Theorem 6. *The local avoidability indices of chain cubes and cyclic cubes are*

$$\lambda(\overline{R}, 3) = 4 \quad and \quad \lambda(\mathring{R}, 3) = 5 .$$

Proof. As in the case of partial words, local $\overline{R}$-cubes cannot be avoided in $\mathcal{A}_3$, since for any letters x and y, the factor $x1y$ is a local $\overline{R}$-cube. Since local $\overline{R}$-overlaps are 4-avoidable by Theorem 3, we have $\lambda(\overline{R}, 3) = 4$.

Next, assume that there exists a locally $(\mathring{R}_4, 3)$-free word w containing infinitely many occurrences of each letter in $\mathcal{A}_4$. Let $\mathcal{A} = \{0, 2\}$ or $\mathcal{B} = \{1, 3\}$. The word w can be factored into blocks where each block contains only letters in $\mathcal{A}$ or in $\mathcal{B}$ and the blocks are maximal in the sense that the neighbour blocks have a different alphabet. By symmetry, we may assume that a block ends with 0 and the next block starts with 1. In order to avoid local $\mathring{R}_4$-cubes, the letter preceding 01 must be 2. Let $201z$ be a factor in w. It is straightforward to verify that z begins with either 311 or 331.

We can also verify that a factor $x \in \mathcal{B}^4$ in w is always followed by either 1 or 3 in order to keep w globally $\mathring{R}_4$-overlap-free. Without loss of generality, we may assume that x begins with 1. There are five possibilities: $w_1 = 1131$, $w_2 = 1133$, $w_3 = 1311$, $w_4 = 1313$ and $w_5 = 1331$. By the symmetry of the relation $\mathring{R}_4$, we may assume that the word w_i is followed by 0. In order to avoid local $\mathring{R}$-cubes, the word w_1 must be followed by 0220. However, the letter preceding w_1 must be 3 and hence the factor $3w_10220 = 311.310.220$ is a local $\mathring{R}$-cube. This is impossible. The word w_20 ends with an $\mathring{R}$-cube 330 and the word w_30 ends with an $\mathring{R}$-cube 110. If the word w_4 is followed by 0, then the words w_400, w_402 and w_403 are $\mathring{R}$-cubes and the word w_401 ends with the local $\mathring{R}$-cube 301. In order to avoid local $\mathring{R}$-cubes, the word w_5 must be followed by 022002 and preceded by 31. However, the word $31w_5022002 = 3113.3102.2002$ is a local $\mathring{R}$-cube. Again, this is a contradiction.

Hence, a factor $x \in \mathcal{B}^4$ in w is always followed by either 1 or 3 and in the word z there are no occurrences of the letters 0 and 2. This is a contradiction. Thus, local $\mathring{R}$-cubes are not 4-avoidable, and by Theorem 3, it follows that $\lambda(\mathring{R}, 3) = 5$.

Finally, we consider local repetitions of order $k > 3$.

Theorem 7. *For $k > 3$, we have*

$$\lambda(R_\uparrow, k) = 2, \quad \lambda(\overline{R}, k) = 3 \quad and \quad \lambda(\mathring{R}, k) = 4.$$

Proof. Let t be the Thue-Morse word $\tau^\omega(a)$. By construction, the word t consists of blocks $\tau^5(a)$ and $\tau^5(b)$. Replace the blocks $\tau^5(a)$ by the words

$$abbabaabbaaba\diamond babaababbaabbabaab,$$

where one b in $\tau^5(a)$ is replaced by a hole. Denote this new partial word by $\hat{t}$. We may easily verify by hand or with computer experiments that $\hat{t}$ does not contain any local $R_\uparrow$-repetitions $u_1 u_2 u_3 u'$, where $u_1 \; R_\uparrow \; u_2 \; R_\uparrow \; u_3$, $|u_1| \le 7$ and $u' \; R_\uparrow \; \mathrm{pref}_{|u'|}(u_3)$.

Next, assume that $\hat{t}$ contains a local $R_\uparrow$-repetitions $w = u_1 u_2 u_3 u'$ and $p = |u_1| = |u_2| = |u_3| > 7$. Then the word $u_1 u_2 x$, where x is the first letter of u_3, must contain at least one position i such that the letter in that position is a hole and the letter in the position $i - p$ or $i + p$ in the factor $u_1 u_2 x$ is a. Otherwise, we could replace all occurrences of holes in $u_1 u_2 x$ by the original letter b and obtain an overlap in t. This is a contradiction with the overlap-freeness of the Thue-Morse word.

Without loss of generality, assume that in the position $i + p$ there is $w_{i+p} = a$. First, let $i \ge 2$. Since w_i is a hole, the letter $w_{i-1} = a$ by the construction and, by compatibility, the letter w_{i+p-1} must be a. Note that w_{i+p-1} cannot be a hole, since holes in $\hat{t}$ are always followed by the letter b. Since the Thue-Morse word can be decomposed into blocks ab and ba, we conclude that $w_{i+p-2} w_{i+p-1} w_{i+p} w_{i+p+1}$ consists of two blocks $ba.ab$. Note again that after or before aa there cannot be any holes. Since $w_{i+2} = a$ and there are no holes after the letter b, we must have $w_{i+p+2} = a$. Assume that $w_{i+p+3} = \diamond$, which implies that $w_{i+p+4} = b$. However, $w_{i+4} = a$ and this is a contradiction with the compatibility of w_{i+p+4} and w_{i+4}. Hence, we have $w_{i+p+3} = w_{i+3} = b$. After $w_{i+p+3} = b$ there cannot be a hole. Thus, $w_{i+p+4} = w_{i+4} = a$. However, we obtain $w_{i+p} \cdots w_{i+p+4} = ababa$, which is a contradiction with the overlap-freeness of the original word t.

Second, let $i = 1$. If $w_{i+p-1} = a$, then we get a contradiction as above. Hence, assume that $w_{i+p-1} = b$. If $w_{i+p+1} w_{i+p+2} = \diamond b$, then the letter w_{i+p+2} is not compatible with the letter $w_{i+2} = a$. Therefore, we must have $w_{i+p+1} = w_{i+1} = b$ and $w_{i+p+2} = w_{i+2} = a$, since no holes are possible after $w_{i+p-1} w_{i+p} w_{i+p+1} = bab$. After $w_{i+p-1} \cdots w_{i+p+2} = baba$ there cannot be a hole and we must have $w_{i+p+3} = w_{i+3} = b$. Thus, we obtain an overlap $w_{i+p-1} \cdots w_{i+p+3} = babab$, which is again a contradiction with the overlap-freeness of t.

Hence, the partial word $\hat{t}$ does not contain any local repetitions of order $k > 3$ and we conclude that $\lambda(R_\uparrow, 3^+) = 2$. As in the proof of Theorem 5, we notice that in $\overline{R}_3$ the letter 1 corresponds to a hole. Hence, by replacing a with 0, b with 2 and $\diamond$ with 1 in $\hat{t}$, we obtain a locally $(\overline{R}, 3^+)$-free infinite word w. Moreover, as in the proof of Theorem 5, we obtain a locally $(\mathring{R}, 3^+)$-free word from w by replacing every other occurrence of 1 with 3. Thus, by (4), we then have $\lambda(\overline{R}, 3^+) = 3$ and $\lambda(\mathring{R}, 3^+) = 4$.

6   Conclusions

We have considered global and local avoidability indices of partial words, chain relations and cyclic relations. A summary of the results is given in Table 1.

Table 1. Avoidability indices of the relations $\overline{R}$, $\mathring{R}$ and $R_\uparrow$

	$\overline{R}$		$\mathring{R}$		$R_\uparrow$	
	γ	λ	γ	λ	γ	λ
2	6	6	7	7	-	-
2^+	4	4	5	5	3	-
3	3	4	4	5	2	-
3^+	3	3	4	4	2	2

References

1. Allouche, J.-P., Shallit, J.: The ubiquitous Prouhet-Thue-Morse sequence. In: Ding, C., Helleseth, T., Niederreiter, H. (eds.) Sequences and Their Applications: Proceedings of SETA 1998, pp. 1–16. Springer, London (1998)
2. Berstel, J., Boasson, L.: Partial words and a theorem of Fine and Wilf. Theoret. Comput. Sci. 218, 135–141 (1999)
3. Blanchet-Sadri, F.: Algorithmic Combinatorics on Partial Words. Chapman & Hall/CRC Press, Boca Raton (2007)
4. Blanchet-Sadri, F., Mercaş, R., Scott, G.: A generalization of Thue freeness for partial words. Theoret. Comput. Sci. 410(8-10), 793–800 (2009)
5. Blanchet-Sadri, F., Mercaş, R., Rashin, A., Willett, E.: An Answer to a Conjecture on Overlaps in Partial Words Using Periodicity Algorithms. In: Dediu, A.H., Ionescu, A.M., Martín-Vide, C. (eds.) LATA 2009. LNCS, vol. 5457, pp. 188–199. Springer, Heidelberg (2009)
6. Blanchet-Sadri, F., Mercaş, R., Simmons, S., Weissenstein, E.: Avoidable Binary Patterns in Partial Words. In: Dediu, A.-H., Fernau, H., Martín-Vide, C. (eds.) LATA 2010. LNCS, vol. 6031, pp. 106–117. Springer, Heidelberg (2010)
7. Blanchet-Sadri, F., Black, K., Zemke, A.: Unary Pattern Avoidance in Partial Words Dense with Holes. In: Dediu, A.-H., Inenaga, S., Martín-Vide, C. (eds.) LATA 2011. LNCS, vol. 6638, pp. 155–166. Springer, Heidelberg (2011)
8. Currie, J.D.: Pattern avoidance: themes and variations. Theoret. Comput. Sci. 339(1), 7–18 (2005)
9. Dekking, F.M.: Strongly non-repetitive sequences and progression-free sets. Journal of Combinatorial Theory, Series A 27(2), 181–185 (1979)

10. Erdős, P.: Some unsolved problems. Magyar Tudományos Akadémia Matematikai Kutató Intézete Közl. 6, 221–254 (1961)
11. Halava, V., Harju, T., Kärki, T.: Relational codes of words. Theoret. Comput. Sci. 389(1-2), 237–249 (2007)
12. Halava, V., Harju, T., Kärki, T.: Interaction properties of relational periods. Discrete Math. Theor. Comput. Sci. 10, 87–112 (2008)
13. Halava, V., Harju, T., Kärki, T.: Square-free partial words. Inform. Process. Lett. 108, 290–292 (2008)
14. Halava, V., Harju, T., Kärki, T., Séébold, P.: Overlap-freeness in infinite partial words. Theoret. Comput. Sci. 410, 943–948 (2009)
15. Kärki, T.: Repetition-freeness with cyclic relations and chain relations. Fund. Inform. 116(1-4), 157–174 (2012)
16. Keränen, V.: Abelian squares are avoidable on 4 letters. In: Kuich, W. (ed.) ICALP 1992. LNCS, vol. 623, pp. 41–52. Springer, Heidelberg (1992)
17. Krieger, D., Ochem, P., Rampersad, N., Shallit, J.: Avoiding approximate squares. In: Harju, T., Karhumäki, J., Lepistö, A. (eds.) DLT 2007. LNCS, vol. 4588, pp. 278–289. Springer, Heidelberg (2007)
18. Leech, J.: A problem on strings of beads. Math. Gazette 41, 277–278 (1957)
19. Manea, F., Mercaş, R.: Freeness of partial words. Theoret. Comput. Sci. 389(1-2), 265–277 (2007)
20. Thue, A.: Über unendliche Zeichenreihen. Norske Vid. Skrifter I Mat.-Nat. Kl. 7, 1–22 (1906)
21. Thue, A.: Über die gegenseitige Lage gleicher Teile gewisser Zeichenreihen. Norske Vid. Skrifter I Mat.-Nat. Kl. 1, 1–67 (1912)

On Quasiperiodic Morphisms

Florence Levé[1] and Gwénaël Richomme[2,3]

[1] Laboratoire MIS, 33 rue Saint Leu, 80039 Amiens Cedex 1 - France
[2] LIRMM (CNRS, Univ. Montpellier 2) - UMR 5506 - CC 477,
161 rue Ada, 34095, Montpellier Cedex 5 - France
[3] Univ. Paul-Valéry Montpellier 3, Dpt MIAp, Route de Mende,
34199 Montpellier Cedex 5, France

Abstract. Weakly and strongly quasiperiodic morphisms are tools introduced to study quasiperiodic words. Formally they map respectively at least one or any non-quasiperiodic word to a quasiperiodic word. Considering them both on finite and infinite words, we get four families of morphisms between which we study relations. We provide algorithms to decide whether a morphism is strongly quasiperiodic on finite words or on infinite words.

1 Introduction

The notion of quasiperiodicity we consider in this paper is the one introduced in the area of Text Algorithms by Apostolico and Ehrenfeucht [1] in the following way: "a string w is quasiperiodic if there is a second string $u \neq w$ such that every position of w falls within some occurrence of u in w". In 2004, Marcus extended this notion to right infinite words and he opened six questions [14]. Four of them were answered in [9] (see also [15]). In particular, we proved the existence of a Sturmian word which is not quasiperiodic.

In [10], we proved that a Sturmian word is not quasiperiodic if and only if it is an infinite Lyndon word. The proof of this result was based on the S-adicity of Sturmian words (Sturmian words form a family of non-periodic words that can be infinitely decomposed over four basic morphisms – see [2] for more properties on Sturmian words) and on a characterization of morphisms that preserve Lyndon words [16]. In [10], we introduced strongly quasiperiodic morphisms as those morphisms that map all infinite words to quasiperiodic ones, and weakly quasiperiodic morphisms that map at least one non-quasiperiodic word to a quasiperiodic one. We characterized Sturmian morphisms that are strongly quasiperiodic and those that are not weakly quasiperiodic.

With Glen [5], the previous results were extended to the class of episturmian words. All quasiperiodic episturmian words were characterized (unlike the Sturmian case, they do not correspond to infinite episturmian Lyndon words). Two proofs were provided for this result. The first one used connections between quasiperiodicity and return words, the second one used S-adic decompositions of episturmian words, and a characterization of strongly quasiperiodic on infinite words episturmian morphisms.

J. Karhumäki, A. Lepistö, and L. Zamboni (Eds.): WORDS 2013, LNCS 8079, pp. 181–192, 2013.
© Springer-Verlag Berlin Heidelberg 2013

Observe that strongly and weakly quasiperiodic morphisms were considered in the context of infinite words. In this paper we consider also these morphisms with respect to finite words. After basic definitions (Sect. 2), in Sect. 3, we study existing relations between the four so-defined families of morphisms. Algorithms to check if a morphism is strongly quasiperiodic are provided in Sect. 4 and 5. In Sect. 6, we provide sufficient conditions for a morphism to be weakly quasiperiodic on infinite words.

2   Quasiperiodic Words and Morphisms

We assume readers are familiar with combinatorics on words, morphisms and automata (see for instance [12]). We let ε denote the empty word, $|w|$ denote the length of a word w, and $|w|_a$ denote the number of occurrences of a letter a in w. Let us recall that, if some words w, u, p and s verify $w = ups$, then p is called a *prefix* of w, s a *suffix* of w and u a *factor* of w. A factor, prefix or suffix is said to be *proper* if it differs from the whole word. An *internal* factor of a word is any occurrence of a factor except its prefixes and suffixes. For a word u and an integer k, u^k denotes the word obtained by concatenating k copies of u and u^ω denotes the infinite periodic word obtained by concatenating infinitely many copies of u.

Given a non-empty word q, q-quasiperiodic words (or strings) are defined in the introduction. Equivalently a finite word w is q-*quasiperiodic* if $w \neq q$ and there exist words p, s and u such that $w = qu$, $q = ps$, $p \neq \varepsilon$, and $su = q$ or su is a q-quasiperiodic word. The word q is called a *quasiperiod* of w. It is called *the quasiperiod* of w if w has no smaller quasiperiod. For instance, the word $w = abababababababababa$ is aba-quasiperiodic and $ababa$-quasiperiodic. The word aba is the quasiperiod of w.

A word w is said *quasiperiodic* if it is q-quasiperiodic for some word q. Otherwise w is called *superprimitive*. The quasiperiod of any quasiperiodic word w is superprimitive. The definition of quasiperiodicity extends naturally to infinite words.

Let us recall that a morphism f is an application on words such that for all words u and v, $f(uv) = f(u)f(v)$. Such a morphism is defined by images of letters. A well-known morphism is the Fibonacci morphism φ defined by $\varphi(a) = ab$, $\varphi(b) = a$. In [9], we proved that the infinite Fibonacci word, the fixed point of φ, has infinitely many quasiperiods that are superprimitive. The first ones are aba, $abaab$, $abaababaa$.

Notice that from now on, we will only consider non-erasing morphisms (images of non-empty words differ from the empty word). As mentioned in the introduction, *strongly quasiperiodic on infinite words morphisms* were introduced as a tool to study quasiperiodicity of some infinite words. They are the morphisms that map any infinite word to a quasiperiodic infinite word. Also we introduced *weakly quasiperiodic on finite words morphisms* that map at least one non-quasiperiodic infinite word to a quasiperiodic one. Examples are provided in the next section. It is interesting to observe that a morphism that is not weakly quasiperiodic on infinite words could be called a quasiperiodic-free morphism as it maps any non-quasiperiodic infinite word to another non-quasiperiodic word. This allows to relate the current study to the stream of works around power-free morphisms. In this context, it is natural to consider the previous notions on finite words. Thus in this paper, we will also consider *strongly quasiperiodic on finite words morphisms* that map any finite word to a quasiperiodic word, and *weakly quasiperiodic on finite words morphisms* that map at least one finite non-quasiperiodic word to a quasiperiodic word.

3 Relations

In this section, we show that the basic relations between the different families of morphisms are the ones described in Fig. 1.

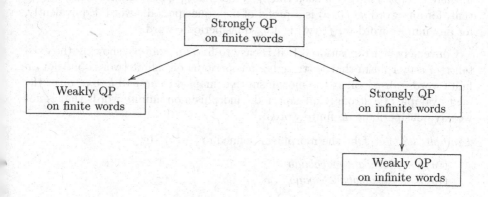

Fig. 1. Basic relations

Let us first observe that it follows the definitions that any strongly quasiperiodic on finite (resp. infinite) words morphism is also a weakly quasiperiodic on finite (resp. infinite) words morphism. The next result proves the last relation of Fig. 1. Its proof uses Lemma 3.2.

Proposition 3.1. *Any strongly quasiperiodic on finite words morphism is strongly quasiperiodic on infinite words.*

Lemma 3.2. *Let f be a morphism. Assume the existence of two words u and v and of an integer k such that $|f(u)^k| \geq |f(v)|$. If $f(u)$ and $f(u^k v u^k)$ are quasiperiodic, then their quasiperiods are equal.*

Proof. Let q_u be the quasiperiod of $f(u)$ and let q be the quasiperiod of the word $f(u^k v u^k)$.

If $|q| < |q_u|$, then q is a prefix and a suffix of q_u and as $f(u)$ is a factor of a q-quasiperiodic word, it is also q-quasiperiodic (we have $f(u) \neq q$ for length reason). This contradicts the fact that, by definition, q_u is the smallest quasiperiod of $f(u)$.

So $|q_u| \leq |q|$. Assume $|q| \geq 2|f(u^k)|$. So by choice of k, $|q| \geq |f(u^k)| + |f(v)|$. This implies that the prefix occurrence of q in $f(u^k v u^k)$ overlaps the suffix occurrence. More precisely $q = q_1 q_2 = q_2 q_3$ with $|q_1 q_2| \geq 2|f(u^k)|$ and $|q_1| = |q_3| \leq |f(u^k)|$: we have $|q_2| \geq |q_1|$. By a classical result (see [11, Lem. 1.3.4]), there exist words x and y with $xy \neq \varepsilon$ and an integer ℓ such that $q_1 = xy$, $q_2 = (xy)^\ell x$ and $q_3 = yx$. For length reason, $\ell \neq 0$ so that q is xyx-quasiperiodic. This contradicts the fact that q is superprimitive.

Thus $|q| < 2|f(u^k)|$. As q is both prefix and suffix-comparable with $f(u^k)$ which is q_u-quasiperiodic, as $|q_u| \leq |q|$, and as q is superprimitive, $q = q_u$.   □

Proof of Proposition 3.1. Assume f is strongly quasiperiodic on finite words. Let α be a letter and let q_α be the quasiperiod of $f(\alpha)$. By Lemma 3.2, for any word u, there exists an integer k such that $f(\alpha^k u \alpha^k)$ is q_α-quasiperiodic. This implies that, for any word u, $f(\alpha u)$ is a prefix of a q_α-quasiperiodic word. Equivalently, for any infinite word $\mathbf{w}$, $f(\alpha \mathbf{w})$ is a q_α-quasiperiodic word.   □

Conversely to Proposition 3.1, it is easy to find an example showing the existence of a morphism that is strongly quasiperiodic on infinite words but not on finite words. Just look at the morphism that maps a to aa and b to a, or at the next example of a strongly quasiperiodic morphism on infinite words that is not weakly quasiperiodic on finite words.

Example 3.3. Let f be the morphism defined on $\{a, b\}^*$ by

$$f(a) = abaababaababababaab$$
$$f(b) = abaabaababababababaab.$$

It is straigthforward that $f(\mathbf{w})$ is aba-quasiperiodic for any infinite word $\mathbf{w}$. Let us prove that f is not weakly quasiperiodic on finite words. Assume by contradiction the existence of a non-quasiperiodic word u such that $f(u)$ is quasiperiodic. Observe $u \neq a$, $u \neq b$ and the quasiperiod of u ends with ab. An exhaustive verification allows to see that no proper prefix of $f(a)$ nor $f(b)$ could be a quasiperiod of $f(u)$. Hence $f(a)$ or $f(b)$ is a prefix of the quasiperiod q of $f(u)$. Observing this implies $|q| \geq |f(a)| = |f(b)|$, we deduce that $f(a)$ or $f(b)$ is a suffix of q. As $f(a)$ and $f(b)$ are not internal factors of $f(aa)$, $f(ab)$, $f(ba)$, $f(bb)$, $q = f(q')$ for some word q'. Moreover u is q'-quasiperiodic, a contradiction.

The next examples show that the other converses of the relations presented in Fig. 1 are false.

Example 3.4. The morphism that maps a to aa and b to bb is weakly quasiperiodic on finite words (as $f(a)$ is quasiperiodic), but we let readers verify that it is not weakly quasiperiodic on infinite words. Thus f is not strongly quasiperiodic on infinite words and, as a consequence of Proposition 3.1, it is not strongly quasiperiodic on finite words.

Example 3.5. The morphism f defined by $f(a) = ba$ and $f(b) = bba$ is weakly quasiperiodic on infinite words since for all word $w \in a\{a, b\}^\omega$, $f(w)$ is bab-quasiperiodic. But $f(ba^\omega) = bb(ab)^\omega$ is not quasiperiodic, and so f is not strongly quasiperiodic on infinite words. By Proposition 3.1, f is not strongly quasiperiodic on finite words.

4 Deciding Strong Quasiperiodicity on Finite Words

The next lemma which is a direct consequence of Lemma 3.2 is the key observation to decide whether a morphism is strongly quasiperiodic on finite words.

Lemma 4.1. *If f is a strongly quasiperiodic on finite words morphism, then for any word u and any letter α, the quasiperiod of $f(u)$ is a factor of $f(\alpha^3)$ of length less than $2|f(\alpha)|$.*

Proof. Assume f is strongly quasiperiodic on finite words. Let u be a word and let q_u be the quasiperiod of $f(u)$. Let i be an integer such that $|f(\alpha^i)| \geq 2|q_u|$ ($|f(\alpha)| \neq 0$ as $f(\alpha)$ is quasiperiodic). Let k be an integer such that $|f(u^k)| \geq |f(\alpha^i)|$. By Lemma 3.2, the quasiperiod of $f(u^k \alpha^i u^k)$ is q_u. As $|f(\alpha)^i| \geq 2|q_u|$, q_u must be a factor of $f(\alpha)^i$. As q_u is superprimitive, $|q_u| < 2|f(\alpha)|$. Consequently q_u is a factor of $f(\alpha)^3$. □

Observe now that, given two words u and q, it follows the definition of quasiperiodicity that the q-quasiperiodicity of $f(u)$ implies that, for each nonempty proper prefix π of $f(u)$, $\pi = xps$ with $xp = \varepsilon$, $xp = q$ or xp is the longest q-quasiperiodic prefix of π if $|\pi| > |q|$, and ps a prefix of q. Based on this remark, we introduce an automaton that will allow to recognize words u such that $f(u)$ is q-quasiperiodic (or q or the empty word ε), for a given word q and a given morphism f. Note that a quasiperiod may have several borders, that is, proper suffixes that are prefixes. For instance, the word $q = abacaba$ has ε, a and aba as borders. Thus while processing the automaton, one cannot determine with precision which will be the word p occurring in the previous observation until the reading of the next letters. Therefore the constructed automaton will just remind (instead of initial p) the longest suffix p of π such that ps is a prefix of q.

Definition 4.2. *Let f be a morphism over A^* and q be a non-empty word. We denote $\mathcal{A}_q(f)$, or simply $\mathcal{A}_q$, the automaton (A, Q, i, F, Δ) where:*

- *the states, the elements of Q, are the pairs (p, s) such that ps is a proper prefix of q;*
- *the initial state i is the pair $(\varepsilon, \varepsilon)$;*
- *the final states, the elements of F, are the pairs of the form (p, ε), with p a prefix of q;*
- *the transitions, the elements of Δ, are triples $((p_1, s1), a, (p_2, s_2))$ where $(p_1, s1) \in Q$, $(p_2, s_2) \in Q$ and one of the two following situations holds:*
  1. If q does not occur in $p_1 s_1 f(a)$ and $|q| > |s_1 f(a)|$, then

- $s_1 f(a) = s_2$,
- p_2 *is the longest suffix of p_1 such that $p_2 s_1 f(a)$ is a proper prefix of q.*

2. *If q occurs in $p_1 s_1 f(a)$*
   - *there exist a suffix x of p_1 and a word y such that $x s_1 f(a) = y s_2$ with $y = q$ or y is q-quasiperiodic,*
   - *p_2 is the longest suffix of y such that $p_2 s_2$ is a proper prefix of q.*

The automaton defined in the previous definition is deterministic. It should be emphasized that given a state (p, s) and a letter a, there may not exist a state (p', s') such that a transition $((p, s), a, (p', s'))$ exists. We let readers verify the next observation and its corollary.

Fact 4.3. *Any state (p, s) in $\mathcal{A}_q$ is reached by reading a word u if and only if there exist words π, p and s, such that $f(u) = \pi p s$ with $\pi p = \varepsilon$, $\pi p = q$ or πp is a q-quasiperiodic word, and, ps is the longest prefix of q that is a suffix of $f(u)$.*

Lemma 4.4. *A word u is recognized by $\mathcal{A}_q$ if and only if $f(u) = \varepsilon$ or $f(u) = q$ or $f(u)$ is q-quasiperiodic.*

Let us give some examples of automata following the previous definition. Notice that we just construct the states that are accessible from $(\varepsilon, \varepsilon)$.

Example 4.5. Let f be the morphism defined by $f(a) = ab$, $f(b) = aba$. The automaton $\mathcal{A}_{aba}$ is the following one.

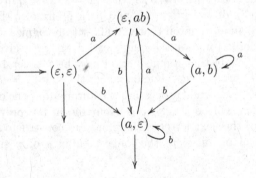

Example 4.6. Let f be the morphism defined by $f(a) = abaaba$, $f(b) = baabaaba$. Here follow automata $\mathcal{A}_{aba}$ and $\mathcal{A}_{baaba}$.

Example 4.7. Let f be the morphism defined by $f(a) = aabaab$, $f(b) = aabaaaba$ and $f(c) = aabaababaabaa$. Here follows automaton $\mathcal{A}_{aabaa}$.

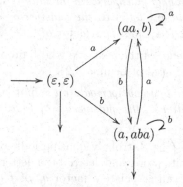

Let $\mathcal{Q}(f)$ be the set of all words q such that, for all letters α in A, $|q| \leq 2|f(\alpha)|$ and q is a factor of $f(\alpha)^3$. Following Lemma 4.1, $\mathcal{Q}(f)$ is the set of all possible quasiperiods of a word of the form $f(u)$. Thus Lemma 4.4 implies the next characterization of strongly quasiperiodic morphisms on finite words.

Proposition 4.8. *A morphism f is strongly quasiperiodic on finite words if and only if, for each letter α, the word $f(\alpha)$ is quasiperiodic, and*

$$A^* = \bigcup_{q \in \mathcal{Q}(f)} \mathcal{L}(\mathcal{A}_q)$$

where $\mathcal{L}(\mathcal{A}_q)$ is the language recognized by the automaton $\mathcal{A}_q$.

As $\mathcal{Q}(f)$ is finite, and as it is decidable whether a finite word is quasiperiodic [1,3,7] (see also [6] for optimality of the complexity of these algorithms), we can conclude:

Corollary 4.9. *It is decidable whether a morphism is strongly quasiperiodic on finite words.*

To end this section, let us illustrate Proposition 4.8. If f is the morphism considered in Example 4.6 ($f(a) = abaaba$, $f(b) = baabaaba$), as aba and $baaba$ belong to $\mathcal{Q}(f)$, as $\mathcal{L}(\mathcal{A}_{aba}) = \varepsilon \cup a\{a,b\}^*$ and $\mathcal{L}(\mathcal{A}_{baaba}) = \varepsilon \cup b\{a,b\}^*$, as $f(a)$ and $f(b)$ are quasiperiodic, we can conclude by Proposition 4.8 that f is strongly quasiperiodic on finite words.

Now consider the morphism defined by $f(a) = ab$, $f(b) = aba$. We have $\mathcal{Q}(f) = \{a, b, ab, ba, aba\}$. By Example 4.5, $\mathcal{L}(\mathcal{A}_{aba}) = \varepsilon \cup \{a,b\}^*b$. We let readers verify that $\mathcal{L}(\mathcal{A}_a) = \mathcal{L}(\mathcal{A}_b) = \mathcal{L}(\mathcal{A}_{ba}) = \emptyset$ and $\mathcal{L}(\mathcal{A}_{ab}) = a^*$. Thus f is not strongly quasiperiodic. As the set $\mathcal{L}(\mathcal{A}_{aba})$ contains non-quasiperiodic words, this morphism f is weakly quasiperiodic.

5   Deciding Strong Quasiperiodicity on Infinite Words

We now show how to adapt the ideas of the previous section to the study of strongly quasiperiodic on infinite words morphisms. First we adapt Lemma 4.1.

Lemma 5.1. *If f is a strongly quasiperiodic on infinite words morphism, then for any infinite word $\mathbf{w}$ and any letter α, the quasiperiod of $f(\mathbf{w})$ is a factor of $f(\alpha^3)$ of length less than $2|f(\alpha)|$ that is a factor of $\mathcal{Q}(f)$.*

This result is a consequence of the next one whose proof is similar to the one of Lemma 4.1 (without the need of Lemma 3.2).

Lemma 5.2. *If f is a strongly quasiperiodic on infinite words morphism, then for any word u and any letter α, the quasiperiod of $f(u\alpha^\omega)$ is a factor of $f(\alpha^3)$ of length less than $2|f(\alpha)|$.*

Proof of Lemma 5.1. Let f be a strongly quasiperiodic on infinite words morphism. Let $\mathbf{w}$ be an infinite word and let α be a letter. With each prefix p of $\mathbf{w}$, by Lemma 5.2, one can associate a factor q_p of $f(\alpha^3)$ such that $f(p\alpha^\omega)$ is q_p-quasiperiodic. As the set of factors of $f(\alpha^3)$ is finite, there exists one, say q, which is associated with an infinity of prefixes of $\mathbf{w}$. This implies $\mathbf{w}$ is q-quasiperiodic. $\qquad\square$

Now we adapt the automaton used in the previous section in order to have a tool to determine if the image of an infinite word is q-quasiperiodic for a given morphism and a given word q.

Definition 5.3. *Let f be a morphism over A^* and q be a non-empty word. Let $\mathcal{A}'_q(f)$, or simply $\mathcal{A}'_q$, denote the automaton (A, Q, i, F', Δ) where Q, i, Δ are defined as in Definition 4.2, and $F' = Q$.*

Lemma 5.4. *An infinite word $f(\mathbf{w})$ is q-quasiperiodic if and only if all its prefixes are recognized by $\mathcal{A}'_q$.*

As a consequence of Lemmas 5.1 and 5.4, we get the next characterization of strongly quasiperiodic morphisms on infinite words.

Proposition 5.5. *A morphism f is strongly quasiperiodic on infinite words if and only if*

$$A^* = \bigcup_{q \in \mathcal{Q}(f)} \mathcal{L}(\mathcal{A}'_q)$$

where $\mathcal{L}(\mathcal{A}'_q)$ is the language recognized by the automaton $\mathcal{A}'_q$.

The proof of Proposition 5.5 is a consequence of the previous definition and lemmas. To make all clearer, just observe that, if a word u is recognized by $\mathcal{A}'_q$ then all its prefixes are also recognized.

As an example to illustrate Proposition 5.5, one can consider the morphism f defined by $f(a) = ab$, $f(b) = aba$. Example 4.5 shows that $\mathcal{A}'_{aba} = \{a, b\}^*$ and so f is strongly quasiperiodic on infinite words.

In the same way, one can verify that the morphism f defined by $f(a) = abaaba$ and $f(b) = aabaaba$ is strongly-quasiperiodic. More precisely, the image of any infinite word beginning with a is $abaa$-quasiperiodic and the image of any word beginning with b is $aaba$-quasiperiodic.

As a consequence of Proposition 5.5, we have the next result.

Corollary 5.6. *It is decidable whether a morphism is strongly quasiperiodic on infinite words.*

6 On Weakly Quasiperiodic Morphisms

We now consider the decidability of the questions: given a morphism f, is f weakly quasiperiodic on finite words? Is it weakly quasiperiodic on infinite words? Note that this is equivalent to asking for the decidability of the question: given a morphism, are all images of non-quasiperiodic words also non-quasiperiodic? We provide some partial answers.

Let us recall that a morphism f is said *prefix* (resp. *suffix*) if for all letters a and b, $f(a)$ is not a prefix (resp. a suffix) of $f(b)$.

Lemma 6.1. *Any non-prefix or non-suffix non-erasing morphism defined on an alphabet of cardinality at least two is weakly quasiperiodic on finite and infinite words.*

Proof. If $f(a)$ is a prefix of $f(b)$ then, for all $k \geq 1$, the finite word $f(b^k a)$ is $f(ba)$-quasiperiodic. The infinite word $f(bab^\omega)$ is also $f(ba)$-quasiperiodic. The morphism f is weakly quasiperiodic both on finite words and on infinite words.

If $f(a)$ is a suffix of $f(b)$ then, for all $k \geq 1$, the finite word $f(ab^k)$ is $f(ab)$-quasiperiodic. The infinite word $f(ab^\omega)$ is $f(ab)$-quasiperiodic (it is even periodic). The morphism f is weakly quasiperiodic both on finite words and on infinite words.

Corollary 6.2. *Any non-injective non-erasing morphism defined on an alphabet of cardinality at least two is weakly quasiperiodic on finite and infinite words.*

Proof. If f is not injective, there exist two different words u and v such that $f(u) = f(v)$. If $f(u)$ and $f(v)$ are powers of same word then f is erasing: a contradiction. Otherwise, we can assume that u and v begin with different letters. Thus f is not prefix and so, by Lemma 6.1, it is weakly quasiperiodic on finite and infinite words.

Proposition 6.3. *Let f be a non-erasing morphism and let u be a primitive word over $\{a, b\}$. If $f(u)$ is not primitive then f is weakly quasiperiodic on finite words. Moreover, if $|u|_a \geq 1$ and $|u|_b \geq 1$, then f is weakly quasiperiodic on infinite words.*

We first need an intermediate result.

Lemma 6.4. *If $f(a^i b^j)$ is not primitive for some integers $i \geq 1$, $j \geq 1$, then one of the words $f(ab^\omega)$, $f(aba^\omega)$, $f(ba^\omega)$, $f(bab^\omega)$ is quasiperiodic.*

Proof. Assume first $i \geq 2$, $j \geq 2$. By Lyndon-Schützenberger's characterization of solutions of the equation $x^i y^j = z^k$ when $i \geq 2$, $j \geq 2$, $k \geq 2$ [13], we deduce that $f(a)$ and $f(b)$ are powers of a same word: $f(ab^\omega)$ is quasiperiodic, as any image of a finite (of length at least 2) or of an infinite word.

Now consider case $j = 1$. Let u be the primitive word such thay $f(a^i b) = u^k$ ($k \geq 2$). If $|f(a)^{i-1}| \geq |u|$, the words $f(a)^i$ and u^k share a common prefix of length at least $|f(a)| + |u|$. By Fine and Wilf's theorem [4], $f(a)$ and u are powers of a same word. It follows that $f(a)$ and $f(b)$ are also powers of a same word. We conclude as in case $i, j \geq 2$.

Now consider the case $|u| \geq |f(a)^i|$. From $f(a)^i f(b) = u^k$, we get $u = f(a)^i x$, $f(b) = xu^{k-1}$ for some word x. Hence $f(b) = x(f(a)^i x)^{k-1}$ and the word $f(bab^\omega)$ is $x(f(a)^i x)$-quasiperiodic.

It remains to consider the case $|f(a)^{i-1}| < |u| < |f(a)^i|$. In this case, for some words x and y, $u = f(a)^{i-1}x$, $f(a) = xy$ and y is a prefix of u. In particular, for some word z, $f(a) = xy = yz$. By a classical result in Combinatorics on Words (see [11, Lem. 1.3.4]), $x = \alpha\beta$, $y = (\alpha\beta)^\ell \alpha$, $z = \beta\alpha$: $f(a) = (\alpha\beta)^{\ell+1}\alpha$, $u = [(\alpha\beta)^{\ell+1}\alpha]^{i-1}\alpha\beta$. Now observe that $yf(b) = u^{k-1} = [[(\alpha\beta)^{\ell+1}\alpha]^{i-1}\alpha\beta]^{k-1}$. When $i \geq 2$, $f(b) = \beta\alpha[(\alpha\beta)^{\ell+1}\alpha]^{i-2}\alpha\beta[[(\alpha\beta)^{\ell+1}\alpha]^{i-1}\alpha\beta]^{k-2}$, and when $i = 1$, $f(b) = \beta(\alpha\beta)^{k-\ell-2}$. In both cases, $f(aba^\omega)$ is $\alpha\beta\alpha$-quasiperiodic.

When $i = 1$, the non-primitivity of $f(ab^j)$ is equivalent to the non-primitivity of $f(b^j a)$. Thus exchanging the roles of a and b, we end the proof of the lemma.   □

Proof of Proposition 6.3. First if u contains only the letter a or only the letter b, we have $u = a$ or $u = b$ and f is weakly quasiperiodic on finite words. Assume from now on that $|u|_a \geq 1$ and $|u|_b \geq 1$. If $|u|_a = 1$, then there exist integers i, j such that $u = b^i ab^j$ with $i + j \geq 1$. As $f(u)$ is not primitive, also $f(ab^{i+j})$ is not primitive: f is weakly quasiperiodic on finite words. By Lemma 6.4, f is also weakly quasiperiodic on infinite words. The result follows similarly when $|u|_b = 1$. Now consider the case $|u|_a \geq 2$ and $|u|_b \geq 2$. A seminal result by Lentin and Schützenberger states that if f is a morphism defined on alphabet $\{a, b\}$, such that for a non-empty word u, $f(u)$ is not primitive then there exists a word v in $a^*b \cap ab^*$ such that $f(v)$ is not primitive [8, Th. 5]. We are back to the previous cases.   □

The converse of Proposition 6.3 is false. Indeed as shown by the morphism f defined by $f(a) = ababa$, $f(b) = ab$, a morphism can be weakly quasiperiodic on finite words or on infinite words and be primitive preserving (the image of any primitive word is primitive). Nevertheless observe that when we consider the problem of deciding if a morphism is weakly quasiperiodic on infinite words, we can assume that all images of letters are primitive. Indeed any morphism f such that $f(a)$ is a non-empty power of a for each letter a is not weakly quasiperiodic: for any word (finite of length at least 2 or infinite) w, $f(w)$ is quasiperiodic if and only if w is quasiperiodic. In consequence, to determine whether a morphism f is weakly quasiperiodic or not, one can substitute f by the morphism r_f where $r_f(a)$ is the primitive root of $f(a)$. Note that images of letters by r_f are primitive words.

For all weakly quasiperiodic on infinite words morphisms met until now, there exist non-empty words u and v such that the infinite word uv^ω is not quasiperiodic while $f(uv^\omega)$ is quasiperiodic. This situation also holds in the next lemma (when **w** in the hypothesis is not quasiperiodic) whose proof is omitted. We conjecture that this holds in all cases. Bounding the length of u and v could lead to a procedure to check whether a morphism is weakly quasiperiodic on infinite words.

Lemma 6.5. *Let f be a morphism, and let $\mathbf{w}$ be an infinite word such that $f(\mathbf{w})$ is q-quasiperiodic for some word q such that $2|q| \leq |f(\alpha)|$ for each letter α. Then:*

1. *$\mathbf{w} = (a_1 \ldots a_k)^\omega$ with $a_1, \ldots, a_k$ pairwise different letters, or,*
2. *there exist words x, y, z and letters a and b such that $|xyz|_a = 0$, $|z|_b = 0$, $xay(bz)^\omega$ is not quasiperiodic and $f(xay(bz)^\omega)$ is q-quasiperiodic. Moreover in this case, we can find x, y and z such that any letter occurs at most once in each of these words.*

7 Conclusion

To conclude this paper on links between quasiperiodicity and morphisms, we point out another question. Given a morphism f prolongable on a letter a, can we decide whether the word $f^\omega(a) = \lim_{n \to \infty} f^n(a)$ is quasiperiodic? We are convinced that a better knowledge of weakly and strongly quasiperiodic on infinite words morphisms could bring answers to the previous question. We suspect in particular that if f is a strongly quasiperiodic on infinite words morphism and if it is prolongable on a, then $f^\omega(a)$ is quasiperiodic. Conversely it should be true that if $f^\omega(a)$ is quasiperiodic and $f(a)$ is not a power of a then f is weakly quasiperiodic on infinite words. The next result states partially that.

Proposition 7.1. *Let f be a non-erasing morphism and a be a letter such that $f^\omega(a)$ is a quasiperiodic infinite word but not a periodic word. If all letters are growing with respect to f ($\lim_{n \to \infty} |f^n(a)| = \infty$), then f is weakly quasiperiodic on infinite words.*

Observe that the converse of the previous proposition does not hold. The morphism f defined by $f(a) = a$, $f(b) = ba$ does not generate an infinite quasiperiodic word (f does not generate its fixed point a^ω and ba^ω is not quasiperiodic), but it is weakly quasiperiodic on infinite words as $f(ab^\omega)$ is aba-quasiperiodic.

It is an open problem to state Proposition 7.1 for arbitrary morphims generating a quasiperiodic infinite word.

The proof of Proposition 7.1 is a consequence of Lemma 6.5 and the following one.

Lemma 7.2. *Let f be a non-erasing morphism. If, for some integer $k \geq 1$, the morphism f^k is weakly quasiperiodic, then f is weakly quasiperiodic.*

Proof. Assume $f^k(\mathbf{w})$ is quasiperiodic for some integer $k \geq 1$ and for some non-quasiperiodic infinite word $\mathbf{w}$. Let i be the smallest integer such that $f^i(w)$ is quasiperiodic. Observe that $i \geq 1$ and that $f^{i-1}(w)$ is not quasiperiodic. As $f^i(\mathbf{w}) = f(f^{i-1}(\mathbf{w}))$, f is weakly quasiperiodic on infinite words.   □

Proof of Proposition 7.1. Let f be a morphism and let a be a letter such that $f^\omega(a)$ is a quasiperiodic infinite word. Let q be the quasiperiod of $f^\omega(a)$. Assume that all letters of f are growing. As all letters are growing with respect to f, for some $k \geq 1$, f^k verifies the hypothesis of Lemma 6.5: f^k is weakly quasiperiodic on infinite words. By Lemma 7.2, f is also weakly quasiperiodic on infinite words.   □

References

1. Apostolico, A., Ehrenfeucht, A.: Efficient detection of quasiperiodicities in strings. Theoret. Comput. Sci. 119, 247–265 (1993)
2. Berstel, J., Séébold, P.: Sturmian words. In: Lothaire, M. (ed.) Algebraic Combinatorics on Words. Encyclopedia of Mathematics and its Applications, vol. 90, pp. 45–110. Cambridge University Press (2002)
3. Brodal, G.S., Pedersen, C.N.S.: Finding maximal quasiperiodicities in strings. In: Giancarlo, R., Sankoff, D. (eds.) CPM 2000. LNCS, vol. 1848, pp. 397–411. Springer, Heidelberg (2000)
4. Fine, N.J., Wilf, H.S.: Uniqueness theorems for periodic functions. Proc. Amer. Math. Soc. 16, 109–114 (1965)
5. Glen, A., Levé, F., Richomme, G.: Quasiperiodic and Lyndon episturmian words. Theoret. Comput. Sci. 409(3), 578–600 (2008)
6. Groult, R., Richomme, G.: Optimality of some algorithms to detect quasiperiodicities. Theoret. Comput. Sci. 411, 3110–3122 (2010)
7. Iliopoulos, C.S., Mouchard, L.: Quasiperiodicity: from detection to normal forms. Journal of Automata, Languages and Combinatorics 4(3), 213–228 (1999)
8. Lentin, A., Schützenberger, M.P.: A combinatorial problem in the theory of free monoids. In: Bose, R.C., Dowling, T.W. (eds.) Combinatorial Mathematics and its Applications, pp. 128–144. Univ. North Carolina Press (1969)
9. Levé, F., Richomme, G.: Quasiperiodic infinite words: some answers. Bull. Eur. Assoc. Theor. Comput. Sci. EATCS 84, 128–238 (2004)
10. Levé, F., Richomme, G.: Quasiperiodic Sturmian words and morphisms. Theoret. Comput. Sci. 372(1), 15–25 (2007)
11. Lothaire, M.: Combinatorics on Words. Encyclopedia of Mathematics and its Applications, vol. 17. Addison-Wesley (1983); Reprinted in the Cambridge Mathematical Library. Cambridge University Press, UK (1997)
12. Lothaire, M.: Algebraic Combinatorics on Words. Encyclopedia of Mathematics and its Applications, vol. 90. Cambridge University Press (2002)
13. Lyndon, R.C., Schützenberger, M.-P.: The equation $a^m = b^n c^p$ in a free group. Michigan Math. J. 9, 289–298 (1962)
14. Marcus, S.: Quasiperiodic infinite words. Bull. Eur. Assoc. Theor. Comput. Sci. EATCS 82, 170–174 (2004)
15. Marcus, S., Monteil, T.: Quasiperiodic infinite words: multi-scale case and dynamical properties. Technical Report arXiv:math/0603354, arxiv.org (2006)
16. Richomme, G.: Lyndon morphisms. Bull. Belg. Math. Soc. Simon Stevin 10(5), 761–786 (2003)

Enumerating Abelian Returns
to Prefixes of Sturmian Words

Zuzana Masáková and Edita Pelantová

Department of Mathematics FNSPE, Czech Technical University in Prague
Trojanova 13, 120 00 Praha 2, Czech Republic
{zuzana.masakova,edita.pelantova}@fjfi.cvut.cz

Abstract. We follow the works of Puzynina and Zamboni, and Rigo et al. on abelian returns in Sturmian words. We determine the cardinality of the set $\mathcal{APR}_\mathbf{u}$ of abelian returns of all prefixes of a Sturmian word $\mathbf{u}$ in terms of the coefficients of the continued fraction of the slope, dependingly on the intercept. We provide a simple algorithm for finding the set $\mathcal{APR}_\mathbf{u}$ and we determine it for the characteristic Sturmian words.

Keywords: Abelian return word, Sturmian word, interval exchange.

1 Introduction

Although Sturmian sequences have been studied for more than 70 years, new properties and characterizations still appear. Return words, introduced by Durand [6], were used in 2001 for one of such equivalent definitions. Vuillon [17] has shown that an infinite word is a Sturmian word if and only if each of its factors has exactly two return words. In 2011, Puzynina and Zamboni [11] use an abelian modification of the notion of return words for deriving yet another equivalent characterization of Sturmian words. The adjective 'abelian' is used when in a word w, we are interested only in the number of occurrences of a letter a and not in the order of letters. Formally, two finite words w, w' over an alphabet $\mathcal{A}$ are *abelian equivalent*, denoted $w \sim_{\mathrm{ab}} w'$, if $|w|_a = |w'|_a$ for every $a \in \mathcal{A}$, where $|w|_a$ stands for the number of occurrences of the letter a in the word w. In order to define abelian return words to a factor w of length $|w| = n$ in an infinite word $\mathbf{u} = u_0 u_1 u_2 \cdots$, denote by $n_1 < \cdots < n_i < n_{i+1} < \cdots$ the consecutive occurrences of factors which are abelian equivalent to w, i.e. $u_{n_i} u_{n_i+1} \cdots u_{n_i+n-1} \sim_{\mathrm{ab}} w$, and $u_j u_{j+1} \cdots u_{j+n-1} \not\sim_{\mathrm{ab}} w$ for $n_i < j < n_{i+1}$. Then the factors $v = u_{n_i} u_{n_i+1} \cdots u_{n_{i+1}-1}$ are called abelian return words to w. Given a factor w in $\mathbf{u}$, the set of abelian return words of w in $\mathbf{u}$ is denoted by $\mathcal{AR}_{w,\mathbf{u}}$. The main result of Puzynina and Zamboni [11] is that an aperiodic recurrent infinite word $\mathbf{u}$ is Sturmian if and only if every factor of $\mathbf{u}$ has two or three abelian return words, i.e. $\#\mathcal{AR}_{w,\mathbf{u}} \in \{2,3\}$ for any factor w in $\mathbf{u}$. If a factor has three abelian return words R_1, R_2, R_3, then for their length one has $|R_1| + |R_2| = |R_3|$, see [12]. We will show that in fact $R_3 = R_1 R_2$ (cf. Theorem 8).

Rigo et al. [14] have studied the set of abelian returns to all prefixes of a Sturmian word $\mathbf{u}$, denoted by $\mathcal{APR}_\mathbf{u} = \bigcup \{\mathcal{AR}_{w,\mathbf{u}} : w \text{ is a prefix of } \mathbf{u}\}$, and

J. Karhumäki, A. Lepistö, and L. Zamboni (Eds.): WORDS 2013, LNCS 8079, pp. 193–204, 2013.

showed that for a Sturmian word **u** with intercept ρ, the set $\mathcal{APR}_\mathbf{u}$ is finite if and only if $\rho \neq 0$. In Theorem 16 we determine the cardinality of the set $\mathcal{APR}_\mathbf{u}$ dependingly on the intercept ρ and the continued fraction of the slope α. We provide an algorithm for listing the elements of $\mathcal{APR}_\mathbf{u}$ explicitly. We provide $\mathcal{APR}_\mathbf{u}$ for every characteristic Sturmian word (Proposition 18), extending thus the result of Rigo et. al [14] who show that $\mathcal{APR}_\mathbf{f} = \{0, 1, 01, 10, 001\}$ for the Fibonacci word **f**.

For our purposes, we present Sturmian words as codings of exchange T : $[0, 1) \rightarrow [0, 1)$ of two intervals. The main tool for obtaining our results is the study of itineraries under the first return map induced by T to a subinterval $I \subset [0, 1)$.

2   Some Facts about Sturmian Words

Sturmian words are usually defined as infinite aperiodic words having for every $n \in \mathbb{N}$ exactly $n + 1$ different factors of length n. For details about definition and basic properties of Sturmian words see [9]. For our purposes, it is useful to consider the equivalent characterization of Sturmian words as codings of exchange of two intervals. For an $\alpha \in (0, 1)$ we consider the exchange T of two intervals of length α and $1 - \alpha$, namely $T : [0, 1) \rightarrow [0, 1)$ given by the prescription,

$$T(x) = \begin{cases} x + 1 - \alpha & \text{if } x \in [0, \alpha) =: J_0, \\ x - \alpha & \text{if } x \in [\alpha, 1) =: J_1. \end{cases} \tag{1}$$

If α is irrational, then the orbit of any given $\rho \in [0, 1)$ is infinite, and the sequence $\rho, T(\rho), T^2(\rho), T^3(\rho), \ldots$ can be coded by an infinite word $\mathbf{u}_{\alpha,\rho} = u_0 u_1 u_2 \cdots$ over the alphabet $\{0, 1\}$ given naturally by

$$u_n = \begin{cases} 0 & \text{if } T^n(\rho) \in J_0, \\ 1 & \text{if } T^n(\rho) \in J_1. \end{cases}$$

Such an infinite word is Sturmian with slope α and intercept ρ. It is well known that any Sturmian word can be obtained by coding an orbit of a 2-interval exchange for some irrational slope α and intercept ρ, or by a similar exchange of intervals where the intervals J_0, J_1 are semi-open from the other side.

All Sturmian words $\mathbf{u}_{\alpha,\rho}$ of the same slope α have the same language $\mathcal{L}(\alpha)$, i.e. the same set of factors. Among Sturmian words with the same slope, one is exceptional – the so-called characteristic word – namely the one with intercept $\rho = 1 - \alpha$. We denote $\mathbf{u}_{\alpha,1-\alpha} = \mathbf{c}_\alpha$. Among the exceptional properties of $\mathbf{c}_\alpha$ is that every prefix w of $\mathbf{c}_\alpha$ is a left-special factor, i.e. both $0w$ and $1w$ belong to the language $\mathcal{L}(\alpha)$.

For any factor $w \in \mathcal{L}(\alpha)$, there is an interval $J_w \subset [0, 1)$, the cylinder of w, such that the prefix of length n of the infinite word $\mathbf{u}_{\alpha,\rho}$ is equal to w, taking any intercept $\rho \in J_w$. The $n + 1$ subintervals J_w for $w \in \mathcal{L}(\alpha) \cap \{0, 1\}^n$ form a partition of $[0, 1)$ and their boundary points are determined by the n numbers $\alpha, T^{-1}(\alpha), \ldots, T^{-n+1}(\alpha)$.

For every fixed n, the lengths of intervals J_w take at most 3 values, where the longest is the sum of the two shorter ones. This is the statement of the so-called three-gap theorem, which was independently proved by several authors, for example [15,16]. The length of J_w corresponds to the frequency of the factor w in $\mathbf{u}_{\alpha,x}$, as mentioned in [5]. These lengths take values – here denoted by $\delta_{k,s}$ – in a discrete set, which is described in terms of the continued fraction of the parameter $\alpha = [0, a_1, a_2, a_3, \dots]$. For an overview about three gap theorem and related results, see [2]. The values $\delta_{k,s}$ are important for our further considerations, that is why we provide them here explicitly. Recall that the numerators p_k and the denominators q_k of the convergents $\frac{p_k}{q_k}$ of α satisfy the recurrence relation $p_k = a_k p_{k-1} + p_{k-2}$, $q_k = a_k q_{k-1} + q_{k-2}$, with initial values $p_0 = a_0 = 0$, $q_0 = 1$, and $p_{-1} = 1$, $q_{-1} = 0$, so that the recurrence holds for every $k \geq 1$. Denoting

$$\delta_{k,s} := \left| (s-1)(p_k - \alpha q_k) + p_{k-1} - \alpha q_{k-1} \right|, \quad \text{for } k \geq 0, \ 1 \leq s \leq a_{k+1}, \quad (2)$$

one has $\delta_{k,s} < \delta_{k',s'} \iff ks \succ_{\text{lex}} k's'$.

It is known [10] that Sturmian words are balanced, which means that for every pair of factors w, w' of the same length $|w| = |w'|$ one has $\big||w|_0 - |w'|_0\big| \leq 1$. This implies that for any n, the number $|w|_0$ of letters 0 in a factor w of length n can take only two values. In accordance with [14], we call the factors w with higher number $|w|_0$ *light*, and the other ones *heavy*.

It can be shown that the union of intervals J_w over all light factors w is again an interval. The same is true for heavy factors. The statement of the following lemma can be derived for example from the proof of Lemma 8 of [3] or the proof of Theorem 8 of [14].

Lemma 1. *A prefix of length n of the infinite word $\mathbf{u}_{\alpha,\rho}$ is light if and only if $\rho \in \left[0, T^{-n+1}(\alpha)\right)$. A prefix of length n of the infinite word $\mathbf{u}_{\alpha,\rho}$ is heavy if and only if $\rho \in \left[T^{-n+1}(\alpha), 1\right)$.*

3   Abelian Returns of Sturmian Factors

The main tool for describing abelian return to prefixes of Sturmian words is the study of return time to a subinterval I of $[0, 1)$ under the transformation T from (1).

Let T be an exchange of two intervals as in (1). To every subinterval $I \subset [0, 1)$ we can associate a mapping $r : I \to \{1, 2, 3, \dots\}$, the so-called return time to I, by setting

$$r(x) = \min\{n \in \mathbb{N}, \ n \geq 1 : T^n(x) \in I\}.$$

The prefix of length $r(x)$ of the Sturmian word $\mathbf{u}_{\alpha,x}$ coding the orbit of the point x is called an I-itinerary under T and denoted $R(x)$.

With these notions we can formulate the connection between abelian returns to a prefix of a word $\mathbf{u}_{\alpha,\rho}$ and the I-itineraries following from Lemma 1.

Lemma 2. *Let w be a factor of a Sturmian word $\mathbf{u}_{\alpha,\rho}$ of length $|w| = n$ for some $n \in \mathbb{N}$. Put $I = [0, T^{-n+1}(\alpha))$ if w is light and $I = [T^{-n+1}(\alpha), 1)$ otherwise. Then v is an abelian return to w if and only if v is an I-itinerary.*

As a consequence we have the following description of the set $\mathcal{APR}_{\mathbf{u}_{\alpha,\rho}}$.

Corollary 3. *Let $\alpha, \rho \in [0, 1)$, α irrational. Let $\mathbf{u}$ be a Sturmian word with slope α and intercept ρ. Then the set of abelian return words of prefixes of $\mathbf{u}$ satisfies*

$$\mathcal{APR}_{\mathbf{u}} = \mathcal{R}_\rho^\alpha \cup \mathcal{R}_\rho'^\alpha \,,$$

where

$$\mathcal{R}_\rho^\alpha = \bigcup_{\rho < \beta \leq 1} \left\{ R \, : \, R \text{ is a } [0, \beta)\text{-itinerary} \right\},$$

$$\mathcal{R}_\rho'^\alpha = \bigcup_{0 \leq \gamma < \rho} \left\{ R \, : \, R \text{ is a } [\gamma, 1)\text{-itinerary} \right\}.$$

Proof. Let w be a prefix of length n of the word $\mathbf{u}$ which is light. This means that for its intercept ρ one has $\rho \in J_w \subset [0, T^{-n+1}(\alpha))$. According to Lemma 2, if v is an abelian return to w, then it is an I-itinerary, where $I = [0, T^{-n+1}(\alpha))$. Thus $v \in \mathcal{R}_\rho^\alpha$. Similarly, if w is a heavy prefix of length n of the word $\mathbf{u}$, we derive that its abelian return words satisfy $v \in \mathcal{R}_\rho'^\alpha$.

For the other inclusion, we will use the following claim which follows from the properties of the transformation T, see [8].

Fact 1 *Let $\alpha \in (0, 1)$ be irrational and let T be defined by (1). Denote $S_\beta = \{ R \, : \, R$ is a $[0, \beta)$-itinerary$\}$. Then for any $\beta_0 \in (0, 1)$ there exists a neighbourhood H_{β_0} such that $S_{\beta_0} \subset S_\beta$ for any $\beta \in H_{\beta_0}$.*

Let $\rho \leq \beta_0 < 1$. If $\beta_0 = T^{-n+1}(\alpha)$ for some n, then the set S_{β_0} of I-itineraries for the interval $I = [0, \beta_0) = [0, T^{-n+1}(\alpha))$ is, according to Lemma 2, formed by abelian returns to the prefix of $\mathbf{u}$ of length n. If $\beta_0 \neq T^{-n+1}(\alpha)$ for all $n \in \mathbb{N}$, we use the fact that $\{T^{-n}(\alpha) \, : \, n \in \mathbb{N}\}$ is dense in $[0, 1)$. By Fact 1, we find $\beta = T^{-n+1}(\alpha)$ sufficiently close to β_0, so that $S_{\beta_0} \subset S_\beta$. Since $S_\beta \subset \mathcal{APR}_{\mathbf{u}}$, the proof is established.

Remark 4. Note that $\mathcal{R}_\rho^\alpha$ is the set of all abelian returns to all light prefixes of the Sturmian word $\mathbf{u}_{\alpha,\rho}$. Similarly, $\mathcal{R}_\rho'^\alpha$ is the set of all abelian returns to all heavy prefixes of the Sturmian word $\mathbf{u}_{\alpha,\rho}$.

4   First Return Map for Sturmian Systems

In the previous section we have explained that for determining the set $\mathcal{APR}_{\mathbf{u}}$ for a given Sturmian word $\mathbf{u}$, it is important to derive what are the I-itineraries under the transformation (1), in particular, for intervals I of the type $I = [0, \beta)$ resp. $I = [\gamma, 1)$. We provide such description in Theorem 8.

First we recall the notion of k-interval exchange transformations. Let $J_0 \cup J_1 \cup \cdots \cup J_{k-1} = [0, 1)$ be a partition of $[0, 1)$ into intervals closed from the left and open from the right. Let $t_0, t_1, \ldots, t_{k-1}$ be constants such that the mapping T defined by $T(x) = x + t_j$ for $x \in J_j$ is a bijection $T : [0, 1) \to [0, 1)$. For example, the transformation (1) is an exchange of two intervals. Clearly, intervals $T(J_0)$, $T(J_1), \ldots, T(J_{k-1})$ also form a partition of $[0, 1)$. Their ordering in the interval $[0, 1)$ is usually specified by a permutation on $\{0, 1, \ldots, k-1\}$.

For a general exchange $T : [0, 1) \to [0, 1)$ of k intervals it was proven in [8] that the induced map (or first return map to I) $T_I : I \to I$ given by $T_I(x) = T^{r(x)}(x)$ is an exchange of at most $k + 2$ intervals. For $k = 3$, this result can be stated in a stronger form: If T is an exchange of three intervals with permutation (321), then for any interval I, the induced map T_I is either again an exchange of three intervals with permutation (321), or exchange of two intervals, see Theorem 4.1 in [4]. In this paper, T is an exchange of two intervals. The following statement about induced maps is a reformulation of Proposition 4.5. of [7].

Proposition 5. *Let $T : [0, 1) \to [0, 1)$ be given by (1). Let $I = [c, c + \delta)$, where $0 \leq c < c + \delta \leq 1$. Then the induced map T_I is*

- *an exchange of two intervals, if $\delta = \delta_{k,s}$ for some $k \geq 0$, $1 \leq s \leq a_{k+1}$, where $\delta_{k,s}$ is defined in (2);*
- *an exchange of three intervals with permutation (321), otherwise.*

As it was already mentioned, the values $\delta_{k,s}$ represent lengths of cylinders J_w of factors w of the Sturmian word. In particular, choosing $I = J_w$, the induced map T_I is an exchange of two intervals, and the return time $r(x)$ therefore takes two values for $x \in I$. The result of Vuillon [17] states a stronger fact, namely that the I-itineraries $R(x)$ take also only two values for $x \in I$, and these are the classical return words to the factor w. If $I \subset [0, 1)$ is chosen arbitrarily, the above theorem implies that the return time $r(x)$ for $x \in I$ takes at most three values. The I-itinerary $R(x)$ can however take, in general, more than three values. For, if $R(x) \neq R(y)$, but $R(x)$ and $R(y)$ are still abelian equivalent, then $r(x) = r(y)$.

Example 6. Let $\alpha = \frac{1}{\tau}$, where $\tau = \frac{1}{2}(1 + \sqrt{5})$ is the golden ratio. In this case, the transformation $T : [0, 1) \to [0, 1)$ is of the form

$$T(x) = \begin{cases} x + 1 - \frac{1}{\tau} & \text{if } x \in [0, \frac{1}{\tau}), \\ x - \frac{1}{\tau} & \text{if } x \in [\frac{1}{\tau}, 1). \end{cases}$$

Consider the interval $I = [\frac{1}{\tau^3}, \frac{1}{\tau} + \frac{1}{\tau^4})$. Define

$$I_1 = [\tfrac{1}{\tau^3}, \tfrac{1}{\tau^2}), \quad I_2 = [\tfrac{1}{\tau^2}, \tfrac{1}{\tau^2} + \tfrac{1}{\tau^5}), \quad I_3 = [\tfrac{1}{\tau^2} + \tfrac{1}{\tau^5}, \tfrac{1}{\tau}), \quad I_4 = [\tfrac{1}{\tau}, \tfrac{1}{\tau} + \tfrac{1}{\tau^4}).$$

Let us list for every subinterval I_j the corresponding return time $r(x)$, the induced map $T_I(x)$, and the I-itinerary $R(x)$, where $x \in I_j$:

$x \in I_1$	$r(x) = 1$	$T_I(x) = x + \frac{1}{\tau^2}$	$R(x) = 0$
$x \in I_2$	$r(x) = 3$	$T_I(x) = x + \frac{1}{\tau^4}$	$R(x) = 010$
$x \in I_3$	$r(x) = 2$	$T_I(x) = x - \frac{1}{\tau^3}$	$R(x) = 01$
$x \in I_4$	$r(x) = 2$	$T_I(x) = x - \frac{1}{\tau^3}$	$R(x) = 10$

We see that the induced map T_I is an exchange of three intervals I_1, I_2, and $I_3 \cup I_4$ with permutation (321). However, the I-itineraries are four different words.

In the previous example we have seen that for a general subinterval $I \subset [0, 1)$, the set of I-itineraries may have four elements, and one can derive from [8] that this is the maximal possible number, when inducing on a subinterval under an exchange of two intervals. We will focus on the case when I has the form $I = [0, \beta)$ for some $\beta < 1$ and show that then

$$\#S_\beta = \#\{R : R \text{ is a } [0, \beta)\text{-itinerary}\} \leq 3 \,.$$

Before that, we give example of a special case of the choice of I.

Example 7. Let $I = [0, \beta)$ where $\alpha < \beta \leq 1$. For determining all I-itineraries, denote by l the non-negative integer such that

$$1 - (l + 1)\alpha < \beta \leq 1 - l\alpha \,.$$

The interval I splits into three subintervals,

$$I_1 = [0, \beta + (l+1)\alpha - 1), \quad I_2 = [\beta + (l+1)\alpha - 1, \alpha), \quad I_3 = [\alpha, \beta),$$

for which the return time and the itinerary are constant, as seen in the table below.

$x \in I_1$	$r(x) = l + 1$	$T_I(x) = x + 1 - (l+1)\alpha$	$R(x) = 01^l$
$x \in I_2$	$r(x) = l + 2$	$T_I(x) = x + 1 - (l+2)\alpha$	$R(x) = 01^{l+1}$
$x \in I_3$	$r(x) = 1$	$T_I(x) = x - \alpha$	$R(x) = 1$

When $\beta = 1 - l\alpha$, the interval $[\beta + (l + 1)\alpha - 1, \alpha)$ vanishes, and thus the induced map T_I is an exchange of two intervals. Otherwise, it is an exchange of three intervals with permutation (321).

Theorem 8. *Let T be an exchange of two intervals as in (1). Let $0 < \beta \leq 1$. Then for the interval $I = [0, \beta)$ there exist words R and R', $R \prec_{lex} R'$, such that the I-itinerary $R(x)$ of every $x \in I$ under T satisfies $R(x) \in \{R, R', RR'\}$.*

Proof. Consider first the case when $\alpha \in I = [0, \beta)$. The first return map to I is given in Example 7 together with the I-itineraries $R = 01^l$, $R' = 1$, and $R'' = RR' = 01^{l+1}$. We can therefore restrict our considerations to an interval $I = [0, \beta)$ such that $\alpha \notin I$. Let K be an interval $K \subset [0, 1)$. We distinguish three types of events for K.

Event a) for K occurs if $\alpha \in T^k(K)$ for some $k \geq 1$.
Event b) for K occurs if $T^l(K) \cap I \neq \emptyset$ for some $l \geq 1$, while $T^l(K) \not\subset I$.
Event c) for K occurs if $T^m(K) \subset I$ for some $m \geq 1$.

Consider first $K = I$. Since the transformation T is minimal (only trivial subsets $A \subset [0, 1)$ satisfy $T(A) \subset A$), the first event which occurs for K is either a) or b).

Case 1. Let the first event be a). Since the left end-point of K is $0 = T(\alpha)$, necessarily $\alpha = T^{-1}(0)$ is an inner point of $T^k(K)$. Put $I_3 = T^{-k}(T^k(I) \cap [\alpha, 1))$. Then $T^{k+1}(I_3) \subset I = [0, \beta)$. Clearly, every $x \in I_3$ satisfies $r(x) = k+1$ and $R(x)$ is constant on I_3, denote $R(x) = R'$. Note that the last letter of R' is 1 and thus it is lexicographically greater than the I-itinerary $R(x)$ of every $x \in I \setminus I_3$.

Put now $K = I \setminus I_3$. If for such K the first occurring event is c) then the I-itinerary $R(x)$ is constant on $I \setminus I_3$, say $R(x) = R$. We obviously have $R' = w1$, $R = w0v$ for some non-empty words $w, v \in \{0, 1\}^*$, and thus indeed $R \prec_{\text{lex}} R'$. The transformation T_I induced by T on I is the exchange of two intervals $I_1 = I \setminus I_3$ and I_3.

Suppose, on the other hand, that the first occurring event for $K = I \setminus I_3$ is not c). Then T_I is necessarily an exchange of three intervals and the first occurring event is b). For, if it were a), then T_I is not an injective map, which is a contradiction. Put $I_1 = T^{-l}(T^l(I \setminus I_3) \cap I)$. For every $x \in I_1$, we have $r(x) = l > k+1$, and $R(x) = R$ is constant on I_1.

Denote $I_2 = (I \setminus I_1) \setminus I_3$. For every $x \in I_2$, we have $r(x) > l$. As T_I is an exchange of three intervals, we must have $r(x)$ constant on I_2, equal to the sum of return times for I_3 and I_1, namely $r(x) = k + 1 + l$. Necessarily $K = I_2$ encounters first the event c) ($T^{k+1+l}(I_2) \subset I$), and thus also $R(x)$ is constant on I_2, say R'', and we know that it is of length $k + l + 1$.

Let us describe R''. By construction, necessarily R is a prefix of R''. Consider the union $I_3 \cup T^l(I_2)$. It is an interval, since the right end-point of I_3 is β, and by the definition of I_1, the left end-point of $T^l(I_2)$ is β. Set $K = I_3 \cup T^l(I_2)$. For every point x in K, the smallest index j such that $T^j(x) \in I$ is $j = k + 1$. This corresponds to the fact that the first event for K is c), $T^{k+1}(K) = T^{k+1}(I_3 \cup T^l(I_2)) \subset I$. We derive that the suffix of R'' of length $k + 1$ is the same as the I-itinerary of points in I_3, namely R'. Thus, indeed, $R'' = RR'$.

Case 2. Let the first event for $K = I$ be b). Set $I_1 = T^{-l}(T^l(I) \cap I)$. Obviously, the return time $r(x) = l$ and the I-itinerary $R(x)$ is constant on I_1. Denote $R = R(x)$ for $x \in I_1$. The I-itinerary of every $x \in I \setminus I_1$ has R as a prefix. Thus R is the smallest among I-itineraries on I.

From injectivity of T_I, one derives that for $K = I \setminus I_1$, first event to occur is a) for some $k \geq l$. Set $I_3 = T^{-k}(T^k(I \setminus I_1) \cap [\alpha, 1))$. For every $x \in I_3$, $r(x) = k+1$ and $R(x) = R'$ is constant on I_3.

Put $I_2 = (I \setminus I_1) \setminus I_3$. If $I_2 = \emptyset$, then T_I is the exchange of two intervals I_1 and I_3, and the proof is finished. If not, then the return time $r(x) = k + l + 1$ is constant on I_2, and thus for $K = I_2$ neither event a) nor event b) may occur sooner than c). We have $T^{k+l+1}(I_2) \subset I$ and the I-itinerary on I_2 is also constant, say R''. Let us describe R''. We already know that R is a prefix of R''. Consider the union $I_3 \cup T^l(I_2)$. It is an interval, for which first occurs event c) with $T^{k+1}(I_3 \cup T^l(I_2)) \subset I$. Thus R' is a suffix of R''.

Case 3. It may happen that for $K = I$ event a) and event b) occur at the same time, i.e. $k = l$. Then we set $I_1 = T^{-l}(T^l(I) \cap I)$, $I_3 = T^{-k}(T^k(I) \cap [\alpha, 1))$ and $I_2 = (I \setminus I_1) \setminus I_3$. Denoting the I-itinerary $R(x)$ for $x \in I_1$ by $R(x) = R = w$, then $R(x) = R' = w1$ for $x \in I_3$, and $R(x) = R'' = ww1$ for $x \in I_2$.

Remark 9. So far, we have considered the transformation defined on intervals closed from the left. In the statement of Theorem 8 we could write all intervals closed from the right, the result would be the same.

With regard to Lemma 2 and Remark 9, Theorem 8 has the following consequence.

Corollary 10. *For every factor w of a Sturmian word $\mathbf{u}$ there exist factors w_1, w_2 such that the set of abelian returns to the factor w satisfies $\mathcal{AR}_{w,\mathbf{u}} \in \{w_1, w_2, w_1 w_2\}$.*

Proof. If w is a light factor of $\mathbf{u}$, then the statement is contained in Theorem 8. If w is heavy, then consider factor $E(w)$ and the Sturmian word $E(\mathbf{u})$ where application of E means that we interchange $0 \leftrightarrow 1$. Thus $E(w)$ is a light factor of $E(\mathbf{u})$, for which the statement holds. Clearly, v is an abelian return to w in $\mathbf{u}$ if and only if $E(v)$ is an abelian return to $E(w)$ in $E(\mathbf{u})$.

Theorem 8 thus provides, as a consequence, an alternative proof of what has appeared in [12], namely that if a given factor w of a Sturmian word $\mathbf{u}$ has three abelian return words, then their lengths l_1, l_2, l_3 satisfy $l_1 + l_2 = l_3$.

For calculating the cardinality of $\mathcal{APR}_{\mathbf{u}}$ we need by Corollary 3 to determine the cardinality of the sets $\mathcal{R}_\rho^\alpha$ and $\mathcal{R}_\rho'^\alpha$ of abelian returns of all light and heavy prefixes, respectively. In fact, it suffices to study abelian returns to light prefixes, due to the symmetry mentioned in the proof of Corollary 10. The following lemma is a consequence of the fact that $\mathbf{u}$ is a Sturmian word with slope α and intercept ρ if and only if $E(\mathbf{u})$ is a Sturmian word with slope $1 - \alpha$ and intercept $1 - \rho$.

Lemma 11. *Let $\alpha, \rho \in (0,1)$, α irrational. Then $\mathcal{R}_\rho'^\alpha = E(\mathcal{R}_{1-\rho}^{1-\alpha})$, where $E : \{0,1\}^* \to \{0,1\}^*$ is determined by $E(a) = 1-a$, for $a \in \{0,1\}$, i.e. interchanging 0 and 1.*

We use the notation (2) and Proposition 5.

Corollary 12. *Let $\alpha, \rho \in (0,1)$, where $\alpha = [0, a_1, a_2, a_3, \ldots]$ is irrational. Let $(k,s) \in \mathbb{N}^2$, $1 \leq s \leq a_{k+1}$, be minimal in lexicographic order such that $\rho \geq \delta_{k,s}$. Then*

$$\#\mathcal{R}_\rho^\alpha = 1 + a_1 + a_2 + \cdots + a_k + s.$$

Proof. Let $\tilde{\delta} < \delta$ be two consecutive values of the form $\delta_{k,s}$. For the interval $I = [0, \delta)$ we have two I-itineraries, i.e. $S_\delta = \{R, R'\}$. According to Proposition 5 and Theorem 8, for β satisfying $\tilde{\delta} < \beta < \delta$, the set S_β has three elements, by Fact 1 not depending on β, i.e. $S_\beta = \{R, R', RR'\}$, when $R \prec_{\text{lex}} R'$. Moreover, $S_{\tilde{\delta}} \subset \{R, R', RR'\}$. Since shortening of the interval I yields longer I-itineraries, necessarily $RR' \in S_{\tilde{\delta}}$, i.e. $S_{\tilde{\delta}} = \{R, RR'\}$ or $S_{\tilde{\delta}} = \{R', RR'\}$. It follows that every open interval $(\tilde{\delta}, \delta)$ with $\rho < \delta$ contributes to $\mathcal{R}_\rho^\alpha$ with one new itinerary. One therefore has

$$\#\mathcal{R}_\rho^\alpha = 2 + \#\{\delta > \rho : \delta = \delta_{i,j} \text{ for some } i \in \mathbb{N}, 1 \leq j \leq a_{i+1}\}, \qquad (3)$$

where the summand 2 corresponds to the two itineraries 0 and 1 obtained for the length $1 = \delta_{0,1}$.

Remark 13. For any irrational α, if $\rho = 0$, then there are infinitely many values $\delta_{k,s} > \rho$. Therefore $\#\mathcal{R}_0^\alpha = +\infty$ and hence by Corollary 3 also $\#\mathcal{APR}_\mathbf{u} = +\infty$ for any Sturmian word $\mathbf{u}$ with zero intercept, as shown already in [14].

Let us calculate several initial values of the decreasing sequence $(\delta_{k,s})$.

Example 14. Let $\mu = [0, a_1, a_2, a_3, \ldots]$, with $a_1 \geq 2$, and $\nu = [0, 1, b_2, b_3, \ldots]$. The sequence $\delta_{k,s}$ corresponding to μ has elements

$$\delta_{0,1} = 1 > \delta_{0,2} = 1 - \mu > \delta_{0,3} = 1 - 2\mu > \ldots >$$
$$> \delta_{0,a_1} = 1 - (a_1 - 1)\mu > \delta_{1,1} = \mu > \delta_{1,2} = (a_1 + 1)\mu - 1 > \ldots \qquad (4)$$

The sequence $\delta_{k,s}$ corresponding to ν has elements

$$\delta_{0,1} = 1 > \delta_{1,1} = \nu > \delta_{1,2} = 2\nu - 1 > \delta_{1,3} = 3\nu - 2 > \ldots >$$
$$\delta_{1,b_2} = b_2\nu - b_2 + 1 > \delta_{2,1} = 1 - \nu > \quad \ldots \qquad (5)$$

Proposition 15. *Let* $\alpha, \rho \in (0,1)$, α *irrational,* $\mathbf{u} = \mathbf{u}_{\alpha,\rho}$.

1. *If* $\max\{\alpha, 1 - \alpha\} \leq \rho < 1$, *then* $\mathcal{R}_\rho^\alpha = \{0, 1, 01\}$.
2. *If* $0 < \rho \leq \min\{\alpha, 1 - \alpha\}$, *then* $\mathcal{R}_\rho^\alpha = \{0, 1, 10\}$.
3. *For any* $\rho \in (0, 1)$, *we have* $\mathcal{R}_\rho^\alpha \cap \mathcal{R}_\rho'^\alpha = \{0, 1\}$.
4. *For any* $\rho \in (0, 1)$, *we have* $\{0, 1, 01, 10\} \subset \mathcal{APR}_\mathbf{u}$.

Proof. In Example 14, consider $\mu = \min\{\alpha, 1 - \alpha\}$ and $\nu = 1 - \mu = \max\{\alpha, 1 - \alpha\}$. In both (4) and (5) we see that the second largest (after $\delta_{0,1}$) value of the decreasing sequence $(\delta_{k,s})$, $k \geq 0$, $1 \leq s \leq a_{k+1}$ is $\max\{\alpha, 1 - \alpha\}$. Relation (3) then implies that $\#\mathcal{R}_\rho^\alpha = 3$. In fact, as seen from Theorem 8, $\mathcal{R}_\rho^\alpha = \{0, 1, 01\}$. From the proof of Corollary 12 it is obvious that $\{0, 1, 01\} \subset \mathcal{R}_\rho^\alpha$ for any $\rho \in (0, 1)$. By symmetry, we can derive for $0 < \rho \leq \min\{\alpha, 1 - \alpha\}$ that $\mathcal{R}_\rho'^\alpha = \{0, 1, 10\}$, cf. Lemma 11, and we have $\{0, 1, 10\} \subset \mathcal{R}_\rho'^\alpha$ for any $\rho \in (0, 1)$. Combining the above and using Corollary 3, we have statement 4 of the proposition.

In order to prove statement 3, realize how the I-itineraries of an interval of the form $I = [0, \beta)$ arise. Directly from the definition of the transformation (1), we see that if $\beta \leq \alpha$, then for every $x \in [0, \beta)$ the $[0, \beta)$-itinerary $R(x)$ of x has the prefix 0. If $\beta > \alpha$, then the $[0, \beta)$-itinerary of $x \in [\alpha, \beta)$ is $R(x) = 1$; for every $x \in [0, \alpha)$, the $[0, \beta)$-itinerary $R(x)$ of x has the prefix 0. Thus the only element of $\mathcal{R}_\rho^\alpha$ not having prefix 0 is the word 1. Similarly, the only element of $\mathcal{R}_\rho'^\alpha = E(\mathcal{R}_{1-\rho}^{1-\alpha})$ not having prefix 1 is the word 0. The statement follows.

For simplicity of notation, the following theorem is stated for Sturmian words whose slope α satisfies $\alpha < \frac{1}{2}$.

Theorem 16. *Let* $\alpha, \rho \in (0,1)$, $\alpha = [0, a_1, a_2, \dots]$ *irrational,* $a_1 \geq 2$. *Let* **u** *be a Sturmian word with slope* α *and intercept* ρ.

(i) *Let* $\rho \in (\alpha, 1 - \alpha)$. *Then* $\#\mathcal{APR}_{\mathbf{u}} \in \{a_1 + 3, a_1 + 4\}$.

(ii) *Let* $\rho \notin (\alpha, 1 - \alpha)$. *Let* $(k, s) \in \mathbb{N}^2$, $1 \leq s \leq a_{k+1}$, *be minimal in lexicographic order such that* $\min\{\rho, 1 - \rho\} \geq \delta_{k,s}$. *Then* $\#\mathcal{APR}_{\mathbf{u}} = 2 + a_1 + \cdots + a_k + s$.

Proof. We will use the formula $\mathcal{APR}_{\mathbf{u}} = \mathcal{R}_\rho^\alpha \cup E(\mathcal{R}_{1-\rho}^{1-\alpha})$ (as derived from Corollary 3 combined with Lemma 11). Since $\alpha = [0, a_1, a_2, \dots]$, $a_1 \geq 2$, we have $1 - \alpha = [0, 1, a_1 - 1, a_2, a_3, \dots]$. Let us first prove statement (i). Substituting $\mu = \alpha$ and $\nu = 1 - \alpha$ into the prescriptions (4) and (5) for the sequences $\delta_{k,s}$ in Example 14, we see that they start with the same values

$$1 > 1 - \alpha > 1 - 2\alpha > \cdots > 1 - (a_1 - 1)\alpha > \alpha > \cdots$$

In order to determine the cardinality of $\mathcal{R}_\rho^\alpha$ by (3), we find an index $i \in \{2, \dots, a_1\}$ such that

$$1 - i\alpha \leq \rho < 1 - (i - 1)\alpha. \tag{6}$$

Then $\#\mathcal{R}_\rho^\alpha = 2 + i$. Obviously, $E(\mathcal{R}_{1-\rho}^{1-\alpha})$ has the same cardinality as $\mathcal{R}_{1-\rho}^{1-\alpha}$, which is determined by finding an index $l \in \{2, \dots, a_1\}$ such that

$$1 - l\alpha \leq 1 - \rho < 1 - (l - 1)\alpha, \tag{7}$$

whence $\#E(\mathcal{R}_{1-\rho}^{1-\alpha}) = 2 + l$.

Since the intersection of $\mathcal{R}_\rho^\alpha$ and $\mathcal{R}_\rho'^\alpha = E(\mathcal{R}_{1-\rho}^{1-\alpha})$ contains by statement 3 of Proposition 15 exactly two elements, we can conclude that $\#\mathcal{APR}_{\mathbf{u}} = 2 + i + l$. Let us find the relationship between i and l.

Inequality (7) can be rewritten as $(l - 1)\alpha < \rho \leq l\alpha$. Using $1/(a_1 + 1) < \alpha < 1/a_1$ we verify that

$$(l - 1)\alpha < 1 - (a_1 - l + 1)\alpha < l\alpha.$$

We have to distinguish two cases.

a) If $(l-1)\alpha < \rho < 1 - (a_1 - l + 1)\alpha$, then $i = a_1 - l + 2$, and thus $\#\mathcal{APR}_{\mathbf{u}} = a_1 + 4$.

b) If $1 - (a_1 - l + 1)\alpha \leq \rho \leq l\alpha$, then $i = a_1 - l + 1$, and consequently $\#\mathcal{APR}_{\mathbf{u}} = a_1 + 3$.

In order to show the second statement of the theorem, consider $\rho \notin (\alpha, 1 - \alpha)$. Let first $\rho \leq \min\{\alpha, 1 - \alpha\}$. From Corollary 12, we derive $\#\mathcal{R}_\rho^\alpha = 1 + a_1 + a_2 + \cdots + a_k + s$, where $k \geq 0$ and $1 \leq s \leq a_{k+1}$ are minimal integers such that $\rho = \min\{\rho, 1 - \rho\} \geq \delta_{k,s}$. By statement 2 of Proposition 15, we have $\#\mathcal{R}_\rho'^\alpha = 3$. Together with statement 3 of Proposition 15, we conclude that $\mathcal{APR}_{\mathbf{u}} = \mathcal{R}_\rho^\alpha \cup \mathcal{R}_\rho'^\alpha = 2 + a_1 + a_2 + \cdots + a_k + s$. The proof for $\rho \geq \max\{\alpha, 1 - \alpha\}$ is similar.

So far, we were interested only in the cardinality in the set $\mathcal{APR}_\mathbf{u}$. However, we can also provide an algorithm for explicit description of its elements. For that, we need the following fact.

Proposition 17. *Let J, I be intervals such that $J \subset I \subset [0,1)$. Let T_I be an exchange of two intervals and denote by P, P' the two I-itineraries under T. Let also $(T_I)_J$ be an exchange of two intervals and denote by Q, Q' the two J-itineraries under T_I. Then T_J is an exchange of two intervals and the two J-itineraries under T are constructed from Q, Q' by applying the morphism*

$$\sigma : \{0,1\}^* \to \{0,1\}^* \quad \text{defined by} \quad \sigma(0) = P, \ \sigma(1) = P'. \tag{8}$$

Explicit description of the set $\mathcal{R}_\rho^\alpha$ is then given using the following algorithm derived from Corollary 12 and its proof. If k_0, s_0 are minimal indices such that $\delta_{k_0,s_0} \leq \rho$, then the number of elements, say N, in $\mathcal{R}_\rho^\alpha$ is equal to

$$N = 1 + a_1 + a_2 + \cdots + a_{k_0} + s_0. \tag{9}$$

Input: $\alpha, \rho \in (0,1)$, α irrational.

Output: $\mathcal{R}_\rho^\alpha$.

Step 1: Determine N according to (9).

Step 2: $\varepsilon := \alpha$, $R := 0$, $R' := 1$, $\mathcal{R} := \{0,1\}$.

Step 3: Repeat $N - 1$ times:
$\mathcal{R} := \mathcal{R} \cup \{RR'\}$,
if $\varepsilon > \frac{1}{2}$ then
$\quad R := R, \ R' := RR', \ \varepsilon := \frac{2\varepsilon - 1}{\varepsilon}$,
if $\varepsilon < \frac{1}{2}$ then
$\quad$ if $RR' \prec_{\text{lex}} R'$ then $R := RR', \ R' := R'$ else $R := R', \ R' := RR'$,
$\quad \varepsilon := \frac{\varepsilon}{1-\varepsilon}$,

Step 4: $\mathcal{R}_\rho^\alpha := \mathcal{R}$.

Note that the parameter ε in the algorithm corresponds to the slope of the induced transformation in each step, cf. Proposition 17.

Using the above algorithm, one can describe the set $\mathcal{APR}_{\mathbf{c}_\alpha} = \mathcal{R}_{1-\alpha}^\alpha \cup \mathcal{R}_{1-\alpha}'^\alpha$ of abelian return words to prefixes of a characteristic Sturmian word $\mathbf{c}_\alpha$.

Proposition 18. *Let $\alpha = [0, a_1, a_2, \cdots]$ be an irrational in $(0,1)$. For the characteristic Sturmian word $\mathbf{c}_\alpha$ we have*

$$\mathcal{APR}_{\mathbf{c}_\alpha} = \begin{cases} \{0, 01, 1, 10, 110, \ldots, 1^{a_1}0\} & \text{if } \alpha < \frac{1}{2}, \\ \{1, 10, 0, 01, 001, \ldots, 0^{a_2+1}1\} & \text{otherwise.} \end{cases}$$

Applying Proposition 18 to the case $\alpha = \frac{1}{\tau} = [0,1,1,1,\ldots]$, we obtain that the set of abelian returns to the prefixes of the Fibonacci word $\mathbf{f} = \mathbf{c}_{1/\tau}$ is $\mathcal{APR}_\mathbf{f} = \{0, 1, 01, 10, 001\}$, as shown by a different technique (specific for the Fibonacci word) in [14].

Acknowledgements. We wish to thank K. Břinda for numerical experiments on the Fibonacci word. We acknowledge financial support by the Czech Science Foundation grant 13-03538S.

References

1. Adamczewski, B.: Codages de rotations et phénomènes d'autosimilarité. J. Théor. Nombres Bordeaux 14, 351–386 (2002)
2. Alessandri, P., Berthé, V.: Three distance theorems and combinatorics on words. L'Enseignement Mathématique 44, 103–132 (1998)
3. Ambrož, P., Frid, A., Masáková, Z., Pelantová, E.: On the number of factors in codings of three interval exchange. Discrete Math. Theor. Comput. Sci. 13, 51–66 (2011)
4. Baláži, P., Masáková, Z., Pelantová, E.: Characterization of Substitution Invariant Words Coding Exchange of Three Intervals. INTEGERS: Electronic Journal of Combinatorial Number Theory 8, A20 (2008)
5. Berthé, V.: Fréquences des facteurs des suites sturmiennes. Theoret. Comput. Sci. 165, 295–309 (1996)
6. Durand, F.: A characterization of substitutive sequences using return words. Discrete Mathematics 179, 89–101 (1998)
7. Guimond, L.S., Masáková, Z., Pelantová, E.: Combinatorial properties of infinite words associated with cut-and-project sequences. J. Théor. Nombres Bordeaux 15, 697–725 (2003)
8. Keane, M.: Interval exchange transformations. Math. Z. 141, 25–31 (1975)
9. Lothaire, M.: Algebraic combinatorics on words. Encyclopedia of Mathematics and its Applications, vol. 90. Cambridge University Press, Cambridge (2002)
10. Morse, M., Hedlund, G.: Symbolic dynamics II: Sturmian sequences. Amer. J. Math. 61, 1–42 (1940)
11. Puzynina, S., Zamboni, L.: Abelian returns in Sturmian words. J. Comb. Theory, Series A 120, 390–408 (2013)
12. Puzynina, S., Zamboni, L.: Abelian returns in Sturmian words. Presentation at 8th International Conference WORDS, Prague (2011), http://words2011.fjfi.cvut.cz/files/slides/2-8-Puzynina.pdf
13. Rampersad, N., Rigo, M., Salimov, P.: A note on abelian returns in rotation words (2012) (preprint), http://hdl.handle.net/2268/135708
14. Rigo, M., Salimov, P., Vandomme, E.: Some properties of abelian return words. Journal of Integer Sequences 16, A 13.2.5 (2013)
15. Slater, N.B.: Gaps and steps for the sequence $n\alpha$ mod 1. Math. Proc. Cambridge Phil. Soc. 63, 1115–1123 (1967)
16. Sós, V.: On the distribution mod 1 of the sequence $n\alpha$. Ann. Univ. Sci. Budapest. Eötös Sect. Math. 1, 127–134 (1958)
17. Vuillon, L.: A characterisation of Sturmian words by return words. Europ. J. Combin. 22, 263–275 (2001)

Regular Ideal Languages
and Synchronizing Automata[*]

Rogério Reis and Emanuele Rodaro[**]

Centro de Matemática, Universidade do Porto
R. Campo Alegre 687, 4169-007 Porto, Portugal
rvr@dcc.fc.up.pt, emanuele.rodaro@fc.up.pt

Abstract. We introduce the notion of reset left regular decomposition of an ideal regular language and we prove that there is a one-to-one correspondence between these decompositions and strongly connected synchronizing automata. We show that each ideal regular language has at least a reset left regular decomposition. As a consequence each ideal regular language is the set of synchronizing words of some strongly connected synchronizing automaton. Furthermore, this one-to-one correspondence allows us to formulate Černý's conjecture in a pure language theoretic framework.

1 Introduction

Since, in the context of this paper, we are not interested in automata as languages recognizer but just on the action of its transition function δ on the set of states Q, let us consider a deterministic finite automaton (DFA) as a tuple $\mathscr{A} = \langle Q, \Sigma, \delta \rangle$, where the initial and final states are deliberately omitted from the definition. But, because in some point of this work we refer to an automaton as a language recognizer, we also call a DFA a tuple $\mathscr{B} = \langle Q', \Sigma', \delta', q_0, F \rangle$ and the language recognized by $\mathscr{B}$ is the set $L[\mathscr{B}] = \{u \in \Sigma^* : \delta'(q_0, u) \in F\}$. A DFA $\mathscr{A} = \langle Q, \Sigma, \delta \rangle$ is called synchronizing if there exists a word $w \in \Sigma^*$ "sending" all the states into a single one, i.e. $\delta(q, w) = \delta(q', w)$ for all $q, q' \in Q$. Any such word is said to be synchronizing (or reset) for the DFA $\mathscr{A}$. This notion has been widely studied since the work of Černý in 1964 [11] and his well known conjecture regarding the length of the shortest reset word. For more information on synchronizing automata we refer the reader to the survey by Volkov [12]. In what follows, when there is no ambiguity on the choice of the action δ of the automaton, we use the notation $q \cdot u$ instead of $\delta(q, u)$. We extend this action to a subset $H \subseteq Q$ in the obvious way $H \cdot u = \{q \cdot u : q \in H\}$ with the convention $\emptyset \cdot u = \emptyset$, and for a language $L \subseteq \Sigma^*$ we use the notation

---

[*] Work partially supported by the European Regional Development Fund through the programme COMPETE and by the Portuguese Government through the FCT – Fundação para a Ciência e a Tecnologia under the project PEst-C/MAT/UI0144/2011 and CANTE-PTDC/EIA-CCO/101904/2008.
[**] Partialy supported by FCT project SFRH/BPD/65428/2009.

J. Karhumäki, A. Lepistö, and L. Zamboni (Eds.): WORDS 2013, LNCS 8079, pp. 205–216, 2013.
© Springer-Verlag Berlin Heidelberg 2013

$H \cdot L = \{q \cdot u : q \in H, u \in L\}$. We say that $\mathscr{A}$ is *strongly connected* whenever for any $q, q' \in Q$ there is a word $u \in \Sigma^*$ such that $q \cdot u = q'$. In the realm of synchronizing automata this notion is crucial since it is well known that Černý's conjecture is true if and only if it is true for the class of strongly connected synchronizing automata.

In this paper we study the relationship between ideal regular languages and synchronizing automata. A language $I \subseteq \Sigma^*$ is called a *two-sided ideal* (or simply an ideal) if $\Sigma^* I \Sigma^* \subseteq I$. In this work we will consider only ideal languages which are regular. Denote by $\mathbf{I}_\Sigma$ the class of ideal languages on an alphabet Σ. For a given synchronizing automaton $\mathscr{A}$, $\mathrm{Syn}(\mathscr{A})$ denotes the language of all the words synchronizing $\mathscr{A}$. It is a well known fact that $\mathrm{Syn}(\mathscr{A}) = \Sigma^* \mathrm{Syn}(\mathscr{A}) \Sigma^*$ is a regular language which is also an ideal. This ideal is generated by the set of minimal synchronizing words $G = \mathrm{Syn}(\mathscr{A}) \setminus (\Sigma^+ \mathrm{Syn}(\mathscr{A}) \cup \mathrm{Syn}(\mathscr{A}) \Sigma^+)$. This set can also be obtained considering the operators introduced in [6,8]. In case the set of generators G is finite, I is called finitely generated ideal and the synchronizing automata whose set of synchronizing words is finitely generated are called finitely generated synchronizing automata (see [5,7,9]). It is observed in [3] that the minimal deterministic automaton $\mathscr{A}_I = \langle Q', \Sigma, \delta', q_0, \{s\} \rangle$ recognizing an ideal language I is synchronizing with a unique final state s which is fixed by all the elements of Σ. We will refer to such state as *the sink state* for $\mathscr{A}_I$. Furthermore $\mathrm{Syn}(\mathscr{A}_I) = I$. Thus, each ideal language is endowed with at least a synchronizing automaton having I as the set of reset words. Therefore, for each ideal I there is a non-empty set $\mathcal{SA}(I)$ of all the synchronizing automata $\mathscr{B}$ with $\mathrm{Syn}(\mathscr{B}) = I$. In [3] the author introduces the notion of *reset complexity* of an ideal I as the number of states of the smallest automata in $\mathcal{SA}(I)$. In the same paper it is shown that the reset complexity can be exponentially smaller than the state complexity of the language. In [1] it is considered the special case of finitely generated synchronizing automata with the set of the reset words which is a principal ideal $P = \Sigma^* w \Sigma^*$ generated by a word $w \in \Sigma^*$, and it is presented an algorithm to generate a strongly connected synchronizing automaton $\mathscr{B}_w$ with $\mathrm{Syn}(\mathscr{B}_w) = P$ with the same number of states of $\mathscr{A}_P$. Therefore, for an ideal language I the first natural question that arises is wheather or not $\mathcal{SA}(I)$ always contains a strongly connected automaton or not. In Section 3 we answer affirmatively to this question for non-unary ideal languages. However, to study and characterize languages which are the reset words of strongly connected synchronizing automata we need to introduce the following provisional class of *strongly connected ideal language*:

Definition 1. *An ideal language I is called strongly connected whenever $I = \mathrm{Syn}(\mathscr{A})$ for some strongly connected synchronizing automaton $\mathscr{A}$.*

The paper is organized as follows. In Section 2 we introduce the notion of a (reset) left regular decomposition of an ideal, and we prove that strongly connected ideal languages are exactly the ideals having a reset left regular decomposition. We also exhibit a bijection that associates to each strongly connected ideal language I a strongly connected synchronizing automaton $\mathscr{A}$ with $\mathrm{Syn}(\mathscr{A}) = I$. In Section 3 we prove that each ideal language is a strongly connected ideal language. Thus, we can introduce the concept of reset regular decomposition complexity of an ideal and give an equivalent formulation of Černý's conjecture using this notion. Finally we state some open problems and direction of future research.

2   Strongly Connected Ideal Languages

We denote the class of strongly connected ideals on some finite alphabet Σ by $\mathbf{SCI}_\Sigma$ and the class of strongly connected synchronizing automata by $\mathbf{SCSA}_\Sigma$. Here, we characterize the class $\mathbf{SCI}_\Sigma$ using the concept of *reset left regular decomposition* of an ideal I. For $L \subseteq \Sigma^*$ and $u \in \Sigma^*$, let $Lu = \{xu : x \in L\}$, $uL = \{ux : x \in L\}$. The *reverse* operator $\cdot^R$ is such that given a word $u = u_1 u_2 \ldots u_k$, $u^R = u_k \ldots u_2 u_1$. This operator extends naturaly to languages.

Definition 2. *A left regular decomposition is a collection $\{I_i\}_{i \in F}$ of disjoint left ideals I_i of Σ^* for some finite set F such that:*

i) For any $a \in \Sigma$ and $i \in F$, there is a $j \in F$ such that $I_i a \subseteq I_j$.

The decomposition $\{I_i\}_{i \in F}$ is called a reset left regular decomposition if it also satisfies the following extra condition:

ii) Let $I = \uplus_{i \in F} I_i$. For any $u \in \Sigma^*$ if there is an $i \in F$ such that $Iu \subseteq I_i$, then $u \in I$.

Note that if $\{I_i\}_{i \in F}$ is a reset left regular decomposition, then the condition $Iu \subseteq I_i$ implies $u \in I_i$. Since $u \in I$, then $u \in I_j$ for some $j \in F$, hence $Iu \subseteq I_j$. If $j \neq i$ we have both $Iu \subseteq I_i$ and $Iu \subseteq I_j$ and thus $I_i \cap I_j \neq \emptyset$, which is a contradiction. We say that an ideal I has a (reset) left regular decomposition if there is a (reset) left regular decomposition $\{I_i\}_{i \in F}$ such that $I = \uplus_{i \in F} I_i$. The *order* of $\{I_i\}_{i \in F}$ is $|F|$. The notion of right regular decomposition is symmetric: exchange left ideals with right ideals and $I_i a$, Iu with aI_i, uI, respectively. Denote by $\mathbf{RLD}_\Sigma$ ($\mathbf{RRD}_\Sigma$) the class of the reset left (right) regular decompositions. Note that for a given left regular decomposition (reset left regular decomposition) $\{I_i\}_{i \in F}$, then $\{I_i^R\}_{i \in F}$ is a right regular decomposition (reset right regular decomposition). Thus $\cdot^R$ is a bijection between $\mathbf{RLD}_\Sigma \to \mathbf{RRD}_\Sigma$. We have the following characterization.

Theorem 3. *An ideal language I is strongly connected if and only if it has a reset left regular decomposition.*

Proof. Let $\mathscr{A} = \langle Q, \Sigma, \delta \rangle$ be a strongly connected synchronizing automata with $\mathrm{Syn}(\mathscr{A}) = I$. For each $q \in Q$, let:

$$I_q = \{u \in I : Q \cdot u = q\}$$

We claim that $\{I_q\}_{q \in Q}$ is a reset left regular decomposition for I. It is obvious that I_q are left ideals since for any $u \in I_q$ and $v \in \Sigma^*$, we get $Q \cdot vu \subseteq Q \cdot u = \{q\}$, i.e. $Q \cdot vu = \{q\}$. Let $q, q' \in Q$ with $q \neq q'$ and assume $I_q \cap I_{q'} \neq \emptyset$ and let

$u \in I_q \cap I_{q'}$. By definition, we have $q = Qu = q'$, which is a contradiction. Hence $I_q \cap I_{q'} = \emptyset$. Clearly $\uplus_{q \in Q} I_q \subseteq I$. Conversely if $u \in I$, since it is a reset word, then $Qu = q'$ for some $q' \in Q$, i.e. $u \in I_{q'}$ and so we have the decomposition $\uplus_{q \in Q} I_q = I$. Moreover for any $a \in \Sigma$, if $u \in I_q$, then $Q \cdot ua = q \cdot a$, thus $I_q a \subseteq I_{q \cdot a}$ and so condition i) of the Definition 2 is fulfilled. Thus it remains to prove that condition ii) is also satisfied. Suppose that $Iw \subseteq I_{\bar{q}}$ for some $\bar{q} \in Q$. Take any $q \in Q$, we claim that $qw = \bar{q}$ and so $w \in \mathrm{Syn}(\mathscr{A}) = I$. Take any $u' \in I$, thus $Q \cdot u' = q'$ for some $q' \in Q$. Since $\mathscr{A}$ is strongly connected, there is $u'' \in \Sigma^*$ such that $q' \cdot u'' = q$. Thus $u = u'u'' \in I$ satisfies $Q \cdot u = q$. Since $Iw \subseteq I_{\bar{q}}$ we get $\bar{q} = Q \cdot (uw) = q \cdot w$, i.e. $q \cdot w = \bar{q}$.

Conversely suppose that I has a reset left regular decomposition $\{I_i\}_{i \in F}$. We associate a DFA $\mathscr{A}(\{I_i\}_{i \in F}) = \langle \{I_i\}_{i \in F}, \Sigma, \eta \rangle$ in the following way. By condition i) of Definition 2 for any I_i and $a \in \Sigma$ there is a $j \in F$ with $I_i \cdot a \subseteq I_j$. Thus we define $\eta(I_i, a) = I_j$. This function is well defined. Let $j, k \in F$ with $j \neq i$, such that $I_i \cdot a \subseteq I_j, I_k$, then $I_i \cdot a \subseteq I_j \cap I_k$, hence $I_j \cap I_k \neq \emptyset$, which is a contradiction. Hence $\mathscr{A}(\{I_i\}_{i \in F})$ is a well defined DFA. It is straightforward to check that $\eta(I_i, u) = I_k$ for $u \in \Sigma^*$ if and only if $I_i u \subseteq I_k$. We prove that $\mathscr{A}(\{I_i\}_{i \in F})$ is strongly connected. Indeed take any $i, j \in F$ and let $w \in I_j$. Since I_j is a left ideal, then $I_i w \subseteq I_j$. Hence $I_i w \subseteq I_j$ implies $\eta(I_i, w) = I_j$ and so $\mathscr{A}(\{I_i\}_{i \in F})$ is strongly connected. We need to prove that $I \subseteq \mathrm{Syn}(\mathscr{A}(\{I_i\}_{i \in F}))$. Let $u \in I$, since $\{I_i\}_{i \in F}$ is a decomposition, $u \in I_j$ for some $j \in F$. Since I_j is a left ideal, we get $I_i u \subseteq I_j$ for any $i \in F$. Hence $\eta(I_i, u) = I_j$ for all $i \in F$, i.e. $u \in \mathrm{Syn}(\mathscr{A}(\{I_i\}_{i \in F}))$. Conversely, let $u \in \mathrm{Syn}(\mathscr{A}(\{I_i\}_{i \in F}))$. By the definition $\eta(I_i, u) = I_j$ for some $j \in F$ and for all $i \in F$. Therefore $I_i u \subseteq I_j$ which implies $Iu \subseteq I_j$ and so by ii) of Definition 2 we get $u \in I$. $\square$

It is straightforward to check that the correspondence given in the proof of Theorem 3 is a bijection between the classes $\mathbf{RLD}_\Sigma$ and $\mathbf{SCSA}_\Sigma$. We state this fact in the following theorem.

Theorem 4. *The map* $\mathcal{A} : \mathbf{RLD}_\Sigma \to \mathbf{SCSA}_\Sigma$ *defined by*

$$\mathcal{A} : \{I_i\}_{i \in F} \mapsto \mathscr{A}(\{I_i\}_{i \in F}) = \langle \{I_i\}_{i \in F}, \Sigma, \eta \rangle$$

with $\eta(I_i, a) = I_j$ *for* $a \in \Sigma$ *if and only if* $I_i a \subseteq I_j$ *is a bijection with inverse given by* $\mathcal{I} : \mathbf{SCSA}_\Sigma \to \mathbf{RLD}_\Sigma$ *defined by*

$$\mathcal{I} : \mathscr{B} = \langle Q, \Sigma, \delta \rangle \mapsto \{I_q\}_{q \in Q} = \{\{u \in \Sigma^* : \delta(Q, u) = q\}\}_{q \in Q}$$

The following corollary characterizes the case of ideals on a unary alphabet.

Corollary 1. *Let* I *be an ideal over a unary alphabet* $\Sigma = \{a\}$. *Then* I *is strongly connected if and only if* $I = \Sigma^*$.

Proof. Since the alphabet is unary we have $I = a^* a^m a^*$ for some $m \geq 0$. Suppose that I is strongly connected, then by Theorem 3 there is a reset left regular decomposition $\{I_i\}_{i \in F}$ of I. Assume $a^m \in I_j$ for some $j \in F$. We claim $|F| = 1$. Indeed, since I_j is a left ideal we have $a^* a^m \subseteq I_j$, hence

$I = a^*a^ma^* = a^*a^m \subseteq I_j$, i.e. $I = I_j$. Therefore, by Theorem 4 the only strongly connected synchronizing automaton having I as set of reset words is the automaton with one state and a loop labelled by a. Hence $I = a^*$. On the other hand, if $I = a^*$ then I is the set of reset words of the synchronizing automaton with one state and a loop labelled by a, which is strongly connected, i.e. I is strongly connected.   □

From this Corollary we can assume henceforth that the ideals considered are taken over an non-unary alphabet Σ. Given a strongly connected ideal language I with $\mathrm{Syn}(\mathscr{B}) = I$ for some strongly connected synchronizing automaton $\mathscr{B} = \langle Q, \Sigma, \delta \rangle$, there is an obvious way to calculate the associated reset left regular decomposition $\mathcal{I}(\mathscr{B})$. It is well known that I is recognized by the power automaton of $\mathscr{B}$ defined by $\mathcal{P}(\mathscr{B}) = \langle 2^Q, \Sigma, \delta, Q, \{\{q\} : q \in Q\}\rangle$, where 2^Q denotes the set of subsets of Q, the initial state is the set Q and the final set of states is formed by all the singletons. Thus, for each $q \in Q$ we can associate the DFA $\mathcal{P}(\mathscr{B})_q = \langle 2^Q, \Sigma, \delta, Q, \{q\}\rangle$ and so we can calculate the associated reset left regular decomposition by $\mathcal{I}(\mathscr{B}) = \{L[\mathcal{P}(\mathscr{B})_q]\}_{q \in Q}$. A first and quite natural issue is to calculate the reset left regular decompositions of the reset words of the Černý's series $\mathscr{C}_n = \langle \{1, \ldots, n\}, \{a, b\}, \delta_n\rangle$, where a acts like a ciclic permutation $\delta_n(i, a) = i + 1$ for $i = 1, \ldots, n - 1$ and $\delta_n(n, a) = 1$, while b fixes all the states except the last one: $\delta_n(i, b) = i$ for $i = 1, \ldots, n - 1$ and $\delta_n(n, b) = 1$ (see Fig. 1).

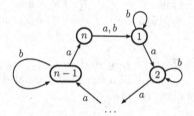

Fig. 1. The Černý's automaton $\mathscr{C}_n$

For example, in the case of $\mathscr{C}_4$ the associated reset left regular decomposition is the one given by

$$L[\mathcal{P}(\mathscr{C})_1] = (((a^*b)(b + ab + a^4)^*(a^3b + (a^2b(b + a^2)^*ab)))((b + ab^*a^3) +$$
$$+ ((ab^*ab)(b + a^2)^*)ab))^*(ab^*a^2b)(b + ((ab^*ab^*)(a(a + b))))^*$$
$$L[\mathcal{P}(\mathscr{C})_2] = L[\mathcal{P}(\mathscr{C})_1]ab^*$$
$$L[\mathcal{P}(\mathscr{C})_3] = L[\mathcal{P}(\mathscr{C})_1]ab^*ab^*$$
$$L[\mathcal{P}(\mathscr{C})_4] = L[\mathcal{P}(\mathscr{C})_1]ab^*ab^*a.$$

In general, for $\mathscr{C}_n$ it is not difficult to see that $|\delta_n(\{1, \ldots, n\}, ux)| = 1$ and $|\delta_n(\{1, \ldots, n\}, u)| > 1$ for some word $u \in \{a, b\}^*$ and a letter $x \in \{a, b\}$ if and only if $\delta_n(\{1, \ldots, n\}, u) = \{n, 1\}$ and $x = b$. Thus, if $|\delta_n(Q, w)| = 1$, then there is a prefix $w'b$ of w with $\delta_n(Q, w') = \{n, 1\}$. Therefore, it is straightforward to check that in this case the decompositions are given by

$$L[\mathcal{P}(\mathscr{C})_1] = \{w \in \Sigma^* \ : \ \delta_n(\{1, \ldots, n\}, w) = \{1\}\}$$
$$L[\mathcal{P}(\mathscr{C})_\ell] = L[\mathcal{P}(\mathscr{C})_1](ab^*)^{\ell-1} \quad \text{for } \ell = 2, \ldots, n-1$$
$$L[\mathcal{P}(\mathscr{C})_n] = L[\mathcal{P}(\mathscr{C})_1](ab^*)^{n-2}a.$$

By Theorem 3 if I is strongly connected, we can associate the non-empty set $\mathcal{R}(I)$ of all the reset left regular decompositions of I. We have the following lemma.

Lemma 1. Let $\{I_i\}_{i \in F}$ be a reset left regular decompositions of I and let $\{J_k\}_{k \in H}$ be a left regular decomposition of an ideal J. If $I \subseteq J$, then the non-empty elements of $\{I_i \cap J_k\}_{i \in F, k \in H}$ form a reset left regular decomposition of I.

Proof. Let $T \subseteq F \times H$ be the set of all the pairs of indices (i, j) for which $I_i \cap J_j \neq \emptyset$ and rename the set $\{I_i \cap J_k\}_{(i,k) \in T}$ by $\{S_j\}_{j \in T}$. It is clear that each S_j is a left ideal and $S_j \cap S_t = \emptyset$ for $j \neq t$. Furthermore $\uplus_{j \in T} S_j = I$. Condition i) is also verified. Take any S_j and suppose that $S_j = I_i \cap J_k$ for some $(i, k) \in T$, and let $a \in \Sigma$. Then $I_i a \subseteq I_s$, $J_k a \subseteq J_t$ for some $s \in F, t \in H$. Hence $(I_i \cap J_k)a = I_i a \cap J_k a \subseteq I_s \cap J_t = S_h$ for some $h \in T$, i.e. $S_j a \subseteq S_h$. Let us prove that reset condition ii) is also fulfilled. Assume $Iu \subseteq S_t$ for some $t \in T$ and $u \in \Sigma^*$. Thus $S_t = I_i \cap J_k$, for some $i \in F, k \in H$, hence $S_t \subseteq I_i$ which implies $Iu \subseteq I_i$. Hence $u \in I$ since $\{I_i\}_{i \in F}$ is a reset left regular decompositions of I. $\square$

Given $\mathcal{I}, \mathcal{J} \in \mathcal{R}(I)$ with $\mathcal{I} = \{I_i\}_{i \in F}$ and $\mathcal{J} = \{J_k\}_{k \in H}$ by Lemma 1 the family $\mathcal{I} \wedge \mathcal{J} = \{I_i \cap J_k\}_{i \in F, k \in H}$ is still a reset left regular decomposition. Thus we have the following immediate result.

Corollary 2. *The family of the reset left regular decompositions of a strongly connected ideal I is a $\wedge$-semilattice.*

Let $\|I\| = \min\{|u| : u \in I\}$. It is a well known fact that Černý's conjecture holds if and only if it holds for strongly connected synchronizing automata. The following proposition place Černý's conjecture in a purely language theoretic context.

Proposition 5. *Černý's conjecture is true for strongly connected synchronizing automata if and only if for any strongly connected ideal I and any reset left regular decomposition $\{I_i\}_{i \in F}$ of I we have:*

$$|F| \geq \sqrt{\|I\|} + 1$$

Proof. Suppose that Černý's conjecture is true for strongly connected synchronizing automata. Let I be a strongly connected ideal and let $\{I_i\}_{i \in F}$ be a reset left regular decomposition of I. Let $\mathcal{A}(\{I_i\}_{i \in F})$ be the standard synchronizing automata associated to this decomposition as in Theorem 4. This automaton has $|F|$ states, hence there is a synchronizing word $u \in \mathrm{Syn}(\mathcal{A}(\{\mathscr{I}\}_{\in \mathscr{F}})) = I$ with $|u| \leq (|F| - 1)^2$. Thus $|F| \geq \sqrt{|u|} + 1 \geq \sqrt{\|I\|} + 1$.

Conversely, take any strongly connected synchronizing automata $\mathscr{A} = \langle Q, \Sigma, \delta \rangle$ with n states and let $\{I_q\}_{q \in Q}$ be the associated reset left regular decomposition of $I = \mathrm{Syn}(\mathscr{A})$ as in Theorem 4. Since the order of this decomposition is n, then $n \geq \sqrt{\|I\|} + 1$. Thus we have that there is a $u \in \mathrm{Syn}(\mathscr{A})$ with $|u| \leq (n - 1)^2$ and so Černý's conjecture holds for $\mathscr{A}$. $\square$

3   Ideal Languages Are Strongly Connected Ideal Languages

The notion of strongly connected ideal languages (**SCI**$_\Sigma$) has been introduced in Section 2 to study the relationship between strongly connected synchronizing automata and ideal languages. In this section we show that **SCI**$_\Sigma$ = **I**$_\Sigma$. This is done by showing that each ideal language I has at least a reset left regular decomposition. Equivalently, by Theorem 4, I is the set of the reset words of some strongly connected synchronizing automata with the same number of states as the order of this decomposition. However, the construction presented in Theorem 6 provides a reset left regular decomposition for I^R which is in general a double exponential with respect to the state complexity of I^R, and this bound does not seem to be tight. Before we prove the main result of this section we introduce some notions which are crucial for the sequel. Let $\mathscr{C} = \langle Q, \Sigma, \delta \rangle$ be an automaton with n states and a sink state s. Note that for such an automaton $|Q \cdot u| = 1$ if and only if $Q \cdot u = \{s\}$. Fix a word $u \in \Sigma^*$ and a subset $H \subseteq Q$. Assume $u = u_1 \ldots u_r$ for $u_1, \ldots, u_r \in \Sigma$ and $r = |u|$. For $0 \leq i < j \leq r$ we use the standard notation $u[i, j]$ to indicate the factor $u_i u_{i+1} \ldots u_j$ if $i > 0$, otherwise $u[0, j] = u_1 \ldots u_j$ with the convention that $u[0, 0] = \epsilon$ and $u[i, i] = u_i$ if $i > 0$. We introduce a function which is fundamental in the sequel. Let $m = \frac{n^2 + n}{2} + 1$ and let $\mathbb{Z}_m$ be the ring of the integers modulo m. For an integer $t \geq 1$, $[2^Q]_t$ denotes the set of subsets of Q of cardinality t. Let $\mathbb{T}_t = \mathbb{Z}_m([2^Q]_t \uplus \Sigma)$ be the free $\mathbb{Z}_m$-module on $[2^Q]_t \uplus \Sigma$. Let $H \in [2^Q]_t$, $a \in \Sigma$ and $p \in \mathbb{Z}_m([2^Q]_t \uplus \Sigma)$. We denote by $p(H)$, $p(a)$ the coefficients in $\mathbb{Z}_m$ of p with terms H, a, respectively. Note that p can be decomposed as the sum of the two following terms

$$p\langle Q \rangle = \sum_{H \subseteq Q} p(H) H, \quad p\langle \Sigma \rangle = \sum_{a \in \Sigma} p(a) a$$

Fix an element $u \in \Sigma^*$ with $u = u_1 \ldots u_r$ and $H \subseteq Q$ with $|H| > 1$. Let j be the biggest index $1 \leq j \leq r$ such that $|H \cdot u[1, j]| > 1$ and if $j < n$, then $|H \cdot u[1, j + 1]| = 1$. The set $S = H \cdot u[1, j]$ is called the *last set* of (H, u). Let i be the index $1 \leq i \leq r$ such that $u[i, j]$ is the maximal factor of u with $|S| = |H \cdot u[0, k]|$ for all $i \leq k \leq j$. The *tail* of (H, u) is the element of $\mathbb{Z}_m([2^Q]_t \uplus \Sigma)$ with $t = |S| \geq 2$ defined by

$$\mathcal{T}(H, u) = \begin{cases} \sum_{k=i}^{j-1} (H \cdot u[0, k] + u[k + 1, k + 1]), & \text{if } u[0, j] = u \\ \sum_{k=i}^{j} (H \cdot u[0, k] + u[k + 1, k + 1]), & \text{otherwise.} \end{cases}$$

Consider the set $\mathbb{T} = \uplus_{t=2}^{n} \mathbb{T}_t$. For an element $\mathcal{T} \in \mathbb{T}_t$, the integer $t \geq 2$ is called *the index* of $\mathcal{T}$ and it is denoted by $\mathrm{Ind}(\mathcal{T})$. We give to $\mathbb{T}$ a structure of semigroup by introducing an internal binary operation $\diamond$ defined in the following way. Let $\mathcal{T}_1 \in \mathbb{T}_i, \mathcal{T}_2 \in \mathbb{T}_j$, then

$$\mathcal{T}_1 \diamond \mathcal{T}_2 = \begin{cases} \mathcal{T}_{\min\{i,j\}} & \text{if } i \neq j \\ \mathcal{T}_1 + \mathcal{T}_2 & \text{otherwise} \end{cases}$$

Note that $(\mathbb{T}, \diamond)$ has a graded structure with respect to the semilattice $([2, n], \min)$, i.e. $\mathbb{T}_i \diamond \mathbb{T}_j \subseteq \mathbb{T}_{\min\{i,j\}}$. Let $u \in \Sigma^*$, the *tail map* is the function $\tau_u : 2^Q \to \mathbb{T}$ defined by

$$\tau_u(H) = \begin{cases} \mathcal{T}(H, u) & \text{if } |H| > 1 \\ 0_n & \text{otherwise} \end{cases}$$

where 0_n is the zero of $\mathbb{T}_n$. The following lemma is a direct consequence of the definitions.

Lemma 2. *With the above notation for any $u, v \in \Sigma^*$ we have:*

$$\tau_{vu}(T) = \tau_v(T) \diamond \tau_u(T \cdot v)$$

We denote by $\mathrm{Hom}(A, B)$ the set of the maps $f_\cdot : A \to B$. We have the following lemma.

Lemma 3. *Consider the map $\mu : \Sigma^* \to \mathrm{Hom}(2^Q, \mathbb{T})$ defined by $\mu(u) = \tau_u$, then $\mathrm{Ker}(\mu)$ is a left congruence on Σ^*.*

We are now ready to prove the main theorem of this section.

Theorem 6. *Let $I \subseteq \Sigma^*$ be an ideal language, then I is a strongly connected ideal language.*

Proof. Put $J = I^R$. Let $\mathscr{A}_J = \langle Q, \Sigma, \delta, q_0, \{s\} \rangle$ be the minimal DFA recognizing J and let μ be the map of Lemma 3 defined with respect to $\mathscr{A}_J$. We claim that the equivalence classes of the relation $\sim = (J \times J) \cap \mathrm{Ker}(\mu)$ form a reset right regular decomposition of J. By the definition of the map μ, $\mathrm{Ker}(\mu)$ has finite index, thus $\sim$ has also finite index. Since $J = \mathrm{Syn}(\mathscr{A}_J)$, for any $H \subseteq Q$ and $u \in J$ we have $H \cdot u = \{s\}$. Hence it is straightforward to check that $\tau_u = \tau_{uv}$ for any $v \in \Sigma^*$. Therefore the $\sim$-classes are right ideals and form a finite partition $\{J_i\}_{i \in F}$ of J. Furthermore, by Lemma 3, $\mathrm{Ker}(\mu)$ is a left congruences of Σ^*, and so, since J is an ideal, it is also a congruence on J, hence for any J_i and $a \in \Sigma$, we get $aJ_i \subseteq J_j$ for some $j \in F$. Thus condition i) of Definition 2 is satisfied and so $\{J_i\}_{i \in F}$ is a right regular decomposition. We claim that also condition ii) is satisfied. Assume, contrary to our claim, that there are $i \in F$ and $v \in \Sigma^* \setminus J$ such that $vJ \subseteq J_i$. Write $H = Q \cdot v$. Since $\mathrm{Syn}(\mathscr{A}_J) = J$ we get $|H| > 1$. Thus let $t = \min\{|H \cdot r| : r \in \Sigma^* \text{ and } H \cdot r \neq \{s\}\}$ and let $S \in \{H \cdot r : r \in \Sigma^* \text{ and } |H \cdot r| = t\}$. Let $x \in \Sigma^*$ such that $H \cdot x = S$ and let $u = vx$. Note that $u \in \Sigma^* \setminus J$, $uJ \subseteq J_i$ and $Q \cdot u = S$ with $|S| = t$. Since $\mathrm{Syn}(\mathscr{A}_J) = J$ and $\mathscr{A}_J$ is a synchronizing automaton with zero, then there is a synchronizing word $w \in J$ with $|w| < \frac{n^2+n}{2}+1$ where $n = |Q|$ (see [10]). Let T' be the last set of (S,w) and let w' be the maximal prefix of w such that $S \cdot w' = T'$. Thus, there is a letter $a \in \Sigma$ such that $w'a$ is a prefix of w and $|T'a| = 1$. We consider two mutually exclusive cases.

i) Suppose $|T' \cdot b| = 1$ for any $b \in \Sigma$. It is not difficult to check that $\mathcal{T}(Q, uw) = \mathcal{T}(Q, uw'a)$. Since $|\Sigma| > 1$ consider a letter $b \in \Sigma$ with $b \neq a$. Since $Q \cdot uw' = T'$ and $|T' \cdot b| = 1$, we also have $\mathcal{T}(Q, uw'bw) = \mathcal{T}(Q, uw'b)$. Since $uJ \subseteq J_i$ we have $uw, uw'bw \in J_i$ (being $w'bw \in J$). Hence we get

$$\mathcal{T}(Q, uw'a) = \mathcal{T}(Q, uw) = \mathcal{T}(Q, uw'bw) = \mathcal{T}(Q, uw'b)$$

In particular we get $\mathcal{T}(Q, uw'a)\langle \Sigma \rangle = \mathcal{T}(Q, uw'b)\langle \Sigma \rangle$, from which it follows $a = b$, a contradiction.

ii) Thus, we can assume that there is a letter $b \in \Sigma$, such that $|T' \cdot b| > 1$. Since $uw, uw'bw \in J_i$ (being $w, w'bw \in J$), we have $\mathcal{T}(Q, uw'bw) = \mathcal{T}(Q, uw)$. Hence, by Lemma 2 we have

$$\mathcal{T}(Q, uw) = \mathcal{T}(Q, uw'bw) = \mathcal{T}(Q, uw'b) \diamond \mathcal{T}(T, w)$$

with $T = T' \cdot b$. Since $|T'| = t$ is minimal and $|T| > 1$ we have $|T| = |T'| = t$, hence $\mathrm{Ind}(\mathcal{T}(Q, uw'b)) = \mathrm{Ind}(\mathcal{T}(T, w)) = t$. Therefore, by the previous equality and the definition of $\diamond$ we get

$$\mathcal{T}(Q, uw) = \mathcal{T}(Q, uw'bw) = \mathcal{T}(Q, uw'b) + \mathcal{T}(T, w)$$

In particular we have

$$\mathcal{T}(Q, uw)\langle Q \rangle = \mathcal{T}(Q, uw'bw)\langle Q \rangle = \mathcal{T}(Q, uw'b)\langle Q \rangle + \mathcal{T}(T, w)\langle Q \rangle \qquad (1)$$

Furthermore, T' is the last set of $(Q, uw'a)$ and uw' is the maximal prefix of $uw'a$ such that $T' = Q \cdot uw'$, since $|T'| = |T|$ we have that T is the last set of $(Q, uw'b)$ and $uw'b$ is the maximal prefix of $uw'b$ with $T = Q \cdot uw'b$. Thus, by the definition of tail we have $\mathcal{T}(Q, uw'a)\langle Q \rangle = \mathcal{T}(Q, uw'b)\langle Q \rangle$. We have already observed that $\mathcal{T}(Q, uw) = \mathcal{T}(Q, uw'a)$, hence by (1)

$$\mathcal{T}(T, w)\langle Q \rangle = 0 \qquad (2)$$

Let $0 = i_1 < i_2 < \ldots < i_\ell \leq |w|$ be the maximal set of indices such that $T = T \cdot w[0, i_j]$ for all $1 \leq j \leq \ell$. Therefore, by the definition of tail and (2) we have in particular

$$0 = \mathcal{T}(T, w)(T) = \ell \quad \mathrm{mod} \ \frac{n^2 + n}{2} + 1$$

Since $\ell \geq 1$ we have that ℓ is a multiple of $\frac{n^2+n}{2}+1$. However $\ell \leq |w| < \frac{n^2+n}{2}+1$, which is a contradiction.

Therefore $v \in J$ and this concludes the proof of the fact that $\{J_i\}_{i \in F}$ is a reset right regular decomposition. Hence $\{J_i^R\}_{i \in F}$ is a reset left regular decomposition and so by Theorem 3 I is a strongly connected ideal language. $\qquad \square$

Corollary 3. *Let I be an ideal language on Σ such that I^R has state complexity n. Then there is a strongly connected synchronizing automata $\mathscr{B}$ with N states and $\mathrm{Syn}(\mathscr{B}) = I$ such that:*

$$N \le m^{k2^n} \left(\sum_{t=2}^{n} m^{\binom{n}{t}} \right)^{2^n}$$

where $k = |\Sigma|$ and $m = \left(\frac{n^2+n}{2} + 1 \right)$.

This corollary shows a double exponential upper bound for the number of states of the associated strongly connected automaton with respect to the state complexity of the reverse of the ideal language. It is unknown by the authors whether this bound is tight or not. In [1], for instance, it is shown an algorithm that given a principal ideal $I = \Sigma^* w \Sigma^*$ with $|w| = n$ in inputs, it returns a strongly connected synchronizing automaton with $n + 1$ states. Therefore in this case the bound is linear with respect to the state complexity of I^R. Even more recently in this volume [2], it is proven that in case I is finitely generated there is always a strongly connected synchronizing automaton with a number of states upper bounded by $2^{\|I\|}$, and this bound is tight. Similarly to [3], where the author has introduced the notion of reset complexity of an ideal I (indicated by $\mathrm{rc}(I)$) as the number of states of the smallest synchronizing automaton $\mathscr{A}$ with $\mathrm{Syn}(\mathscr{A}) = I$, we can also give a similar notion in the realm of strongly connected synchronizing automata/reset left regular decomposition. By Theorem 6 for any ideal languages I, the set $\mathcal{R}(I)$ of all the reset left regular decompositions of I is non-empty. Thus we can define the *reset regular decomposition complexity of* I as the integer

$$\mathrm{rdc}(I) = \min\{|F| : \{I_i\}_{i \in F} \in \mathcal{R}(I)\}$$

By the correspondence introduced in Theorem 3, $\mathrm{rdc}(I)$ is also the number of states of the smallest strongly connected synchronizing automaton with the set of reset words equal to I. Furthermore $\mathrm{rc}(I) \le \mathrm{rdc}(I)$ holds. The importance of the index $\mathrm{rdc}(I)$ can be also understood by the following theorem where we present a purely language theoretic restatement of Černý's conjecture.

Theorem 7. *Černý's conjecture holds if and only if for any ideal language I we have:*

$$\mathrm{rdc}(I) \ge \sqrt{\|I\|} + 1$$

where $\|I\| = \min\{|w| : w \in I\}$.

Proof. This a consequence of the fact that Černý's conjecture holds if and only if it holds for strongly connected automata and Proposition 5. □

Note that using the well known upper bound $(n^3 - n)/6$ (see [4]) for the shortest reset word of a synchronizing automaton, we have the bound $\mathrm{rdc}(I) \ge \sqrt[3]{6\|I\|}$. In general, a natural issue would be the study of bounds for $\mathrm{rdc}(I)$ depending on the state complexity of I or I^R. As we have already observed, Corollary 3 gives an upper bound to $\mathrm{rdc}(I)$ with respect to the state complexity of I^R which is not known to be tight.

Open Problems

We list some open problems originated by the previous results. Fix an ideal language I.

1. Give a tight upper bound of $\mathrm{rdc}(I)$ with respect to the state complexity of I^R or I.
2. In case I is finitely generated is true that $\mathrm{rdc}(I) \geq \|I\|+1$? The same problem in case I is a principal ideal language has been raised in [1]. This would give a better bound for the shortest synchronizing word for the class of finitely generated synchronizing automata with respect to the bound obtained in [9].
3. The proof of Theorem 6 uses the minimal DFA recognizing I^R. Is there a proof using another automaton associated to I?
4. Recall that $\mathcal{R}(I)$ is the set of all the reset left regular decompositions of I and the order of a decomposition $\mathcal{I} \in \mathcal{R}(I)$ is just the cardinality $|\mathcal{I}|$. We denote by $\mathcal{R}_k(I)$ the set of reset left regular decompositions of I of order $k \geq 1$.
   A quite natural question is whether $\sup\{k \geq 1 : \mathcal{R}_k(I) \neq \emptyset\} = \infty$ or not? In particular, what is the case if we consider I in the class of finitely generated ideals or in the even smaller class of principal ideals? This last case answers to the question whether or not, given a principal ideal I, there can there can be an arbitrarily large strongly connected DFA $\mathscr{A}$ with $\mathrm{Syn}(\mathscr{A}) = I$.
5. By Theorem 3, a naive way to calculate $\mathcal{R}_k(I)$ can be accomplished by building all the strongly connected synchronizing automata with k states and checking if their set of reset words coincides with I. Thus, it is natural to ask whether there is a more "efficient" way to perform this task without passing from the construction of all the automata with k states.

Acknowledgments. The authors thank E. Pribavkina for pointing out the unary case alphabet in Corollary 1.

References

1. Gusev, V., Maslennikova, M., Pribavkina, E.: Principal ideal languages and synchronizing automata. In: Halava, V., Karhumaki, J., Matiyasevich, Y. (eds.) RuFiDimII. TUCS Lecture Notes, vol. 17 (2012)
2. Gusev, V.V., Maslennikova, M.I., Pribavkina, E.V.: Finitely generated ideal languages and synchronizing automata. In: Karhumäki, J., Lepistö, A., Zamboni, L. (eds.) WORDS 2013. LNCS, vol. 8079, pp. 143–153. Springer, Heidelberg (2013)
3. Maslennikova, M.: Reset complexity of ideal languages. In: Bieliková, M., Friedrich, G., Gottlob, G., Katzenbeisser, S., Špánek, R., Turán, G. (eds.) Proc. Int. Conf. SOFSEM 2012, vol. II, pp. 33–44. Institute of Computer Science Academy of Sciences of the Czech Republic (2012)
4. Pin, J.E.: On two combinatorial problems arising from automata theory. Ann. Discrete Math. 17, 535–548 (1983)

5. Pribavkina, E.V., Rodaro, E.: Finitely generated synchronizing automata. In: Dediu, A.H., Ionescu, A.M., Martín-Vide, C. (eds.) LATA 2009. LNCS, vol. 5457, pp. 672–683. Springer, Heidelberg (2009)
6. Pribavkina, E.V., Rodaro, E.: State complexity of prefix, suffix, bifix and infix operators on regular languages. In: Gao, Y., Lu, H., Seki, S., Yu, S. (eds.) DLT 2010. LNCS, vol. 6224, pp. 376–386. Springer, Heidelberg (2010)
7. Pribavkina, E.V., Rodaro, E.: Recognizing synchronizing automata with finitely many minimal synchronizing words is PSPACE-complete. In: Löwe, B., Normann, D., Soskov, I., Soskova, A. (eds.) CiE 2011. LNCS, vol. 6735, pp. 230–238. Springer, Heidelberg (2011)
8. Pribavkina, E.V., Rodaro, E.: State complexity of code operators. International Journal of Foundations of Computer Science 22(07), 1669–1681 (2011)
9. Pribavkina, E.V., Rodaro, E.: Synchronizing automata with finitely many minimal synchronizing words. Information and Computation 209(3), 568–579 (2011), http://www.sciencedirect.com/science/article/pii/S0890540110002063
10. Rystsov, I.: Reset words for commutative and solvable automata. Theoretical Computer Science 172(1-2), 273–279 (1997), http://www.sciencedirect.com/science/article/pii/S0304397596001363
11. Černý, J.: Poznámka k homogénnym eksperimentom s konečnými automatami. Mat.-Fyz. Čas. Slovensk. Akad. Vied. 14, 208–216 (1964) (in slovak)
12. Volkov, M.V.: Synchronizing automata and the Černý conjecture. In: Martín-Vide, C., Otto, F., Fernau, H. (eds.) LATA 2008. LNCS, vol. 5196, pp. 11–27. Springer, Heidelberg (2008)

Another Generalization of Abelian Equivalence: Binomial Complexity of Infinite Words

Michel Rigo[1] and Pavel Salimov[1,2,*]

[1] Dept of Math., University of Liège, Grande traverse 12 (B37),
B-4000 Liège, Belgium
M.Rigo@ulg.ac.be
[2] Sobolev Institute of Math., 4 Acad. Koptyug avenue, 630090 Novosibirsk, Russia

Abstract. The binomial coefficient of two words u and v is the number of times v occurs as a subsequence of u. Based on this classical notion, we introduce the m-binomial equivalence of two words refining the abelian equivalence. The m-binomial complexity of an infinite word x maps an integer n to the number of m-binomial equivalence classes of factors of length n occurring in x. We study the first properties of m-binomial equivalence. We compute the m-binomial complexity of the Sturmian words and of the Thue–Morse word. We also mention the possible avoidance of 2-binomial squares.

1 Introduction

In the literature, many measures of complexity of infinite words have been introduced. One of the most studied is the factor complexity p_x counting the number of distinct blocks of n consecutive letters occurring in an infinite word $x \in A^{\mathbb{N}}$. In particular, Morse–Hedlund theorem gives a characterization of ultimately periodic words in terms of bounded factor complexity. Sturmian words have a null topological entropy and are characterized by the relation $p_x(n) = n + 1$ for all $n \geqslant 0$. Abelian complexity counts the number of distinct Parikh vectors for blocks of n consecutive letters occurring in an infinite word, i.e., factors of length n are counted up to abelian equivalence. Already in 1961, Erdős opened the way to a new research direction by raising the question of avoiding abelian squares in arbitrarily long words [6]. Related to Van der Waerden theorem, we can also mention the arithmetic complexity [1] mapping $n \geqslant 0$ to the number of distinct subwords $x_i x_{i+p} \cdots x_{i+(n-1)p}$ built from n letters arranged in arithmetic progressions in the infinite word x, $i \geqslant 0$, $p \geqslant 1$. In the same direction, one can also consider maximal pattern complexity [7].

As a generalization of abelian complexity, the k-abelian complexity was recently introduced through a hierarchy of equivalence relations, the coarsest being abelian equivalence and refining up to equality. We recall these notions.

* The second author is supported by the Russian President's grant no. MK-4075.2012.1 and Russian Foundation for Basic Research grants no. 12-01-00089 and no. 11-01-00997 and by a University of Liège post-doctoral grant.

J. Karhumäki, A. Lepistö, and L. Zamboni (Eds.): WORDS 2013, LNCS 8079, pp. 217–228, 2013.

Let $k \in \mathbb{N} \cup \{+\infty\}$ and A be a finite alphabet. As usual, $|u|$ denotes the length of u and $|u|_x$ denotes the number of occurrences of the word x as a factor of the word u. Karhumäki *et al.* [8] introduce the notion of *k-abelian equivalence* of finite words as follows. Let u, v be two words over A. We write $u \sim_{ab,k} v$ if and only if $|u|_x = |v|_x$ for all words x of length $|x| \leqslant k$. In particular, $u \sim_{ab,1} v$ means that u and v are *abelian equivalent*, i.e., u is obtained by permuting the letters in v.

The aim of this paper is to introduce and study the first properties of a different family of equivalence relations over A^*, called *k-binomial equivalence*, where the coarsest relation coincide with the abelian equivalence.

Let $u = u_0 \cdots u_{n-1}$ be a word of length n over A. Let $\ell \leqslant n$. Let $t : \mathbb{N} \to \mathbb{N}$ be an increasing map such that $t(\ell - 1) < n$. Then the word $u_{t(0)} \cdots u_{t(\ell-1)}$ is a *subword* of length ℓ of u. Note that what we call subword is also called scattered subword in the literature. The notion of *binomial coefficient* of two finite words u and v is well-known, $\binom{u}{v}$ is defined as the number of times v occurs as a subword of u. In other words, the binomial coefficient of u and v is the number of times v appears as a subsequence of u. Properties of these coefficients are presented in the chapter of Lothaire's book written by Sakarovitch and Simon [12, Section 6.3]. Let $a, b \in A$, $u, v \in A^*$ and p, q be integers. We set $\delta_{a,b} = 1$ if $a = b$, and $\delta_{a,b} = 0$ otherwise. We just recall that

$$\binom{a^p}{a^q} = \binom{p}{q}, \quad \binom{u}{\varepsilon} = 1, \quad |u| < |v| \Rightarrow \binom{u}{v} = 0, \quad \binom{ua}{vb} = \binom{u}{vb} + \delta_{a,b} \binom{u}{v}$$

and the last three relations completely determine the binomial coefficient $\binom{u}{v}$ for all $u, v \in A^*$.

Remark 1. Note that we have to make a distinction between subwords and factors. A factor is a particular subword made of consecutive letters. Factors of u are denoted either by $u_i \cdots u_j$ or $u[i, j]$, $0 \leqslant i \leqslant j < |u|$.

Definition 1. *Let $m \in \mathbb{N} \cup \{+\infty\}$ and u, v be two words over A. We say that u and v are m-binomially equivalent if*

$$\binom{u}{x} = \binom{v}{x}, \quad \forall x \in A^{\leqslant m}.$$

Since the main relation studied in this paper is the m-binomial equivalence, we simply write in that case: $u \sim_m v$.

Since $\binom{u}{a} = |u|_a$ for all $a \in A$, it is clear that two words u and v are abelian equivalent if and only if $u \sim_1 v$. As for abelian equivalence, we have a family of refined relations: for all $u, v \in A^*$, $m \geqslant 0$, $u \sim_{m+1} v \Rightarrow u \sim_m v$.

Example 1. For instance, the four words $ababbba$, $abbabab$, $baabbab$ and $babaabb$ are 2-binomially equivalent. For any w amongst these words, we have the following coefficients

$$\binom{w}{a} = 3, \quad \binom{w}{b} = 4, \quad \binom{w}{aa} = 3, \quad \binom{w}{ab} = 7, \quad \binom{w}{ba} = 5, \quad \binom{w}{bb} = 6.$$

But one can check that they are not 3-binomially equivalent, as an example,

$$\binom{ababbba}{aab} = 3 \text{ but } \binom{abbabab}{aab} = 4$$

indeed, for this last binomial coefficient, aab appears as subwords $w_0 w_3 w_4$, $w_0 w_3 w_6$, $w_0 w_5 w_6$ and $w_3 w_5 w_6$. Considering again the first two words, we find $|ababbba|_{ab} = 2$ and $|abbabab|_{ab} = 3$, showing that these two words are not 2-abelian equivalent. Conversely, the words $abbaba$ and $ababba$ are 2-abelian equivalent but are not 2-binomially equivalent:

$$\binom{abbaba}{ab} = 4 \text{ but } \binom{ababba}{ab} = 5.$$

This paper is organized as follows. In the next section, we present some straightforward properties of binomial coefficients and m-binomial equivalence. In Section 3, we give upper bounds on the number of m-binomial equivalence classes partitioning A^n. Section 3 ends with the introduction of the m-binomial complexity $\mathbf{b}_x^{(m)}$ of an infinite word x. In Section 4, we prove that if x is a Sturmian word then, for any $m \geqslant 2$, $\mathbf{b}_x^{(m)}(n) = n + 1$ for all $n \geqslant 0$. In Section 5 we consider the Thue–Morse word t and show that, for all $m \geqslant 1$, there exists a constant C_m such that $\mathbf{b}_t^{(m)}(n) \leqslant C_m$ for all $n \geqslant 0$. For instance, binomial coefficients of t were considered in [3]. Due to space limitations, we only give details for the cases $m = 2, 3$. In the last section, we evoke the problem of avoiding 2-binomial squares.

2   First Properties

We denote by $\mathbf{B}^{(m)}(v)$ the equivalence class of words m-binomially equivalent to v. Binomial coefficients have a nice behavior with respect to the concatenation of words.

Proposition 1. *Let p, s and $e = e_0 e_1 \cdots e_{n-1}$ be finite words. We have*

$$\binom{ps}{e} = \sum_{i=0}^{n} \binom{p}{e_0 e_1 \cdots e_{i-1}} \binom{s}{e_i e_{i+1} \cdots e_{n-1}}.$$

We can also mention some other basic facts on m-binomial equivalence.

Lemma 1. *Let u, u', v, v' be finite words and $m \geqslant 1$.*

- *If $u \sim_m v$, then $u \sim_\ell v$ for all $\ell \leqslant m$.*
- *If $u \sim_m v$ and $u' \sim_m v'$, then $uu' \sim_m vv'$.*

Proof. Simply note for the second point that, for all $x = x_0 \cdots x_{\ell-1}$ of length $\ell \leqslant m$, $\binom{uu'}{x}$ is equal to

$$\sum_{i=0}^{\ell} \binom{u}{x[0, i-1]} \binom{u'}{x[i, \ell-1]} = \sum_{i=0}^{\ell} \binom{v}{x[0, i-1]} \binom{v'}{x[i, \ell-1]} = \binom{vv'}{x}.$$

Remark 2. Thanks to the above lemma, we can endow the quotient set $A^*/\sim_m$ with a monoid structure using an operation $\circ : A^*/\sim_m \times A^*/\sim_m \to A^*/\sim_m$ defined by $\mathbf{B}^{(m)}(p) \circ \mathbf{B}^{(m)}(q) = \mathbf{B}^{(m)}(r)$ if the concatenation $\mathbf{B}^{(m)}(p).\mathbf{B}^{(m)}(q)$ is a subset of $\mathbf{B}^{(m)}(r)$. In particular, one can take $r = pq$. If a word v is factorized as $v = pus$, then the m-equivalence class $\mathbf{B}^{(m)}(v)$ is completely determined by p, s and $\mathbf{B}^{(m)}(u)$.

3   On the Number of k-Binomial Equivalence Classes

For 2- and 3-abelian equivalence, the number of equivalence classes for words of length n over a binary alphabet are respectively $n^2 - n + 2$ and $\Theta(n^4)$. In general, for k-abelian equivalence, the number of equivalence classes for words of length n over a ℓ-letter alphabet is $\Theta(n^{(\ell-1)\ell^{k-1}})$ [8]. We consider similar results for m-binomial equivalence (proofs can be found in [15]).

Lemma 2. *Let $u \in A^*$, $a \in A$ and $\ell \geqslant 0$. We have*

$$\binom{u}{a^\ell} = \binom{|u|_a}{\ell} \quad \text{and} \quad \sum_{|v|=\ell} \binom{u}{v} = \binom{|u|}{\ell}.$$

Lemma 3. *Let A be a binary alphabet, we have*

$$\#(A^n/\sim_2) = \sum_{j=0}^{n}((n-j)j+1) = \frac{n^3 + 5n + 6}{6}.$$

Proposition 2. *Let $m \geqslant 2$. Let A be a binary alphabet, we have*

$$\#(A^n/\sim_m) \in \mathcal{O}(n^{2((m-1)2^m+1)}).$$

We denote by $\mathrm{Fac}_x(n)$ the set of factors of length n occurring in x.

Definition 2. *Let $m \geqslant 1$. The m-binomial complexity of an infinite word x counts the number of m-binomial equivalence classes of factors of length n occurring in x,*

$$\mathbf{b}_x^{(m)} : \mathbb{N} \to \mathbb{N}, \; n \mapsto \#(\mathrm{Fac}_x(n)/\sim_m).$$

Note that $\mathbf{b}_x^{(1)}$ corresponds to the usual abelian complexity denoted by ρ_x^{ab}.

If p_x denotes the usual factor complexity, then for all $m \geqslant 1$, we have

$$\mathbf{b}_x^{(m)}(n) \leqslant \mathbf{b}_x^{(m+1)}(n) \quad \text{and} \quad \rho_x^{ab}(n) \leqslant \mathbf{b}_x^{(m)}(n) \leqslant p_x(n). \tag{1}$$

4   The m-Binomial Complexity of Sturmian Words

Recall that a *Sturmian word* x is a non-periodic word of minimal (factor) complexity, that is, $p_x(n) = n + 1$ for all $n \geqslant 0$. The following characterization is also useful.

Theorem 1. *[13, Theorem 2.1.5] An infinite word $x \in \{0,1\}^\omega$ is Sturmian if and only if it is aperiodic and balanced, i.e., for all factors u, v of the same length occurring in x, we have $||u|_1 - |v|_1| \leqslant 1$.*

The aim of this section is to compute the m-binomial complexity of a Sturmian word as expressed by Theorem 2. We show that any two distinct factors of length n occurring in a Sturmian words are never m-binomially equivalent. First note that Sturmian words have a constant abelian complexity. Hence, if x is a Sturmian word, then $\mathbf{b}_x^{(1)}(n) = 2$ for all $n \geqslant 1$.

Theorem 2. *Let $m \geqslant 2$. If x is a Sturmian word, then $\mathbf{b}_x^{(m)}(n) = n + 1$ for all $n \geqslant 0$.*

Remark 3. If x is a right-infinite word such that $\mathbf{b}_x^{(1)}(n) = 2$ for all $n \geqslant 1$, then x is clearly balanced. If $\mathbf{b}_x^{(2)}(n) = n+1$, for all $n \geqslant 0$, then the factor complexity function p_x is unbounded and x is aperiodic. As a consequence of Theorem 2, an infinite word x is Sturmian if and only if, for all $n \geqslant 1$ and all $m \geqslant 2$, $\mathbf{b}_x^{(1)}(n) = 2$ and $\mathbf{b}_x^{(m)}(n) = n + 1$.

Before proceeding to the proof of Theorem 2, we first recall some well-known fact about Sturmian words. One of the two symbols occurring in a Sturmian word x over $\{0, 1\}$ is always isolated, for instance, 1 is always followed by 0. In that latter case, there exists a unique $k \geqslant 1$ such that each occurrence of 1 is always followed by either $0^k 1$ or $0^{k+1} 1$ and x is said to be of *type* 0. See for instance [14, Chapter 6]. More precisely, we have the following remarkable fact showing that the recoding of a Sturmian sequence corresponds to another Sturmian sequence. Note that $\sigma : A^\omega \to A^\omega$ is the shift operator mapping $(x_n)_{n \geqslant 0}$ to $(x_{n+1})_{n \geqslant 0}$.

Theorem 3. *Let $x \in \{0,1\}^\omega$ be a Sturmian word of type 0. There exists a unique integer $k \geqslant 1$ and a Sturmian word $y \in \{0,1\}^\omega$ such that $x = \sigma^c(\mu(y))$ for some $c \leqslant k + 1$ and where the morphism $\mu : \{0,1\}^* \to \{0,1\}^*$ is defined by $\mu(0) = 0^k 1$ and $\mu(1) = 0^{k+1} 1$.*

Corollary 1. *Let $x \in \{0,1\}^\omega$ be a Sturmian word of type 0. There exists a unique integer $k \geqslant 1$ such that any factor occurring in x is of the form*

$$0^r 10^{k+\epsilon_0} 10^{k+\epsilon_1} 1 \cdots 0^{k+\epsilon_{n-1}} 10^s \tag{2}$$

where $r, s \leqslant k + 1$ and $\epsilon_0 \epsilon_1 \cdots \epsilon_{n-1} \in \{0,1\}^*$ is a factor of the Sturmian word y introduced in the above theorem.

Let $\epsilon = \epsilon_0 \cdots \epsilon_{n-1}$ be a word over $\{0, 1\}$. For $m \leqslant n - 1$, we define

$$S(\epsilon, m) := \sum_{j=0}^{m} (n - j)\epsilon_j \quad \text{and} \quad S(\epsilon) := S(\epsilon, n - 1). \tag{3}$$

Remark 4. Let $v = 0^r 10^{k+\epsilon_0} 10^{k+\epsilon_1} 1 \cdots 0^{k+\epsilon_{n-1}} 10^s$ of the form (2), we have

$$\binom{v}{01} = r(n+1) + \sum_{j=0}^{n-1} (k + \epsilon_j)(n-j) = r(n+1) + S(\epsilon_0 \cdots \epsilon_{n-1}) + k\frac{n(n+1)}{2}.$$

We need a technical lemma on the factors of a Sturmian word.

Lemma 4. *Let $n \geqslant 1$. If u and v are two distinct factors of length n occurring in a Sturmian word over $\{0,1\}$, then $S(u) \not\equiv S(v) \pmod{n+1}$.*

Proof. Consider two distinct factors u, v of length n occurring in a Sturmian word y. For $m < n$, we define $\Delta(m) := |u_0 u_1 \cdots u_m|_1 - |v_0 v_1 \cdots v_m|_1$. Due to Theorem 3, we have $|\Delta(m)| \leqslant 1$. Note that, if there exists i such that $\Delta(i) = 1$ then, for all $j > i$, we have $\Delta(j) \geqslant 0$. Otherwise, we would have $|v[i+1,j]|_1 - |u[i+1,j]|_1 > 1$ contradicting the fact that y is balanced. Similarly, for all $j < i$, we also have $\Delta(j) \geqslant 0$.

Since u and v are distinct, replacing u with v if needed, we may assume that there exists a minimal $i \in \{0, \ldots, n-1\}$ such that $\Delta(i) = 1$. From the above discussion and the minimality of i, $\Delta(j) = 0$ for $j < i$ and $\Delta(j) \in \{0,1\}$ for $j > i$.

From (3), for any $j < n$, we have

$$\Delta(j+1) > \Delta(j) \Rightarrow S(u, j+1) - S(v, j+1) = S(u,j) - S(v,j) + (n-j)$$
$$\Delta(j+1) = \Delta(j) \Rightarrow S(u, j+1) - S(v, j+1) = S(u,j) - S(v,j)$$
$$\Delta(j+1) < \Delta(j) \Rightarrow S(u, j+1) - S(v, j+1) = S(u,j) - S(v,j) - (n-j).$$

In view of these observations, the knowledge of $\Delta(0), \Delta(1), \ldots$ permits to compute $(S(u,j) - S(v,j))_{0 \leqslant j < n}$ and we deduce that $0 < S(u) - S(v) < n+1$ concluding the proof.

Proof (Proof of Theorem 2). Let x be a Sturmian word of type 0 and $m \geqslant 2$. From (1), we have, for all $\ell \geqslant 0$,

$$\mathbf{b}_x^{(2)}(\ell) \leqslant \mathbf{b}_x^{(m)}(\ell) \leqslant p_x(\ell) = \ell + 1.$$

We just need to show that any two distinct factors of length ℓ in x are not 2-binomially equivalent, i.e., $\ell + 1 \leqslant \mathbf{b}_x^{(2)}(\ell)$.

Proceed by contradiction. Assume that x contains two distinct factors u and v that are 2-binomially equivalent. In particular, $\binom{u}{00} = \binom{v}{00}$ and $\binom{u}{11} = \binom{v}{11}$. Hence we get $|u| = |v|$ and $|u|_1 = |v|_1 = n$. From Corollary 1, there exist $k \geqslant 1$ and a Sturmian word y such that

$$u = 0^r 10^{k+\epsilon_0} 10^{k+\epsilon_1} 1 \cdots 0^{k+\epsilon_{n-1}} 10^s, \quad v = 0^{r'} 10^{k+\epsilon'_0} 10^{k+\epsilon'_1} 1 \cdots 0^{k+\epsilon'_{n-1}} 10^{s'}$$

where $\epsilon = \epsilon_0 \epsilon_1 \cdots \epsilon_{n-1}$ and $\epsilon' = \epsilon'_0 \epsilon'_1 \cdots \epsilon'_{n-1}$ are both factors of y.

Since $u \sim_2 v$, it follows $\binom{u}{01} = \binom{v}{01}$. From Remark 4, we get

$$r(n+1) + S(\epsilon) + k\frac{n(n+1)}{2} = r'(n+1) + S(\epsilon') + k\frac{n(n+1)}{2}.$$

Otherwise stated, we get $S(\epsilon) - S(\epsilon') = (r'-r)(n+1)$ contradicting the previous lemma.

5   The Case of the Thue–Morse Word

The *Thue–Morse* word $t = 0110100110010110100101100110 \cdots$ is the infinite word $\lim_{n \to \infty} \varphi^n(a)$ where $\varphi : 0 \mapsto 01$, $1 \mapsto 10$. The factor complexity of the Thue–Morse word is well-known [2,5]: $p_t(0) = 1$, $p_t(1) = 2$, $p_t(2) = 4$ and

$$p_t(n) = \begin{cases} 4n - 2 \cdot 2^m - 4 & \text{if } 2 \cdot 2^m < n \leqslant 3 \cdot 2^m \\ 2n + 4 \cdot 2^m - 2 & \text{if } 3 \cdot 2^m < n \leqslant 4 \cdot 2^m \end{cases}$$

and the abelian complexity of t is obvious.

Lemma 5. *We have* $\mathbf{b}_t^{(1)}(2n) = 3$ *and* $\mathbf{b}_t^{(1)}(2n+1) = 2$ *for all* $n \geqslant 1$.

The main result of this section is the following one. It is quite in contrast with the Sturmian case because here, the Thue–Morse word exhibits a bounded m-binomial complexity.

Theorem 4. *Let* $m \geqslant 2$. *There exists* $C_m > 0$ *such that the m-binomial complexity of the Thue–Morse word satisfies* $\mathbf{b}_t^{(m)}(n) \leqslant C_m$ *for all* $n \geqslant 0$.

For the sake of presentation, we first show that the 2-binomial complexity of the Thue–Morse word is bounded by a constant.

Theorem 5. *There exists* $C_2 > 0$ *such that the 2-binomial complexity of the Thue–Morse word satisfies* $\mathbf{b}_t^{(2)}(n) \leqslant C_2$ *for all* $n \geqslant 0$.

Proof. Any factor v of t admits a factorization of the kind $p\varphi(u)s$ with $p, s \in \{0, 1, \varepsilon\}$ and where u is a factor of t. Using Remark 2, it is therefore enough to prove that, for all n,

$$\#\{\mathbf{B}^{(2)}(v) \mid \exists u \in \mathrm{Fac}_t(n) : v = \varphi(u)\} \leqslant 9. \tag{4}$$

Recall from the proof of Lemma 3 that the 2-binomial equivalence class of a word v of length $2n$ over a binary alphabet $\{0, 1\}$ is completely determined by its length, $|v|_0$ and $\binom{v}{01}$, i.e.,

$$\#\{\mathbf{B}^{(2)}(v) \mid \exists u \in \mathrm{Fac}_t(n) : v = \varphi(u)\}$$
$$= \#\{(\binom{v}{0}, \binom{v}{1}, \binom{v}{00}, \binom{v}{01}, \binom{v}{10}, \binom{v}{11}) \mid \exists u \in \mathrm{Fac}_t(n) : v = \varphi(u)\}$$
$$= \#\{(|v|_0, \binom{v}{01}) \mid \exists u \in \mathrm{Fac}_t(n) : v = \varphi(u)\}.$$

Fix $n \geqslant 1$. Consider an arbitrary factor $u = u_0 \cdots u_{n-1} \in \mathrm{Fac}_t(n)$ and the corresponding factor $v = \varphi(u) = v_0 \cdots v_{2n-1}$ of t of length $2n$. From Lemma 5, $|v|_0$ takes at most three values (depending on n).

Let us compute the possible values taken by the coefficient $\binom{v}{01}$. Consider an occurrence of 01 as a subword of v, i.e., a pair (i, j), $i < j \leqslant n - 1$, such that $v_i v_j = 01$. There are two possible cases:

- If $i = 2m$ and $j = 2m+1$, for some $m \geqslant 0$, then $u_m = 0$ because $v_{2m}v_{2m+1} = \varphi(u_m)$. There are $|u|_0$ such occurrences.
- Otherwise, we have $i \in \{2m, 2m + 1\}$, $j \in \{2m', 2m' + 1\}$ with $m' > m$. For all m (resp. m'), exactly one letter of the factor $v_{2m}v_{2m+1} = \varphi(u_m)$ (resp. $v_{2m'}v_{2m'+1} = \varphi(u'_m)$) is 0 and the other one is 1. Hence, for any $i \in \{0, \ldots, n-2\}$, j can take a value of the $n-1-i$ values in $\{i+1, \ldots, n-1\}$.

Summarizing these two cases, we have

$$\binom{v}{01} = |u|_0 + \sum_{i=0}^{n-2}(n - 1 - i) = |u|_0 + \frac{n(n - 1)}{2}.$$

From Lemma 5, $|u|_0$ takes at most three values (depending on n) and therefore the same holds for $\binom{v}{01}$. Hence, the conclusion follows.

We now extend the proof of Theorem 5. The first part is to generalize (4).

Lemma 6. *Let $m, k \geqslant 1$. Assume that there exists D such that, for all n,*

$$\#\{\mathbf{B}^{(m)}(v) \mid \exists u \in \mathrm{Fac}_t(n) : v = \varphi^k(u)\} \leqslant D.$$

Then the m-binomial complexity of the Thue–Morse word $\mathbf{b}_t^{(m)}$ is bounded by a constant.

Proof. Let $\ell \geqslant 1$. Let f be a factor of t of length ℓ. This factor is of the form[1] pvs where p (resp. s) is a proper suffix (resp. prefix) of some $\varphi^k(a)$ (resp. $\varphi^k(b)$) where a, b are letters and $v = \varphi^k(u)$ for some factor u of t of length n. In particular, we have $|p|, |q| \leqslant 2^k - 1$. Note that ℓ is of the form $n \cdot 2^k + r$ with $0 \leqslant r \leqslant 2(2^k - 1)$. Hence, for a given f of length ℓ, the corresponding integer n can take at most 2 values which are $\lfloor \ell/2^k \rfloor - 1$ and $\lfloor \ell/2^k \rfloor$. From the assumption, we get

$$\#\{\mathbf{B}^{(m)}(v) \mid \exists u \in \mathrm{Fac}_t(\lfloor \ell/2^k \rfloor - 1) \cup \mathrm{Fac}_t(\lfloor \ell/2^k \rfloor) : v = \varphi^k(u)\} \leqslant 2D.$$

Finally, using Remark 2, we have $\mathbf{B}^{(m)}(f) = \mathbf{B}^{(m)}(p) \circ \mathbf{B}^{(m)}(v) \circ \mathbf{B}^{(m)}(s)$. Since p and s have bounded length, $\mathbf{B}^{(m)}(p)$ and $\mathbf{B}^{(m)}(s)$ take a bounded number of values. Moreover, $\mathbf{B}^{(m)}(v)$ takes at most $2D$ values, hence $\mathbf{b}_t^{(m)}$ is bounded by constant.

From now on, intervals $[r, s]$ (resp. $[r, s)$) will be considered as intervals of integers, i.e., one should understand $[r, s] \cap \mathbb{Z}$ (resp. $[r, s) \cap \mathbb{Z}$).

Aside from the idea of dealing with words of a convenient form, the second key idea of the proof of Theorem 5 is to split the set of occurrences of the subword 01 into two disjoint subsets facilitating the counting. We shall now generalize this idea for m-binomial complexity but some terminology is required. Let v be a word. A subset $T = \{t_1 < t_2 < \ldots < t_n\} \subseteq [0, |v|)$ defines a subword denoted by $v_T = v_{t_1} v_{t_2} \cdots v_{t_n}$.

---

[1] This is the idea of "de-substitution" where t is factorized into consecutive factors of length 2^k.

Definition 3. *If $\alpha_1, \ldots, \alpha_m$ are non-empty and pairwise disjoint subsets of a set X such that $\cup_i \alpha_i = X$, then $\alpha = \{\alpha_1, \ldots, \alpha_m\}$ is a partition of X. Any partition α of a set X is a refinement of a partition β of X if every element of α is a subset of some element of β. In that case, α is said to be finer than β (equivalently β is coarser than α) and we write $\alpha \preceq \beta$. Since $\preceq$ is a partial order, we define a chain as a subset of partitions $\beta^{(1)}, \beta^{(2)}, \ldots$ of X satisfying*

$$\beta^{(1)} \preceq \beta^{(2)} \preceq \cdots .$$

A k-partition $\alpha = \{\alpha_1, \ldots, \alpha_m\}$ of the set $[0, mk)$ is a partition into subsets $\alpha_i = [(i-1)k, ik)$ of size k. In particular, a 2^i-partition is a refinement of a 2^j-partition of $[0, 2^k)$, $i < j \leqslant k$.

Definition 4. *Let X be a set and $T = \{t_1 < t_2 < \ldots < t_n\}$ be a subset of X. A partition $\alpha = \{\alpha_1, \ldots, \alpha_m\}$ of X induces a partition $\alpha_T = \{\gamma_1, \ldots, \gamma_r\}$ of $[1, n]$ defined by*

$$i, j \in \gamma_t \Leftrightarrow \exists s : t_i, t_j \in \alpha_s.$$

Note that for two partitions α, β of X, if $\alpha \preceq \beta$, then $\alpha_T \preceq \beta_T$.

Example 2. Take $X = [0, 7]$ and $T = \{0, 2, 3, 5\}$. Consider the following two partitions of X: $\alpha = \{\{0, 1\}, \{2, 3, 4\}, \{5, 6, 7\}\}$ and $\beta = \{\{0, 1, 2\}, \{3, 4, 5\}, \{6, 7\}\}$. We get $\alpha_T = \{\{1\}, \{2, 3\}, \{4\}\}$ and $\beta_T = \{\{1, 2\}, \{3, 4\}\}$.

Definition 5. *Let $T = \{t_1 < t_2 < \ldots < t_n\}$ and $U = \{u_1 < u_2 < \ldots < u_n\}$ be subsets of X. These subsets are equidistributed with respect to a partition α of X if $\alpha_T = \alpha_U$. These subsets are equidistributed with respect to a chain $\mathfrak{C}$ of partitions of X if $\alpha_T = \alpha_U$ for all $\alpha \in \mathfrak{C}$. We also say that the subsets are $\mathfrak{C}$-equidistributed.*

Example 3. Consider the chain $\mathfrak{C}$ consisting of the 4-partition $\beta = \{[0, 3], [4, 7]\}$ and the 2-partition $\alpha = \{[0, 1], [2, 3], [4, 5], [6, 7]\}$ of the set $[0, 7]$. The subsets $T = \{0, 5\}$, $U = \{1, 2\}$ and $V = \{3, 4\}$ are equidistributed with respect to the 2-partition ($\alpha_T = \alpha_U = \alpha_V = \{\{1\}, \{2\}\}$), but U is not $\mathfrak{C}$-equidistributed to T (resp. V) because $\beta_T = \beta_V = \{\{1\}, \{2\}\}$ and $\beta_U = \{\{1, 2\}\}$.

Example 4. In the last part of the proof of Theorem 5, we have considered the two possible cases for an occurrence of the subword 01 in v. If $T = \{i, j\}$ is a subset of $[0, |v|)$ and α is the 2-partition of $[0, |v|)$, then these cases correspond exactly to the two possible values $\alpha_T = \{1, 2\}$ or $\alpha_T = \{\{1\}, \{2\}\}$.

Let $\mathfrak{C}$ be a chain $\beta^{(1)} \preceq \beta^{(2)} \preceq \cdots$ of partitions of X and $T = \{t_1, \ldots, t_n\}$ be a subset of X. We use nested brackets to represent the induced chain $\beta_T^{(1)} \preceq \beta_T^{(2)} \preceq \cdots$ of partitions of $[1, n]$. The outer (resp. inner) brackets represent the coarsest (resp. finest) partition of $[1, n]$. As an example $[[t_1 t_2]][[t_3][t_4]]$ represents the partition $\{\{1, 2\}, \{3\}, \{4\}\}$ and the coarser partition $\{\{1, 2\}, \{3, 4\}\}$. To get used to these new definitions, we consider another particular statement. (A precise and formal definition of the bracket notation is given in [15].)

Remark 5. Two subsets T and U of size n of X are equidistributed with respect to a chain $\mathfrak{C}$ of partitions of X if and only if they give rise to the same notation of nested brackets. We call it the *type* of T with respect to $\mathfrak{C}$.

Example 5 (continuing Example 3). Consider the subsets $R = \{0, 1, 4, 7\}$ and $S = \{2, 3, 4, 6\}$ of $[0, 7]$. We have $\alpha_R = \alpha_S = \{\{1, 2\}, \{3\}, \{4\}\}$ and $\beta_R = \beta_S = \{\{1, 2\}, \{3, 4\}\}$. Hence R and S are $\mathfrak{C}$-equidistributed and give both rise to the notation $[[t_1 t_2]][[t_3][t_4]]$.

We prove the case of the 3-binomial complexity. The proof of the general case has been treated in [15].

Theorem 6. *There exists $C_3 > 0$ such that the 3-binomial complexity of the Thue–Morse word satisfies $\mathbf{b}_t^{(3)}(n) \leqslant C_3$ for all $n \geqslant 0$.*

Proof. In view of Lemma 6, it is enough to show that there exists a constant D such that, for all n, we have $\#\{\mathbf{B}^{(3)}(v) \mid \exists u \in \mathrm{Fac}_t(n) : v = \varphi^2(u)\} \leqslant D$.

Let $n \geqslant 1$. Let $v = \varphi^2(u)$ with $u \in \mathrm{Fac}_t(n)$. In particular, $|v| = 4n$. Consider the chain $\mathfrak{C}$ consisting of the 2-partition and the 4-partition of $[0, 4n)$. Any subset $T = \{t_1 < t_2 < t_3\}$ of $[0, 4n)$ is $\mathfrak{C}$-equidistributed to a subset of one the following types:

- $[t_1][t_2][t_3]$, i.e., the union of the types $[[t_1]][[t_2]][[t_3]]$, $[[t_1][t_2]][[t_3]]$ and $[[t_1]][[t_2][t_3]]$: the 3 elements of T belong to pairwise distinct subsets of the 2-partition of $[0, 4n)$
- $[[t_1 t_2][t_3]]$ or $[[t_1][t_2 t_3]]$: two elements belong to the same subset of the 2-partition of $[0, 4n)$ and the 3 elements of T belong to the same subset of the 4-partition of $[0, 4n)$.
- $[[t_1 t_2]][[t_3]]$ or $[[t_1]][[t_2 t_3]]$: two elements belong to the same subset of the 2-partition and to the same subset of the 4-partition of $[0, 4n)$.

Let $e = e_0 e_1 e_2$ be a word of length 3. We will count the number of occurrences of the subword $e = v_{t_1} v_{t_2} v_{t_3}$ in v depending on the type of $T = \{t_1, t_2, t_3\}$ with respect to $\mathfrak{C}$.

Assume that the type of T is $[t_1][t_2][t_3]$. Each subset S of the 2-partition of $[0, 4n)$ corresponds to a factor $v_S = 01$ or $v_S = 10$ and v contains $2n$ such factors. Hence the number of subwords e occurring in v for this type takes, for a given n, a unique value which is $\binom{2n}{3}$.

Now assume that the type of T is $[[t_1 t_2][t_3]]$ (similar arguments apply to $[[t_1][t_2 t_3]]$). Each subset S of the 4-partition of $[0, 4n)$ corresponds to a factor v_S which is either $\varphi^2(0) = 0110$ or $\varphi^2(1) = 1001$. Then the number of subwords e occurring in v of this type is

$$\underbrace{\binom{01}{e_0 e_1}}_{0 \text{ or } 1} \underbrace{\binom{10}{e_2}}_{1} |u|_0 + \underbrace{\binom{10}{e_0 e_1}}_{0 \text{ or } 1} \underbrace{\binom{01}{e_2}}_{1} |u|_1 \in \{0, |u|_0, |u|_1\}.$$

Recall that, for a given $n = |u|$, the pair $(|u|_0, |u|_1)$ can take at most three values (see Lemma 5). The number of subwords e occurring in v of this type takes, for a given n, takes at most 4 values[2].

Now assume that the type of T is $[[t_1 t_2]][[t_3]]$ (similar arguments apply to $[[t_1]][[t_2 t_3]]$). Each subset S of the 4-partition of $[0, 4n)$ is a union of two sets S', S'' of the 2-partition of $[0, 4n)$ and we have either $v_{S'} = 01, v_{S''} = 10$ or $v_{S'} = 10, v_{S''} = 01$. They are n subsets of size 4 in the 4-partition of $[0, 4n)$ and we have to pick 2 of them. Hence, the number of subwords e occurring in v for this type is

$$\left(\underbrace{\binom{01}{e_0 e_1} + \binom{10}{e_0 e_1}}_{0 \text{ or } 1} \right) \left(\underbrace{\binom{01}{e_2} + \binom{10}{e_2}}_{2} \right) \binom{n}{2}$$

and this quantity, for a given n, takes at most 2 values.

We have proved that, for all $|e| = 3$ and $v = \varphi^2(u)$ with $u \in \mathrm{Fac}_t(n)$, $\binom{v}{e}$ takes at most $1 + 2 \cdot 4 + 2 \cdot 2 = 13$ values (these values depend on n, but the *number* of values is bounded without any dependence to n). Note that $\mathbf{B}^{(3)}(v)$ is determined from $\mathbf{B}^{(2)}(v)$ and by the values of $\binom{v}{e}$ for the words e of length 3. To conclude the proof, note that $\#\{\mathbf{B}^{(2)}(v) \mid \exists u \in \mathrm{Fac}_t(n) : v = \varphi^2(u)\}$ is bounded by $\#\{\mathbf{B}^{(2)}(v) \mid \exists z \in \mathrm{Fac}_t(2n) : v = \varphi(z)\} \leqslant 9$ using (4). Consequently, we have shown that $\#\{\mathbf{B}^{(3)}(v) \mid \exists u \in \mathrm{Fac}_t(n) : v = \varphi^2(u)\} \leqslant 9 \cdot 13^8$ for all $n \geqslant 1$.

Remark 6. By computer experiments, $\mathbf{b}_t^{(2)}(n)$ is equal to 9 if $n \equiv 0 \pmod 4$ and to 8 otherwise, for $10 \leqslant n \leqslant 1000$. Moreover, $\mathbf{b}_t^{(3)}(n)$ is equal to 21 if $n \equiv 0 \pmod 8$ and to 20 otherwise, for $8 \leqslant n \leqslant 500$.

6   A Glimpse at Avoidance

It is obvious that, over a 2-letter alphabet, any word of length $\geqslant 4$ contains a square. On the other hand, there exist square-free infinite ternary words [12]. In the same way, over a 3-letter alphabet, any word of length $\geqslant 8$ contains an abelian square, i.e., a word uu' where $u \sim_1 u'$. But, over a 4-letter alphabet, abelian squares are avoidable, see for instance [10]. So a first natural question in that direction is to determine, whether or not, over a 3-letter alphabet 2-binomial squares can be avoided in arbitrarily long words. Naturally, a 2-*binomial square* is a word of the form uu' where $u \sim_2 u'$. Note that, for abelian equivalence, the longest ternary word which is 2-abelian square-free has length 537 [9].

As an example, $u = 121321231213123132123121312$ is a word of length 27 without 2-binomial squares but this word cannot be extended without getting a 2-binomial square. Indeed, $u1$ (resp. $u3$) ends with a square of length 8 (resp. 26).

Consider the 13-uniform morphism of Leech [11] which is well-known to be square-free, $g : a \mapsto abcbacbcabcba, b \mapsto bcacbacabcacb, c \mapsto cabacbabcabac$.

---

[2] A close inspection shows that if $|u| = 2n$, then $|u|_0, |u|_1 \in \{n - 1, n, n + 1\}$, if $|u| = 2n + 1$, then $|u|_0, |u|_1 \in \{n, n + 1\}$.

In the submitted version of this paper, we conjectured that the infinite square-free word $g^\omega(1)$ avoids 2-binomial squares. For instance, we can prove that

$$u \sim_2 v \Leftrightarrow g(u) \sim_2 g(v).$$

Nevertheless, M. Bennett has recently shown that the factor of length 508 occurring in position 845 is a 2-binomial square [4].

Acknowledgments. The idea of this binomial equivalence came after the meeting "Representing streams" organized at the Lorentz center in December 2012 where Jean-Eric Pin presented a talk, *Noncommutative extension of Mahlers theorem on interpolation series*, involving binomial coefficients on words. Jean-Eric Pin and the first author proposed independently to introduce this new relation.

References

1. Avgustinovich, S.V., Fon-Der-Flaass, D.G., Frid, A.E.: Arithmetical complexity of infinite words. In: Ito, M., Imaoka, T. (eds.) Words, Languages & Combinatorics III, pp. 51–62. World Scientific Publishing (2003)
2. Brlek, S.: Enumeration of factors in the Thue-Morse word. Discrete Appl. Math. 24, 83–96 (1989)
3. Berstel, J., Crochemore, M., Pin, J.-E.: Thue–Morse sequence and p-adic topology for the free monoid. Disc. Math. 76, 89–94 (1989)
4. Currie, J.: Personal communication (June 3, 2013)
5. de Luca, A., Varricchio, S.: On the factors of the Thue-Morse word on three symbols. Inform. Process. Lett. 27, 281–285 (1988)
6. Erdős, P.: Some unsolved problems. Magyar Tud. Akad. Mat. Kutató Int. Közl. 6, 221–254 (1961)
7. Kamae, T., Zamboni, L.: Sequence entropy and the maximal pattern complexity of infinite words. Ergodic Theory Dynam. Systems 22, 1191–1199 (2002)
8. Karhumäki, J., Saarela, A., Zamboni, L.Q.: On a generalization of Abelian equivalence and complexity of infinite words, arXiv:1301.5104
9. Huova, M., Karhumäki, J.: Observations and problems on k-abelian avoidability. In: Combinatorial and Algorithmic Aspects of Sequence Processing (Dagstuhl Seminar 11081), pp. 2215–2219 (2011)
10. Keränen, V.: Abelian squares are avoidable on 4 letters. In: Kuich, W. (ed.) ICALP 1992. LNCS, vol. 623, pp. 41–52. Springer, Heidelberg (1992)
11. Leech, J.: A problem on strings of beads. Math. Gazette 41, 277–278 (1957)
12. Lothaire, M.: Combinatorics on Words. Cambridge Mathematical Library. Cambridge University Press (1997)
13. Lothaire, M.: Algebraic Combinatorics on Words. Encyclopedia of Mathematics and its Applications, vol. 90. Cambridge University Press (2002)
14. Pytheas Fogg, N., Berthé, V., Ferenczi, S., Mauduit, C., Siegel, A. (eds.): Substitutions in dynamics, arithmetics and combinatorics. Lecture Notes in Mathematics, vol. 1794. Springer, Berlin (2002)
15. Rigo, M., Salimov, P.: Another Generalization of Abelian Equivalence: Binomial Complexity of Infinite Words (long version) (preprint, 2013), http://hdl.handle.net/2268/149313

Weakly Unambiguous Morphisms
with Respect to Sets of Patterns with Constants

Aleksi Saarela*

Department of Mathematics and Statistics
University of Turku, FI-20014 Turku, Finland
amsaar@utu.fi

Abstract. A non-erasing morphism is weakly unambiguous with respect to a pattern if no other non-erasing morphism maps the pattern to the same image. If the size of the target alphabet is at least three, then the patterns for which there exists a length-increasing weakly unambiguous morphism can be characterized using the concept of loyal neighbors of variables. In this article this characterization is generalized for patterns with constants. Two different generalizations are given for sets of patterns.

1 Introduction

Many fundamental topics of combinatorics on words are defined in terms of morphisms. One example is equality sets and the Post Correspondence Problem: Given two morphisms f and g, does there exist a non-empty word w such that $f(w) = g(w)$. Another example is given by word equations: A solution of a word equation $u = v$ is a morphism h such that $h(u) = h(v)$. For more on these and several other topics related to morphisms, see [5]. Also the theory of codes is concerned with morphisms [1], as is the theory of pattern languages [7].

This central role of morphisms in combinatorics on words means that it is important to understand the behavior of morphisms. For example, this might lead to the study of fixed points of morphisms, see e.g [6] and [11], or to the concept of unambiguity of morphisms, which is the topic of this paper.

A morphism is said to be unambiguous with respect to a pattern (or a word) if no other morphism maps the pattern to the same image. Unambiguity of morphisms was introduced by Freydenberger, Reidenbach and Schneider [4]. Two questions that have been studied in many papers [4,3,10,9] are:

- For which patterns does there exist an unambiguous morphism?
- For which patterns does there exist a non-erasing unambiguous morphism?

Unambiguity is closely related to pattern languages, see e.g [8].

Many variations of unambiguity of morphisms exist. For example, it is possible to study unambiguity in the free semigroup, that is, assume that all morphism

---

* Supported by the Academy of Finland under grant 257857.

J. Karhumäki, A. Lepistö, and L. Zamboni (Eds.): WORDS 2013, LNCS 8079, pp. 229–237, 2013.

are non-erasing. This leads to the definition of weakly unambiguous morphisms:
A non-erasing morphism is said to be weakly unambiguous with respect to a
pattern if no other non-erasing morphism maps the pattern to the same image.
Trivially, every 1-uniform morphism is weakly unambiguous with respect to every
pattern, so the interesting question in this case is the following:

- For which patterns does there exist a non-erasing length-increasing weakly
  unambiguous morphism?

This question was studied by Freydenberger, Nevisi and Reidenbach [2]. Questions on unambiguity of morphisms often lead to complicated technical considerations, but the results on weakly unambiguous morphisms are relatively elegant.
If the target alphabet is unary, then the question is quite simple, although not
trivial. If the size of the target alphabet is at least three, then a characterization
can be obtained by using so called loyal neighbors of variables. The binary case
is complicated and only partial results are known.

In many questions about morphism, there can be constants (or terminal symbols), i.e. letters which must be mapped to themselves. For example, constants
are often used in the theory of pattern languages. However, unambiguity has
mostly been studied from the point of view of constant-free patterns. In this
article weak unambiguity is studied for patterns with constants. We concentrate
on the case of target alphabets with at least three letters. If the definition of loyal
neighbors of variables is extended for patterns with constants in the right way,
then also the characterization from [2] can be extended quite straightforwardly.

As another generalization, weak unambiguity with respect to several patterns
is studied in this paper. If the patterns are constant-free, then a characterization that is similar to the one in [2] can be found easily. However, if the two
generalizations are studied at the same time, that is there are many patterns
with constants, then the situation is more complicated. The same characterization works only if the size of the target alphabet is at least two more than the
number of patterns.

There is also another way to generalize unambiguity for sets of patterns.
Instead of considering every pattern separately, they can be treated, in a sense,
as a single pattern. Weak unambiguity and loyal neighbors can then be defined
for sets of patterns and an analogous characterization can be proved.

Although this paper concentrates on weakly unambiguous morphisms, and
only on the case of ternary or larger alphabets, it seems likely that unambiguity
with respect to patterns with constants and with respect to multiple patterns
could be studied also more generally.

2   Patterns with Constants

Let Σ be an alphabet of *constants* and Ξ an alphabet of *variables*. A word
$\alpha \in (\Xi \cup \Sigma)^+$ is called a *pattern*. If $\alpha \in \Xi^*$, then α is *constant-free*. If Γ is the
set of those variables that appear in α, then α is a Γ-*pattern*.

The *empty word* is denoted by ε, the length of a word w by $|w|$, and the
number of occurrences of a letter a in w by $|w|_a$.

A *morphism* is a mapping $h : (\Xi \cup \Sigma)^* \to \Sigma^*$ such that $h(\alpha\beta) = h(\alpha)h(\beta)$ for all $\alpha, \beta \in (\Xi \cup \Sigma)^*$ and $h(a) = a$ for all $a \in \Sigma$. Thus all morphisms are assumed to be constant-preserving. A morphism h is *non-erasing* if $h(x) \neq \varepsilon$ for all $x \in \Xi$. A non-erasing morphism h is *Γ-increasing* if $|h(x)| \geq 2$ for some $x \in \Gamma$. Two morphisms h and g are *Γ-equivalent* if $h(x) = g(x)$ for all $x \in \Gamma$. This is denoted by $h \sim_\Gamma g$, and non-equivalence is denoted by $h \nsim_\Gamma g$

Let α be a Γ-pattern. A non-erasing morphism h is *weakly unambiguous with respect to α* if there is no non-erasing morphism $g \nsim_\Gamma h$ such that $h(\alpha) = g(\alpha)$. It is easy to see that if h is not Γ-increasing, then h is weakly unambiguous with respect to every Γ-pattern. Thus we study the following question: Given a Γ-pattern α, does there exist a Γ-increasing morphism that is weakly unambiguous with respect to α?

Example 1. Let $\Xi = \{x, y\}$ and $\Sigma = \{a, b\}$. Consider the pattern xay. The morphism defined by $x \mapsto a, y \mapsto ba$ is weakly unambiguous with respect to xay, because no other non-erasing morphism maps xay to $aaba$. The morphism defined by $x \mapsto a, y \mapsto ab$ is not weakly unambiguous with respect to xay, because also the morphism defined by $x \mapsto aa, y \mapsto b$ maps xay to $aaab$.

If the alphabet Σ is unary, say $\Sigma = \{a\}$, then the addition of constants in patterns is not very interesting. Let $\alpha \in (\Xi \cup \{a\})^+$ and let α' be the pattern obtained from α by removing every occurrence of a. For all morphisms h and g, $h(\alpha) = g(\alpha)$ if and only if $h(\alpha') = g(\alpha')$. Thus h is weakly unambiguous with respect to α if and only if it is weakly unambiguous with respect to the constant-free pattern α' and the result in [2] can be used directly.

If the alphabet Σ is binary, then only partial results are known on weak unambiguity of morphisms with respect to constant-free patterns. In this article we concentrate on the case where Σ has at least three letters, since this case is well-understood for constant-free patterns.

Let $\alpha = a_0 a_1 \ldots a_n a_{n+1}$, where $a_0 = a_{n+1} = \varepsilon$ and $a_1, \ldots, a_n \in \Xi \cup \Sigma$. The set of *left neighbors of x in α* is

$$L_\alpha(x) = \{a_i \mid 0 \leq i \leq n, a_{i+1} = x\},$$

and the set of *right neighbors of x in α* is

$$R_\alpha(x) = \{a_i \mid 1 \leq i \leq n+1, a_{i-1} = x\}.$$

Both $L_\alpha(x)$ and $R_\alpha(x)$ are subsets of $\Xi \cup \Sigma \cup \{\varepsilon\}$.

It was defined in [2] that if α is a constant-free pattern, then a variable x has *loyal neighbors in α* if at least one of the following two conditions is satisfied:

$$\varepsilon \notin L_\alpha(x) \text{ and } R_\alpha(y) = \{x\} \text{ for all } y \in L_\alpha(x),$$
$$\varepsilon \notin R_\alpha(x) \text{ and } L_\alpha(y) = \{x\} \text{ for all } y \in R_\alpha(x).$$

This definition must be generalized for patterns with constants. This is done by treating the constants in the same way as the beginning and end of the pattern (or in the same way as ε in $L_\alpha(x)$ and $R_\alpha(x)$). So, given a pattern α with constants, a variable x has *loyal neighbors in* α if at least one of the following two conditions is satisfied:

$$L_\alpha(x) \subseteq \Xi \text{ and } R_\alpha(y) = \{x\} \text{ for all } y \in L_\alpha(x), \tag{1}$$
$$R_\alpha(x) \subseteq \Xi \text{ and } L_\alpha(y) = \{x\} \text{ for all } y \in R_\alpha(x). \tag{2}$$

Theorem 6 justifies that this is the right definition.

Example 2. Let $\Xi = \{x, y, z, t\}$, $\Sigma = \{a\}$, and $\alpha = xayzyt$. The variable y has loyal neighbors in α because $R_\alpha(y) = \{z, t\}$ and $L_\alpha(z) = L_\alpha(t) = \{y\}$. The other variables do not have loyal neighbors in α:

- x does not, because $\varepsilon \in L_\alpha(x)$ and $a \in R_\alpha(x)$.
- z does not, because $L_\alpha(z) = \{y\}$ but $R_\alpha(y) \neq \{x\}$, and $R_\alpha(z) = \{y\}$ but $L_\alpha(y) \neq \{x\}$.
- t does not, because $L_\alpha(t) = \{y\}$ but $R_\alpha(y) \neq \{t\}$, and $\varepsilon \in R_\alpha(t)$.

Next we will characterize, in the case $\#\Sigma \geq 3$, those Γ-patterns with respect to which there exists a Γ-increasing weakly unambiguous morphism. There are many similarities between the proofs here and the proofs in [2]. The proofs are self-contained, so we do not need to refer to any previous results.

Lemma 3. *Let* $u_1, \ldots, u_n, v_1, \ldots, v_n \in \Sigma^*$. *If* $u_1 \ldots u_n$ *is a factor of* $v_1 \ldots v_n$, *then either* $u_i = v_i$ *for all* i *or* u_i *is a proper factor of* v_i *for some* i.

Proof. Let $v_1 \ldots v_n = u_0 u_1 \ldots u_n u_{n+1}$ and consider the numbers

$$k_i = |v_1 \ldots v_i| - |u_0 \ldots u_i|$$

for $i \in \{0, \ldots, n\}$.

If $k_i = 0$ for all i, then $u_i = v_i$ for all i.

If $k_i < 0$ for some i, then let j be the largest index such that $k_j < 0$. Because $k_n \geq 0$, it must be $j < n$, and $k_{j+1} \geq 0$. This means that u_{j+1} is a proper factor of v_{j+1}.

If $k_i > 0$ for some i, then let j be the smallest index such that $k_j > 0$. Because $k_0 \leq 0$, it must be $j > 0$, and $k_{j-1} \leq 0$. This means that u_j is a proper factor of v_j. □

Lemma 4. *Let* α *be a* Γ-pattern *and* h *a non-erasing morphism. If there is* $x \in \Gamma$ *such that* $|h(x)| > 1$ *and* x *has loyal neighbors in* α, *then* h *is not weakly unambiguous with respect to* α.

Proof. Assume that (1) is satisfied for x (the case where (2) is satisfied is symmetric). It must be $x \notin L_\alpha(x)$, because it is not possible that $R_\alpha(x) = \{x\}$. Let $h(x) = au$ where $a \in \Sigma$ and $u \in \Sigma^+$. If g is the morphism defined by $g(x) = u$, $g(y) = h(y)a$ for all $y \in L_\alpha(x)$ and $g(z) = h(z)$ for all $z \in \Xi \smallsetminus L_\alpha(x) \smallsetminus \{x\}$, then $h(\alpha) = g(\alpha)$. □

Lemma 5. *Let α be a Γ-pattern and x a variable that does not have loyal neighbors in α. Let $a, b, c \in \Sigma$ be different letters such that $L_\alpha(x) \cap \Sigma \neq \{a\}$ and $R_\alpha(x) \cap \Sigma \neq \{b\}$. The morphism h defined by $h(x) = ab$ and $h(y) = c$ for all $y \in \Xi \setminus \{x\}$ is weakly unambiguous with respect to α.*

Proof. We assume that $g \approx_\Gamma h$ is a Γ-increasing morphism such that $h(\alpha) = g(\alpha)$ and derive a contradiction. Let $\alpha = a_1 \ldots a_n$, where $a_1, \ldots, a_n \in \Xi \cup \Sigma$. Lemma 3 is used with $g(a_1), \ldots, g(a_n)$ as $u_1, \ldots, u_n$ and $h(a_1), \ldots, h(a_n)$ as $v_1, \ldots, v_n$. Because $g \approx_\Gamma h$, it follows from Lemma 3 that there is an i such that $g(a_i)$ is a proper factor of $h(a_i)$. In particular, $|h(a_i)| > |g(a_i)| \geq 1$, so $a_i = x$. Thus $g(x)$ is a proper factor of $h(x) = ab$. By symmetry, it can be assumed that $g(x) = a$. Then $g(y)$ cannot contain a's for any variable $y \in \Gamma \setminus \{x\}$, because otherwise $g(\alpha)$ would contain more a's than $h(\alpha)$.

Let $|\alpha|_x = k$ and
$$\alpha = w_0 x w_1 x \ldots w_{k-1} x w_k.$$
If $j = |w_0 \ldots w_{i-1}|_a + i$ for some $i \in \{1, \ldots, k\}$, then the jth a in $h(\alpha) = g(\alpha)$ is followed by b. Thus $g(y)$ begins with b for all $y \in R_\alpha(x)$. This means that $\varepsilon, d \notin R_\alpha(x)$ for all $d \in \Sigma \setminus \{b\}$. By the definition of b, $R_\alpha(x) \subseteq \Xi$.

The number of b's in $h(\alpha)$ is
$$|\alpha|_b + |\alpha|_x$$
and in $g(\alpha)$ it is at least
$$|\alpha|_b + \sum_{y \in R_\alpha(x)} |\alpha|_y.$$
These numbers should be the same, but because x does not have loyal neighbors in α,
$$|\alpha|_x < \sum_{y \in R_\alpha(x)} |\alpha|_y.$$
This is a contradiction. □

Theorem 6. *Let $\#\Sigma \geq 3$ and let α be a Γ-pattern. There is a Γ-increasing morphism h that is weakly unambiguous with respect to α if and only if at least one variable does not have loyal neighbors in α.*

Proof. Assume first that all variables have loyal neighbors in α and h is a Γ-increasing morphism. Then some variable x satisfies the conditions of Lemma 4, so h is not weakly unambiguous with respect to α.

Assume then that a variable x does not have loyal neighbors in α. Because $\#\Sigma \geq 3$, the three letters of Lemma 5 exist, and there is a Γ-increasing morphism that is weakly unambiguous with respect to α. □

Theory of word equations was mentioned in the introduction as one area where morphisms are important. Theorem 6 can be formulated in terms of word equations, although this is probably just a curiosity.

Corollary 7. *Let $\alpha \in (\Xi \cup \Sigma)^+$. There is a $\beta \in \Sigma^+$ such that $|\beta| > |\alpha|$ and the word equation $\alpha = \beta$ has a unique non-erasing solution if and only if at least one variable does not have loyal neighbors in α.*

3 Many Patterns

Weak unambiguity can be generalized for sets of patterns in two ways. The first way is to study the existence of morphisms that are weakly unambiguous with respect to multiple patterns. The next theorem proves a result about constant-free patterns.

Theorem 8. *Let $\#\Sigma \geq 3$ and let α_i be a constant-free Γ_i-pattern for each $i \in \{1, \ldots, n\}$. Let $\Gamma = \bigcap_{i=1}^{n} \Gamma_i$. There is a Γ-increasing morphism h that is weakly unambiguous with respect to every α_i if and only if at least one variable does not have loyal neighbors in any α_i.*

Proof. Assume first that for every variable x there is an index i_x such that x has loyal neighbors in α_{i_x}. Assume also that h is a Γ-increasing morphism. There is a variable x such that $|h(x)| > 1$. By Lemma 4, h is not weakly unambiguous with respect to α_{i_x}.

Assume then that a variable x does not have loyal neighbors in any α_i. Because the patterns are constant-free, any three letters a, b, c satisfy the conditions of Lemma 5, and there is a Γ-increasing morphism that is weakly unambiguous with respect to every α_i. □

To generalize Theorem 8 for patterns with constants, a larger alphabet Σ is needed.

Theorem 9. *Let $\#\Sigma \geq n+2$ and let α_i be a Γ_i-pattern for each $i \in \{1, \ldots, n\}$. Let $\Gamma = \bigcap_{i=1}^{n} \Gamma_i$. There is a Γ-increasing morphism h that is weakly unambiguous with respect to every α_i if and only if at least one variable does not have loyal neighbors in any α_i.*

Proof. Assume first that for every variable x there is an index i_x such that x has loyal neighbors in α_{i_x}. Assume also that h is a Γ-increasing morphism. There is a variable x such that $|h(x)| > 1$. By Lemma 4, h is not weakly unambiguous with respect to α_{i_x}.

Assume then that a variable x does not have loyal neighbors in any α_i. There can be at most n letters a such that $L_{\alpha_i}(x) \cap \Sigma = \{a\}$ for some i, so there is a letter a such that $L_{\alpha_i}(x) \cap \Sigma \neq \{a\}$ for all i. There can be at most n letters b such that $R_{\alpha_i}(x) \cap \Sigma = \{b\}$ for some i, so there is a letter $b \neq a$ such that $R_{\alpha_i}(x) \cap \Sigma \neq \{b\}$ for all i. By Lemma 5, there is a Γ-increasing morphism that is weakly unambiguous with respect to every α_i. □

The next example shows that the assumption $\#\Sigma \geq n + 2$ in Theorem 9 is necessary. Finding a characterization for smaller alphabets remains an open question. It is of course possible that this question is very complicated, like in the binary case for patterns with constants.

Example 10. Let $\Xi = \{x, y_1, y_2, z_1, z_2, t_1, t_2\}$ and $\Sigma = \{a_1, \ldots, a_n, b\}$. Let $a_0 = a_n$ and

$$\alpha_i = y_1 y_2 a_i x z_1 z_2 x a_{i+1} t_1 t_2$$

for $i \in \{0, \ldots, n - 1\}$. The variable x does not have loyal neighbors in any α_i, but there does not exist a Ξ-increasing morphism that would be weakly unambiguous with respect to every α_i. This can be seen as follows. If h would be a Ξ-increasing morphism that is weakly unambiguous with respect to α_0, then $|h(x)| > 1$ by Lemma 4, because all variables except x have loyal neighbors in α_0. If $h(x)$ starts with a_i, say $h(x) = a_i u$, and g is the morphism defined by $g(x) = u$, $g(y_2) = h(y_2)a_i$, $g(z_2) = h(z_2)a_i$ and $g(s) = h(s)$ for other variables s, then $h(\alpha_i) = g(\alpha_i)$. Similarly, if $h(x)$ ends with a_{i+1}, then h is not weakly unambiguous with respect to α_i. The only possibility is that $h(x) = bub$. But if g is the morphism defined by $g(x) = b$, $g(z_1) = ubh(z_1)$, $g(z_2) = h(z_2)bu$ and $g(s) = h(s)$ for other variables s, then $h(\alpha) = g(\alpha)$.

4   Sets of Patterns

The second way to generalize weak unambiguity for sets of patterns is to use the following definitions.

If A is a set of patterns and Γ is the set of those variables that appear in some $\alpha \in A$, then A is a Γ-set of patterns.

Let A be a Γ-set of patterns. A non-erasing morphism h is *weakly unambiguous with respect to A* if there is no non-erasing morphism $g \approx_\Gamma h$ such that $h(\alpha) = g(\alpha)$ for every $\alpha \in A$.

The set of *left neighbors of x in A* is

$$L_A(x) = \bigcup_{\alpha \in A} L_\alpha(x)$$

and the set of *right neighbors of x in A* is

$$R_A(x) = \bigcup_{\alpha \in A} R_\alpha(x)$$

A variable x has *loyal neighbors in A* if at least one of the following two conditions is satisfied:

$$L_A(x) \subseteq \Xi \text{ and } R_A(y) = \{x\} \text{ for all } y \in L_A(x), \tag{3}$$
$$R_A(x) \subseteq \Xi \text{ and } L_A(y) = \{x\} \text{ for all } y \in R_A(x). \tag{4}$$

Lemmas 11 and 12 and Theorem 13 are simple modifications of Lemmas 4 and 5 and Theorem 6.

Lemma 11. *Let A be a Γ-set of patterns and h a non-erasing morphism. If there is $x \in \Gamma$ such that $|h(x)| > 1$ and x has loyal neighbors in A, then h is not weakly unambiguous with respect to A.*

Proof. Assume that (3) is satisfied for x (the case where (4) is satisfied is symmetric). It must be $x \notin L_A(x)$, because it is not possible that $R_A(x) = \{x\}$. Let $h(x) = au$ where $a \in \Sigma$ and $u \in \Sigma^+$. If g is the morphism defined by $g(x) = u$, $g(y) = h(y)a$ for all $y \in L_A(x)$ and $g(z) = h(z)$ for all $z \in \Xi \setminus L_A(x) \setminus \{x\}$, then $h(\alpha) = g(\alpha)$ for every $\alpha \in A$. □

Lemma 12. *Let A be a Γ-set of patterns and x a variable that does not have loyal neighbors in A. Let $a, b, c \in \Sigma$ be different letters such that $L_A(x) \cap \Sigma \neq \{a\}$ and $R_A(x) \cap \Sigma \neq \{b\}$. The morphism h defined by $h(x) = ab$ and $h(y) = c$ for all $y \in \Xi \setminus \{x\}$ is weakly unambiguous with respect to A.*

Proof. We assume that $g \approx_\Gamma h$ is a Γ-increasing morphism such that $h(\alpha) = g(\alpha)$ for all $\alpha \in A$ and derive a contradiction. There is a $\Gamma_1 \subseteq \Gamma$ and a Γ_1-pattern $\alpha_1 \in A$ such that $g \approx_{\Gamma_1} h$. Let $\alpha_1 = a_1 \dots a_n$, where $a_1, \dots, a_n \in \Xi \cup \Sigma$. Lemma 3 is used with $g(a_1), \dots, g(a_n)$ as $u_1, \dots, u_n$ and $h(a_1), \dots, h(a_n)$ as $v_1, \dots, v_n$. Because $g \approx_{\Gamma_1} h$, it follows from Lemma 3 that there is an i such that $g(a_i)$ is a proper factor of $h(a_i)$. In particular, $|h(a_i)| > |g(a_i)| \geq 1$, so $a_i = x$. Thus $g(x)$ is a proper factor of $h(x) = ab$. By symmetry, it can be assumed that $g(x) = a$. Then $g(y)$ cannot contain a's for any variable $y \in \Gamma \setminus \{x\}$, because otherwise $g(\alpha)$ would contain more a's than $h(\alpha)$ for some $\alpha \in A$.

Consider any $\alpha \in A$. Let $|\alpha|_x = k$ and

$$\alpha = w_0 x w_1 x \dots w_{k-1} x w_k.$$

If $j = |w_0 \dots w_{i-1}|_a + i$ for some $i \in \{1, \dots, k\}$, then the jth a in $h(\alpha) = g(\alpha)$ is followed by b. Thus $g(y)$ begins with b for all $y \in R_\alpha(x)$. This means that $\varepsilon, d \notin R_\alpha(x)$ for all $d \in \Sigma \setminus \{b\}$. By the definition of b, $R_A(x) \subseteq \Xi$.

The combined number of b's in all words $h(\alpha)$ is

$$\sum_{\alpha \in A} (|\alpha|_b + |\alpha|_x)$$

and in all words $g(\alpha)$ it is at least

$$\sum_{\alpha \in A} (|\alpha|_b + \sum_{y \in R_A(x)} |\alpha|_y).$$

These numbers should be the same, but because x does not have loyal neighbors in A,

$$\sum_{\alpha \in A} |\alpha|_x < \sum_{\alpha \in A} \sum_{y \in R_\alpha(x)} |\alpha|_y.$$

This is a contradiction. □

Theorem 13. *Let $\#\Sigma \geq 3$ and let A be a Γ-set of patterns. There is a Γ-increasing morphism h that is weakly unambiguous with respect to A if and only if at least one variable does not have loyal neighbors in A.*

Proof. Assume first that all variables have loyal neighbors in A and h is a Γ-increasing morphism. Then some variable x satisfies the conditions of Lemma 11, so h is not weakly unambiguous with respect to A.

Assume then that a variable x does not have loyal neighbors in A. Because $\#\Sigma \geq 3$, the three letters of Lemma 12 exist, and there is a Γ-increasing morphism that is weakly unambiguous with respect to A. □

References

1. Berstel, J., Perrin, D., Reutenauer, C.: Codes and Automata. Cambridge University Press (2010)
2. Freydenberger, D., Nevisi, H., Reidenbach, D.: Weakly unambiguous morphisms. Theoret. Comput. Sci. 448, 21–40 (2012)
3. Freydenberger, D., Reidenbach, D.: The unambiguity of segmented morphisms. Discrete Appl. Math. 157(14), 3055–3068 (2009)
4. Freydenberger, D., Reidenbach, D., Schneider, J.: Unambiguous morphic images of strings. Internat. J. Found. Comput. Sci. 17(3), 601–628 (2006)
5. Harju, T., Karhumäki, J.: Morphisms. In: Rozenberg, G., Salomaa, A. (eds.) Handbook of Formal Languages, vol. 1, pp. 439–510. Springer (1997)
6. Head, T.: Fixed languages and the adult languages of 0L schemes. Int. J. Comput. Math. 10(2), 103–107 (1981)
7. Mateescu, A., Salomaa, A.: Aspects of classical language theory. In: Rozenberg, G., Salomaa, A. (eds.) Handbook of Formal Languages, vol. 1, pp. 175–251. Springer (1997)
8. Reidenbach, D.: Discontinuities in pattern inference. Theoret. Comput. Sci. 397(1-3), 166–193 (2008)
9. Reidenbach, D., Schneider, J.: Restricted ambiguity of erasing morphisms. Theoret. Comput. Sci. 412(29), 3510–3523 (2011)
10. Schneider, J.: Unambiguous erasing morphisms in free monoids. RAIRO Inform. Theor. Appl. 44(2), 193–208 (2010)
11. Shallit, J., Wang, M.W.: On two-sided infinite fixed points of morphisms. Theoret. Comput. Sci. 270(1-2), 659–675 (2002)

On Infinite Words Determined by L Systems

Tim Smith

College of Computer and Information Science, Northeastern University
Boston, MA 02115, USA
smithtim@ccs.neu.edu

Abstract. A deterministic L system generates an infinite word α if each word in its derivation sequence is a prefix of the next, yielding α as a limit. We generalize this notion to arbitrary L systems via the concept of prefix languages. A prefix language is a language L such that for all $x, y \in L$, x is a prefix of y or y is a prefix of x. Every infinite prefix language determines an infinite word. Where C is a class of L systems (e.g. 0L, DT0L), we denote by $\omega(C)$ the class of infinite words determined by the prefix languages in C. This allows us to speak of infinite 0L words, infinite DT0L words, etc. We categorize the infinite words determined by a variety of L systems, showing that the whole hierarchy collapses to just three distinct classes of infinite words: $\omega(\text{PD0L})$, $\omega(\text{D0L})$, and $\omega(\text{CD0L})$.

1 Introduction

L systems are parallel rewriting systems which were originally introduced to model growth in simple multicellular organisms. With applications in biological modelling, fractal generation, and artificial life, L systems have given rise to a rich body of research [11,9]. L systems can be restricted and generalized in various ways, yielding a hierarchy of language classes.

The simplest L systems are D0L systems (deterministic Lindenmayer systems with 0 symbols of context), in which a morphism is successively applied to a start string or "axiom". The resulting sequence of words comprises the language of the system. If the morphism is prolongable on the start string, then each word in the derivation sequence will be a prefix of the next, yielding an infinite word as a limit. An infinite word obtained in this way is called an infinite D0L word.

Two well-studied generalizations of D0L systems are 0L systems, which introduce nondeterminism by changing the morphism to a finite substitution, and DT0L systems, in which the morphism is replaced by a set of morphisms or "tables". In each case, there is no longer just one possible derivation sequence; rather, there are many possible derivations, depending on which letter substitutions or tables are chosen at each step. This raises the question of under what conditions such a system can be said to determine an infinite word.

We answer this question with the concept of a prefix language. A prefix language is a language L such that for all $x, y \in L$, x is a prefix of y or y is a prefix of x. Every infinite prefix language determines an infinite word. Where C is a class of L systems (e.g. 0L, DT0L), we denote by $\omega(C)$ the class of infinite words

J. Karhumäki, A. Lepistö, and L. Zamboni (Eds.): WORDS 2013, LNCS 8079, pp. 238–249, 2013.

determined by the prefix languages in C. This allows us to speak of infinite 0L words, infinite DT0L words, etc.

With this notion in place, we categorize the infinite words determined by a variety of L systems. We consider four production features (D,P,F,T) and five filtering features (E,C,N,W,H). Each production feature may be present or absent, and at most one filtering feature may be present, giving a total of $2^4 \cdot 6 = 96$ classes of L systems. We show that this whole hierarchy collapses to just three classes of infinite words: $\omega(\text{PD0L})$, $\omega(\text{D0L})$, and $\omega(\text{CD0L})$. Our results appear in Figure 1.

The inclusions among these three classes are proper, giving $\omega(\text{PD0L}) \subset \omega(\text{D0L}) \subset \omega(\text{CD0L})$. The class $\omega(\text{CD0L})$ contains exactly the morphic words, while $\omega(\text{D0L})$ properly contains the pure morphic words.

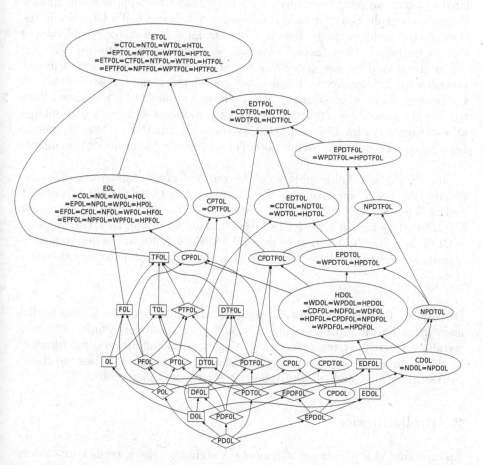

Fig. 1. Inclusion diagram showing classes of L systems colored by the infinite words they determine. Green classes (diamonds) determine exactly $\omega(\text{PD0L})$, blue classes (rectangles) determine exactly $\omega(\text{D0L})$, and yellow classes (ellipses) determine exactly $\omega(\text{CD0L})$. Inclusions and equalities are from [9].

Proof Techniques. We obtain our categorization results by showing that all infinite languages in certain classes of L systems have infinite subsets in certain smaller classes of L systems. This limits the infinite words of the larger class to the infinite words of the smaller class. That every infinite T0L language has an infinite D0L subset was shown in [12] using a pumping lemma for T0L languages. With this result, we show that every infinite ET0L language has an infinite CD0L subset, and we make further use of the pumping lemma to show that every infinite PT0L language has an infinite PD0L subset. A separate argument shows that every infinite ED0L (EPD0L) language has an infinite D0L (PD0L) subset.

Related Work. Prefix languages were investigated by Book [3], who formulated a "prefix property" intended to allow languages to "approximate" infinite sequences, and showed that for certain classes of languages, if a language in the class has the prefix property, then it is regular. Languages whose complement is a prefix language, called "coprefix languages", have also been studied [2].

The iterative processes underlying L systems have been investigated in connection with infinite words. Pansiot [10] considered various classes of infinite words obtained by iterated mappings. Culik & Karhumäki [5] considered iterative devices generating infinite words. Culik & Salomaa [6] investigated infinite words associated with D0L and DT0L systems; their notion of "strong uniform convergence" is equivalent to our notion of a language "determining" an infinite word.

Our results on infinite subsets can be restated in the framework of set immunity [13]. For a language class C, a language L is C-immune iff L is infinite and no infinite subset of L is in C. For example, our result that every infinite ET0L language has an infinite CD0L subset could be stated: no ET0L language is CD0L-immune. In addition to categorizing the infinite words determined by L systems, our results characterize the immunity relationships among these systems.

Outline of Paper. The paper is organized as follows. Section 2 gives preliminary definitions and propositions. Section 3 gives results on infinite subsets of certain classes of L systems. Section 4 categorizes the infinite words determined by the hierarchy of L systems. Section 5 separates and characterizes the classes $\omega(\text{PD0L})$, $\omega(\text{D0L})$, and $\omega(\text{CD0L})$. Section 6 gives our conclusions.

2   Preliminaries

An **alphabet** A is a finite set of symbols. A **string** (or finite word) is an element of A^*. We denote the empty string by λ. A **language** is a subset of A^*. An **infinite word** (or stream) is an element of A^ω. A (symbolic) **sequence** S is an element of $A^* \cup A^\omega$. A **prefix** of S is a string x such that $S = xS'$ for some sequence S'. A **subword** (or factor) of S is a string x such that $S = wxS'$ for some string w and sequence S'. For a nonempty string x, x^ω denotes the infinite word $xxx\cdots$. Such a word is called **purely periodic**. An infinite word of the form xy^ω, where x and y are strings and $y \neq \lambda$, is called **ultimately periodic**.

A **morphism** on an alphabet A is a map h from A^* to A^* such that for all $x, y \in A^*$, $h(xy) = h(x)h(y)$. Notice that $h(\lambda) = \lambda$. The morphism h is **nonerasing** if for all $a \in A$, $h(a) \neq \lambda$. The morphism h is a **coding** if for all $a \in A$, $|h(a)| = 1$. The morphism h is a **weak coding** if for all $a \in A$, $|h(a)| \leq 1$. The morphism h is an **identity** if for all $a \in A$, $h(a) = a$. For a language L, we define $h(L) = \{h(x) \mid x \in L\}$. A string $x \in A^*$ is **mortal** (for h) if there is an $m \geq 0$ such that $h^m(x) = \lambda$. The morphism h is **prolongable** on a symbol a if $h(a) = ax$ for some $x \in A^*$, and x is not mortal. In this case $h^\omega(a)$ denotes the infinite word $a\, x\, h(x)\, h^2(x)\, \cdots$. An infinite word α is **pure morphic** if there is a morphism h and symbol a such that h is prolongable on a and $\alpha = h^\omega(a)$. An infinite word α is **morphic** if there is a morphism h, coding e, and symbol a such that h is prolongable on a and $\alpha = e(h^\omega(a))$. Every purely periodic word is pure morphic, and every ultimately periodic word is morphic. For results on morphic words, see [1].

A **finite substitution** on A is a map σ from A^* to 2^{A^*} such that (1) for all $x \in A^*$, $\sigma(x)$ is finite and nonempty, and (2) for all $x, y \in A^*$, $\sigma(xy) = \{x'y' \mid x'$ is in $\sigma(x)$ and y' is in $\sigma(y)\}$. Notice that $\sigma(\lambda) = \{\lambda\}$. σ is **nonerasing** if for all $a \in A$, $\sigma(a) \not\ni \lambda$. For a language L, we define $\sigma(L) = \{x' \mid x'$ is in $\sigma(x)$ for some $x \in L\}$.

2.1   Prefix Languages

A **prefix language** is a language L such that for all $x, y \in L$, x is a prefix of y or y is a prefix of x. A language L **determines** an infinite word α iff L is infinite and every $x \in L$ is a prefix of α. For example, the infinite prefix language $\{\lambda, ab, abab, ababab, \dots\}$ determines the infinite word $(ab)^\omega$. The following propositions are basic consequences of the definitions.

Proposition 1. *A language determines at most one infinite word.*

Proposition 2. *A language L determines an infinite word iff L is an infinite prefix language.*

Notice that while a language determines at most one infinite word, an infinite word may be determined by more than one language. In particular, we will make use of the following fact.

Proposition 3. *If a language L determines an infinite word α and L' is an infinite subset of L, then L' determines α.*

For a language class C, let $\omega(C) = \{\alpha \mid \alpha$ is an infinite word and some $L \in C$ determines $\alpha\}$.

2.2   L Systems

Many classes of L systems appear in the literature. Following [9], we consider four production features (D,P,F,T) and five filtering features (E,C,N,W,H). Each production feature may be present or absent, and at most one filtering feature may be present, for a total of $2^4 \cdot 6 = 96$ classes of L systems.

Feature	Meaning	Example
none		A **0L system** is a tuple $G = (A, \sigma, w)$ where A is an alphabet, σ is a finite substitution on A, and w is in A^*. The language of G is $L(G) = \{s \in \sigma^i(w) \mid i \geq 0\}$.
D	Deterministic	A **D0L system** is a tuple $G = (A, h, w)$ where A is an alphabet, h is a morphism on A, and w is in A^*. The language of G is $L(G) = \{h^i(w) \mid i \geq 0\}$.
P	Propagating	A **PD0L** system is a D0L system (A, h, w) such that h is nonerasing.
F	Finite axiom set	A **DF0L system** is a tuple $G = (A, h, F)$ where A is an alphabet, h is a morphism on A, and F is a finite set of strings in A^*. The language of G is $L(G) = \{h^i(f) \mid f \in F \text{ and } i \geq 0\}$.
T	Tables	A **DT0L system** is a tuple $G = (A, H, w)$ where A is an alphabet, H is a finite nonempty set of morphisms on A (called "tables"), and w is in A^*. The language of G is $L(G) = \{s \mid h_i \cdots h_1(w) = s$ for some $h_1, \ldots, h_i \in H$.
E	Extended	An **ED0L system** is a tuple $G = (A, h, w, B)$ where A and B are alphabets and $B \subseteq A$, h is a morphism on A, and w is in A^*. The language of G is $L(G) = \{s \in B^* \mid h^i(w) = s$ for some $i \geq 0\}$.
H	Homomorphism	An **HD0L system** is a tuple $G = (A, h, w, g)$ such that $G' = (A, h, w)$ is a D0L system and g is a morphism on A. The language of G is $L(G) = \{g(s) \mid s$ is in $L(G')\}$.
C	Coding	A **CD0L** system is an HD0L system (A, h, w, g) such that g is a coding.
N	Nonerasing	An **ND0L** system is an HD0L system (A, h, w, g) such that g is nonerasing.
W	Weak coding	A **WD0L** system is an HD0L system (A, h, w, g) such that g is a weak coding.

These features combine to form complex L systems. For example, an **EPD0L system** is an ED0L system (A, h, w, B) such that h is nonerasing. A **T0L system** is a tuple $G = (A, T, w)$ where A is an alphabet, T is a finite nonempty set of finite substitutions on A (called "tables"), and w is in A^*. The language of G is $L(G) = \{s \mid \sigma_i \cdots \sigma_1(w) \ni s$ for some $\sigma_1, \ldots, \sigma_i \in T\}$. If for all $\sigma \in T$, σ is nonerasing, then G is a **PT0L system**. See [11] and [9] for more definitions.

We call an L system G **infinite** iff $L(G)$ is infinite. When speaking of language classes, we denote the class of D0L languages simply by D0L, and similarly with other classes. An **L system feature set** is a subset of $\{D,P,F,T\}$ $\cup \{E,C,N,W,H\}$ containing at most one of $\{E,C,N,W,H\}$. Let $\mathscr{L}(S)$ be the language class of L systems with feature set S. For example, $\mathscr{L}(\{C,D,T\}) = $ CDT0L. From the definitions of the features, we have the following inclusions.

Proposition 4 (Structural inclusions)
Let S be an L system feature set. Then:

- $\mathscr{L}(S \cup \{D\}) \subseteq \mathscr{L}(S)$,
- $\mathscr{L}(S \cup \{P\}) \subseteq \mathscr{L}(S)$,
- $\mathscr{L}(S) \subseteq \mathscr{L}(S \cup \{F\})$, *and*
- $\mathscr{L}(S) \subseteq \mathscr{L}(S \cup \{T\})$.

Let S be an L system feature set containing none of $\{E,C,N,W,H\}$. Then:

- $\mathscr{L}(S) \subseteq \mathscr{L}(S \cup \{E\})$,
- $\mathscr{L}(S) \subseteq \mathscr{L}(S \cup \{C\})$,
- $\mathscr{L}(S \cup \{C\}) \subseteq \mathscr{L}(S \cup \{N\}) \subseteq \mathscr{L}(S \cup \{H\})$, *and*
- $\mathscr{L}(S \cup \{C\}) \subseteq \mathscr{L}(S \cup \{W\}) \subseteq \mathscr{L}(S \cup \{H\})$.

Beyond these structural inclusions, many relationships are known among the language classes; see [9]. In comparing L system classes, [9] considers two languages to be equal if they differ by the empty word only; otherwise, propagating classes would be automatically different from nonpropagating ones. See Figure 1 for a depiction of the known inclusions and equalities.

3   Infinite Subsets of L Systems

In this section we show that all infinite languages in certain classes of L systems have infinite subsets in certain smaller classes of L systems. This limits the infinite words of the larger class to the infinite words of the smaller class. We make use of a pumping lemma for T0L systems from [12]. A T0L system $G = (A, T, w)$ is **pumpable** iff there are $a, b \in A$ such that (1) some $s_0 \in L(G)$ contains a, and (2) for some composition t of tables from T, $t(a)$ includes a string s_1 containing distinct occurrences of a and b and $t(b)$ includes a string s_2 containing b. The next two theorems appear in [12].

Theorem 5 (Smith). *A T0L system is infinite iff it is pumpable.*

Theorem 6 (Smith). *Every infinite T0L language has an infinite D0L subset.*

Theorem 7. *Every infinite PT0L language has an infinite PD0L subset.*

Proof. Take any infinite PT0L language L with PT0L system $G = (A, T, w)$. By Theorem 5, G is pumpable for some $a, b \in A$, $s_0, s_1, s_2 \in A^*$, and composition t of tables from T. Let h be a morphism on A such that $h(a) = s_1$, $h(b) = s_2$

unless $a = b$, and for every other $c \in A$, $h(c) = s$ for some $s \in t(c)$. Since t is a composition of tables from T, t is nonerasing, hence h is nonerasing. Further, for all $i \geq 0$, $h^i(s_0)$ is in $t^i(s_0)$, so $h^i(s_0)$ is in L. A simple induction shows that for all $i \geq 0$, $h^i(s_0)$ contains a and at least i copies of b. Hence the language of the PD0L system (A, h, s_0) is an infinite subset of L. $\quad\square$

Theorem 8. *Let $G = (A, h, w, B)$ be an infinite ED0L system. Then there are $a \geq 0, b \geq 1$ such that the language of the D0L system $(A, h^b, h^a(w))$ is an infinite subset of $L(G)$.*

Proof. Let alph(s) be the set of symbols which appear in the string s. Since $L(G)$ is infinite, there is an $m \geq 0$ such that the sequence w, $h(w)$, $h^2(w)$, ..., $h^m(w)$ contains more than $2^{|B|}$ strings in $L(G)$. For every $s \in L(G)$, alph(s) $\subseteq B$. Hence there is a $C \subseteq B$ and i, j such that $0 \leq i < j \leq m$ and alph($h^i(w)$) = alph($h^j(w)$) = C. Then for any string s such that alph(s) = C, alph($h^{j-i}(s)$) = C. Let $a = i$ and $b = j - i$. Then for every $n \geq 0$, alph($h^{a+bn}(w)$) = C. Hence for every $n \geq 0$, $h^{a+bn}(w)$ is in $L(G)$. So take the D0L system $G' = (A, h^b, h^a(w))$. We have $L(G') \subseteq L(G)$. Suppose some string s occurs twice in the derivation sequence of G'. Then s occurs twice in the derivation sequence of G, making $L(G)$ finite, a contradiction. So $L(G')$ is infinite. Therefore $L(G')$ is an infinite subset of $L(G)$. $\quad\square$

Corollary 9. *Every infinite ED0L language has an infinite D0L subset.*

Corollary 10. *Every infinite EPD0L language has an infinite PD0L subset.*

Proof. Take any infinite EPD0L system $G = (A, h, w, B)$. By Theorem 8, there are $a \geq 0, b \geq 1$ such that the language of the D0L system $G' = (A, h^b, h^a(w))$ is an infinite subset of $L(G)$. Since h is nonerasing, h^b is nonerasing. Hence $L(G')$ is an infinite PD0L subset of $L(G)$. $\quad\square$

Theorem 11. *Every infinite ET0L language has an infinite CD0L subset.*

Proof. Take any infinite ET0L language L. By Theorem 2.7 of [9], ET0L = CT0L. Hence there is a coding e and T0L language L' such that $L = e(L')$. Since L is infinite, L' is infinite. Then by Theorem 6, L' has an infinite D0L subset L''. Since L'' is infinite and e is a coding, $e(L'')$ is infinite. Since $L'' \subseteq L'$, $e(L'') \subseteq e(L')$. Therefore $e(L'')$ is an infinite CD0L subset of L. $\quad\square$

Theorem 12. *Let S be an L system feature set not containing F. Then every infinite $\mathscr{L}(S \cup \{F\})$ language has an infinite $\mathscr{L}(S)$ subset.*

Proof. Take any infinite L system G with feature set $S \cup \{F\}$. Since G has a finite axiom set, $L(G)$ is a finite union of $\mathscr{L}(S)$ languages. Then since $L(G)$ is infinite, one of these $\mathscr{L}(S)$ languages is infinite. Therefore $L(G)$ has an infinite $\mathscr{L}(S)$ subset. $\quad\square$

Theorem 13. *Let C and D be language classes such that every infinite language in C has an infinite subset in D. Then $\omega(C) \subseteq \omega(D)$.*

Proof. Take any $\alpha \in \omega(C)$. Some $L \in C$ determines α. Then L is infinite, so L has an infinite subset L' in D. Then L' determines α. So α is in $\omega(D)$. Hence $\omega(C) \subseteq \omega(D)$. $\quad\square$

4 Categorizations

In this section we categorize the infinite words determined by each class of L systems. We partition the 96 classes into three sets, called Set_1, Set_2, and Set_3, and show that for every $C_1 \in Set_1$, $C_2 \in Set_2$, and $C_3 \in Set_3$, $\omega(C_1) = \omega(\text{PD0L})$, $\omega(C_2) = \omega(\text{D0L})$, and $\omega(C_3) = \omega(\text{CD0L})$.

4.1 PD0L Classes

Let Set_1 = {PD0L, PDF0L, P0L, PF0L, PDT0L, PDTF0L, PT0L, PTF0L, EPD0L, EPDF0L}.

Theorem 14. *For every $C \in Set_1$, every infinite C language has an infinite PD0L subset.*

Proof. Take any $C \in Set_1$. By structural inclusion, $C \subseteq \text{PTF0L}$ or $C \subseteq \text{EPDF0L}$. By Theorem 12, every infinite PTF0L language has an infinite PT0L subset. By Theorem 7, every infinite PT0L language has an infinite PD0L subset. Hence every infinite PTF0L language has an infinite PD0L subset. By Theorem 12, every infinite EPDF0L language has an infinite EPD0L subset. By Corollary 10, every infinite EPD0L language has an infinite PD0L subset. Hence every infinite EPDF0L language has an infinite PD0L subset. Hence every infinite C language has an infinite PD0L subset.   □

Theorem 15. *For every $C \in Set_1$, $\omega(C) = \omega(PD0L)$.*

Proof. Take any $C \in Set_1$. By structural inclusion, $\text{PD0L} \subseteq C$. Hence $\omega(\text{PD0L}) \subseteq \omega(C)$. By Theorem 14, every infinite C language has an infinite PD0L subset. Then by Theorem 13, $\omega(C) \subseteq \omega(\text{PD0L})$. Therefore $\omega(C) = \omega(\text{PD0L})$.   □

4.2 D0L Classes

Let Set_2 = {D0L, DF0L, 0L, F0L, DT0L, DTF0L, T0L, TF0L, ED0L, EDF0L}.

Theorem 16. *For every $C \in Set_2$, every infinite C language has an infinite D0L subset.*

Proof. Take any $C \in Set_2$. By structural inclusion, $C \subseteq \text{TF0L}$ or $C \subseteq \text{EDF0L}$. By Theorem 12, every infinite TF0L language has an infinite T0L subset. By Theorem 6, every infinite T0L language has an infinite D0L subset. Hence every infinite TF0L language has an infinite D0L subset. By Theorem 12, every infinite EDF0L language has an infinite ED0L subset. By Corollary 9, every infinite ED0L language has an infinite D0L subset. Hence every infinite EDF0L language has an infinite D0L subset. Hence every infinite C language has an infinite D0L subset.   □

Theorem 17. *For every $C \in Set_2$, $\omega(C) = \omega(D0L)$.*

Proof. Take any $C \in Set_2$. By structural inclusion, $\text{D0L} \subseteq C$. Hence $\omega(\text{D0L}) \subseteq \omega(C)$. By Theorem 16, every infinite C language has an infinite D0L subset. Then by Theorem 13, $\omega(C) \subseteq \omega(\text{D0L})$. Therefore $\omega(C) = \omega(\text{D0L})$.   □

4.3   CD0L Classes

Let Set_3 = {CD0L, ND0L, WD0L, HD0L, CPD0L, NPD0L, WPD0L, HPD0L, CDF0L, NDF0L, WDF0L, HDF0L, CPDF0L, NPDF0L, WPDF0L, HPDF0L, E0L, C0L, N0L, W0L, H0L, EP0L, CP0L, NP0L, WP0L, HP0L, EF0L, CF0L, NF0L, WF0L, HF0L, EPF0L, CPF0L, NPF0L, WPF0L, HPF0L, EDT0L, CDT0L, NDT0L, WDT0L, HDT0L, EPDT0L, CPDT0L, NPDT0L, WPDT0L, HPDT0L, EDTF0L, CDTF0L, NDTF0L, WDTF0L, HDTF0L, EPDTF0L, CPDTF0L, NPDTF0L, WPDTF0L, HPDTF0L, ET0L, CT0L, NT0L, WT0L, HT0L, EPT0L, CPT0L, NPT0L, WPT0L, HPT0L, ETF0L, CTF0L, NTF0L, WTF0L, HTF0L, EPTF0L, CPTF0L, NPTF0L, WPTF0L, HPTF0L}.

Theorem 18. *For every* $C \in Set_3$, *every infinite* C *language has an infinite CD0L subset.*

Proof. Take any $C \in Set_3$. By structural inclusion, $C \subseteq$ ETF0L or $C \subseteq$ HTF0L. By Theorem 2.7 of [9], ETF0L = HTF0L = ET0L. So $C \subseteq$ ET0L. By Theorem 11, every infinite ET0L language has an infinite CD0L subset. Hence every infinite C language has an infinite CD0L subset. $\square$

Theorem 19. *For every* $C \in Set_3$, $\omega(C) = \omega(CD0L)$.

Proof. Take any $C \in Set_3$. By Theorem 18, every infinite C language has an infinite CD0L subset. Then by Theorem 13, $\omega(C) \subseteq \omega(CD0L)$.

Next, by structural inclusion, CPD0L $\subseteq C$ or EP0L $\subseteq C$ or EPDT0L $\subseteq C$. By Theorem 2.4 of [9], EP0L = C0L, so CPD0L $\subseteq$ EP0L. By Theorem 2.6 of [9], CPDT0L $\subseteq$ EPDT0L, so CPD0L $\subseteq$ EPDT0L. Hence CPD0L $\subseteq C$. Now by Theorem 2.3 of [9], CPDF0L = CDF0L. Hence CD0L $\subseteq$ CPDF0L. Hence $\omega(CD0L) \subseteq \omega(CPDF0L)$. By Theorem 12, every infinite CPDF0L language has an infinite CPD0L subset. Then by Theorem 13, $\omega(CPDF0L) \subseteq \omega(CPD0L)$. Hence $\omega(CD0L) \subseteq \omega(CPD0L) \subseteq \omega(C)$.

Therefore $\omega(C) = \omega(CD0L)$. $\square$

5 ω(PD0L), ω(D0L), and ω(CD0L)

In this section, we separate the three classes of infinite words obtained in the previous section, giving $\omega(PD0L) \subset \omega(D0L) \subset \omega(CD0L)$. We observe that $\omega(D0L)$ properly contains the pure morphic words and we show that $\omega(CD0L)$ contains exactly the morphic words.

5.1   Separating the Classes

From Theorem 2.3 of [10], the infinite words generated by iterating nonerasing morphisms are a proper subset of the pure morphic words, which in turn are a proper subset of the morphic words. Our classes ω(PD0L), ω(D0L), and ω(CD0L) are defined more generally using prefix languages, but similar arguments serve to separate them.

Theorem 20. $\omega(PD0L) \subset \omega(D0L)$.

Proof. By structural inclusion, $\omega(\text{PD0L}) \subseteq \omega(\text{D0L})$. To separate the two classes, we use an infinite word from [4]. Let $A = \{0, 1, 2\}$. Let f be a morphism on A such that $f(0) = 01222$, $f(1) = 10222$, and $f(2) = \lambda$. Let $\alpha = f^\omega(0) = 01222102221022201222\ldots$ Then α is a pure morphic word, hence α is in $\omega(\text{D0L})$. In [4] it is shown that there is no nonerasing morphism g on A such that $g^\omega(0) = \alpha$. We generalize this result to show that α is not in $\omega(\text{PD0L})$. First, we show that if g is a nonerasing morphism on A and $g(\alpha) = \alpha$, then g is an identity morphism. We adapt the proof of Example 3 in [4].

Let τ be the Thue-Morse word $\tau = 01101001\ldots = u^\omega(0)$, where u is a morphism on $\{0, 1\}$ such that $u(0) = 01$ and $u(1) = 10$. Let d be a morphism on A such that $d(0) = 0$, $d(1) = 1$, and $d(2) = \lambda$. As observed by [4], $d(\alpha) = \tau$. Notice that the only subwords of α in $\{0, 1\}^*$ are in $\{\lambda, 0, 1, 01, 10\}$ and the only subwords of α in $\{2\}^*$ are in $\{\lambda, 2, 22, 222\}$. Notice also that α does not contain the subword 212.

Suppose g is a nonerasing morphism on A and $g(\alpha) = \alpha$. Suppose $g(2)$ is not in 2^*. Let $s = d(g(2))$. Then s is not empty. Since 222 is a subword of α and $g(\alpha) = \alpha$, $g(222)$ is a subword of α. Then since $d(\alpha) = \tau$, τ contains $d(g(222)) = sss$, a contradiction, since τ is known to be cubefree. So $g(2)$ is in 2^*. Then since α contains $g(222)$, and 2222 is not a subword of α, and g is nonerasing, $g(2) = 2$.

Suppose $g(0) \neq 0$. Then since α starts with 0, $g(0) = 01x$ for some $x \in A^*$. Since 1222 is a subword of α, $g(1222) = g(1)\,222$ is a subword of α. Then since 2222 is not a subword of α, $g(1)$ cannot end with 2. So $g(1) = ya$ for some $y \in A^*$ and $a \in \{0, 1\}$. Now since 10 is a subword of α, so is $g(10) = ya01x$. But α contains no subword of the form $a01$, a contradiction. So $g(0) = 0$.

Suppose $g(1) \neq 1$. Then since α begins with 012, $g(1) = 12z$ for some $z \in A^*$. Since 2221 is a subword of α, $g(2221) = 22212z$ is a subword of α, a contradiction, since α does not contain the subword 212. So $g(1) = 1$. Then g is an identity morphism.

So suppose α is in $\omega(\text{PD0L})$. Then there is a PD0L system $G = (A, h, w)$ such that $L(G)$ determines α. Since h is nonerasing, $h(\alpha)$ is an infinite word. Suppose $h(\alpha) \neq \alpha$. Then there is a prefix p of α such that $h(p)$ is not a prefix of α. Since $L(G)$ determines α, p is a prefix of some s in $L(G)$. Then $h(p)$ is a prefix of $h(s)$. But then since $h(s)$ is in $L(G)$, $h(p)$ is a prefix of α, a contradiction. So $h(\alpha) = \alpha$. Then from above, h is an identity morphism. But then $h(w) = w$, so $L(G)$ is finite, a contradiction. Therefore α is not in $\omega(\text{PD0L})$. Hence $\omega(\text{PD0L}) \subset \omega(\text{D0L})$. $\qquad\square$

Theorem 21. $\omega(D0L) \subset \omega(CD0L)$.

Proof. By structural inclusion, $\omega(\text{D0L}) \subseteq \omega(\text{CD0L})$. Let $\alpha = \text{abba}^\omega$. Since α is ultimately periodic, α is morphic, hence α is in $\omega(\text{CD0L})$. Suppose α is in $\omega(\text{D0L})$. Then there is a D0L system $G = (A, h, w)$ such that $L(G)$ determines α. Clearly $h(\text{a})$ cannot include b, and if $h(\text{a}) = \lambda$, $L(G)$ is finite, a contradiction. So since $h(\text{a})$ must be a prefix of α, $h(\text{a}) = \text{a}$. Then a $h(\text{b})\, h(\text{b})$ is a prefix of α, hence $h(\mathbf{b}) = \lambda$ or $h(\mathbf{b}) = \mathbf{b}$. But then $L(G)$ is finite, a contradiction. So α is not in $\omega(\mathrm{D0L})$. Hence $\omega(\mathrm{D0L}) \subset \omega(\mathrm{CD0L})$.   □

5.2 Characterizing the Words in Each Class

That $\omega(\mathrm{D0L})$ includes every pure morphic word is immediate from the definitions. In [8], the infinite word $\mathbf{aab}^\omega$ is given as an example of an infinite D0L word which is not pure morphic. Hence $\omega(\mathrm{D0L})$ properly contains the pure morphic words. Next, we show that $\omega(\mathrm{CD0L})$ contains exactly the morphic words. The **adherence** of a language L, denoted Adherence(L), is the set $\{\alpha \mid \alpha$ is an infinite word and for every prefix p of α, there is an $s \in L$ such that p is a prefix of $s\}$.

Lemma 22. *Suppose L is in D0L and α is in Adherence(L). Then α is morphic.*

Proof. From [7], either (1) α is ultimately periodic, or (2) $\alpha = w\,x\,h(x)\,h^2(x)\cdots$ for some morphism h and strings w, x such that $h(w) = wx$ and x is not mortal. If (1), α is morphic. If (2), α is an infinite D0L word, so by Proposition 10.2.2 of [8], α is morphic.   □

Theorem 23. *α is in $\omega(CD0L)$ iff α is morphic.*

Proof. That $\omega(\mathrm{CD0L})$ includes every morphic word is immediate from the definitions. So take any $\alpha \in \omega(\mathrm{CD0L})$. Then there is a CD0L system $G = (A, h, w, e)$ such that $L(G)$ determines α. Then $L(G)$ is infinite. Hence the language L of the D0L system (A, h, w) is infinite. As noted in [7], a language has empty adherence iff the language is finite. Therefore there is an $\alpha' \in$ Adherence(L). By Lemma 22, α' is morphic. Now for any prefix p of α', there is a string s in L with p as a prefix. Then $e(p)$ is a prefix of $e(s)$. Then since $e(s)$ is in $L(G)$, $e(p)$ is a prefix of α. So for every prefix p of α', $e(p)$ is a prefix of α. Since e is a coding, $e(\alpha')$ is infinite. So $e(\alpha') = \alpha$. Then because a coding of a morphic word is still a morphic word, α is morphic. Hence α is in $\omega(\mathrm{CD0L})$ iff α is morphic.   □

6 Conclusion

In this paper we have categorized the infinite words determined by L systems, showing that a variety of classes of L systems collapse to just three classes of infinite words. To associate L systems with infinite words, we used the concept of prefix languages. This concept can be applied not just to L systems, but to arbitrary language classes, offering many opportunities for further research. That is, where C is any language class, we denote by $\omega(C)$ the class of infinite words determined by the prefix languages in C. Then for a given language class, we can ask what class of infinite words it determines. From the other direction, for a given infinite word, we can ask in what language classes it can be determined. It is hoped that work in this area will help to build up a theory of the complexity of infinite words with respect to what language classes can determine them.

Acknowledgments. I want to thank my advisor, Rajmohan Rajaraman, for supporting this work, encouraging me, and offering many helpful comments and suggestions.

References

1. Allouche, J.P., Shallit, J.: Automatic Sequences: Theory, Applications, Generalizations. Cambridge University Press, New York (2003)
2. Berstel, J.: Properties of infinite words: Recent results. In: Monien, B., Cori, R. (eds.) STACS 1989. LNCS, vol. 349, pp. 36–46. Springer, Heidelberg (1989)
3. Book, R.V.: On languages with a certain prefix property. Mathematical Systems Theory 10, 229–237 (1977)
4. Cassaigne, J., Nicolas, F.: Quelques propriétés des mots substitutifs. Bulletin of the Belgian Mathematical Society-Simon Stevin 10(5), 661–677 (2003)
5. Culik, K., Karhumäki, J.: Iterative devices generating infinite words. Int. J. Found. Comput. Sci. 5(1), 69–97 (1994)
6. Culik, K., Salomaa, A.: On infinite words obtained by iterating morphisms. Theoretical Computer Science 19(1), 29–38 (1982)
7. Head, T.: Adherences of D0L languages. Theoretical Computer Science 31(1-2), 139–149 (1984)
8. Honkala, J.: The equality problem for purely substitutive words. In: Combinatorics, Automata, and Number Theory, pp. 505–529. Cambridge University Press, Cambridge (2010)
9. Kari, L., Rozenberg, G., Salomaa, A.: L systems. In: Rozenberg, G., Salomaa, A. (eds.) Handbook of Formal Languages, vol. 1, pp. 253–328. Springer-Verlag New York, Inc., New York (1997)
10. Pansiot, J.J.: On various classes of infinite words obtained by iterated mappings. In: Nivat, M., Perrin, D. (eds.) Automata on Infinite Words. LNCS, vol. 192, pp. 188–197. Springer, Heidelberg (1985)
11. Rozenberg, G., Salomaa, A.: Mathematical Theory of L Systems. Academic Press, Inc., Orlando (1980)
12. Smith, T.: Infiniteness and boundedness in 0L, DT0L, and T0L systems. In: Dediu, A.-H., Martín-Vide, C., Truthe, B. (eds.) LATA 2013. LNCS, vol. 7810, pp. 535–546. Springer, Heidelberg (2013)
13. Yamakami, T., Suzuki, T.: Resource bounded immunity and simplicity. Theoretical Computer Science 347(1-2), 90–129 (2005)

Sets Represented as the Length-n Factors of a Word

Shuo Tan and Jeffrey Shallit

School of Computer Science, University of Waterloo, Waterloo, ON N2L 3G1, Canada
{s22tan,shallit}@uwaterloo.ca

Abstract. Let Σ denote a finite alphabet. We say that a subset of Σ^n is *representable* if it occurs as the set of all length-n factors of a finite word. In this paper we consider the following problems: how many different subsets of Σ^n are representable? If a subset is representable, how long a word do we need to represent it? How many such subsets are represented by words of length t? For the first problem, we give upper and lower bounds of the form α^{2^n} in the binary case, where $\alpha > 1$ is a real number. For the second problem, we give a weak upper bound and some experimental data. For the third problem, we give a closed-form formula in the case where $n \leq t < 2n$.

1 Introduction

Let w, x, y, z be finite words. If $w = xyz$, we say that y is a *factor* of w. De Bruijn proved [1] the existence of a set of binary words $(b_n)_{n \geq 1}$ with the property that every binary word of length n appears as a factor of b_n (and, in fact, appears exactly once in b_n). Here we are thinking of b_n interpreted as a circular word. For example, consider the case where $n = 2$, where we can take $b_2 = 0011$. Interpreted circularly, the factors of length 2 of b_2 are $00, 01, 11, 10$, and these factors comprise all the binary words of length 2.

However, not every subset of $\{0, 1\}^n$ can be represented as the factors of some finite word. For example, the set $\{00, 11\}$ cannot equal the set of all factors of any word w — interpreted in the ordinary sense or circularly — because the set of factors of any w containing both letters must contain either 01 or 10.

This raises the natural question, how many different non-empty subsets S of $\{0, 1\}^n$ can be represented as the factors of some word w? (Note that, unlike [8], we do *not* insist that each element of S appear exactly once in w.) We give upper and lower bounds for this quantity for circular words, both of the form α^{2^n} for a real number $\alpha > 1$. Our upper bound has $\alpha = \sqrt[4]{10} \doteq 1.78$ while our lower bound has $\alpha = \sqrt{2} \doteq 1.41$.

If the set of length-n factors of a word w (considered circularly) equals S, we say that w *witnesses* S. We study the length of the shortest witness for subsets of $\{0, 1\}^n$, and give an upper bound.

Restriction on the length of a witness leads us to another interesting problem. Let $T(t, n)$ denote the number of subsets of $\{0, 1\}^n$ witnessed by some word of

J. Karhumäki, A. Lepistö, and L. Zamboni (Eds.): WORDS 2013, LNCS 8079, pp. 250–261, 2013.

length $t \geq n$. Is there any characterization of $T(t, n)$? We focus on ordinary (non-circular) words for this question and derive a closed-form formula for $T(t, n)$ in the case where $n \leq t < 2n$.

Algorithmic versions of related problems have been widely studied in the literature under the name "shortest common superstring" and "representing word". For example, Gallant, Maier, and Storer [4] proved that the following decision problem is NP-complete:

Instance: A set S of words and an integer K.

Question: Is there a word w of length $\leq K$ containing each word in S (and possibly others) as a factor?

Recently, Blanchet-Sadri and Simmons [5] studied the representability of sets by finite partial words, which are sequences containing holes that match all letters. They showed that whether a given set is represented by some partial word of exactly h holes can be decided in polynomial time. However, the combinatorial problems that we study in this paper seem to be new.

2 Preliminaries

Let $\Sigma = \{0, 1\}$ denote the alphabet. Let $F_n(w)$ denote the set of length-n factors of an ordinary (non-circular) word w, and let $C_n(w)$ denote the set of length-n factors of w where w is interpreted circularly. For example, if $w = 001$, then $F_2(w) = \{00, 01\}$, while if $w = 001$ is interpreted circularly, then $C_2(w) = \{00, 01, 10\}$.

We say that a word w *witnesses* (resp., *circularly witnesses*) a subset S of Σ^n if $F_n(w) = S$ (resp., $C_n(w) = S$). A subset S of Σ^n is *representable* (resp., *circularly representable*) if there exists a non-empty word (resp., circular word) that witnesses S. Let R_n denote the set of all non-empty representable subsets of Σ^n, and let $\mathring{R}_n$ denote the set of all non-empty circularly representable subsets of Σ^n.

Let $\mathrm{sw}(S)$ (resp., $\mathrm{scw}(S)$) denote the length of the shortest non-circular witness (resp., circular witness) for S. Let μ_n (resp., ν_n) denote the maximum length of the shortest non-circular (resp., circular) witness over all representable subsets of Σ^n.

A *de Bruijn word* b_n of order n over the alphabet Σ is a shortest circular witness for the set Σ^n. It is known [1] that the length of a de Bruijn word of order n over Σ is 2^n.

For convenience, we let $w[i]$ denote the i'th letter of w and $w[i..j]$ denote the factor of w with length $j - i + 1$ that starts with the i'th letter of w. Thus $w = w[1..n]$ where $n = |w|$.

3 Bounds on the Size of $\mathring{R}_n$

In this section, we give lower and upper bounds on the size of $\mathring{R}_n$, both of which are of the form α^{2^n}. Our lower bound has $\alpha = \sqrt{2}$ while our upper bound has $\alpha = \sqrt[4]{10}$. Note that our lower bound also works for the size of R_n, since every circularly representable subset is also representable.

3.1   Lower Bound

Our argument for the lower bound derives from constructing a set of circularly representable subsets.

Proposition 1. *Let b_n be any de Bruijn word of order n. Then $|C_{n+1}(b_n)| = 2^n$.*

Proof. Every de Bruijn word of order n is of length 2^n; thus there are 2^n length-$(n+1)$ factors of b_n (considered circularly). These length-$(n+1)$ factors are pairwise distinct, for if $w \in \Sigma^{n+1}$ appears more than once as a factor of b_n, then $w[1..n]$ appears more than once as a factor of b_n. However, every length-n factor appears only once in b_n, a contradiction. Hence $|C_{n+1}(b_n)| = 2^n$. $\square$

Lemma 2. *Given a de Bruijn word b_n, let Y denote the set $\Sigma^{n+1}\backslash C_{n+1}(b_n)$. For any $y \in Y$, the set $\{y\} \cup C_{n+1}(b_n)$ is circularly witnessed by a word w for which both the length-2^n prefix and the length-2^n suffix equal b_n.*

Proof. We construct such a witness for $\{y\} \cup C_{n+1}(b_n)$.

Let $w = b_n b_n b_n b_n$. Let $y_1 = y[1..n]$ and $y_2 = y[2..n+1]$. Let i_1 denote the index of the first occurrence of y_1 in w; namely, the index i_1 is the minimal integer such that $y_1 = w[i_1..i_1 + n - 1]$. Let i_2 denote the index of the last occurrence of y_2 in w; namely, the index i_2 is the maximal integer such that $y_2 = w[i_2..i_2 + n - 1]$.

We argue that the first occurrence of y_1 does not overlap the last occurrence of y_2. We have $i_1 \leq 2^n$, since every possible factor of length n appears in the circular word b_n. Similarly, we obtain $i_2 > 3 \cdot 2^n - n$. Thus we have

$$i_1 + n - 1 - i_2 < -2 \cdot 2^n + 2n - 1 < 0,$$

and hence the first occurrence of y_1 does not overlap the last occurrence of y_2.

Now consider the circular word

$$w_y = b_n b_n w[1..i_1 - 1]w[i_1..i_1 + n - 1]w[i_2 + n - 1]w[i_2 + n..2^{n+2}]b_n b_n.$$

We argue that w_y is a witness for $\{y\}\cup C_{n+1}(b_n)$. For one direction, every element of $\{y\}\cup C_{n+1}(b_n)$ appears as a length-$(n+1)$ factor of w_y. This is a consequence of the following two facts:

1. $b_n b_n$ witnesses $C_{n+1}(b_n)$.
2. $w[i_1..i_1 + n - 1]w[i_2 + n - 1] = y[1..n]y[n + 1] = y$.

For the other direction, we can see that all factors of length $n + 1$ in w_y are elements of $\{y\} \cup C_{n+1}(b_n)$ by inspection. Note that the length-2^n prefix and the length-2^n suffix of w_y both equal b_n. Hence we conclude that there exists a word for which the prefix and the suffix equal b_n and this circular word circularly witnesses $\{y\} \cup C_{n+1}(b_n)$. $\square$

Example 3. Let $n = 2$. One of the de Bruijn words of order 2 is $b_2 = 0011$. We have $C_3(b_2) = \{001, 011, 110, 100\}$. Thus $Y = \{000, 010, 101, 111\}$. Let $y = 010$.

The following circular word demonstrates that the set $\{y\} \cup C_{n+1}(b_n)$ is representable:

$$w_{010} = \underbrace{(00110011)}_{b_2 b_2}(\underbrace{0}_{w[1..i_1-1]})(\underbrace{01}_{w[i_1..i_1+n-1]=y_1})(\underbrace{0}_{w[i_2+n-1]})(\underbrace{011}_{w[i_2+n..2^n+2]})\underbrace{(00110011)}_{b_2 b_2}.$$

Proposition 4. *Given a de Bruijn word b_n, let Y denote the set $\Sigma^{n+1} \setminus C_{n+1}$ (b_n). For any subset $S \subseteq Y$, the set $S \cup C_{n+1}(b_n)$ is a circularly representable subset of Σ^{n+1}.*

Proof. We have proved this proposition for the case where $|S| = 1$ by Lemma 2. Now we turn to the general case. Let $S = \{s_1, s_2, \ldots, s_m\}$. By Lemma 2, for each $1 \leq i \leq m$, there exists a circular word w_i that witnesses $\{s_i\} \cup C_{n+1}(b_n)$ and both the prefix and the suffix of w_i equal b_n. We argue that the circular word $w_S = w_1 w_2 \cdots w_m$ witnesses $S \cup C_{n+1}(b_n)$.

First, for any $1 \leq i \leq m$, s_i appears in w_i and thus in w_S. Moreover, every element of $C_{n+1}(b_n)$ appears in the prefix of w_S: $b_n b_n$. Thus, it suffices to show that every length-$(n+1)$ factor of w_S is a member of $S \cup C_{n+1}(b_n)$. This is shown by the fact that for any $1 \leq i < m$, both the suffix of w_i and the prefix of w_{i+1} equal b_n, which implies that the concatenation of t_i and t_{i+1} does not produce any new factor of length $n+1$ in w_S.

Thus, we conclude that for any subset S of Y, there exists a witness for the set $S \cup C_{n+1}(b_n)$. $\qquad\square$

Corollary 5. *A lower bound for the size of $\mathring{R}_{n+1}$ is $2^{2^n} = \sqrt{2}^{2^{n+1}}$.*

3.2 Upper Bound

An obvious upper bound for $|\mathring{R}_n|$ is 2^{2^n}, since $\mathring{R}_n \subseteq 2^{\Sigma^n}$, where $|2^{\Sigma^n}| = 2^{2^n}$. In this section, we will show that a tighter upper bound is α^{2^n}, where $\alpha = \sqrt[4]{10}$.

Definition 6. *Let $S \subseteq \Sigma^{n+1}$ and $T \subseteq \Sigma^n$. We say that S is incident on T if there exists a circular word w such that w witnesses both S and T.*

Example 7. For example, we fix $n = 3$. Let $w = 0110$. Then w is a witness for the set $S = \{0110, 1100, 1001, 0011\} \in \mathring{R}_4$ and $T = \{011, 110, 100, 001\} \in \mathring{R}_3$. It follows that S is incident on T. Note that $w' = 01100110$ is also a witness for S, and a witness for T as well.

In fact we can argue that if S is incident on T, then every word that witnesses S also witnesses T.

Proposition 8. *Every set $S \in \mathring{R}_{n+1}$ is incident on exactly one set in $\mathring{R}_n$.*

Proof. Let

$$T = \{t \in \Sigma^n : \text{there exists } w \in S \text{ such that } t \text{ is a length-}n \text{ prefix or suffix of } w\}.$$

Then a word w which witnesses S also witnesses T. Thus S is incident on T. Moreover, if S is incident on T and T', then every witness of S must also witness T and T'. Thus we have $T = T'$. So we conclude that every set $S \in \mathring{R}_{n+1}$ is incident on exactly one set in $\mathring{R}_n$.   □

Now we give a partition of $\mathring{R}_{n+1}$. Let

$$\mathring{R}_{n+1}[T] = \{S \in \mathring{R}_{n+1} : S \text{ is incident on } T\}.$$

Proposition 8 implies that $\{\mathring{R}_{n+1}[T]\}_{T \subseteq \Sigma^n}$ is a pairwise disjoint partition of the set $\mathring{R}_{n+1}$. Namely, (1) for every $T_1 \neq T_2$, we have $\mathring{R}_{n+1}[T_1] \cap \mathring{R}_{n+1}[T_2] = \emptyset$ and (2) $\bigcup_{T \in \mathring{R}_n} \mathring{R}_{n+1}[T] = \mathring{R}_{n+1}$.

Thus we have $|\mathring{R}_{n+1}| = \sum_{T \subseteq \Sigma^n} |\mathring{R}_{n+1}[T]|$. So to give an upper bound for $|\mathring{R}_{n+1}|$, it suffices to give a upper bound for the size of $\mathring{R}_{n+1}[T]$.

Definition 9. *Let x be a word of length n. We say that $P_x = \{0x, 1x\}$ is a pair of order n w.r.t. x, that $S_x = \{0x, 1x, x0, x1\}$ is a skeleton of order n w.r.t. x, and $N_x = \{0x0, 0x1, 1x0, 1x1\}$ is a net of order n w.r.t. x. We also say that a set S contains P_x (resp., S_x and N_x) if $P_x \subseteq S$ (resp., $S_x \subseteq S$ and $N_x \subseteq S$).*

For any $T \subseteq \Sigma^n$, let $\sigma(T)$ denote the number of skeletons of order $n-1$ in T and let $\rho(T)$ denote the number of pairs of order $n-1$ in T. We have the following proposition:

Proposition 10. *For any $T \subseteq \Sigma^n$, we have $|\mathring{R}_{n+1}[T]| \leq 7^{\sigma(T)}$.*

Before giving the proof for Proposition 10, we introduce another definition.

Definition 11. *A set R is feasible for a set $T \subseteq \Sigma^n$ if there exists $S \in \mathring{R}_{n+1}[T]$ such that $R \subseteq S$.*

We observe that $\Sigma^{n+1} = \bigcup_{x \in \Sigma^{n-1}} N_x$ and thus any subset $S \subseteq \Sigma^{n+1}$ is a disjoint union of subsets of nets of order $n-1$. Formally, for any subset $S \subseteq \Sigma^{n+1}$, we have $S = \bigcup_{x \in \Sigma^{n-1}} R_x$, where $R_x \subseteq N_x$.

Proof (of Proposition 10). Let F_x denote the set of feasible subsets (for T) of the net N_x. If $S \in R_{n+1}[T]$, then S is a disjoint union of feasible subsets (for T) of nets. Thus we have $|R_{n+1}[T]| \leq \prod_{x \in \Sigma^n} |F_x|$. In order to prove this proposition, it now suffices to show that for any $x \in \Sigma^{n-1}$, the following condition holds.

- if $S_x \subseteq T$, then $|F_x| \leq 7$;
- otherwise $|F_x| \leq 1$.

For any $x \in \Sigma^{n-1}$, we consider all the possible feasible subsets of N_x. Let F denote any feasible subset of N_x.

- For the first case where $S_x \subseteq T$, we have the following properties:
  1. Either $0x0 \in F$ or $0x1 \in F$ since $0x \in T$;
  2. Either $1x0 \in F$ or $1x1 \in F$ since $1x \in T$;

3. Either $0x0 \in F$ or $1x0 \in F$ since $x0 \in T$;

4. Either $0x1 \in F$ or $1x1 \in F$ since $x1 \in T$.

Hence we have at most 7 possible feasible subsets of N_x which are listed as follows: $\{0x0, 1x1\}$, $\{0x0, 0x1, 1x1\}$, $\{0x0, 1x0, 1x1\}$, $\{0x0, 0x1, 1x0, 1x1\}$, $\{0x0, 0x1, 1x0\}$, $\{0x1, 1x0\}$, $\{0x1, 1x0, 1x1\}$. Thus $|F_x| \leq 7$.

– For the second case where $S_x \not\subseteq T$, we argue that $|F_x| \leq 1$. Without loss of generality, suppose $0x \notin T$. It follows that:

1. $0x0$ and $0x1$ cannot occur in F since $0x \notin T$;

2. $1x0 \in F$ if and only if $x0 \in T$;

3. $1x1 \in F$ if and only if $x1 \in T$;

Hence, F is fixed. It follows that $|F_x| \leq 1$.

By finishing the argument on the above two cases, we conclude that $|\mathring{R}_{n+1}[T]| \leq 7^{\sigma(T)}$. □

Now, we are close to the core part. Instead of computing the number of skeletons, which is quite complex, we consider the number of pairs.

Proposition 12. *The size of the set $|\mathring{R}_{n+1}|$ is bounded by $10^{2^{n-1}}$.*

Proof. Let $L_{k,i}$ denote the number of subsets $T \in \mathring{R}_n$, such that $|T| = k$ and $\rho(T) = i$. There are in total 2^{n-1} pairs in Σ^n, and we first choose i pairs from them. Then, we choose the other $k - 2i$ elements which do not form any pair from the remaining $2^n - 2i$ elements (which forms $2^{n-1} - i$ pairs); it is equivalent to pick $k - 2i$ pairs from the remaining $2^{n-1} - i$ pairs and randomly choose one element from each selected pair. Thus, we have

$$L_{k,i} = \binom{2^{n-1}}{i}\binom{2^{n-1} - i}{k - 2i}2^{k-2i}.$$

Note that $k \geq 2i$ since a set of k elements can contain at most $\lfloor \frac{k}{2} \rfloor$ pairs and the term $L_{k,i}$ vanishes when $k - 2i > 2^{n-1} - i$. Thus we have

$$|\mathring{R}_{n+1}| = \sum_{T \subseteq \Sigma^n} |\mathring{R}_{n+1}[T]| \leq \sum_{k=0}^{2^n}\sum_{i=0}^{\lfloor \frac{k}{2} \rfloor} L_{k,i}7^i.$$

The inequality holds since we count the number of pairs instead of the number of skeletons and the number of pairs is always greater than or equal to the number of skeletons. Then we can see that

$$|\mathring{R}_{n+1}| \leq \sum_{k=0}^{2^n}\sum_{i=0}^{\lfloor \frac{k}{2} \rfloor} \binom{2^{n-1}}{i}\binom{2^{n-1} - i}{k - 2i}2^{k-2i}7^i \leq \sum_{i=0}^{2^{n-1}}\binom{2^{n-1}}{i}7^i\sum_{k=2i}^{2^n}\binom{2^{n-1} - i}{k - 2i}2^{k-2i}$$

by writing $L_{k,i}$ in closed form. Note that

$$\sum_{k=2i}^{2^n}\binom{2^{n-1} - i}{k - 2i}2^{k-2i} = \sum_{k=0}^{2^n - 2i}\binom{2^{n-1} - i}{k}2^k = \sum_{k=0}^{2^{n-1} - i}\binom{2^{n-1} - i}{k}2^k = 3^{2^{n-1} - i}.$$

So we have

$$|\mathring{R}_{n+1}| \le \sum_{i=0}^{2^{n-1}} \binom{2^{n-1}}{i} 7^i 3^{2^{n-1}-i} = 10^{2^{n-1}}.$$

□

Proposition 12 directly implies the upper bound we claimed in the beginning of this section.

4   Shortest Witness

Recall that μ_n (resp., ν_n) is the maximum length of the shortest non-circular witness (resp., circular witness) over all subsets of Σ^n. The quantities of μ_n and ν_n are of interest since we can enumerate all sequences of length less than or equal to μ_n (resp., ν_n) in order to list all the representable (resp., circularly representable) subsets of Σ^n. In this section we obtain an upper bound on μ_n and ν_n.

We need the following result of Hamidoune [7, Prop. 2.1].

Proposition 13. *Let $G = (V, E)$ be a directed graph on n vertices. If G is strongly connected (that is, if there is a directed path from every vertex to every vertex), then there is a Hamiltonian walk of length at most $\lfloor (n+1)^2/4 \rfloor$. Furthermore, this bound is best possible.*

From this we immediately get

Proposition 14. *An upper bound for μ_n and ν_n is $2^{2n-2} + 2^{n-1}$.*

5   Numerical Results

It is not feasible to enumerate every single word to verify whether a subset is circularly representable (or non-circularly representable). For this reason, we exploit ideas from graph theory.

Formally, we define $G_n = (V_n, E_n)$, where

$V_n = \{(S, u, v) : S \subseteq \Sigma^n \text{ and } u, v \in \Sigma^n\}$ and
$E_n = \{((S, u, v), (S \cup \{x\}, u, x)) : S \subseteq \Sigma^n, \ u, v, x \in \Sigma^n, \text{ and } v[2..n] = x[1..n-1]\}.$

We say that a node (S, u, v) is *valid* if S is witnessed by a non-circular word w for which the length-n prefix is u and the length-n suffix is v.

We use a breadth-first search strategy to compute all the possible valid nodes in G_n. Let I denote a subset of nodes $\{(\{u\}, u, u) : u \in \Sigma^n\}$ in G_n. Nodes in G_n that are connected to any node in I can be proven valid by induction. Thus, a breadth-first search begins with the subset I and enumerates all nodes that are connected to nodes in I.

The relation between valid nodes in G_n and non-empty representable subsets of Σ^n is that any subset $S \subseteq \Sigma^n$ is representable if and only if there exist

$u, v \in \Sigma^n$ such that (S, u, v) is valid. This relation can be proved by induction. Similarly, any subset $S \subseteq \Sigma^n$ is circularly representable if and only if there exists $u \in \Sigma^n$ such that (S, u, u) is valid and the minimum distance d between (S, u, u) and nodes in I satisfies the inequality $d \geq n - 1$.

With the above properties, we can enumerate all the possible non-empty representable (or circularly representable) subsets of order n. Our results are shown in the following table. The last two columns give words w of length ν_n (resp., μ_n) for which no shorter word witnesses $C_n(w)$ (resp., $F_n(w)$).

n	$|\mathring{R}_n|$	$|R_n|$	ν_n	μ_n	longest circ. witness	longest witness
1	3	3	2	2	01	01
2	6	14	4	5	0011	00110
3	27	121	9	10	000100111	0001011100
4	973	5921	24	24	000010001011100011101111	000010010101100101101111
5	2466131	20020315	82	77	—	—

6 Fixed-Length Witnesses

We now turn to a related question. We fix a length n and we ask, how many different subsets of Σ^n can we obtain by taking the (ordinary, non-circular factors) of a word of length t? We call this quantity $T(t, n)$. As we will see, for $t < 2n$, there is a relatively simple answer to this question.

In order to compute $T(t, n)$, we consider the number of words that witness the same subset of Σ^n. Suppose $S \subseteq \Sigma^n$. Let $C_t(S)$ denote the number of words of length t that witness S. Then we have

$$T(t, n) = 2^t - \sum_{\substack{S \subseteq \Sigma^n \\ C_t(S) > 1}} (C_t(S) - 1).$$

It suffices to characterize what subsets S satisfy $C_t(S) > 1$ and to determine $C_t(S)$.

For $t < 2n$, we have such a characterization by Theorem 15 below. Before stating the theorem, we first introduce some notation.

Let w be a word. Let $\mathrm{Pref}(w)$ denote the set of prefixes of w. A *period* p of w is a positive integer such that w can be factorized as $w = s^k s'$, with $|s| = p$, $s' \in \mathrm{Pref}(s)$, and $k \geq 1$. Let $\pi(w)$ denote the minimal period of w.

The *root* of a word w is the prefix of w with length $\pi(w)$. Let $r(w)$ denote the root of w. Two words w and w' are *conjugate* if there exist $u, v \in \Sigma^*$ such that $w = uv$ and $w' = vu$; w and w' are *root-conjugate* if their roots $r(w)$ and $r(w')$ are conjugate.

The following theorem is crucial for our work and of independent interest.

Theorem 15. *Let t, n, k be such that $t = n + k$, $n \geq k + 1$, and $k \geq 0$. Let w and w' be distinct words of length t over an arbitrary alphabet. Then $F_n(w) = F_n(w')$ iff $\pi(w) = \pi(w') \leq k + 1$ and w, w' are root-conjugate.*

One direction is easy: if w and w' are root-conjugate with period $p \leq k+1$, then there are p places to begin, and considering consecutive factors of length $n + p - 1$ gives exactly p distinct length-n factors.

For the other direction, we need three lemmas.

Lemma 16. *(Fine-Wilf theorem [3, Theorem 1]) Let w_1, w_2 be two words. If w_1 and w_2 have a common prefix of length $\pi(w_1) + \pi(w_2) - 1$, then $r(w_1) = r(w_2)$.*

Lemma 17. *For any $w \in \Sigma^+$, if there exists a factorization $w = xyz$ such that $xy = yz$ and $x, y, z \in \Sigma^+$, then w is periodic with $\pi(w) \leq |x|$.*

Proof. By the Lyndon-Schützenberger theorem [6, Lemma 2], there exist $u \in \Sigma^+, v \in \Sigma^*$ and an integer $e \geq 0$ such that $x = uv, y = (uv)^e u, z = vu$. Thus $w = (uv)^{e+2} u$. Thus w is periodic with $\pi(w) \leq |x|$. □

Lemma 18. *Let t, n, k be integers such that $t = n + k$, $n \geq k + 1$, and $k \geq 0$. Let w be a word of length t with $\pi(w) \leq k + 1$. If w' is any word such that $F_n(w) = F_n(w')$, then w and w' are root-conjugate.*

Carpi and de Luca proved a stronger proposition [2, Proposition 6.2] which directly implies this lemma. We first introduce some relevant notation from that paper.

A factor s of a word w is said to be *right-special* in w if there exist two distinct symbols a and b such that sa and sb are factors of w. Let R_w denote the minimal length m such that there exists no factor of length m that is right-special. A factor s of a word w is said to be *right-extendable* (resp., *left-extendable*) in w if there exists a symbol a such that sa is a factor of w (resp., as is a factor of w). Let K_w and H_w denote the length of the shortest factor which is not right-extendable (resp., left-extendable). A word is *semiperiodic* if $R_w < H_w$.

Proof (of Lemma 18). Carpi and de Luca proved [2, Lemma 3.2] that $\pi(w) > R_w$. Also, we have $H_w \geq \pi(w)$ since the length-$(\pi(w) - 1)$ prefix of w is left-extendable. Thus w is semiperiodic. Moreover we have $F_n(w) = F_n(w')$ where $n \geq k + 1 \geq \pi(w) \geq 1 + R_w$. Then we can apply [2, Proposition 6.2] to prove this lemma. □

Proof (of Theorem 15). We give a proof for Theorem 15 by induction on k.

The base case is when $k = 0$. In this case $t = n$ and thus $F_n(w) = \{w\}$ and $F_n(w') = \{w'\}$. Thus $w = w'$, contradicting the fact that w and w' are distinct.

Now we deal with the induction step. We assume the result holds for $k - 1$ and we prove it for k. For convenience, we let $p_i(w)$ denote the length-i prefix of the word w; let $s_i(w)$ denote the length-i suffix of the word w.

We first consider the case where $H_w < n$. We have $p_n(w) \in F_n(w) = F_n(w')$. If $p_n(w) \neq p_n(w')$, then there exists $a \in \Sigma$ such that $a p_{n-1}(w) \in F_n(w')$.

Thus we have $ap_{n-1}(w) \in F_n(w)$ which leads to the contradiction that $H_w \geq |ap_{n-1}(w)| = n$. Hence $p_n(w) = p_n(w')$.

Now let $s = w[2..t]$ and $s' = w'[2..t]$. Clearly $|s| = |s'| = t-1$. The prefix $p_n(w)$ appears only once as a factor of w, otherwise $p_{n-1}(w)$ is left-extendable in w which contradicts the fact that $H_w < n$. Thus we have $F_n(s) = F_n(w)\backslash\{p_n(w)\}$. Similarly we have $F_n(s') = F_n(w')\backslash\{p_n(w)\}$. Thus $F_n(s) = F_n(s')$. Let $k' = k-1$. We have $t - 1 = n + k - 1 = n + k'$ and $n \geq k + 1 > k' + 1$. By induction, we have either

Case 1: $s = s'$; or

Case 2: s and s' are root-conjugate and $\pi(s) = \pi(s') = \rho$, where $\rho \leq k' + 1 = k$.

In Case 1, it follows that $w = w'$, contradicting the fact that w, w' are distinct. In Case 2, we prove that $s = s'$ by showing that their roots are identical. Suppose s and s' have a common prefix of length d. We have $d \geq n-1$, since w and w' have a common prefix of length at least n. If $d \geq \rho$, then the root of s is identical to the root of s'. Otherwise, we have the chain of inequalities $k \geq \rho \geq d+1 \geq n \geq k+1$, which is trivially a contradiction. Thus neither Case 1 nor Case 2 can occur and we are done with the case where $H_w < n$.

Similarly we can prove the induction step when $K_w < n$. Thus it suffices to consider the case where $H_w \geq n$ and $K_w \geq n$. We first claim $\pi(w) \leq k + 1$. There are several cases to settle:

- The first case is when $p_{n-1}(w) = s_{n-1}(w)$ and the occurrence of $p_{n-1}(w)$ and $s_{n-1}(w)$ do not overlap; namely we have $w = p_{n-1}(w)Lp_{n-1}(w)$, where $L \in \Sigma^*$. We have the inequality $n+k = t = |w| = 2|p_{n-1}(w)|+|L| = 2(n-1)+|L|$. Thus $|L| = k + 2 - n$. Hence $\pi(w) \leq |p_{n-1}(w)L| = n - 1 + k + 2 - n = k+1$.
- The second case is when $p_{n-1}(w) = s_{n-1}(w)$ and these occurrences overlap. Formally we put it as follows: there exist $x, y, z \in \Sigma^+$, such that $p_{n-1}(w) = xy = yz$ and $w = xyz$. It follows that $\pi(w) \leq |x| \leq k + 1$ by Lemma 17.
- The last case is when $p_{n-1}(w) \neq s_{n-1}(w)$. Let i_p denote the index of the last occurrence of $p_{n-1}(w)$; namely $i_p = \sup\{i \geq 1 : p_{n-1}(w) = w[i..i + n - 2]\}$. Note that i_p exists since $p_{n-1}(w)$ is left-extendable and $i_p \leq t - n + 2$ since $p_{n-1}(w) \neq s_{n-1}(w)$. We argue that $w_1 = w[1..i_p + n - 2]$ is periodic with $\pi(w_1) \leq i_p - 1 \leq k$. If the first occurrence of $p_{n-1}(w)$ (the prefix of w) overlaps the last occurrence of $p_{n-1}(w)$, then by Lemma 17, we see that w_1 is periodic with $\pi(w_1) \leq i_p - 1 \leq k$. Otherwise, we have $2(n-1) \leq |w_1| \leq t-1$; thus $k = n - 1$ and $|w_1| = 2(n - 1)$. Then we have $w_1 = p_{n-1}(w)p_{n-1}(w)$, where w_1 is periodic with $\pi(w_1) \leq n - 1 = i_p - 1 = k$. For both cases, we have w_1 is periodic with $\pi(w_1) \leq i_p - 1 \leq k$.

Similarly we let i_q denote the index of the first occurrence of $s_{n-1}(w)$ and $w_2 = w[i_q..t]$. We have $1 < i_q \leq t - n + 2$ and $\pi(w_2) \leq t - n + 2 - i_q$. The factors w_1 and w_2 overlap for at least $|w_1| + |w_2| - t \geq \pi(w_1) + \pi(w_2) - 1$ symbols. Let D denote the overlap of w_1 and w_2. We have $|D| \geq \pi(w_1) +

$\pi(w_2) - 1$. Also $\pi(w_1)$ is a period of D since $|D| \geq \pi(w_1)$ and D can be factorized as

$$D = d^l d', \text{ where } d \text{ is conjugate to the root of } w_1, \; d' \in \text{Pref}(d), \text{ and } l \geq 1.$$

By Lemma 16, the overlap D has the same root as w_2. Since root-conjugacy is an equivalence relation, we have w_1 and w_2 are root-conjugate. Let l_1 denote the length of the root of w_1. We argue that w is periodic with $\pi(w) \leq l_1 \leq k + 1$ by the fact that l_1 is also a period of w. It suffices to show that $w[l_1 + i] = w[i]$ for $1 \leq i \leq t - l_1$. For the case where $1 \leq i \leq |w_1| - l_1$, we have $w[i + l_1] = w_1[i + l_1] = w_1[i] = w[i]$; for the other case where $|w_1| - l_1 < i \leq t - l_1$, we have $w[i + l_1] = w_2[i + l_1 - i_q + 1] = w_2[i - i_q + 1] = w[i]$. Thus, we see that w is periodic with $\pi(w) \leq k + 1$.

Finally by Lemma 18, we get that w and w' are root-conjugate and their periods $\pi(w) = \pi(w') \leq k + 1$. By all cases, we finish the induction and complete the proof of Theorem 15. $\qquad\square$

The following corollary gives $T(t, n)$ when $t < 2n$.

Corollary 19. *For $n \leq t < 2n$, we have $T(t, n) = 2^t - \sum_{k=1}^{t-n+1} \frac{k-1}{k} \sum_{d|k} \mu(\frac{k}{d}) 2^d$, where $\mu(\cdot)$ is the Möbius function.*

Proof. Let $k = t - n$. We have $n \geq t - n + 1 = k + 1$. By Theorem 15, we know that for any set $S \subseteq \Sigma^n$, $C_t(S) > 1$ if and only if there exists a word w that witnesses S with $\pi(w) \leq k + 1$. In this case we have $C_t(S) = \pi(w)$; that is, the set of words that witness S is the same as the set of the words that are root-conjugate to w. Thus each S such that $C_t(S) > 1$ corresponds to a set of root-conjugate words, which can be represented by their lexicographically least roots (the Lyndon words).

Thus we have

$$T(t, n) = 2^t - \sum_{\substack{S \subseteq \Sigma^n \\ C_t(S) > 1}} (C_t(S) - 1) = 2^t - \sum_{\substack{w \text{ is a Lyndon word} \\ \pi(w) \leq k+1}} (\pi(w) - 1)$$

$$= 2^t - \sum_{i=1}^{k+1} (i - 1) \cdot L(i),$$

where $k = t - n$ and $L(i) = \frac{1}{i} \sum_{d|i} \mu(\frac{i}{d}) 2^d$ is the number of Lyndon words of length i.

$\qquad\square$

Example 20. To finish this section, we give a table listing some numerical results for $T(t, n)$. The numbers in bold follow from Corollary 19, while the others were computed by brute force.

n \ t	1	2	3	4	5	6	7	8	9	10	11	12	13	14	15	16
1	2	3	3	3	3	3	3	3	3	3	3	3	3	3	3	3
2		4	7	11	12	12	12	12	12	12	12	12	12	12	12	12
3			8	15	27	48	72	94	100	103	101	103	101	103	101	103
4				16	31	59	114	216	391	677	1087	1621	2246	2928	3595	4235
5					32	63	123	242	474	933	1795	3421	6399	11682	20704	35914
6						64	127	251	498	986	1965	3899	7709	15171	29710	57726
7							128	255	507	1010	2010	4013	8001	15969	31789	63256
8								256	511	1019	2034	4058	8109	16193	32367	64671

7 Open Problems and Future Work

1. In Section 3, we gave lower and upper bounds on $|\mathring{R}_n|$, both of the form α^{2^n}. Does the limit $\lim_{n \to \infty} |\mathring{R}_n|^{\frac{1}{2^n}}$ exist?
2. Find better bounds for μ_n and ν_n. For example, is $\mu_n \leq (n-1)2^n$ for $n \geq 2$?
3. It is easy to see that Theorem 15 fails for $n < k + 1$. Indeed, it is possible to have $F_n(x) = F_n(y)$ in this case, and yet $\pi(x) \neq \pi(y)$. For example, take $n = k - 1$ so that $t = 2k - 1$, and consider $x = 0^k 10^{k-2}$ and $y = 0^{k-1} 10^{k-1}$. Then $F_n(x) = F_n(y)$ but $\pi(x) = k + 1$ and $\pi(y) = k$.

   The remaining case is $n = k$, so that $t = 2k$. We conjecture that if x and y are distinct binary words of length $2n$ with $F_n(x) = F_n(y)$ then $\pi(x) = \pi(y)$ and furthermore x and y are root-conjugate. However, it is possible in this case that $\pi(x) > n + 1$. Furthermore it seems that if $\pi(x) > n + 1$, then $x = uv01vu$ and $y = uv10v^R u$ (or vice versa) for some nonempty words u, v where u is the longest palindromic prefix of uv and $\pi(x) = t - |u|$.

References

1. de Bruijn, N.G.: A combinatorial problem. Nederl. Akad. Wetensch., Proc. 49, 758–764 (1946); Indagationes Math. 8, 461–467 (1946)
2. Carpi, A., de Luca, A.: Semiperiodic words and root-conjugacy. Theoret. Comput. Sci. 292, 111–130 (2003)
3. Fine, N.J., Wilf, H.S.: Uniqueness theorems for periodic functions. Proc. Amer. Math. Soc. 16, 109–114 (1965)
4. Gallant, J., Maier, D., Storer, J.A.: On finding minimal length superstrings. J. Comput. System Sci. 20, 50–58 (1980)
5. Blanchet-Sadri, F., Simmons, S.: Deciding representability of sets of words of equal length. Theoret. Comput. Sci. 475, 34–46 (2013)
6. Lyndon, R.C., Schützenberger, M.P.: The equation $a^M = b^N c^P$ in a free group. Michigan Math. J. 9, 289–298 (1962)
7. Hamidoune, Y.O.: Sur les sommets de demi-degré h d'un graphe fortement h-connexe minimal. C. R. Acad. Sci. Paris Sér. A-B 286, A863–A865 (1978)
8. Moreno, E.: De Bruijn sequences and De Bruijn graphs for a general language. Info. Proc. Letters 96, 214–219 (2005)

Author Index